PENGUIN BOOKS

# THE FUTURE OF MOTHERHOOD

Jessie Bernard earned her B.A. and M.A. degrees at the University of Minnesota and her doctorate in sociology at Washington University. One of America's leading authorities on family relationships, she is now professor emerita of sociology at Penn State University. Books by her include *American Family Behavior*, *The Sex Game*, and *The Future of Marriage*. Dr. Bernard, who is a widow, has three children and one grandchild.

JESSIE BERNARD

# The
# Future of
# Motherhood

Penguin Books Inc
*New York · Baltimore*

Penguin Books Inc
72 Fifth Avenue
New York, New York 10011

Penguin Books Inc
7110 Ambassador Road
Baltimore, Maryland 21207

Penguin Books Canada Limited
41 Steelcase Road West
Markham, Ontario, Canada L3R 1B4

First published by The Dial Press, New York, 1974
Published by Penguin Books Inc, 1975

Grateful acknowledgment is made for permission to use the following copy-
righted material.

Extract from "At Wit's End," by Erma Bombeck, used by permission of
Publishers-Hall Syndicate.

Extract from *Women's Two Roles,* by Alva Myrdal and Viola Klein, used by
permission of Humanities Press, Inc., New York, and Routledge & Kegan
Paul, Ltd., London.

Extract from *Are Parents Bad for Children?*, by Graham B. Blaine, Jr.,
copyright © Graham B. Blaine, Jr., 1973, used by permission of Coward,
McCann & Geoghegan, Inc., New York, and Collins-Knowlton-Wing, Inc.

Extracts from *Communities* and *Leaves of Twin Oaks* used by permission
of Community Publications Cooperative.

Extract from "Alternate-Culture Mirror America," by Margarita Donnelly:
Every effort has been made to contact the author. The Dial Press will be
happy to arrange formal acknowledgment and customary payment if the
author will write to them.

# Contents

Foreword      vii

Part One.    **Motherhood As Institution,
Mother As Symbol, and Women**    1

PROLEGOMENA    The Victorian Model for the
Role of Mother    3

CHAPTER 1    Mother Is a Role, Women Are
Human Beings    7

Part Two.    **The First Imperative
and the Future**    17

CHAPTER 2    Why Motherhood?    21
CHAPTER 3    Nonmotherhood    41
CHAPTER 4    How Much Motherhood?    53

Part Three.    **The Second Imperative
and the Future**    65

CHAPTER 5    Storm Signals    69

*Contents*

CHAPTER 6     A Variety of Scripts                                    90

              Part Four.   **Role Severance and Attrition**          107

CHAPTER 7     What Do You Mean, Work?                                 111
CHAPTER 8     The Severed Roles                                       131

              Part Five.   **Gestating the Future**                  153

CHAPTER 9     The Professional Mother                                 157
CHAPTER 10    The Working Mother                                      182
CHAPTER 11    The Other Half                                          196

              Part Six.    **Technologies, Politics,
                           and Economics of Motherhood**              223

CHAPTER 12    Physical and Social Technologies                        227
CHAPTER 13    Medical, Pharmacological, and
              Psychological Technologies                              243
CHAPTER 14    The Politics of Motherhood                              265
CHAPTER 15    The Economics of Motherhood                             286

              Part Seven.  **What To Do About the
                           Future of Motherhood**                     303

CHAPTER 16    Experimental Communities                                309
CHAPTER 17    Revolution via Reform                                   332

              Part Eight.  **Motherhood and the
                           Social Order**                             345

CHAPTER 18    A New Balance                                           348
              Notes                                                   367
              Index                                                   421

# Foreword

This book is concerned with both the way our society institutionalizes one of its most important functions, namely the bearing and rearing of its children, and the forces—technological, political, economic, and ethical—that shape its operation. Motherhood is more than the biological process of reproduction. Much more. As an institution it consists of customs, traditions, conventions, beliefs, attitudes, mores, rules, laws, precepts, and the host of other rational and non-rational norms which deal with the care and rearing of children. It has also, like other institutions, a powerful symbolic component as well.

Although the reproductive aspects of motherhood—such, for example, as conception, gestation, birth, and lactation—have remained fairly constant for untold millennia,[1] variability has been the rule for its institutional aspect. Like most institutions, motherhood has varied widely from time to time and place to place. A major element of anthropological research, in fact, consists of reports on the manifold quaint and curious customs and myths associated with pregnancy, birth, and child rearing. All societies give preponderant responsibility for child rearing to women, though not exclusively to mothers, in the first years of life. But beyond that diversity prevails.

Among the array of child-care and child-rearing practices reported in this research, our own institutions of motherhood do not show up well. Motherhood in a modern industrial society like ours is a phenomenon quite different from motherhood in preliterate and preindustrialized societies. In a modern society, the two basic roles of women—those of mother and productive worker—have been separated with implications for both that we are only now beginning to trace, analyze, and, hopefully, to understand. We have not yet come to terms with this severance. We are, in fact, only beginning to catch a glimpse of the dimensions of the issues with which it confronts us. But it is quite clear that no discussion of motherhood in our day, let alone in the future, can ignore the effect which changes in the roles of mother and worker are having on both. The low birth rate now urgently advocated and the increasing participation of mothers in the labor force, are only the most salient of these changes. The immediate future calls for a reappraisal of both the mother and worker roles of women combined with a search for ways to reintegrate them, both psychologically and structurally.

## II

When we speak of feminine curves we are not usually thinking in terms of statistical trends. But the three curves on the frontispiece represent the most important "feminine" curves of today and tomorrow. The top one tells the story of trends in fertility; the middle and bottom, the story of labor-force participation of mothers of preschool- and school-age children. In and of themselves, these curves are simple enough. The fertility rate, which rose fairly precipitately in the late forties and fifties, has been declining since 1957; the proportion of mothers in the labor force with preschool- and school-age children has been going up.[2] Together these three trends describe a major revolution now in process, the most important "news" today. The contents of this book may be viewed as an extended exegesis of the story reflected in the three curves.

It is a sociological truism that a social system is such an organic entity that no matter where you touch it, the whole thing responds, violently perhaps in some parts, more mildly in others. Thus, although this book begins with the three "feminine" curves, symbolizing the mother and the work roles of women, ultimately it inevitably involves almost every aspect of modern society, political, economic, ethical, with technology pervading all of them. For the several technologies have played a fundamental part in shaping the three curves. They, not women themselves, have changed the roles of women both as workers and as mothers.

## III

Technologies have changed the nature of work, creating new jobs and attenuating and eliminating others.[3] A society is a lumbering and awkward system, but it does have to hang together, however loosely. So if, as seems to be the case in an industrial society, it takes about 40 to 50 percent of the entire labor force to do the types of work which until now have been assigned to women,[4] many things must happen in order for the society to adjust to the situation. For there is little if any likelihood that a modern economy could dispense with the work contributed by women since so many of the newer—like so many of the older—types of work are the kinds that today's women do well.[5] Indeed, "the level of demand for women workers has risen to such an extent that no demographic changes that are at all likely to occur can return us to the situation that existed in 1940. We have . . . passed the point of no return." [6] And women, like men, have had to respond to the exigencies of the times in which they live. They have supplied the work demanded by modern economies.

Women themselves had little to do with the technologies that attenuated their work in the home and took their industrial work out of it, just as they had little to say about the resulting demand for their services outside the home. They reacted rather than acted. Some may have resisted the outward pull. But there was never any possibility that, as a collective whole, they could have halted the technologies which produced industrialization and urbanization and the consequent demand for their services in the labor force. Even while priests, ministers, rabbis, and theologians, not to mention fathers, husbands, and men in general, shouted that woman's place was in the home, slowly, silently, they left the home. These were not members of any women's liberation movement. They were just individuals responding to the world in which they lived. As Jeanne Binstock reminds us, movements like the current feminist one "are really a consequence of technological changes"; this one has appeared "at the historical moment when a sharp reduction in the occupational group known as mothers is mandatory, and the technological capacity to achieve it is available. . . . [for] ideological change can occur only when the technological capacities for achieving it are available." [7] In this case the movement of the women came first and the supporting ideology came later. "Just as the Protestant Ethic lubricated the spread of capitalism, so the women's liberation ideology will lubricate the necessary occupational shift of masses of mothers into the emerging new society." [8]

## IV

Not only has the nature of work been changed by technology but so has the nature of motherhood itself. There was a time when a mother's work could be fitted into the rest of a woman's life without a seam. She could perform her role as mother and as productive worker at the same time and in the same setting. She learned to do a great deal of work with a baby on her left hip. Her work was considerably harder then than it is now but the demands of her children were more moderate. When they could see their mothers busy with household jobs: in the garden, in the yard, tending chickens, cleaning, laundering, cooking, preparing food, mending, sewing, hauling water and firewood—all obviously hard work—it did not occur to them that they were entitled to her full time and attention.

On the farm, in fact, there were useful things for the children themselves, however small, to do. The farm or household was clearly a family enterprise and everyone's hands were needed. "A child was expected to work, did work, and could see that his work was valuable. He found his identity in the contribution he made to what was essentially a family venture. . . . Children grew up in their chores. Progressing from the easiest of farm tasks to the most difficult, they could look forward confidently to taking, in time, the adult place that was clear before them." [9] And in the smaller towns there were yards and nearby fields where a child could play safely when not engaged in chores around the house. Even in cities, children were still offered relatively safe playing space. A woman could get her own work done without fear of her children being endangered. The technologies that produced urbanization and suburbanization have changed all that. Now that the mother's physical work within the home occupies relatively little time, the child makes correspondingly more demands upon her for attention. Responding to these demands can be as stressful as scrubbing a tubful of laundry once was.

The reintegration of the roles of mother and worker constitutes one of our major priorities today, an ethical as well as a political imperative. It is not merely a matter of roles per se, but of the whole world in which women's roles are performed, a matter of whole systems of relationship, a reversal of the trend of change from a world based on love and/or duty to one based on monetary exchange or a "cash-nexus."

## V

Where does one look for the future? In addition to statistical projections based on past and current trends, the young and the educated are the best sources, for it is their attitudes, opinions, and preferences that provide us with clues.

For some purposes—those of politicians, for example, or marketers—majorities are important. But for trying to explore the future, not how many people think one way or another but who they are is what is significant. Thus, for example, in an election or a poll all votes count equally; in the market, similarly, all dollars count the same. But so far as serving as indexes of the future is concerned, some "votes" count more heavily than others. The conservative elderly voter has as much weight in an election as the recently enfranchised eighteen-year-old. But the eighteen-year-old college freshman has more impact on the future than the venerable dowager. Cross-section surveys do not, therefore, always give hints with respect to the future. The size of the segment of a population that holds a particular view does not in and of itself necessarily portend what the future will be, for it may only reflect the past. In order to perceive trends one has to look for what it is that certain components of the public are thinking and doing, especially those who tend to be in the vanguard: the young and the more educated.

A striking example of the predictive validity of the attitudes of young and educated women as clues for the future is the direction of change in public attitude reported by Harris polls in the course of only one year, between 1971 and 1972. The poll asked the respondents if they favored efforts to strengthen or change the status of women in society. By 1972 the older women had arrived at about the same position as that taken by the younger women in 1971; by 1972 the high-school and eighth-grade graduates had arrived at the position taken by college women in 1971; and by 1972 the rural women had arrived at the position taken by the 1971 suburban women.[10] Meanwhile, of course, the young, the educated, and the suburban women had moved on. Among the young, over half (56 percent) favored efforts to strengthen women's status in 1972; among the college educated, 57 percent; and among suburban women, 51 percent. In addition there was also a slight tendency for the proportion of respondents giving a "not sure" response to decline, especially among the college-educated women.

Equally interesting as a clue to the future is the fact that the rate or extent as well as the direction of change between 1971 and 1972 was greater among the women under forty—about 22 percent—than among women fifty and over—about 37 percent; it was greater among the college women—about 30 percent—than among eighth-grade graduates—about 14 percent; and greater among the suburban—about 25 percent—than among the rural women—about 18 percent.[11]

In view of the tendency for the less educated women to be more conservative than the more educated, it is significant for the future that increasing education characterizes each generation. By 1990 it is estimated that half of all women sixty-five years of age and over and more than three-fourths of women twenty-five to sixty-four will be high-school graduates.[12] It is the growing size of the educated population that makes the views of educated women so significant as clues to the future.

Nor can history be ignored in looking for clues. If, for example, there ever were strong, aggressive, competent women, this fact alerts us to the possibilities for the future. To those, therefore, who say that women lack aggressiveness, adventuresomeness, and other admirable qualities, the existence of women with these qualities suggests the fallacy of the generalization. The use of history in a book on the future is justified also on the grounds that although there is no necessary relation between the past and the present or future, the past helps us to see the present more clearly and thus our vision of the future can be calibrated more accurately. No one who traces the history of motherhood, of the home, of child-rearing practices will ever assume the eternal permanence of our own way of institutionalizing them.

A considerable proportion of the literature on motherhood has a psychoanalytic slant. My own orientation is sociological, but I do not think one can reject insights simply because they are not personally convincing. I believe that just as the findings of demographers change over time so, also, will those of the psychoanalysts. I do not think the kinds of things the Freudians have found in the past will necessarily also be found in the future. I do not see the kinds of relationships between the sexes nor between parents and children in the future that will necessarily produce the kinds of neuroses that family relations of the past produced.

## VI

This book is not about the future of marriage nor of the family nor of the female labor force nor about women in general. There is a plethora of books on each of these topics. This one is about women in one particular role. A considerable literature deals with mothers as "factors" or as "variables" in accounting for characteristics of children—their achievement motivation, their political attitudes, their ideologies, their complexes and fixations and compulsions, what-have-you—but the emphasis is on the children, not the women, who remain shadowy wraiths in the background. To be sure, a book on women fulfilling their role as mothers is, by definition, bound to include those in complementary roles—children, husbands, fathers. But in the discussion here they are incidental, peripheral, minor characters in the cast. Attention is focused on the women themselves.

Our society is engaged in rewriting the script for the role of women as mothers. This is no side show, no minor concern that calls for a casual glance when we have time left over after debating defense and the balance of trade. It is the heart of the matter, one of the most momentous projects relevant for the future of our species. Such hyperbole invites a quizzical skepticism. Change, yes. Granted. But "future of our species?" Surely, even when it comes from dedicated environmentalists, an exaggeration? Slightly hysterical?

If the statement were made as a cry of doom, as it sometimes is, it could be so interpreted. But it is not. It is simply a statement of the fact that we are wrestling with a reordering of the lives of women to integrate their diminishing role as mothers and their changing role as workers. Such integration of the lives of women, as Erik Erikson has noted, will not be achieved "without conflict and tension." [13] Nor, it should be further noted, will the conflict and tension be limited to women themselves. Such a massive restructuring of our world, involving as it does the relations of women to men, of wives to husbands, and of mothers to children, does seem to warrant characterization as most momentous for the future of our species. And we are all in this together.

# PART ONE

## Motherhood As Institution, Mother As Symbol, and Women

## The Victorian Model
## for the Role of Mother

Not for the star-crowned heroes, the
    men that conquer and slay,
But a song for those that bore them, the
    mothers braver than they!
With never a blare of trumpets, with
    never a surge of cheers,
They march to the unseen hazard —
    pale, patient volunteers.[1]

---

The bravest battle that ever was fought;
Shall I tell you where and when?
On the maps of the world you will find it not;
It was fought by the mothers of men.[2]

---

Over my heart in the days that have flown,
No love like Mother-love ever has shone;
No other worship abides and endures,
Faithful, unselfish, and patient, like yours.[3]

---

The sweetest face in all the world to me,
Set in a frame of shining golden hair,
With eyes whose language is fidelity,
This is my mother. Is she not most fair?[4]

---

Don't poets know it
    Better than others?
God can't be always everywhere: and, so,
    Invented Mothers.[5]

The home where happiness securely dwells
Was never wrought by charms or magic spells.
A mother made it beautiful, but knew
No magic save what toiling hands can do.[6]

---

No angel, but a dearer being, all dipt
In angel instincts, breathing Paradise,
Interpreter between the gods and men,
Who look'd all native to her place, and yet
On tiptoe seem'd to touch upon a sphere
Too gross to tread, and all male minds perforce
Sway'd to her from their orbits as they moved,
And girdled her with music. Happy he
With such a mother! faith in womankind
Beats with his blood, and trust in all things high
Comes easy to him, and tho' he trip and fall
He shall not blind his soul with clay.[7]

---

For one on the ocean of crime long tossed,
Who loves his mother, is not quite lost.[8]

---

There was a young man loved a maid
Who taunted him. "Are you afraid,"
She asked, "to bring me today
Your mother's head upon a tray?"

He went and slew his mother dead
Tore from her breast her heart so red
Then towards his lady love he raced
But tripped and fell in all his haste.

As the heart rolled on the ground
It gave forth a plaintive sound.
And it spoke, in accents mild:
"Did you hurt yourself, my child?" [9]

---

Mother's arms are made of tenderness,
And sweet sleep blesses the child who lies therein.[10]

. . . of all women in the world, the most pure—and the most
useful as a sanction for adolescent chastity—was Mother. Every
young Victorian heard his father's voice, sounding in his conscience, "Remember your dear, good mother, and never do anything, think anything, imagine anything she would be ashamed
of. . . ."[11]

Mother . . . is a synonym of all that is good. It is a balm for every wound. It is the life of the young, the guiding star of manhood, the joy of old age. . . .[12]

A mother's calm strength, her sense of humor in the small tragedies, her courage, her justice, her loving service to each family member—these are the things that build a home, these are the things that make the mother the center—the heart—of the home. The mother who is truly the heart of the home has achieved that selflessness which enables her to rise to the need of each member of the family. . . . The wise mother will concern herself with all the varied interests of the family members. . . . As the family grows the mother extends her activities to meet the interests of the family outside the home. . . . The mother who has been the heart of the home during her children's early years does not withdraw from that position as the children grow, not even as they leave home. She remains the teacher-friend of her children, whose wise counsel is the bedrock of many a new family.[13]

. . . it is the mother, preeminently the mother, who, forgetful of self, is continually thinking and planning for the welfare and happiness of others; and it is her unselfish life of sacrifice and devotion that calls forth profound expression of man's inherent love for her whose consummate mother-love is the greatest human instrumentality in molding the lives of men and women for lives of usefulness, for spiritual helpfulness and for God.[14]

The noblest and best of earth in every age have honored and revered Mother and motherhood. By voice and pen they have delighted in expressing heartfelt and loving tributes to Mother and to mother-love; to her who has given herself, ofttimes, from starlit dawn to midnight's silent hour in untiring service and devotion to the physical and spiritual needs of her family; who is respected by all men for her charity toward the fallen and oppressed; who is loved for the consolation and comfort and helpfulness extended to the sick and needy and unfortunate, and for her womanly honor and nobility of mind and heart; who is adored for her sweetness and gentleness and purity of life and character—she who has done so much to shape the lives of men and women for the things that are eternal; who is extolled for her tender compassion, her noble self-sacrifice, her boundless mother-love; who is exalted for her living hope and trust in God and in the King of Glory; and whom we glorify for her steadfast-

5

ness and subl/ity of faith which more nearly approaches the divine than anything else we know in life.

Genial, sunshiny, happy. Hers is life's sweetest and tenderest love, a love beautiful and loyal and true, love that never fails. A halo of purity resting on her saintly brow—her face abeam with joy the world cannot give nor take away. Such mothers, though uncrowned, are the real queens of earth.[15]

# CHAPTER ONE

## Mother Is a Role,
## Women Are Human Beings

### A New and Unique Institution

Motherhood as we know it today is a surprisingly new institution. It is also a unique one, the product of an affluent society. In most of human history and in most parts of the world even today, adult, able-bodied women have been, and still are, too valuable in their productive capacity to be spared for the exclusive care of children. They have been necessary for tilling the fields or fishing or gathering. In a study of six cultures around the world, including our own, for example, a team of anthropologists and psychologists found only our culture following our model.[1]

Among the Nyansongo of Kenya, for example, "during much of the day . . . the mother is working the nearby fields and around the house, and the infant is carried and cared for by a child nurse . . . six to ten years old . . . usually an older sibling . . . who plays an important part in the infant's life." [2] Sometimes co-wives help; sometimes fathers do also. For "Nyansongo mothers are over-burdened with an agricultural and domestic work load which limits the attention they can pay to their weaned children. In consequence, they delegate a good deal of care-taking and training to older children in the homestead, and they reduce their maternal role to what they consider its bare essentials. . . . Another important consequence of the mother's heavy work load is that she trains the children to share it with her as soon as they are able." [3] Similarly, among the *Rajputs* of India, "during the months when the baby is too old to lie quietly on a cot and too young to walk itself, it is, if possible, turned over to an older girl to carry when the

7

mother is busy working. As a rule, this caretaker will be an older sister, but a cousin may take the child if the sisters-in-law are on good terms." [4] Old men may also help in baby-tending. And once the child begins to walk, if he is a boy, the men—fathers, uncles, or grandfathers—may take over. And so, too, among the villagers of Taira, Okinawa. "From the time he is a month old until shortly before the arrival of the next baby, he [the infant] is constantly carried during the day-time on the back of . . . an adult or an older child. . . . His carriers include parents, paternal grandparents, unmarried aunts and uncles, older siblings in an extended household, and parents and older siblings in a nuclear household." [5] And the Mixtecans of Mexico where "the transference of the primary caretaking responsibilities from the mother to the sibling group . . . takes place . . . about a year after weaning." [6] And among the residents of Tarong, an Ilocos barrio in the Philippines: "in no household did a mother have sole responsibility for her children—it would be unthinkable. . . . If the house is relatively isolated and the family nuclear, the father may well hold the baby whenever he is not in the fields, bathe it, change its clothes, feed it tidbits. If the house has many women or older girls, he will rarely do more than play with the child while it is still young." [7] After weaning, caretakers may be aunts, grandmothers, siblings, or even fathers. "More often than not . . . the child . . . eventually obtains care from the socially approved source—the neighbor-kin group, both adults and peers." [8] For pre-schoolers there are many caretakers, all the children belonging to all in the housing group. "We all help to raise our children." [9] Among the Alors, "since women are primarily responsible for garden work and the subsistence economy, mothers return to regular field work ten days to two weeks after the birth of the child. It is not customary for the mother to work with the child on her back or even near her, as it is in some societies. Instead the infant is left at home in care of some kin, for example the father, an older sibling of either sex, or a grandmother whose field labor is less effective or necessary than that of a younger woman." [10] By way of contrast, we find that in our society today "parents . . . generally discourage older siblings . . . from assuming responsibility for infants on the grounds that the older child will be irresponsible and that it would also be imposing unduly on him or her. It is thought to be too trying for an older child to face the baby's antisocial behavior and maintain reasonable control over it." [11]

### And Not a Good One

The way we institutionalize motherhood in our society—assigning sole responsibility for child care to the mother, cutting her off from the easy help of others in an isolated household, requiring round-the-clock tender, loving care, and making such care her exclusive activity—is not only new and unique, but not even a good way for either women or—if we accept as a criterion the amount of maternal warmth shown—for children. It may, in fact, be the worst. It is as though we had selected the worst features of all the ways motherhood is structured around the world and combined them to produce our current design.

This charge is based on the findings of the research teams previously quoted. They found that women in cultures where they were given the heaviest load of child care were more changeable in expressing warmth than those in other cultures and more likely to have hostilities not related to the behavior of the children.[12] In fact, the greater the burden of child care assigned to these mothers, the less likely they were to be able to supply the warm care infants require. "Mothers," they reported, "who spend a high proportion of their time caring for children are somewhat more unstable in their emotional reactions to their children than are mothers who do not have such exclusive responsibility."[13] The so-called harassment aspect of child care was also greater among them. Maternal warmth was more likely to occur when there was a grandmother present to spell the mother off. "Mothers who must cope more than others, either with their own children or their children's cousins, are muted in their warmth, while mothers who have the help of a grandmother are free in their expression of affection."[14] Maternal instability likewise decreased when additional caretakers eased the mother's burden and when there were relatively few children requiring her care.

Life-style was also found to be related to maternal warmth. "Mothers who are really isolated from their relatives and substitute caretakers may control expressiveness . . . to avoid further wear and tear on their own frayed nerves and fights among siblings for their own praise and affection.[15] Another study of forty-five cultures for which data were available found a relationship between a high incidence of mother-child households (as, for example, in polygyny) and the inflicting of pain on the child by the nurturant agent. And, conversely, although less markedly, a negative relationship between maternal warmth and incidence of mother-child households.[16]

The two requirements we build into the role of mother—full-time care of children and sole responsibility for them—seem, in brief, to be incompatible with one another, even mutually exclusive. In view of these findings it is sobering to note that in our society we seem to maximize this contradiction in the role so that mothers here "have a significantly heavier burden (or joy) of baby care than the mothers in any other society." [17] Today young mothers who "spend a high proportion of their time caring for children" are corroborating the researchers' report. Yes, they are beginning to tell us, it's true: they find joy in their children, but they do not like motherhood.[18]

### Home and Mother

The isolated home as we know it, like motherhood with which it is intrinsically related, is also a fairly new institution in human history. The privacy of the home originated as a form of protective isolation, though what it was guarding against changed with time. In the fifteenth century, for example, it was protection against the evils of communal festivities. Later it was protection against too great demands being made upon it:

> In the eighteenth century, the family began to hold society at a distance, to push it back beyond a steadily extending zone of private life. The organization of the house altered in conformity with this new desire to keep the world at bay. . . . People began defending themselves against a society whose constant intercourse had hitherto been the source of education, reputation and wealth. . . . The history of modern manners can be reduced in part to this long effort to break away from others, to escape from a society whose pressure had become unbearable.[20]

In the nineteenth century the cloistering of the home was a protection against the evils of industrialization and urbanization.

In the new economic order that accompanied the industrial revolution, hard, driving, competitive men were creating a male-oriented civilization in which a dog-eat-dog philosophy prevailed; the survival of the fittest as it was then interpreted, called for an extremely rugged individualism. Let the best man win. It was a world of achievement at almost any human price.

But even for those who could operate successfully in such an atmosphere, as well as for those who could not, there had to be some place where relief was possible. That place was provided by the sheltering home. And it was woman's role to supply the healing balm to the victors as well as to the victims of the cruel outside world. "The Feminine as the giver of shelter and protection" encompassed "the life of the family and group in the symbol of the house." [21]

### The Queen's Walled Garden

The home was a sacred place. Even for non-believers and agnostics it was a "secular temple," a place for social altruism. In order for the mother to perform her sheltering and protective function she herself had to be protected from the outside world, isolated from it, immured in a walled garden.

> . . . the conception of the home as a source of virtue and emotions which were nowhere else to be found, least of all in business and society . . . made it a place radically different from the surrounding world. It was much more than a house where one stopped at night for temporary rest and recreation—or procreation—in the midst of a busy career. It was a place apart, a walled garden, in which certain virtues too easily crushed by modern life could be preserved, and certain desires of the heart too much thwarted be fulfilled.[22]

This isolated home, protected from the outside world for whatever reason, was the mother's responsibility to maintain as a sanctuary. She ruled over it contributing order, arrangement, decision, as well as faithful and wise counseling. In an essay that has been called "the most important single document . . . for the characteristic idealization of love, woman, and the home in Victorian thought," [23] John Ruskin laid out the province of mothers:

> This is the true nature of home—it is the place of Peace; the shelter, not only from all injury, but from all terror, doubt, and division. In so far as it is not this, it is not home; so far as the anxieties of the outer life penetrate into it, and the inconsistently-minded, unknown, unloved, or hostile society of the outer world is allowed by either husband or wife to cross the threshold, it ceases to be home; it is then only a part of that outer world which you have roofed over, and lighted fire in.

11

But so far as it is a sacred place, a vestal temple, a temple of the hearth watched over by Household Gods . . . so far as it is this, and roof and fire are types only of a nobler shade and light,—shade as of the rock in a weary land, and light as of the Pharos in the stormy sea;—so far it vindicates the name, and fulfills the praise, of Home.[24]

A man might have to sally forth to meet the perils of the outside world, to struggle on that grim, harsh stage, become hardened, but "he guards the woman from all this; within his house, as ruled by her, unless she herself has sought it, need enter no danger, no temptation, no cause of error or offense." [25] George Eliot put it succinctly: "A loving woman's world lies within the four walls of her own home; and it is only through her husband that she is in any electric communication with the world beyond." [26] Protected, sheltered, isolated, safe within the walls of their gardens, women as mothers became the repositories of all the humane virtues. It was the mother who made of home a school of virtue.

## Mother As Symbol

The idealization of the maternal role in society's taboos in-dicates that in the interest of the survival of the species the mother-child relationship has to be buttressed by social regu-lation, and also that this is often not sufficient, and that defi-ciencies have therefore to be covered up by idealization.[27]

Increasingly idealized—by definition loving, gentle, tender, self-sacrificing, devoted, limited in interests to creating a haven for her family—the mother became in time almost a parody. Mothers have been honored from time immemorial, assessed above rubies in value, as the Proverbial woman was, or as the Roman matron was, or the chatelaine of a medieval castle might be. But the mother adored for her self-abnegation, her "altruistic surrender," [28] even for her self-immolation, was a nineteenth-cen-tury Victorian creation. This image reached its heyday at the turn of the century and lingered on until yesterday.

Even today, in fact, one catches glimpses of the Victorian mother in debates about the place of women.[29] The image still lurks behind the battle cry "A woman's place is in the home." It has retained a tenacious hold on our minds long after the environ-ment that created and supported it has disappeared. And its exten-sion into the future is suggested by its persistence in children's schoolbooks, where mother is still the ever-loving homebody.[30]

It has taken a long time to overcome this concept of the home as a walled garden presided over by a cherishing mother, an isolated, cut-off, protected temple where people could huddle together against a cruel outside world. It may be that only certain members of the post-war generation carry no vestige of it. So far as they are concerned, they want no part of it. For them—and even, increasingly, for their mothers as well—the isolated, walled garden became a prison long ago, keeping them in rather than the world out.

Furthermore, the outside world changed, changing the part played both by the home and by the workshop. The home was no longer a sanctuary for men in a hostile world. They were deriving as much—or as little—satisfaction from their work as from their marriages.[31]

## Mothers As Women

Victorian motherhood was a male—and a middle-class—conception. The more female historians study it from the point of view of the women themselves the less authentic it looks. It was never a genuine portrait even of the Victorian mother, let alone the mother of any other age. Women are just not like that. Now or ever.

Mothers in the home were already becoming a "social problem" a hundred years ago. They were already champing at the bit. They were already complaining of being boxed in. Even then they were fretting and wearied by motherhood's "daily round of trivial tasks, occupying the time and absorbing the energies." [32] Then as now they felt shut in "from the larger life of the world, which courses freshly past the home within which they are imprisoned." Many who "once dreamed of great things" sighed "sadly in the thought of the nursery bondage and . . . looked out wistfully on the noble labors awaiting mind and heart in the outer world." [33] Then, as now, those who fretted "under its [motherhood's] burdens of care, threw off from them in every way possible their divinely imposed charge" in order to "escape from the home to society, to find for themselves pleasure, or to make for themselves work other than that providentially ordered." [34] As early as 1879, Ibsen's Nora, in reply to her husband's dictum that "before all else" she was "a wife and mother," said: "that I no longer believe. I believe that before all else I am a human being, just as much as you are—or at least that I should try to become one."

By the turn of the century it was already becoming apparent that there was something wrong about the nineteenth-century model for the role of mother. Women were finding it increasingly difficult to perform it. Invoking the idealized model did no good. "Putting on a Madonna-like pedestal the often impatient, irritable mother who feels chained to her duties, may suffice for the aims of idealism and wishful thinking, but makes life easier neither for mothers nor for children. True, it saves society the feeling that it should change itself." [35] But aggrieved women were not to let "society" spare itself the comfort of standing pat. If they were poor, they were protesting against having too many children; [36] if they were affluent, they were protesting against the confinement of the doll's house. They wanted out.

But never until this very historical moment have women rebelled as many are now doing against the very way we institutionalize motherhood. They are daring to say that although they love children, they hate motherhood. That they object to being assigned sole responsibility for child care. That they object to having child care conceived as their only major activity. That they object to the isolation in which they must perform the role of mother, cut off from help, from one another, from the outside world. For the first time they are protesting the false aura of romanticism with which motherhood is endowed, keeping from young women its terrible "hidden ~~~~lerside," which "is hardly talked about." One young mother feels obsessed with the need to tell people what really happens when you have children," to expose "the terrible weight of responsibility, the way it affects a woman's personality." A group of women, basing their conclusions on their own experiences as participant observers—or, rather, as observant participators—note almost point for point how the way we institutionalize motherhood is bad for women. They call on women to organize "to fight those aspects of our society that make childbearing and child rearing stressful rather than fulfilling experiences." One young woman speaks of "the baby trap." [37] Another writes a book to tell us that "mother's day is over," to inform us that "until now millions of women have secretly shared, and silently endured, a profound guilt: they love their children, but they do not love being mothers." She hopes her book "will end their solitude and reduce their guilt and make them more dignified human beings." [38]

Nor is motherhood as we institutionalize it good for children. The anger and irritability it fosters in women reverberates on the children. "When it is realized how difficult woman's present situation makes her full self-realization, how many desires, rebellious feelings, just claims she nurses in secret, one is frightened at the thought that defenseless infants are abandoned to her care." [39] It is no less serious because "most women have the morality and decency to repress their spontaneous impulses; nevertheless these impulses suddenly flash out at times in angry scenes, slaps, punishments, and the like." The mother may feel remorse; but the child feels the pain.

The "smother-love" fostered in women with no other channel for self-actualization came in time to be resented by the sons and daughters. These children of the women struggling to fill their lives with the mother role were as much victimized as the women themselves. They began to see their mothers as not all that saintly after all. Sometimes, in fact, they saw them as devouring vultures. Instead of honoring mother they had to fight to rid themselves of their enforced dependencies on her. Mothers were attacked as a generation of vipers [40] who had ruined their sons by their momism [41] and had produced sons full of sexual compulsions.[42] The virtues of the nineteenth-century mother were turned inside out: the angels became monsters. The Great Mother archetype became the Terrible Mother archetype.[43] Once worshipfully hoisted on a pedestal, mothers were now pelted with abuse.

> . . . mothers are held responsible for juvenile delinquency, problem children, neurotic children, vandalism, communism, and the many other woes of society. Now, on bearing a child, one automatically loses any semblance of common sense one may have had earlier when one was in business, in a profession or in some other career. . . . [Mothers] are maligned, insulted, and treated like an evil spirit.[44]

Whether the denigration of the mother resulted, as some alleged, from neglect by working mothers or, as others alleged, from "smother-love" by home-bound mothers, whether too little or too much mothering was the basis of the denigration, it was, in fact, quite real. Whatever was wrong in our society, it had to be the mother's fault.

Role, home, and symbol as components of Victorian motherhood were, then, all relatively new when they arose, but they were already in process of becoming anachronisms when the twentieth century inherited them. What we see today is the tail end of a comet, the tail of a model of motherhood that began to disintegrate as it struck the twentieth century. The comet itself was a model of motherhood that appeared in Victorian times in response to a set of circumstances unique in human history, circumstances that resulted finally in the severance of the two most fundamental aspects of human life, family and work. Two worlds separated out, one an outside work world, one an almost cloistered family world.

It was not the protests of mothers that finally battered down the walls of the queen's garden. It was the outside forces that were taking much of the work of women out of the home and attenuating much that remained within it. The shock waves of industrialization and urbanization that began to break at the end of the eighteenth century were to be felt throughout all of nineteenth-century society. Nothing was to be left untouched, even motherhood. The nature of work, the nature of the home, the nature of all human relations, were all to be transformed. We have to go back more than ten thousand years, to the beginnings of agriculture, to find anything comparable to the events we now call *the* industrial revolution, actually only one of many, before and since.

The walls that had surrounded the home proved unable to withstand the maelstrom of industrialism and urbanism. They crumbled first among the poor. Then among the unmarried daughters of the not-so-poor. Then among the valiant well-to-do, among women who began to see the walls as keeping them in rather than as keeping the world out. Then among wives, even mothers. The walls, however symbolic, remain today as only reminders of the past. They have come to be seen by more and more women as gilded cages, if not as prisons.

The current revolt of many women against the role of mother as institutionalized in our society will no more force us to rethink the structure of motherhood today than did the protests of mothers a century ago. But a host of other forces, including—in addition to continuing technological changes—the antinatalism engendered by the environment movement, are already at work to bring about such a restructuring. We can't go home again. Not, at least, to the Victorian home.

# PART TWO

---

# The
# First Imperative
# and the Future

# Introduction

Although reproduction, a biological phenomenon, is not the same as motherhood, still the first imperative of motherhood, however institutionalized, is to reproduce. There can be no motherhood without children. In this sense motherhood has a biological substrate. But it is much more. We cannot interpret the future of motherhood in strictly biological terms.

The role of mother is universally prescribed for women. There are exceptions—members of religious orders, for example, the unmarried, and, though not by design, beautiful women [1]—are excused. But for practically all others, the bearing of children has been almost intrinsic to femaleness, evidence and proof and validation of competence as a female. And practically all women do bear children. But why?

The simplest explanation is in terms of a maternal instinct. But it is extremely difficult to make such an explanation stick. It is true that among mammalians the presence of an infant is enough to bring forth nurturant behavior in most adult females. But the evidence for that kind of maternal instinct is too ambiguous to rely on; it does not explain the presence of the infant in the first place. Further we do not need to posit such an instinct to explain the all-but-universal desire of women to have children. The pressures exerted on girls to become mothers are enough to explain it. Indeed, they are so great as to appear coercive to many women. Chapter 2 looks into some of them.

There was a time when this overwhelming emphasis on the reproductive function of women was tolerable, whether or not it was necessary. Women complied. But at least in the immediate future, the emphasis will be on the muting, not the stimulating, of the desire for children. And questions are being raised with respect to this damping down of the mother role. Will it have deleterious effects on women? If the future of motherhood did, indeed, rest on a maternal instinct, frustrating it could have serious repercussions. If, that is, we were dealing with a built-in biological drive, there might be grounds for concern.

We are not, fortunately, in that kind of bind. We do not have to change nor violate female heredity to moderate fertility. Damping down the maternal role does not run counter to any overwhelming drive and hence run the risk of serious biological harm to women. Since the all-but-universal desire for children does not require an instinct to explain it but can be explained in terms of the pressures exerted on girls, all we really have to do, as Judith Blake tells us, is release the pressures.[2]

Of special interest is the emergence of a movement for non-motherhood, not necessarily anti-motherhood, but simply non-motherhood (Chapter 3). The purpose is not to denigrate motherhood but rather to remove the pressures and make it truly voluntary.

Also of special interest for the future of motherhood is the current call emanating from the environmental movement for reducing the number of babies women have. If women were extravagant in their desire for motherhood or if they had maternal instincts that demanded constant expression there would be cause for concern. Cutting down on babies or rationing them could conceivably have untoward effects on them. Fortunately women are not extravagant in their desire for babies. They are, rather, quite stable and on the moderate side. Left to themselves most would probably settle for one or two (Chapter 4). Women will well survive such a "rationing" of motherhood. So will motherhood.

Demographers report few if any personality differences among women who want many and women who want few babies. This is a good augur for the future.

# CHAPTER TWO

## Why Motherhood?

### Many Differences, One Similarity

There can be, of course, no motherhood, whatever the model for the role, whatever the prescriptions it calls for, or whatever the difficulties it involves, until the babies are born. The first imperative for the role of mother, therefore, has always been: Bear children. Women are the people who bear the children, the people for whom the script is written. The script is the same for all of them; the women themselves are not at all the same. Some find the role congenial, others do not. Some perform it well. Others do not.

Women come in a wide variety of shapes, sizes, colors, talents, temperaments, and degrees of "motherliness." They come in a wide variety of personalities and with different motivations. They differ in standards and styles. They come from a wide variety of backgrounds: Some are rich, some are poor, most are in between; some are educated and some are not. They differ in occupational backgrounds and, most relevantly, as far as motherhood is concerned, in religion.

In one respect, despite all these differences, women are alike. Practically all of them want at least one or two children. Not a single study of young women to date has reported more than a minuscule proportion who did not give motherhood as one life goal.[1] Because of the differences among them, the actual fulfillment and satisfaction they expect do not necessarily follow. Still, for the present, if not the future, anticipation of children is present in practically every young woman in our society.[2]

The combination of these differences and this similarity raises at least two sets of questions relevant for the future: Why is it that despite their differences, almost all females want babies? What are the effects on the performance of the mother role that result when, despite these differences, practically all women become mothers?

Are we dealing here with some female biological constant that will determine the future of motherhood as it has its past, some ineluctable "instinct" that will defy our efforts at control, so that in anticipating the future we face certain constraints on our expectations? In view of intrinsic biology can the top curve in the colophon plunge any further? Will it hit a floor beyond which it cannot fall, a floor determined by a maternal "instinct?" That is the first set of questions and the answer is that although there has to be a floor—the birth rate cannot decline to zero—that floor is not determined by a maternal "instinct"; it is determined, rather, by the institutional pressures operating on girls and women. And these pressures, at least within limits, can presumably be modified.

## Why Motherhood?

The most facile explanation for the all-but-universal desire for children among the most diverse types of women is, simply, animal instinct. All females, regardless of differences among themselves, have a maternal instinct and that is enough to explain their desire for children.

If we were dealing with a strictly theoretical problem there would be no point in tackling this point of view here. But as a practical—even political—matter it has to be faced at the very outset in any discussion of the future of motherhood. For whatever the answer to the question may prove to be, the future is sure to call for only moderate indulgence in motherhood for most women. It is relevant, therefore, to know if we are dealing with some biological constant that will determine the future of motherhood, some ineluctable instinct that will—some might say, should—defy our efforts at control? So that in anticipating the future we face given constraints on what we can expect? It is because questions of this kind are sometimes asked that we must pay our respects to them here.[3]

There are unquestionably numerous reflexes involved in human, as well as in animal, reproduction, including the reflexes that propel the infant from the womb and produce milk in the breasts and the hosts of physiological reflexes that precede them.

No problem here. In this sense there are many "maternal" instincts, present in all women, universal, part of species heredity, as instincts by definition must be.

But the term "maternal instinct" does not usually refer to these reproductive reflexes. It refers rather to the more psychological and social aspects of motherhood. The nearest to evidence for the existence of a maternal instinct in this psychological and social sense is the fact that among mammalians the presence of an infant does, indeed, tend to stimulate nurturant behavior on the part of most [4]—though not all [5]—mothers. Even, one might add, on the part of non-mothers. Many women enjoy holding babies without at the same time wanting to assume total responsibility for them.

And even this provocative fact does not tell us much about the preceding desire for the infant which, when it appears, produces the nurturant or maternal behavior. The "nurturant" instinct is not enough to demonstrate a maternal instinct with the criteria specified above—present in all women, universal, part of species heredity.

One could, in fact, argue the direct opposite to the instinct point of view. If wanting children were indeed instinctive why are such powerful engines of socialization—documented below—required to make girls want them? [6] There is also anthropological evidence of the rejection of motherhood at many times and in many places in the form of abortion and infanticide which have been acceptable human institutions from time immemorial.[7] W. G. Sumner, early in the century, called our attention to the fact that "abortion and infanticide . . . show how early in the history of civilization the burden of children became so heavy that parents began to shirk it." [8]

He reminds us also that we have to distinguish between sexual and parental instincts. He was of the opinion that "if procreation had not been put under the dominion of a great passion, it would have been caused to cease by the burdens it entails." [9] The separation of sexuality from parenthood which human beings have achieved means that the burdens of procreation can be dealt with more expeditiously than by resort to abortion and infanticide.

Nor, finally, can it be demonstrated that there is any biological necessity for maternity in the individual woman, as contrasted with the group. There is no unequivocal evidence that women need motherhood for the sake of health or longevity. The health and longevity of nuns are as good as those of other women. It may be true that some kinds of illnesses are more or less common among non-mothers than among mothers, but the net effect, if any, of motherhood on health and longevity is not demonstrably great. Women can function very well without maternity. A woman may indeed bloom and be at her maximum beauty during pregnancy, but maternity does not improve her health or prolong her life. Before medical science overcame the hazards of childbirth it was one of the great killers. Men, as recorded on New England tomb stones, might "go through" several wives in a lifetime.

The answer to the question, are we up against a biological given so that damping down maternity will wreak destructive effects on women, may be answered in the negative. We do not have to posit a maternal instinct in women that can brook no frustration. The institutional pressures exerted on women to become mothers are more than enough to explain why it is that every little girl automatically replies to the question, "what are you going to be when you grow up?" with a prompt and confident, "mother." Bearing children is, literally, the first imperative for women.

## "Coercive" Motherhood

"I was forty years old," says a suburban housewife, "before it dawned on me that I really had had no choice about becoming a mother. Not that I didn't know all about contraception but that it had never occurred to me that anything else was possible." She felt indignant. She might have chosen motherhood anyway; she was not dissatisfied with her role as mother. But she was resentful that there had been no real choice, no chance to choose. As one demographer has pointed out "being a 'parent' and living in a family setting, are part of the generally unexamined assumptions of human societies." [10] Some of the younger women do not see it in such bland terms; to them there is a more purposeful design back of the insistence on motherhood: "I do not know if it was pure biological urge that made it imperative that I bear a child. I doubt it. The thrust toward my child's conception was fueled by many vested interests. 'They' wanted it. And 'they' delight in it to this very moment. . . . In every childhood fantasy of the future, I pictured myself surrounded by my adoring children. Never did the possibility of choice cross my mind. At best, I would combine motherhood with some sort of career." [11] She was not bitter; she loved her baby. "But nobody told me what the trip was."

Until it is carefully analyzed and called to our attention, it is difficult to see how coercive motherhood is for women, how little choice they really have, how powerful are the forces operating on them. Judith Blake has made such an analysis of "coercive prona-talism" for the Commission on Population Growth and the American Future. Her analysis concentrates on two such coercive forces; "the prescribed primacy of parenthood in the definition of adult sex roles and the prescribed congruence of personality traits with the demands of the sex roles as defined." [12] We define adult sex roles in terms of parenthood and then see to it that girls become the kind of people we say mothers must be and boys the kind of people we say fathers should be.

By emphasizing the "primacy of parenthood" in the lives of women, we foreclose alternative roles for them. We define anything that challenges this primacy as deviant or even pathological. Ms. Blake thus shows that female labor force participation, education for women, and feminism arouse "widespread opposition to the recognized threat [they constitute] to sex-role expectations." [13] Motherhood has to take precedence over everything else in the lives of women. The social sciences and the law bolster this institutionally prescribed primacy. Psychoanalysis, sociology, and legal philosophy have also shored up the traditional controls even when it looked superficially as though they were being overcome. Practically all of the thinking in law, theology, and the social sciences has, in fact, had at its core the fact that women bear children. The institutional structure of our society is based on that rock bottom fact. Motherhood is, after all, woman's destiny; all else is secondary. Yes, girls should be reared to be attractive sex objects to men. Yes, they should be prepared to support themselves and their children "just in case" or "in a pinch." Yes, let them even become artists or scientists or scholars if they wish. But all that is secondary. Motherhood comes first. Even before wifehood. Wives have been discarded for sterility, or even for producing only daughters. This is the institutional ambience in which girls are reared.

The other coercive force Ms. Blake specifies is the socializing process by which the personality traits of girls are shaped to conform to the demands of this ambience. We socialize girls so effectively as children that we hardly need to apply outside pressures when they grow up. We teach them to be "feminine" so that they will not only opt for motherhood but will feel satisfied with it and even fight any change that may threaten it.[14] We build "the perpetuation of pronatalist sex roles into the structure of personality through socialization 'for' personality traits that are congruent with these sex roles, and 'against' traits that could produce conflict with them. Such rigid sex-typing of personality traits doubtless explains, in part, why a change in sex role expectations is so difficult to effect." [15]

### Girls into Mothers

The first step in preparing women for the role of mother is to process them to want children. It has been the function of parents, school, church, law, the media, and governmental policy to achieve this goal.

Thus almost from the moment she is born, the little pink-clad infant is processed to become a mother. It has been noted that if one asks a little boy what he is going to be when he grows up he will reply in a wide variety of ways: fireman, aviator, astronaut. Not so the little girl. She will reply that she is going to be a mother. In school books for small children: "Dick says he will be an engineer. Sally says she will be a Mommy." [16] And so, in these first encounters with her own future, "when a girl looks ahead to the future, she is like Jill, a girl who wants to be a farmer's wife and . . . have lots of children." [17]

There are few surprises in the future of the little girl. When or how often she will become a mother may not be anticipated in advance, but that she will become one is practically beyond doubt. It was estimated that only 1.3 percent of all women as of 1960 would never bear a child,[18] and some of these would be mothers anyway, if not of children of their own bodies, then of children borne by others.

The exact mechanisms involved in socializing girls for motherhood have been assiduously studied by researchers. More than half a century ago Leta Hollingsworth reported on the techniques used to persuade women to have babies. She showed how religion and art have glorified the image of the mother, how public opinion, subsidies, and bounties have encouraged motherhood, and how laws against contraception, abortion, and infanticide have provided negative sanctions.[19] And feminists today have brought the story up to date by showing how the use of toys, the image in story books and on television, games, and school patterns have all slanted the socialization of girls inevitably toward accepting motherhood as an ultimate goal.

On television, for example, motherhood is a continuing theme in all the soap operas:

> Susan, on "As the World Turns," has just had a baby. She is not the only one. Turning the daytime dial, we see that Chris, on "Where the Heart Is," has just had a baby too. Within the past year, babies have also been born to Janet on "Search for Tomorrow," Meredith on "One Life to Live," Edie on "All My Children," Angel on "Love Is a Many-Splendored Thing," Diana on "General Hospital," Linda on "Days of Our Lives," Mary on "Where the Heart Is," Carolee on "The Doctors." . . . and on "Another World" Pat Randolph has twins. There will be more new mothers soon. Susan . . . , Kate . . . , Kathy . . . , India Hillman . . . , Jane . . . , Iris . . . , and Tara . . . , are all pregnant. Actually, the birth rate on daytime TV seems to rival that of Latin America.[20]

Nothing is more horrifying in these stories than loss of ability to have children. "Sandy reacted to her hysterectomy with nothing short of blind hysteria: 'Empty, empty, empty—I'll never feel life inside me again!'" [21] A miscarriage lands a woman in an institution or on the psychiatrist's couch. Male sterility is just as traumatic.

Daytime talk and quiz shows carry the same message. "Television has done a good job with some old messages. 'We've got a big country here,' say the Westerns. 'Motherhood is destiny,' say the soaps. 'Kids are fun for everyone,' imply the evening story lines. 'Life's real and high adventure is wiping up spills,' say the advertisers. Any problems? Drop two Crayolas in water." [22]

An analysis of two thousand television commercials showed that they, too, glorified large families. Motherhood was used to sell a wide variety of products. "Mom, you're incredible. . . . I hope I look as good as you when I grow up." A child decides not to run away from home when Mom fixes the advertised food. Mothers used a certain product, so now their daughters do too, suggesting the inevitability of motherhood. Mothers are shown as synonymous with wisdom. Husband says: "Now that you're expecting, I don't want you to lift a finger." "Having a baby can do great things for your hands." Or your hair: "There's nothing like having a baby to help you discover the best shampoo for your hair." "I'm going to tell *my* mommy *I* want a new baby brother, too." And so on and on.[23]

Fan magazines addressed to young women cater to this world of illusion, this world apotheosizing motherhood. Thus in an interview, a "Special Editorial Adviser to the Motion Picture Fan Magazine on the Creation and Perpetuation of Star Images" (sic) for thirty-five years, tells us how she always made her own stand on the true position of women quite clear "by bringing out the *unnatural* tortures and anxieties that women go through when they choose a career, as opposed to the *natural* tortures and anxieties of just being a wife and mother." [24] In other words, since it can be taken for granted that women are going to suffer, no matter what choices they make, they would do better to suffer as mothers than as careerists. In writing about the glamorous female stars it was always the joys and sorrows of motherhood rather than the triumphs of achievement that sold stars, at least to the female public. When Elizabeth Taylor's unconventional and seemingly ruthless love life was alienating millions of women, the story of her hysterectomy won them back. One could feel only compassion for a woman no longer capable of bearing children. After thirty-five years during which neither time nor tide has held still, the Editorial Adviser's basic convictions remain the same:

> Stardom, especially for a woman, is a dizzying, almost innately evil situation. It denatures her, compromises her, and worst of all, tends to distract her from the *summum bonum* of womanhood. That *summum bonum* is fecundity, the production of children, the defining of herself through that creation. Barrenness, especially through hysterectomy, whether it happens to a childless woman or a woman already a mother, is the greatest tragedy that can befall a woman. The greater her suffering over the loss of her childbearing capacities, the more she is to be pitied; the greater the redemptive power of that loss. The new permissiveness has become a legitimate and boldly dramatic phenomenon so long as it leads to motherhood. Babies have become the great purifiers. In short, no matter how you get there.[25]

Even out-of-wedlock pregnancies are acceptable. A woman can violate every moral canon provided she bears children. That one act redeems her:

> It matters not at all whether a woman smokes pot, employs four-letter words, consorts with Black Panthers, or bears chil-

dren out of love rather than in marriage—so long as she bears. Nor does it matter how wanton and arrogant her past has been, so long as she suffers enormously because of her inability to reproduce.[26]

Nor is the glorification of motherhood limited to the mass media. In a somewhat different style textbooks carry a similar message. They contribute to the emphasis on motherhood by taking it for granted that it is the only option for women, by ignoring the possibility of fulfillment outside of motherhood, by assuming a maternal instinct, and by overemphasis on fertility technology rather than on contraceptive technology.[27] A preliminary overview of the attitude toward motherhood in textbooks quotes one textbook to the effect that "if there is no physical or financial or professional reason for . . . [a] young woman not to have a child, she may be suffering from a neurotic infantilism." It further notes that: the inevitability of motherhood is assumed; the books take it for granted that maternity is the central focus of a woman's whole life; childlessness is problematic or undesirable; there is also a bias against the only child or one-child family; large families are portrayed as happy; and so on.

The results of this campaign have been so successful and all-pervasive that it is no wonder that wanting children has been assumed to be instinctive.

There have been many other theories, in addition to instinct and societal pressures to explain the almost universal desire of women to have children. Proof of biological competency or normal femaleness; competition with one's mother ("a woman's first baby may involve a hostile desire to replace the mother; having a larger or smaller family may also be an attempt to outdo the mother");[28] a desire to punish oneself or others; a desire for immortality; a way to gain attention; a form of becoming mother to the father as well as the child; a way to entrap a man or to force parental approval of a marriage; a way to "escape from freedom"; a way to fill up one's time,[29] are among the many reasons given for why women want babies. Pressure from obstetricians and gynecologists has also been suggested.[30] And one woman writes to Ann Landers to tell her why women want babies: "don't you know that a great many women are . . . insecure and ego-hungry? They need to produce a large family in order to prove their femininity—not to mention adequacy. And don't forget the overweight ladies who find it easier to hide their rolls of fat under a maternity dress than control their mouths and go on a diet." [31] Some young women want the experience of childbirth, just to see what it is like; they want to see the "apparatus in action" so they will know what it is all about. (Taking care of a child is something else again.) Some want the babies when they are infants but not children who grow up and make demands on them. "For any given mother it may be that only one phase—pregnancy, *or* infancy, *or* childhood, etc.—satisfies her need; so that, once her child has passed that stage, she may turn her attention away from him and try to repeat the, to her, most important phase by creating another baby. In this way many a large family comes about as a result of the mother's need to 'hold a baby in her arms.' " [32]

However it is explained—and it is complex enough to call for and justify a variety of explanations—the desire for babies does exist in all kinds of young women. Nor does our ability to trace, step by step, how this desire is socialized into girls in any way detract from its power. An inbred desire is no less potent than an instinctive one. The pain and anguish resulting from deprivation of an acquired desire for children are as real as the pain and anguish resulting from an instinctive one. And, lest the real suffering of women deprived of natural motherhood be unfeelingly brushed aside, here is the cry of a woman destined to remain childless because of her husband's infertility: "Whenever I read in the papers that someone has beat a child to death I cry my eyes out. How I'd love to have had that little one. And then I keep reading about abortions, vasectomies, The Pill, and girls who throw babies in garbage cans and leave them in churches. (A few weeks ago someone left a newborn baby on a plane!) I'm so depressed I could die." [33]

The second question raised above had to do with the effects on the performance of the mother role that result when, despite their differences, practically all women become mothers, some of whom are—like the woman just quoted—"natural mothers" who love children regardless of race, sex, or age and enjoy motherhood as well; some of whom love children but not motherhood or, conversely, motherhood but not children; some of whom love children but only in moderation; and some of whom agree with W. C. Fields. And, finally, some of whom throw babies away.

### Differences in Role Performance

In September, 1972, Lulu, a seven-year-old gorilla in the Central Park zoo, had a baby. She was overjoyed. "When she showed Sunny Jim to her keeper, she hugged and kissed him and, according to reports, was so happy, she was 'laughing and dancing.' She cradles the baby in her arms when she swings around her cage and she nestles him against her cheek. As a matter of fact, she likes him so much, she cuddles him on her chest as she lies on her back kissing his head and kicking her legs in glee." [34] In the Washington zoo, Mgeni-mopaya, a baby gorilla born May 29, was being raised by the zoo-keeper's wife.[35] Apparently his mother did not enjoy motherhood as much as Sunny Jim's did. Female chimpanzees in their natural habitat also differ among themselves in their maternal behavior; some are more nurturant than others.[36] And so, too, female human beings. Some are accepting and loving; some are rejecting.

Quite expectably so. If we forced every girl to become, say, a librarian or nurse or secretary or what-have-you, we would not be surprised if some performed well and others poorly. Or that some enjoyed their work while others did not. We would recognize that they were all different and that a common career would not be equally congenial to all. We show no such logic in the case of mothers. We expect every woman not only to want babies but also to love motherhood. If she does not, we make her feel deviant.

One of the gambits dramatic critics use in reporting on theatrical productions is to compare the way different actors perform the great classic roles. Richard Burton's Hamlet is compared with John Gielgud's, or one actress's Juliet with another's. And this is not merely a superficial ploy to show one's erudition. For the same role can be performed many different ways with astonishingly different and satisfactory results. So, too, with the script for the role of mother. Even when the function is the same— protecting and nurturing small children—the style of performance can change on different stages or in different societies.

The role is extremely congenial to some women; it may even be so for most. These are the ones who are well fitted for it or, perhaps, it is well fitted to them. They are tender and loving and nurturant and taking care of infants and children is a natural vocation for them. But it is not every woman's dish of tea. Some are put off by the demands of motherhood; they are not well fitted for performing the role of mother, or perhaps the role as institutionalized in our society does not fit them. Some are in-between: they would enjoy being mothers if it were not a round-the-clock job. All these widely different women are using the same role-script; their interpretations may vary as widely as those of actresses who play Juliet or Gertrude.

Motherhood may work miraculous changes in women, transforming at least some of them into a close approximation of the model, or a reasonable facsimile thereof, but for the most part women enter motherhood with the full complement of human virtues and defects, as various as all other living beings, and they remain different to the end.

### "Natural Mothers"

There are women who do, indeed, have in great degree the qualities apotheosized in the Victorian model of the role of mother. They are endlessly loving, tender, giving, patient, devoted, sacrificial. They do, in fact, find in motherhood the fulfillment they seek. They are included among the countless women who adopt children, especially those who are willing to adopt the hard-to-place children and most especially those who adopt children even when they have children of their own. They are included among the many women who accept the responsibility for mothering foster children. They are included among the women always and everywhere being sought but not always and everywhere found, for serving in custodial institutions for children of one kind or another or, for that matter, in schools. Here is only one example, in this case of a woman who is willing to work in order to have more—than her present seven—children.

> For the last year, Mrs. Collis, mother of seven, has been trying to adopt Jaime Faustine Terrico Sejas, 18, a boyish-looking Bolivian student who has been living with the Collis family for seven months. The adoption is about to become final, but immigration officials are requiring the youth to leave the country . . . because he violated his immigration status by taking a job. . . . Mrs. Collis and her husband Preston, 49, began their family when she was 19 when they adopted a destitute 7-year-old neighbor girl. "She had no clothes and her mother didn't care about her. . . . I'm very sentimental" . . . Mrs. Collis said she works 56 hours a week as a restaurant manager and cocktail waitress to help support the family. Her

husband polishes eyeglasses for an optical company. "I've
always loved children. If I didn't have to work I'd like to open
a home for kids.[37]

There are more such heroines all across the land who take on
themselves the hardships and the burdens of childrearing, not
only of the blue-eyed blond infant girls so much in demand but
also of inter-racial children, of difficult children, of handicapped
children, of strays of one kind or another. There are not nearly
enough to supply an almost inexhaustible demand.

Also among the "natural" mothers must be included the single
women who adopt children. These women constitute a new group
which, while growing, has not yet been measured. One report
tells us that they are in their late thirties, were themselves reared
in homes with several siblings, are professional workers with incomes, as of 1973, of at least twelve thousand dollars a year. They
adopt children, we are told, "not out of loneliness but out of a
sense of fulness, a desire to love." [38] They sometimes select motherhood in preference to wifehood, a child rather than a husband,[39]
but not all abandon the idea of marriage also. The attitude of some
has been articulated as: "I have done everything I wanted to do;
now I decided to have a family." [40] These women have "motherliness" or "mother-love" in sufficient quantities to take on all the
hardships written into the role of mother [41] with their eyes open,
forewarned. But they have also succeeded in the worker role as
well.

Among the "natural" mothers, the woman who bears a child outside of marriage because she wants it even without marriage
should probably also be included. "Several sociological surveys of
young people," we are told, "in Europe and the United States indicate a growing trend toward and acceptance of 'bachelor mothers.' " [42] Vanessa Redgrave, Mia Farrow, Patty Duke, and Bernadette Devlin, not to mention Ingrid Bergman a generation ago,
illustrate this trend, if, indeed, it is one. The "illegitimate" baby is
increasingly being kept by the mother rather than adopted. The
phenomenon of single mothers is still too new for any role script
to have developed. It does not precisely duplicate the widowed or
divorced mother's situation, for the relationship between the
parents is not the same. The single mother may be willing to share
the child with its father; but, again, she may not. Simone de Beauvoir tells of a woman she knew who wanted "to have a child

belonging wholly to herself," a woman "whose eyes lighted up at the sight of a fine male, not with sexual desire but because she judged him a good begetter." [43] Like Paul's mother in D. H. Lawrence's *Sons and Lovers,* Beauvoir reminds us, such women try "to develop an exclusive association between themselves and their . . . progeny." [44]

The fact that a woman has a high level of such motherliness or nurturance does not, of course, guarantee that she has all the other human virtues also. Social workers, who are usually more particular than God when they place children, often have to face the problem of weighing the relative wisdom of keeping children in a home where the mother has the motherly virtues but also other quite non-motherly ones like, for example, unconventional sexual interests. A husband writes to Ann Landers about his philandering wife who is such a woman, a veritable paragon in every respect but one: "I realize now that my wife's insatiable sexual appetite is an illness and no reflection on my manhood. She's a good mother except for her nymphomania and she's a good wife. A sweeter and more generous person never lived. She's more considerate of my mother than my sisters [are]. Everyone loves her." [45] Another writes that he is not the father of any one of his four children, all of whom, in fact, have different fathers. He decided to keep the family together anyway: "I figured she was a good wife and mother with a sex problem." [46] Obviously one can't have everything. And now, increasingly, we hear of Lesbian women who have all the loving attributes of good mothers.

Then, too, there are the women who love babies but find the role of mother as we institutionalize it irksome. They would love to have babies, would enjoy playing with them, even assuming a great deal of the burdens involved. But that and nothing else? They show the "natural" nurturant response to infants but not the "natural" response to motherhood.

Nor can it be overlooked that, because we exalt the role of mother so highly, there are women who enjoy the status conferred by motherhood but who do not care for babies. There is the professional woman who admitted she had become a mother in order to make her more credible in her academic specialty: What could a nonmother know about child development? And the woman whose daughter says: ". . . My mother never had time for me alone. I think she enjoyed the picture she made walking cross campus with me. But it was for the audience's benefit, not mine.

. . . I felt that my relationship to her was more to project an image at the college of a womanly woman than a genuinely mother-child relationship. . . ." [47]

How "natural" is this kind of motherhood? Quite natural. It is the natural reaction to the pressures to which we subject women. But there is another side to this coin.

## The Other Side of the Coin

Since we pressure *all* young women to want babies, it is inevitable that among them there will be many who do not have the temperament for it. They do not find fulfillment in the role of mother, any more than they would have in many other occupations all worthy, important, honorable, respectable, virtuous, and so on, desirable for some women but not for them. The difference is that they can freely reject these noncongenial occupations. Rejecting motherhood is different.

"I have a cute baby—everybody says so. But I just can't feel warm inside about him the way some mothers seem to. How can I get to liking him more?" [48] There are enough women who do not enjoy motherhood to lead one researcher to conclude that "one of the most important questions before our society today is: how can we help women *enjoy* being mothers and thus provide good maternal care for future generations." [49] Until more research uncovers the causes—in psychology, physiology, sociology, and psychosomatics—she suggests: better medical management, "instruction and research designed to stimulate thinking about positive aspects of motherhood," and counseling help for mothers from "skilled mothers' advisers who concentrate on helping mothers in their problems with their children." [50]

The women who are not natural mothers may have a host of desirable traits, just as motherly women may have a host of undesirable ones. Instead of coercing them into motherhood, making them feel that not becoming a mother is a misfortune or, worse, pitiable, why not appreciate them for their good qualities rather than denigrating them for their lack of maternal aptitude? Or structure motherhood in a more congenial fashion?

## What's the Difference?

What it is, precisely, that differentiates the motherly and the nonmotherly females is not always clear.[51] One study looked for physiological reasons for the difference. It compared women who complained about having to take care of their babies in the hospital with those who enjoyed looking after their babies. There were physiological differences that "indicated that women who disliked looking after their babies were also more likely to have negative feelings about other aspects of their biological role and to be physically less efficient and less productive females." [52] To the extent, if at all, that the quality of mothering depends on physiology, it is, in effect, a constant. It will be the same in the future as in the past. There will be women whose physiology predisposes them to the role of mother and others whose physiology does not so predispose them.

There are also psychoanalytic interpretations of the degree of maternal feeling, but few convincing demographic or, for that matter, psychological ones. Helene Deutsch reports one of her own cases, a German midwife who had chosen her profession in order to have many babies in whom to invest her motherliness. She feared childbirth; "she had to leave the situation of danger to the other woman before she could identify herself with the mother in possession of a child." She showed all the maternal virtues. "No work was too hard for her; she could stand sleepless nights without fatigue." Dr. Deutsch explains the woman's extreme motherliness in terms of an oppressive sense of guilt in relation to her own mother.[53] Dr. Deutsch reports many professional women in her practice similar to the midwife. They were prevented from having children of their own because they repudiated both their own sexuality and their mother's. So they satisfied "very warm and intense maternal feelings in their work." [54]

## Structural Factors

Perhaps we are looking in the wrong places for the explanation of a lack of motherliness. It may be less in the women themselves than in the circumstances of their lives. In 1972, anthropologists were shocked to learn that there exists in Africa a people, the Ik, among whom there is practically no such thing as mother love.[55] The researcher concluded that mother love as we know it may be a luxury. It is possible for a people to be so poor they cannot afford the sacrifice it calls for. In the history of the human species it is conceivable that there have also been other peoples who have disappeared from the face of the earth because they were too poor to be able to afford love, even for their children.

Nor is the experience of the Ik unthinkable in Europe. In eighteenth-century Paris, for example, the poverty of the masses was so grinding that children were unwanted and unloved. "Their chances of survival in their disease-ridden environment were small and many were helped on their way—exposed, abandoned, dumped in the Foundling Hospital. About six thousand to seven thousand children a year were taken in by the hospital, but even so their chances of survival were small—68 percent died within a year of birth and in some bad years, such as 1796-97, the figure rose to 92 percent." [56] (Of the two-thirds who were not abandoned, many were orphaned.) [57] We know that rejection is more likely to occur in poor families, as is violence against children.

Far less extreme than any of these examples are the six cultures reported on by a team of anthropologists and psychologists. They did find that maternal warmth was, indeed, related to life style, being lowest under conditions of both crowding and isolation and highest between these extremes. Maternal instability was also found to be related to household composition and maternal obligations. Instability increased "if mothers have extensive economic or domestic chores, in addition to prolonged responsibility for children." [58] The lesson seems to be that if we want mothers to be warm and stable in their relations with their children we should protect them from both crowded and isolated households, supply them with relief from too much time spent in caretaking, and not impose on them too extensive other obligations. We can improve mothering more by helping the mother than by scolding and blaming her.

There are, in brief, some women who are good mothers under some conditions but not under others. Some have greater "child-tolerance" than others. Aside from the women who are pushed beyond the levels of endurance in the style of motherhood we impose on them, there are others who perform very well if they can be spelled off. Some even find labor-force participation a relief from the demands of mothering.

### How Fulfilling Is Motherhood?

In view of the universally instilled dream of self-fulfillment by way of motherhood it is legitimate to ask to what extent motherhood actually provides such self-fulfillment. A survey of women made in the fall of 1971 reported that more than half of the respondents—53 percent—said that they received their major satisfactions from motherhood.[59] But another study of housewives re-

37

ported that only 38 percent of the 979 comments made by 568 women in reply to the question, "What are the satisfactions of the homemaker's role?" had to do with children.[60] If self-fulfillment is a major reason for having children, it does not always bring the expected results.

The degree of self-fulfillment depends, of course, on the nature of the self that is being fulfilled. One study tackled the question in terms of differences among women in three "needs" or "motivations" assumed to characterize all human beings, namely: "affiliation" or, in less pretentious terms, sociability; power; and achievement. For women who scored high on these three needs or motivations, the evidence was not very reassuring with respect to fulfillment by way of motherhood, which would not (except in retrospect) [61] satisfy their need for sociability, for the exercise of power, or for a sense of achievement.

Despite the close tie between mother and child, this study did not show it to be a satisfactory one for fulfilling the mother's need for sociability. The obligatory nature of the love and the authoritative status of the mother precluded such need fulfillment in relations with her children and the demands of motherhood itself may interfere with fulfillment in relations with other people. In fact, "the negative impact that motherhood can have on the affiliative interests of women perhaps takes its greatest toll in women whose greatest contacts with the outside world are generally minimal," [62] especially mothers of preschoolers.

The need for achievement can be derived from motherhood, the authors of the study note, in any of three ways: just becoming a mother could be considered an achievement; child rearing itself could be seen as an achievement; and the achievements of the children themselves could be vicariously satisfying. The authors found all three modes operating. The first seemed most important for high-school educated mothers and the second for college-educated women, but this depended to a large extent on the feedback they got from others for their high-level child rearing. The third, vicarious, way to win a sense of achievement through children tended to have a negative effect when children were grown since, in the very nature of things, the children of most women turn out to be just plain run-of-the-mill human beings. "The disappointment a mother feels about her child's failure to achieve her grand expectations for his accomplishments may be the reason why women with high achievement motivation are more likely to mention feeling inadequate about not spending enough time with their children. They may want to avoid contacts that remind them of their own disappointments." [63] Motherhood in and of itself, in brief, does not seem to be a clear-cut path to self-fulfillment among high-achievement women.

In a sex long denied formal power in the outside world, motherhood would seem to be a "natural" source of self-fulfillment for those with high power motivation. In the case of women with a high-school education, it did, in fact, seem to be so. "Power motivation seemed especially important for high-school-educated women, who perhaps more than any other group, feel that controlling children is an important potential source of gratification, and lack of control a potential source of difficulty." [64] The authors were struck by the fact that among these women, the power motivation persisted even into the adult years of their children. Among women with less education and among those with more, motherhood as a source of gratification of the power drive disappeared when their children grew up.[65]

### The Current Scene

On both the institutional and the personal side, challenges are being addressed to the emphasis on motherhood as the destiny of all women. It is increasingly recognized that the future is sure to call for only very modest indulgence in childbearing and that we can no longer persist in our pronatalist attitudes.

A variety of ways have been suggested for reducing the desire for babies. One commonly suggested proposal to achieve this goal is greater encouragement of labor-force participation by women.[66] More esoteric ideas have to do with the possibility that we could "androgenize" women, that is, give them the hormone androgen, for androgenized women apparently tend to be less interested in motherhood than other women.[67] No one has yet suggested Skinnerian behavior modification by means of "aversive conditioning." But someone doubtless will in time. Girls will be given an electric shock whenever they see a picture of an adorable baby until the very thought of motherhood becomes anathema to them or they will be rewarded with a stunning make-up kit every time they draw a mustache on the picture of an adorable infant in an ad.

To the extent that women want babies because of the pressures we have exerted on girls, the pressures will certainly have to be relaxed. All we have to do to moderate the desire for motherhood,

Judith Blake suggests, is simply to refrain from positively encouraging women to have babies as our present policies and practices do. That would reduce the desire for babies to a manageable level.

On the personal side there are now many—at least some—women who are no longer willing to accept the first imperative of the prescribed script for women. They are beginning to examine the "generally unexamined assumptions of human society." And finding them invalid at least for them. They may still want babies after their examination of the assumptions. But when one woman really did begin to examine them she was "appalled at what she saw." For her and for others like her, "mother's day is over."

There is, in fact, now in process a movement not only to reduce the pressures but positively to counteract them. The goal for the future is to make nonmotherhood as well as motherhood a genuine option for those who prefer it, to make one as esteemed and acceptable as the other. No projection of the future of motherhood can ignore the nascent movement to encourage the so-called child-free marriage.

## CHAPTER THREE

## Nonmotherhood

And our sex is not without learning.
This I say, that those who have never
Had children, who know nothing of it,
In happiness have the advantage
Over those who are parents.
The childless, who never discover
Whether children turn out as a good thing
Or as something to cause pain, are spared
Many troubles in lacking this knowledge.

(Euripides, *Medea*, translated by Rex Warner
Phoenix Books, 1955, lines 1089–1097)

### The Child-Free Marriage

Despite the motherhood myth, Euripides was right on target. In a study of the periods in life in which contentment was greatest, the years when there were no children in the home rated highest. About 90 percent of childless wives eighteen to twenty-nine were satisfied with their lives and more than half were very happy. Fewer than 10 percent ever worried about having a nervous breakdown. Among women with preschoolers in the home, on the other hand, fewer said they were satisfied with life as a whole, and even fewer, that they were very happy.[1]

In addition to women incapable of bearing children [2]—who, in view of the advances in medical technology may be a vanishing breed [3]—there must always have been at least some women who did not, for one reason or another, wish to become mothers at all, who wished to "know nothing of it." One study suggests 5 percent; [4] another 9 percent.[5] Actually, true choice for all women with respect to motherhood will not be a reality until the enormous pressures on women to make them want children are abated, and until contraception has achieved enough success so that no unwanted babies are born. When we do arrive at this state, the reluctant or unwilling mother will disappear from the scene. Only women who are willing to make the sacrifices called for will then make the decision in favor of motherhood. Only then will genuine self-selection for motherhood become a reality.

In the meanwhile the emergence of a movement to delegitimize motherhood as the sole career for women is worthy of serious consideration. It is epitomized in an organization, the National Organization for Non-Parents—NON—which was launched in 1972.[6] It is not nonmotherhood in and of itself, but the emergence of women who admit, even proclaim, their preference for nonmotherhood that is new and important. Removal of the stigma from nonmotherhood is one of its major contributions. But even more important is giving nonmotherhood a positive, valued, desirable status in and of itself. And like so many other groups formerly invisible in our society, these women have now surfaced, become visible, found one another, come to share common experiences and help other women who would like to make the same decision.

A distinction has to be made before further comments. Nonmotherhood is not the same as "antinatalism." Antinatalism is a technical term used by students of population to refer to policies designed to hold down the birth rate. It addresses itself to programs which have the effect of discouraging childbearing. It looks at tables and graphs; the women fade in the background. NON is an activist translation of the term, but its emphasis is on specific, concrete men and women. What it seeks is genuine options for them. Antinatalist policies tend to be manipulative; NON tries to be enlightening. Antinatalism works by way of laws and legislation, NON by way of personal relationships.

Although the women in this movement are not especially involved with population movements, including Zero Population Growth, the NON movement as a whole does invoke concern with population and environmental protection as one—but only one—of its sanctions. It seeks to cooperate with Planned Parenthood, Zero Population Growth, and Coalition for a National Population Policy; but its eye is on human beings. And although the women in NON view themselves as feminists, they take issue with some members of the women's liberation movement who assume motherhood as a taken-for-granted goal, or at least expectation, for all women, as current customs do.[7]

It is doubtful that a movement for nonmotherhood would have arisen without these other movements to serve as precursors, or that the increase in the proportion of women who say they want no children would have been so rapid. In 1967, only 1.3 percent of wives eighteen to twenty-four said they wanted no children; in 1971—only four years later—the proportion had trebled to 3.9 percent.[8] NON did not, of course, precipitate this increase; but it illuminates the thinking and feeling behind it.

### SELF-SELECTION FOR NONMOTHERHOOD

Is it an impossible dream that maybe, some day, women will boycott (girlcott) the Motherhood Myth? Will sisters listen to each other? Will they act on the Truth as revealed in the Misery of their daily lives? Now, we can dare to look at it and . . . BINGO! We can know it doesn't have to happen this way. It is not inevitable that to gain social acceptance we accept a Life Sentence. We can change that. We can tell our sons and daughters that there is a choice; that to choose not to have children is a sound moral decision which would benefit society. . . . Can we change our consciousness so that we can hear our own wisdom?[9]

If the answer to this question is yes, what difference would it make? Who would choose not to have children? Two psychologists have recently asked precisely that question.

"If . . . we no longer consign all women to a single role [that of mother] but instead offer real options, what will the self-selection of mothers be like?"[10] What of nonmothers? Research on self-selection for nonmotherhood in the form of voluntarily child-free marriages is relatively new so we do not yet have a very good idea of who the people are who select this option or why. One thing that early research reports do show, however, is that at least up to now, drift rather than clear-cut decision has characterized the process. One study of fifty-two such couples found, for example, that only about a third of the women entered marriage with a proviso of childlessness as part of the contract. Most of them had arrived at this attitude during adolescence but they were unable to specify just what it was that had led them to it. A small number of them had been "converted" to the idea of child-free marriage during the engagement period, presumably in discussion with their future husbands. Among the remaining two-thirds, however, childlessness was not a matter of clear-cut decision, either before or even after marriage, but rather the result of a series of decisions to postpone having children. They simply kept putting off the time until they had decided that they did not want children after all.[11]

There has not yet been time to make thoroughgoing analyses of the third of the young women who had actually selected themselves out of motherhood before marriage rather than drifting into it after marriage. But there is a study of high school students who stated that they did not wish to have children which—although we know many of them will change their minds in time—gives us a clue, admittedly not a wholly reliable one, but acceptable as a start. The young women who in their ecological fervor might foreswear motherhood at sixteen, might also succumb to the pressures toward motherhood at twenty-six or thirty-six. But, for what they are worth, here are the results.[12]

The study was made in the fall of 1972; it included 357 students 15 to 17 years of age. Understandably, the proportion intending to have no children was larger—more than two-and-a-half times greater, in fact—among male (23.2 percent) than among female students (9.4 percent).[13] But the young men seemed less certain about their reasons. The heavy impact of religion on attitudes toward childbearing which shows up in all studies of fertility showed up here too, much more in the case of the young women than of the young men. Although such an impersonal reason for not having children as "pessimism with respect to the future quality of life" ranked fairly high, personal reasons—loss of personal freedom, financial cost, responsibility, and reduction of happiness in marriage—ranked higher. The relative weight assigned to the several reasons was roughly the same for both sexes, both ranking loss of personal freedom highest and reduction of marital happiness lowest. The specific reasons given may or may not reflect a thought-through decision; they may be simple rationalizations. That they have reasons at all is interesting. In any event, reasons given by respondents in a survey do not necessarily explain.

## Personality Explanations for Nonmotherhood

There are as many reasons for not wanting children as for wanting them. There have no doubt always been some women who remained child-free as a matter of conscience or principle: a hereditary disease, for example, or physical disability that made child care impossible. Not, of course, to mention the women in religious orders who foreswore motherhood on religious grounds. At the other end of the spectrum there no doubt have always been some women who remained child-free for more mundane reasons: fear of losing their youthful beauty, lowered level of living, or the other sacrifices involved. And, between these extremes, as the following passionate cry illustrates, some have rejected motherhood as a form of protest.

> I remember with bitterness that "our mother the church" told women for two thousand years (more or less) that their mission in life was to have children. That was the only purpose of marriage and of their existence. . . . No love. Absolutely no sex without an eye to procreation. The mother of God coredemptress with her son. The mother of the children of man to be Mary's handmaiden on earth—to sacrifice herself to lead the little ones to Christ. That makes me sick. . . . I think I've been so "mad" I avoided having children as a resistance measure. How dare they reduce me to a servant status. Mary's handmaiden indeed! Who is she that she should be a model for me? [14]

In view of the almost casual way in which most child-free women actually fall into nonmotherhood, it seems gratuitous to attempt to explain their childlessness in terms of personality characteristics. Still, psychiatrists especially, but also others concerned with understanding human behavior, are prone to seek such explanations. They reject the reasons given by the women themselves and seek more esoteric explanations.

Helene Deutsch, for example, reported one case of a nonmother whose attitude was in reality one of motherliness.

> The patient was twice forced into a respectable middle-class marriage by friends who wanted to save her from a prostitute's life. Both marriages were, of course, unsuccessful. The words "motherhood" and "motherliness" aroused her abhorrence

and disgust, and this spread to all words ending in "hood" or "liness." An absolutely unmotherly woman, one would say. And yet . . . in her instinctual life she was nothing else but mother. . . . In this case one can put the responsibility for the whole neurotic picture on . . . an overstrong primary mother attachment.[15]

Anyway it makes interesting reading.

More recently psychiatrists in this country have put forth somewhat modified versions. One, for example, speaks not of primary mother attachment among nonmothers but of dependencies. These women are narcissistic and have conflicts between their own desires to be taken care of and the demands made by motherhood to take care of children. "These are people who can't tolerate the idea of caring for children, who have no margin of love to spare them." [16] A psychologist traces the motivation of child-free women to the "narcissistic entitlement" which the other-directed child-rearing practices of the 1950s fostered.[17] He also invokes the dependency explanation: "many of these young adults are ambivalent about relinquishing the role of the one who is cared for and taking on that of the one who does the caring." [18] Another speaks in ominous terms of "the disappointed womb" and Erikson's "inner space" that is never filled. He finds many college students today who "feel strangely empty," unrelated to basic biological things.[19] A family therapist sees these women expressing something like a herd instinct, reacting to the dangers of overpopulation, crowding, pollution and nuclear war; but a child psychiatrist sees nonmotherhood as a form of rationalization by young people of their own ambivalence. "They ask questions like, 'Why add to the population explosion? Why create people who will have to face all the problems that are approaching in the next century?' " [20]

The most important aspect of these several explanations is not the specific contents—neurotic over-strong primary mother attachment or the dependencies or the narcissistic entitlements or the role-ambivalence or the herd instinct—but the implication of deviance they imply. Not one "explains" the women who prefer nonmotherhood as strong, autonomous women able to resist coercive pressures. No one emphasizes their strengths. It is always something bordering on the pathological. It does take a great deal of ego-strength to stand up to the pressures propelling women into motherhood. There will be no genuine freedom for women until the status of nonmotherhood ceases to be denigrated, until it becomes de-stigmatized, until it is viewed as a dignified life style, in no sense abnormal or pathological, until women cease to be threatened by disappointed wombs. Insistence on nonmotherhood as an honorable status is not at all the same as imposing it on resistant women. It is merely another attempt to de-stigmatize a perfectly legitimate choice of life style. Attempts to stereotype child-free women are in any event premature. They are doubtless as varied among themselves as are other women.

### Is Nonmotherhood Dysfunctional?

The "experts" quoted above may find little admirable in the women who choose nonmotherhood. But a psychologist at the University of Rhode Island does. And bemoans their decision for, in her opinion, they belong to the "cream of the crop."

Bernice E. Lott, studying the attitudes of college women toward motherhood and feminism, was disturbed by what seemed to her undesirable results of self-selection for nonmotherhood by women with qualities she admired. She found that there was a relationship between attitudes toward women's liberation and attitudes toward motherhood. The women who were favorable to one tended to be unfavorable to the other. "Although proliberation women ranked child rearing as more creative than did antiliberation women, they ranked themselves as less interested in personally engaging in this activity. Proliberation women said they were far less eager than [antiliberation women] to have children." [21] She cites another study at the University of Kentucky which reported that proliberation women tended to have strong desires for autonomy, for independence, for self-sufficiency, and for freedom from external control; they tended to be less authoritarian. In contrast, the women opposed to the liberation movement "emerged as self-protective, fearful of danger, risk avoiding, resistant to change, and low in curiosity and flexibility." [22] The dysfunctional implications of these two sets of results struck Lott forcibly. So in answer to her own question, "who wants the children?" she replies, not those who would make the best mothers:

> If we consider the pictures of the pro- and anti-liberation college women . . . and then ask which one would make the better mother, my answer is immediate and unhesitating. On any

47

criterion of competence for motherhood, my choice is for the independent, flexible, and democratically oriented proliberation woman. But who do we find planning to have the children and desiring to rear them? Not those who would make the best mothers but those with the least desirable characteristics.[23]

Not here "narcissistic entitlement" or "disappointed wombs" but women with strengths and flexibility. And the future self-selected mothers come through as fearful, inflexible, self-protective. We have here, then, one answer to the question raised by the two psychologists quoted above, "what will the self-selection of mothers be like?" It is not altogether reassuring.

### Who's More Selfish Than Whom?

The terms narcissistic and dependencies and mother-fixation and rationalization used by the professional analysts imply what the man-on-the-street calls plain selfishness. At any rate, the implication is clearly that the women are self-centered, unwomanly, if not deviant, in selecting other goals than motherhood. And, it must be admitted, those who are in favor of promoting non-motherhood do indeed play up hedonistic arguments. Many of them do so deliberately, on principle, to raise our consciousness about our priorities. Why is self-realization by way of work or career inferior to self-realization by way of motherhood? What is so sacred about self-sacrifice? What is so intrinsically noble about wanting children? Or so ignoble, for that matter, about pleasure? It is noteworthy, one must add parenthetically, that even those who make a big point of the pleasurable rewards of non-motherhood do add that these child-free women are also engaged in worthwhile activities. True, they have more fun than mothers, but they also do good.[24]

Conversely, it has been pointed out that the reasons for wanting children are equally, if not more, narcissistic and may be equally, if not more, selfish than the reasons for not wanting them. Those who want children as a guarantee of immortality; to keep the family name; to take care of them in their later years; to achieve for them; "just for the experience"; for "self-fulfillment"; and for any of the myriad other reasons often given for wanting children are no less narcissistic or selfish than those women who choose non-motherhood.

### Some Gains

One of the more obvious gains from the acceptance of non-motherhood is the elimination of the reluctant mother, the woman who really does not want children but feels she really has to because otherwise she is viewed as strange. She is out of things. Among women who talk only about their children she is an outsider. If the pressures are released she will feel freer to reject motherhood.

Nonmotherhood also promises gains for the women we have called "nestlings"; [25] the women who want many babies; the women who, as soon as one child outgrows the bassinet, want another to replace it; the women who have a natural calling for child-bearing. The current emphasis on small, if not child-free, families could hurt them and genuine concern has been expressed for their anticipated frustration. A number of palliatives have been proposed to assuage their feelings of deprivation. One is to offer substitute uses for their time in jobs; another is in foster-care or adoption of other children; another is in offering their services to children who need them in one situation or another. Instead of these unsatisfactory alternatives, nonmotherhood among some women will make it possible for the nestlings to have more of their own. By foregoing motherhood themselves, some women would make available to the nestlings the "privilege" of having more children than the "permitted" two. Every woman who "surrendered" the privilege of bearing her "quota" of two would make it "permissible" for another woman to have four. The use of quotation marks is not inadvertent. They imply a situation of control quite beyond current standards but not, perhaps, wholly unthinkable.[26] But they do make possible an interesting apologia for nonmotherhood if one is needed.

The release of pressure on some women to have children and the channeling of childbearing to women who preferred it would go a long way toward making the specialization of motherhood a distinct career. Some women would choose it as a life work while others would select different professions.

Another gain would accrue to women, a gain subtle and not easy to perceive. So long as women want babies they will be expected to "pay" for them. They are, it can be argued, "getting their money's worth" and therefore have no right to complain of the costs or of any of the sacrifices. If more and more women have a genuine option not to have children, there will be more incentive to "pay" them for selecting the motherhood option in the form of help with services of all kinds.

### The Unwritten Script

Nonmotherhood is, obviously, not proposed for all women; nor, for that matter, necessarily for a majority of women. But the very fact of its acceptance as a legitimate life style without penalties attached is an important force in shaping the future of motherhood itself. Women will no longer be viewed only as potential or actual mothers.

The seeming growth of nonmotherhood does not reflect any change in the genes of women; they are no less women for their changing attitude toward motherhood. Women today have virtually the same genetic inheritance as women of say, one, two, three centuries ago, for human heredity is remarkably stable. So any differences in their behavior have to be the result of the world in which they live.

The actual behavior of people often changes long before the scripts for their roles are rewritten.[27] Women began to respond to urbanism and industrialism long before the scripts for their roles were revised.[28] And the scripts are only now beginning to catch up with the twenty-first century. The examples of marriage and motherhood are cases in point. Paul Glick and Arthur Norton have shown us that since the late 1950s, "the trend of the first-marriage rate has continued to decline while divorce and remarriage rates rose sharply." They conclude that the simultaneous diminution of first marriage and acceleration of divorce in recent years suggests an unprecedented modification of life styles and values relating to marriage.[29] Two interesting trends are discernible: one is the de facto "serial monogamy" about which there has been so much discussion in recent years as we try to bring our role conceptions into line with actual behavior and the other is the apparent growing preference for a single life-style among young women. The second of these trends is more relevant here. The proportion of women who have married at a given age has been going up for half a century; but it appears now to be wavering if not showing symptoms of actual decline. Women born in the 1940s will have set the all-time record for marriage: more than 97 percent will have married before they reach their mid-forties. But women who entered their twenties in the last decade are not following their example. The decline in "propensity to marry" might, Glick recognizes, merely represent a postponement; it might represent a preference among women for a single life style; it might represent postponement by young men trying to catch up on their war-interrupted careers; or it might represent a reaction against the experience of their mothers who had been early-marriers and bearers of many children. It might also reflect the new kind of relationship—"cohabitation"—developing among young people, especially on university campuses,[30] a relationship in which motherhood is definitely not contemplated. Any change in the script for marriage inevitably implies a change in the script for motherhood as well.

The script for motherhood was prescribing nineteenth century behavior long after women began to respond to twentieth century conditions. They are now beginning to respond to twenty-first century conditions, especially though not exclusively as delineated in the environmental movement. A host of technological and industrial, as well as demographic, trends impinge on the role of mother. The script is only now beginning to catch up with them, and slowly. The birth rate changes more rapidly than does the script for motherhood. The slow emergence of nonmotherhood as a respectable option for women may be one more example of this lag between actual behavior and modification of role scripts to fit it. We are only now working out the script for nonmotherhood.

### Preview

Here is a preview of the script:

I strongly urge all mothers to be honest with themselves, their families, and each other—and with their sons and daughters and other young people when they arrive at the threshold of parenthood. The next time you feel an impulse to ask a childless couple when they are going to start their family, don't. Check that compulsion to talk about the boundless joys of motherhood and boast about your own children unless you honestly temper your words with the negatives. Don't tell a carefree, child-free young wife that she'll never know the delight of having a small child present her with a Mother's Day gift unless you also tell her she'll also never know how dreadful it is to sit up all night with a feverish child.

To young women who have not yet taken that irreversible step to motherhood, I want to offer . . . [these] words.

51

. . . People who try to manipulate you into having children are being rude, crude, and thoughtless. It's no one's business if your ovaries aren't functioning—and no one's business if they are. You don't need to justify a decision not to have children—to anyone. You are entitled, indeed you are obliged, to make your own judgments in these matters, and unless those urging you to have children are also willing to finance the venture and help you take care of the products of their busybodying, you don't owe them even a polite answer. . . .

If you don't want children or are not certain that you are ready to have them, stick to your guns. It makes no sense to enter into a lifetime contract making you responsible for another human being for the singular reason of pleasing or pacifying someone else who will bear no responsibility for the child you are being urged to have.[31]

It may not be too long now before Amy Vanderbilt puts it into the etiquette books.

## CHAPTER FOUR

## How Much Motherhood?

### Retrenchment

The future calls for an end to the glorification of the large family.[1] There is even a future for nonmotherhood, though it is not likely in the cases of a majority or even a large proportion of women. A moderate retrenchment—say a reduction to one or two children per woman—is not, however, out of the question for even the immediate future. Indeed, although labor-force projections in the early seventies were resting heavily on the assumption of a two-child family for the eighties, by December, 1972, statisticians were adding projections based on a 1.8-child family.[2] Motherhood will continue to call for a relatively minor investment of time in the lives of women.

### A Backward Glance

There is among some women an anxious foreboding that the strong antinatalism generated by the environmental movement will deprive them of the large families they want to build their whole lives around. They feel defensive because they do not want to do anything else with their lives but rear children. They fear they will be deprived of the privilege of bearing as many children as they want.

The post-war recrudescence of the feminine mystique in the 40s and 50s, only now beginning to recede, has made us forget that the desire for large families had, until then, already been unusual for a long time. In the early years of the century the two-child family was already a desideratum for many women.[3] Since they did not have all that good control over the matter, they took it for granted that they would have some children, but they tried to postpone them and to space them to keep the number down. The young woman who had a baby too soon after marriage, even beyond the respectable nine months, was pitied. It was too bad. Better luck next time. They were reacting against the 19th century enslavement to maternity of so many women.

Anne Firor Scott, for example, tells us about the Southern ladies whose lives of constant pregnancy had seemed to them to be not worth living. Their letters and diaries were filled with anguish for, in the general romanticization of motherhood, then, as until yesterday, it was "only in private women could give voice to the misery of endless pregnancies, with attendant illness, and the dreadful fear of childbirth." [4] Even upper-class women. "My heart almost sinks within me at the thought of feeding another child," one writes to her mother.[5] The young wife of a North Carolina planter longed for death. She was nothing but trouble. "I'm not fit for anything but to have children, and that is nothing but trouble and sorrow." [6] Later in the century an urban mother, trying to assuage the despair of her thirty-eight-year-old daughter in yet another unwanted pregnancy, advised her that if she nursed the baby long enough she might never have to endure another.[7] Children, yes, to be sure. But, oh please, not so many!

Margaret Sanger in the early years of the twentieth century was still reporting the same state of affairs. She was receiving myriads of letters from women filled with despair at their ceaseless childbearing. Not from frivolous, selfish, indolent women but from "the typical American mother . . . worshipped in our popular songs, stories and motion pictures, . . . heroically willing to make any sacrifice to their children."

> They work like slaves to provide food, clothing, shelter and education for the ever-growing brood. The majority of them are uncomplaining, long-suffering, thinking first of the well-being and the future happiness of the boys and girls they have brought into the world. . . . From this slave mother is exacted a triple tax: her own health is broken down; the well-being of her older children is jeopardized; and the last-born infants are brought into the world with progressively decreasing chances of survival.[8]

Margaret Sanger then reproduces a spate of such letters. Here is one of them:

> I am thirty-five. In seventeen years of married life have brought eight children into the world and went down in the grave after three I failed to get. We bought us a little home to start with and oh, the struggle! Have both worked like slaves, I with my own efforts have kept the family in what we had to buy, have sold $300.00 worth of butter, eggs and chickens. He raises what he can for us to eat and saves a little and in this way we have managed to pay for our little home, but have no conveniences whatever. Sometimes I've had only my husband to wait on me when the children came and in every instance have been on the job, slinging pots and pans when my baby was two weeks old and strange to say am still well. I have six children in school and two under my feet, am milking five cows, sell from seventy-five to one hundred pounds of butter a month, fix a package for parcel post every day.
>
> I have milked six cows at six o'clock and brought a baby into the world at nine.
>
> My baby is nine months old and the thoughts of another almost kills me.
>
> Oh! tell me how to keep from having another. Don't open the door of heaven to me and then shut it in my face.
>
> Oh! please tell me, I feel like it's more important to raise what I have than to bring more.[9]

It's hard to brush that aside. Or romanticize it, either.

Motherhood on such a scale could exact an enormous toll. Only exceptional women came through the ordeal unscathed. Fortunately those days are gone forever for most women. Few are going to be exposed to motherhood on that scale. The fear now anticipated by some women is just the reverse, not enough motherhood to fill a life. Not too many children but rather not enough children to fill the void. This, they tell us, is not the 19th century; we are more affluent now; we have more technological aids; we have better medical care. We are entitled to as many children as we want.

Actually, as it turns out, relatively few want all that many. Though young women in their maternal enthusiasm may—as they used to, though no more—say that they would like to have a dozen children—it was a code word for femininity—they rarely wanted anything like that many. Nor, for that matter, will the young ecology enthusiast who says she wants no children at all, necessarily bear no children. Both extremes are comparatively rare. Most women fall in between.

### Desired Number of Children

Demographers make distinctions among desired number of children, expected number, actual number, and ideal number.[10] All vary over time and some vary within the lifetime of individual couples. But there are also some fairly stable aspects both overall and family by family.

Different as women may be, they are similar in the fact that it does not take very many children to satisfy whatever maternal "instinct" or desire for children has been so assiduously cultivated in them. Before control of conception became widely feasible, the number of children a woman bore had little to do with her own preference in the matter. It was all very well for wise men to tell her to delay marriage or to practice continence, as the Malthusians did in the nineteenth century, or for theologians to tell her to bear as many as she could, as they had been saying for a good many centuries. When it came right down to it, children were, in fact, literally Acts of God over which women had little control. This situation has become less and less true so far as a growing number of women are concerned. Increasingly the differences among women in the number of children borne "are attributable to differences in desired family size." [11] And in this respect, despite all their differences, women are remarkably alike; they are also remarkably moderate. They tend to remain within the two- to four-child range. Sometimes the number wanted moves in one direction, toward an average of two and sometimes in the other direction, toward an average of four.[12] Unfortunately, even this modest desire may prove excessive for the future. In 1971, the movement was toward the lower limit; among youngsters fifteen to twenty-one, 58 percent said they wanted two or less children; only 17 percent said they wanted four or more.[13]

### Ideal Number of Children

The number of children people consider ideal is somewhat higher than the number they want or expect to have. In 1966 a summary of thirteen studies dealing with ideal family size found that for the most part the number considered ideal remained fairly consistently between two and four, but that there had been a tendency to shift away from the two-child family toward the four-child ideal in the preceding quarter century, in the era of the feminine mystique.[14] Since then there has been a shift in the other direction, toward the two-child family.

Why do women's preferences change over time in the number of children they consider ideal? One team of researchers confess that they do not know for sure. They "cannot identify with certainty all the causes of the changes in attitudes toward [ideal] family size, nor can we measure precisely the influence of any cause. We simply note that changes in attitudes have occurred and emphasize that they will probably occur again." [15] They suggest that fluctuations in ideals over time may be due to economic conditions, but they do not dismiss the idea that "such intangibles as 'fashion' " may also play a part.

It may seem bizarre to view as a matter of fashion anything so fundamental as ideal family size. But so it seems to be. Sometimes, as in the post-war years, the ideal of many children was fashionable, sometimes, as currently, few children. In the precipitate decline of the early 1970s, the movement toward population control was undoubtedly a significant influence.

One important addendum. In only two years between 1943 and 1966—1947 and 1955—did men express an ideal number of children that was larger than the ideal women expressed. In only three years (1941, 1945, and 1952) was there no difference between the sexes. In the other eighteen years, the women's ideal was larger than the men's. "In so far as women want them [large families], their reactions cannot be ascribed to male pressure." [16] Men are not nearly so pressured toward parenthood as are women.

An interesting relationship between age and ideal family size is worth at least a parenthetical comment. In every year since 1936, more older than younger women expressed a preference for large families as an ideal.[17] And in a retrospective study of women re-interviewed twenty years after the first interview, the ideal number of children which had declined in the early years of motherhood, when the women were in the midst of the pressures of infant- and child-care, had bounced back to the pre-motherhood size of 3.1.[18] In a quite different kind of study, a team of psychologists found that mothers in later years endow early motherhood with a nostalgic aura. When it's all over, apparently, the "retired" older women tend to glorify the early years of active motherhood.[19] "Enjoy them while you can," they tell the harassed young mother. "They'll grow away from you all too soon."

### Expected Babies

Since overall, if not woman-by-woman, the average number of babies expected tends to conform to the average number of babies actually borne, the number of such expected babies is used as the basis for projecting the future. It is therefore interesting to note the precipitate decline in expectations in the early seventies. Among white women—data for all races are not available before 1967—the decline was about one third between 1955 and 1972, from 3.2 percent among eighteen- to twenty-four-year-old women in 1955 to 2.2 percent in 1972; from 3.1 percent among the twenty-five- to twenty-nine-year-olds in 1955 to 2.4 percent in 1972.[20] Among wives eighteen to twenty-four years of age, the proportion expecting zero or one child more than doubled between 1955 and 1972; the proportion expecting four or more declined about four-fifths.[21]

### Actual Versus Wanted Family Size

Taken as a whole, the average number of children wanted early in marriage corresponds quite well with the average number actually borne by the end of the child-bearing years. Woman-by-woman, however, there is no such close correspondence. In the overall figures, for example, those who have fewer than they said they wanted and those who have more, cancel one another out.[22] Thus, those who said they wanted 2.0 children had 2.5 and those who said they wanted 6.0 had 5.6. The first figures reflected accidential conceptions and the second, a change of heart. Especially, it might be noted here, a change of heart with experience. One study made in 1954, for example, reported that just before they were married the women said they wanted 3.2 children; a year later that number was down to 2.7. "Evidently the introduction to the cares of motherhood," the researchers note laconically "at first reduces the number of children many would like to have." [23]

But so, also, does not being introduced to the cares of motherhood. For it was found that "the longer a couple delays the occurrence of a 'wanted' birth, the more opportunity the wife has to acquire role patterns not defined in terms of early child-care responsibility. At some point that next birth may no longer be so desirable." [24] The same change has been reported for the so-called child-free marriage. Especially if the "acquired role patterns" include a job.[25]

Overall, the actual number of babies women have falls short of the expressed ideal number.[26] But women vary in their success in achieving exactly the size they want.[27] About 41 percent succeed. Only 14 percent were two or more children—in either direction—away from their mark.[28]

## Structural Factors and Motherhood

A variety of structural factors have been found to be related to the number of children women have. We know, for example, from numerous studies that women with foreign family backgrounds, rural women, working class women, poor women, and less educated women have more babies than their counterparts, women, that is, who are native, urban, white-collar, affluent, and more educated. Two structural factors—income and religion—are especially noteworthy.

One of the first extensive studies to explore differences in family size was made in Indianapolis during the depression. The question then was why were people not having babies? Literally scores of variables were canvassed and a lot was learned and a host of hypotheses generated. We learned, for example, that although in the total population poor women had more babies than middle-class women, among women who controlled conception the relationship was reversed: the poor women had fewer children than the middle-class women. The very rich, with nurses, nannies, governesses, and maids to help carry the load, had more than the middle class. It was assumed by some theorists that the differential between the poor and the more affluent was a result of differences in access to contraceptive information. Once such information was universally available there would be a direct rather than an inverse relationship between income and family size; people would have only as many children as they felt they could afford.

These theorists viewed children as "consumer durables." [29] People had children for the same reasons they had cars. They made the same kinds of calculations in both cases. This conceptualization led to the conclusion that in time the rich would have more babies than the poor because they could afford more. We wouldn't have to worry about supporting poor welfare children. Poor people would see that they couldn't afford them and so stop having them.

Not so at all, replied a sociologist. The "children-as-consumer-durables" theory ignored such equally potent structural factors as religion. Actually the studies that seemed to support the economist's thesis were invalid and those that did support it did so because of some other non-economic factor: "the relationship predicted by an *economic* interpretation of fertility—a rise in family-size preference with rising income—is not actually found unless some powerful pro-natalist *non*-economic influence, such as Catholicism, is at work." [30] She points out the defects in the analogy between "demand" for economic goods and "desire" for a family. Economic goods are purchased within the constraints of income or credit; you just can't buy more than you can pay for. There are no similar controls over the "acquisition" of even wanted children. The decision to have children is supported, even encouraged if not actually any longer enjoined, rather than curbed, whether or not people can afford them, especially by conservative religious denominations. And, once children are "acquired," they cannot, like other "consumer durables" be disposed of or exchanged for other goods that produce greater "utility" than the children. "In fact, by creating public support for the dominance of family 'values' over economic rationality, reproductive and social institutions are geared to *prevent* economic factors from inhibiting reproduction." [31] Women are taught to believe that God would provide.

And it is, indeed, true that religion has been found to play an enormous part in family size.[32] In any one income bracket, the Catholic women have more children than the non-Catholic women and within any one religious group, the active or devout have more children than the inactive or less devout. Other things being equal, Jewish women have fewer children than non-Jewish women. Protestant women fall between the Catholic and the Jewish.[33]

Characteristics related to structural factors are not, however, necessarily related to any individual personality traits of the women themselves. They are determined by the women's position in society or in the cultural matrix that shapes them. And even these differences among women are becoming smaller as all kinds of "differential birth rates" are declining. The future is headed toward "demographic homogenization."

But how about individual personality differences among women? Are there any such individual personality differences that distinguish women who want many from women who want few children? The questions are important for the future. If the differences among women are due primarily to structural factors, attempts to influence family size will have to work through these structural factors. If the differences are due primarily to differences in personality, attempts to influence family size will have to work through them.

If the differences among women in wanted family size are related to individual personality differences, they will survive structural changes. They will also answer the question raised by the two psychologists: "if . . . we no longer consign all women to a single role [that of mother] but instead offer real options, what will the self-selection of mothers be like?" [34] In Chapter 3 we commented on this question from the point of view of women selected out of motherhood; here we look at it from the point of view of women selected into motherhood.

### Self-Selection for Motherhood

The idea of official—as contrasted with self—selection for motherhood was an old nineteenth-century fantasy that had to do with the eugenics movement. It was based on biological grounds; women would be selected for motherhood by bureaucrats on the basis of their genetic endowment. What would be selected? The answer: strong biological specimens. The idea, though still propounded from time to time, is too naïve for current acceptance.

But the question now asked by the psychologists is more interesting. What kinds of selection for motherhood would result if women themselves had free, un-coerced, genuine choices as between motherhood and other life patterns? Would only "motherly" women select abundant child-bearing? women who found self-fulfillment in motherhood? women whose sociability, achievement, and power motivations were satisfied in the role of mother? And, perhaps more to the point, would such self-selection be auspicious for the children? Can we take it for granted that such self-selection would guarantee children the close, warm mothering that we are told they need? Would such self-selected women always be the best people to be in charge of the care of children? Is wanting lots of children enough? Is even "motherliness" enough? Demographers have been at great pains to try to answer the question of individual differences as related to fertility in another context but the results are relevant here also. Just what is it about women who bear many children that distinguishes them from those who bear fewer? The answers to date have been surprisingly barren.

The Indianapolis study was one of the first to go beyond merely structural factors and to look for differences in attitudes and other personality variables among women who had many and women who had few babies.[35] Later studies have pursued the same problem with continually improved instruments. So far the researchers have found no clear-cut relationships between attitudes seemingly closely related to desire for children and number of children actually borne.

It was once hypothesized, for example, that people on the make, ambitious, climbing up the social ladder as hard as they could would be likely to have few children in order not to encumber themselves in the upward climb. Not, in fact so. The number of children women have is not related to: whether they feel they are achieving their life goals, how satisfied they are with their husbands' jobs, their perception of their husbands' opportunities to get ahead, their aspirations for their children's education, their drive to get ahead, how willing they are to sacrifice conviction and social interests in order to get ahead, whether they perceive the effect of another child as unfavorable for getting ahead, the relevance of finances for having another child, how prone they are to buying on installment credit, their social class identification, their social class aspirations, and their interest in social manners.[36] Some who were high on these characteristics had many children, some had few, if any; and vice versa. Those with many and those with few children were not distinguishable on the basis of at least these characteristics.

The Indianapolis study of couples who controlled conception found that size of planned family was directly related to feelings of economic security. But later studies of national samples did not find family size related to how secure the women felt economically. In fact, the wife's feeling of economic security was negatively related in one study to number of pregnancies. It is only in families that plan family size that the feeling of economic security is positively related. Some of the differences can be accounted for in terms of the kinds of samples studied.[37] Still, it does seem strange that feelings of economic security cannot be demonstrably and unequivocally shown to be related to family size. Or better, perhaps, family size to feelings of security.

Equally irrelevant to the number of children a woman had was a brace of personality traits which one could logically expect to be related to it, such, for example, as "manifest anxiety, ambiguity tolerance, impulse gratification, need achievement, nurturance needs, preference for working alone, self-awareness, and compulsiveness." [38]

Strangest of all, and seemingly incredible, was the finding that there was little relationship between a woman's "liking for children" and the number she actually bore.[39] Nor between her adjustment to the mother role and the number of children she had. Or, for that matter, adjustment to the role of wife itself. Or finding babies enjoyable. Nor—and this is a really stunning surprise—did the availability of help with child care make any difference in the number of children borne, except perhaps among Jews.[40] Whew!

There is something encouraging for the future of motherhood in these unexpected research findings. A considerable amount of concern has been expressed about the frustration women may be expected to experience when motherhood comes to take a smaller and smaller proportion of their lives and as the environmentally optimum number of children per mother declines. But if a "liking for children" or "adjustment to the role of mother" is just as likely to be associated with a small as with a large number of children, the implication is that two children can satisfy the imputed "maternal instinct" of women as well as half a dozen.

Whatever it is, in brief, that distinguishes women who have many babies from those who have few, it is more likely· to be related to their cultural and class background than to anything intrinsic in their own personalities. The women who bear children may vary greatly in their capacity for nurturance, but those who have many do not differ from those who have few in any of the personality traits the demographers have been able to measure by the questions they have asked. The women who bear many and the women who bear few children, whatever the script for the role may be, are just run-of-mill human beings like anyone else. Structural factors seem to make the difference.

Actually, in sum, the similarities among women with respect to child bearing are more striking than the differences. The enormous pressures exerted on them until now to have babies has guaranteed that they would all want and have at least two children; but the costs of motherhood have guaranteed that they would want not more than three or four, no matter how many they actually had. This conclusion is justified by the finding that of the roughly one-fifth of unwanted pregnancies resulting in births between 1960 and 1965, most were fourth, fifth, and sixth or higher parities.[41]

Returning, finally, to the question raised by the two psychologists with respect to self-selection for motherhood—if we give women real choices between motherhood and other options—we may conclude that among women who select motherhood at all (as compared with those who reject it entirely), those in any given income or ethnic or cultural group who have few children will not differ greatly from those who have many.[42]

Though many young women seem not to know it, just having a baby is only the first step in motherhood. There is a whole lifetime beyond. For, as Judith Blake reminds us, contrary to the economists' conception, a baby is not just a "consumer durable," which, like a car or a boat, can be returned, exchanged, or discarded when it is no longer satisfying. Motherhood is for keeps. It is forever. There is more beyond the delivery. Much more. As the young mother learns right away.

# PART THREE

---

# The Second
# Imperative
# and the Future

# Introduction

If bearing children is the first imperative of motherhood, the
second is protecting and socializing them. For many centuries,
even millennia, just keeping infants alive was a major task of
motherhood, successful only half the time in some epochs and
some places. But even when the sheer physical survival of most
infants could be taken for granted, the task of motherhood was not
greatly ameliorated. We are, in fact, in the presence of an anomaly
here. As affluence has brought more technological help to the
mother, it has provided less personal help to her so that the role of
mother has become more difficult. It is thus little easier today than
it was when "mothers . . . wept tears of bitterness over their infant daughters, at the thought of the sufferings which they were
destined to undergo while they cherished the decided wish that
these daughters would never marry." [1] Motherhood was difficult
then because of the physical hardships involved; it is hard today
because of the psychological hazards involved. For the way we institutionalize motherhood, giving mothers the exclusive responsibility for the care of children and making this care their exclusive
activity, has destructive effects on women as well as on children.
Its costs are great and women are beginning to rebel against it.

The question is sometimes asked, are the interests of mothers
and children antagonistic? Can they both be served? Or is the self-
sacrifice built into the Victorian model for the role of mother intrinsic to it and essential for the welfare of children? One answer
is suggested in Chapter 5. If we want women to be able to provide
the tender-loving-care essential for the development of children

we must protect them against the pressures our way of institutionalizing motherhood subjects them to. Both mothers and children benefit from such relief.

The socialization as well as the protection of children has been a preoccupation of parents, especially of mothers, for millennia. The scripts have changed over time. But two such scripts—one based on a stern disciplinary conception of human nature and the other on a gentler, more permissive one—have tended to alternate or even coexist. One, following Calvin, views the infant as wired for sin and calling for strong controls; the other, following Rousseau, views the infant as born trailing clouds of glory, who should be protected from the contaminating world. The immediate future, as projected on the basis of past trends, will see a swing back to a more disciplinary point of view after the permissiveness of the recent past.

# CHAPTER FIVE

## Storm Signals

### Keeping Infants Alive

A woman has traditionally provided for care of children through the first two or three years of life, whether she supplied it herself or shared it with others. Just keeping infants alive was a major part of the mother's role. When an infant was almost as likely to die as to survive, a large component of motherhood was, in fact, simply one of warding off death. Once past infancy, until the fifteenth century in Europe at least, the child was—and even today in preliterate societies still is—on its own. It mingled with the general community; motherhood became, accordingly, attenuated.

One of the first scientific treatises on infant care appeared—apparently, though not really—incongruously, in Aristotle's *Politics*. Here, he laid down the fundamentals for the role of mother before and after the child's birth:

> The women should take care of their bodily health during pregnancy, not leading a life of indolence, nor yet adopting a scanty diet. [Were women even then worried about losing their figures?] This care of their bodies may be easily secured by the legislator, if he ordains that they should daily take a certain walk to render due service to the gods whose function it is to provide over childbirth. But their minds, unlike their bodies, should at such times be comparatively indolent and free from anxiety, as we see that children are affected by the state of the mother during pregnancy.

Babies were to be hardened to temperature changes soon after birth, fed plenty of milk, given freedom to cry and kick, not swaddled. When they got older they were not to be left too much in the company of slaves nor exposed to bad language or bad examples.

Centuries later, Aristotle's script for infant care was not being followed. The attitude recommended for child care is reflected in a sixteenth-century French how-to-do-it book on child care:

> She [the nanny] rejoices when the child is happy, and feels sorry for the child when he is ill; she picks him up when he falls, she binds him when he tosses about, and she washes and cleans him when he is dirty. She brings the child up and teaches him to talk: she pronounces the words as if she had a stammer, to teach him to talk better and more rapidly. . . . She carries him in her hands, then on her shoulder, then on her lap, to play with him when he cries; she chews the child's meat for him when he has no teeth so that he can swallow profitably and without danger; she plays with the child to make him sleep and she binds his limbs to keep them straight so that he has no stiffness in his body, and she bathes and annoints him to nourish his flesh.[1]

Aristotle would not have approved. The infant swaddled; cared for by a servant; given an example of stammering? But please note: she carried the infant in her hands, then on her shoulder, then on her lap, she played with it when it cried. Whatever else she may have been doing wrong, she was doing a great deal that was right. Chewing the child's food may not have been very salutary for the infant's physical health, but supplying the physical contact and social stimulation was extremely salutary for its emotional health.

The emphasis on physical care of the infant was an important component in any script for the role of mother because until modern medicine made infancy safe, parents could expect to lose almost as many children as they saved. They could not afford to become too attached to infants if, as was probable, they might lose them. In France, Philippe Ariès reminds us, an infant who died was buried as casually as a pet cat or dog, for "he was such an unimportant little thing, . . . inadequately involved in life." [2] Such seeming callousness was almost inevitable.[3] Mothers did, of course, grieve at the loss of their babies,[4] but there was no certain recourse against early death. One had to live with the precarious state of infant survival until modern science came to the rescue.

By the twentieth century the physical care of infants reflected the advances made in preventive measures. "Attention was focused on safe methods of infant feeding, of hygiene and sanitation in the nursery and the kitchen, culminating in the concept of prevention of diseases through routine well-baby care, and immunization schedules." [5] And as the twentieth century passed its mid-point, preventive measures were beginning to reach the fetus long before birth.[6]

One of the most spectacular feats of science in the nineteenth and twentieth centuries was precisely this lowering of the infant mortality rate. No amount of punctilious conformity to any child-care method could have guaranteed infant survival without the science, technology, engineering, and sanitation that cleaned up the environment and warded off lethal infections by innoculation. More than mothering alone was called for, as it is, of course, to this day.

As a result of these health measures, the situation has improved to the extent that relatively few women lose any of their children. Just keeping babies alive is no longer the all-encompassing charge of motherhood.

Once the scientific break-through for infant survival had been achieved, we discovered that health care was not enough. It might no longer be difficult to keep infants fed, clean, and dry,[7] but it was not easy to keep them emotionally well. If physical care were all that was called for, motherhood would be a cinch. Transforming the infant into a human being takes a good deal more.[8]

## Marasmus and Tender Loving Care

In the twentieth century a spate of research studies began to report on *marasmus*, a wasting away of infants as a result of inadequate amounts of loving attention. A pediatrician, Dr. Henry Chapin, in a paper presented at the American Pediatric Society in 1915, reported that most babies less than a year old who entered hospitals or children's institutions died. In one such institution, in fact, all infants were entered as "hopeless," anticipating the usual result of the "care" they would receive. A hint as to the reasons came from the experience of a Düsseldorf institution in which Old Anna wandered around carrying a baby on both hips. When a case looked hopeless, it was turned over to her. She just cuddled the sick infants and she usually succeeded in healing them. Later Dr. René Spitz conducted a two-year experiment in which the amount of affection bestowed on the children differed; in the "Nursery" the mothers took care of them, in the Foundling Home, over-worked nurses. The development of the Foundling children was severely retarded. Over a five year period of observation, none of the Nursery children died; 37 percent of the Foundling children died.[9] During World War II work by Anna Freud on children in London during the blitz showed that although the children taken care of by nurses developed in the first months normally physically, their later emotional development was on a more brittle level.[10] John Bowlby at midcentury had built up the concept of "maternal deprivation" to an almost alarming extent.[11]

Meanwhile new research approaches were corroborating the importance of physical contact in the development of infants and small children. The work of the Harlows at the University of Wisconsin in the fifties and sixties [12] and of James Prescott on neurological, psychological, and anthropological data,[13] all documented the lethal or at least devastatingly retarding effects of severe "maternal deprivation," especially deprivation of physical contact. This research was convincing. It left no doubt that infants who suffered from insufficient body contact, rocking motion, social stimulation and response from their caretakers, suffered serious psychological and developmental consequences.

There is, therefore, a sad irony in the fact that although many preliterate societies optimize the conditions for supplying such physical contact and social stimulation—there is always someone available to carry the infant about or play with it in a social setting—we make it as hard as possible to supply these essentials by making one person alone responsible for supplying them all by herself in an isolated household.[14] The situation in marasmus is quite different from that of germ diseases. Public sanitation could remove a great deal of the danger of germ diseases from the responsibility of mothers. It could not supply the body contact and movement and smiling face that the infant's emotional health also demanded. However superior we are in physical hygiene, we are less advanced than many preliterate communities in social and emotional hygiene.

## Mothering: Psychological or Structural?

There is a great deal to be said about individual differences among women in temperament, in maternalism, and in knowledge as related to their ability to perform the role of mother.[15] Some perform the role well and some poorly, almost regardless of circumstances. But there is also a great deal to be said about the setting in which the role is performed. For in addition to individual differences there are also cultural differences in the way the role is institutionalized. And these, too, have to be taken into account. Thus, for example, a team of psychologists and anthropologists cited in Chapter 1 reported that women who lived in isolated households behaved differently from those who lived in crowded households, those who had help from those who did not, those who worked in the fields from those who did not. They concluded that "the pressures impinging upon the growing child are much more in the nature of by-products of the horde of apparently irrelevant considerations that impinge upon the parents. These considerations of household composition, size of family, work load, etc., determine the time and energy that mothers have available to care for children. They determine the range and content of mother-child relations and the context in which these relations must take place." [16] The isolated mother-child household, for example, has been found to be related to lack of physical affection and, more decisively, to the inflicting of pain.[17] Yet in our society we stage motherhood in precisely this unfavorable setting:

A small family, consisting of parents and children only, normally lives in a confined, relatively isolated, cell-like space, side by side with similar families in similar accommodation. This means that members of the family are more closely penned up together than in the past, which puts a greater strain on emotional relations between mother and child. In comparison with village conditions, which (without showing them in an unduly favourable light) can be said to have offered a relatively constant environment for thousands of years, the area of the known and emotionally familiar has notably shrunk so far as the town child is concerned. Opportunities of escape to other members of the family are more restricted [for the mother as well as for the child]. In other words, the whole ambivalent emotional tension of the child is predominantly concentrated on the mother [as well as vice versa, so that she] often feels overburdened by this and feels more ambivalently towards the child in consequence. . . . To a greater or lesser extent the child becomes the object on which she discharges her unpleasure tensions.[18]

In brief, it is as much the way we structure motherhood as it is the way the individual women themselves think or feel that determines how they perform the maternal role.

Increasingly, therefore, it is being asked, what good does it do to research patiently the nature of child development and the part the mother plays in fostering it if we then stage the script in a way that makes it all but impossible for so many well-meaning and conscientious women to perform it in an optimal manner? If, in effect, we combine all the circumstances that research shows to be antithetical to the warmth in mother-child relationships which we know children need, and then ask women to overcome them? If we specify tender-loving-care and then make it so difficult to bestow it?

## Structural Defects and Results

The mutually incompatible requirements we build into the role of mother—tender-loving-care round the clock and exclusive responsibility for the care of children—lead to anxiety and guilt and, combined with our life style—the isolated household which deprives mothers of help—to the stresses of fatigue. The impact of all these defects does not fall equally on all women, nor do all necessarily feel the weight of each one. Some mothers must contend with the additional burden of poverty. And some—extremely wealthy women, for example, and women securely cocooned within an ethnic enclave—may escape all of them. But for a large proportion of mothers the weight is heavy. No one, of course, is "to blame." No one deliberately planned how to make motherhood so hard. But that is the result that has been achieved.

The evidence for this charge does not come in the form of neatly designed research findings presented in neatly organized tables. It comes, rather, in the form of the personal experiences of mothers themselves. For even after the team of psychologists and anthropologists had called our attention to the change in the early 1960s, it did not even occur to most researchers of the American scene to question the way we structured motherhood. But now an incipient "revolt of the mothers"—already presaged a century ago [19]—is beginning to suggest that we may not have mothers to kick around much longer.

## Storm Signals

Storm signals are now being raised. "The hidden underside [of motherhood] is hardly talked about," cries one young mother, so she feels "obsessed with the need to tell people what really happens when you have children." [20] She feels she must expose "the terrible weight of responsibility, the way it affects a woman's personality." [21] And a group of women, basing their conclusions on their own experiences as observant participators, as well as on relevant scientific research, note almost point for point how the way we institutionalize the role of mother is bad for women. They call on women to organize "to fight those aspects of our society that make childbearing and child rearing stressful rather than fulfilling experiences." [22]

Before documenting in detail their charges that motherhood as we structure it is not good for either women or children and in order to forestall the blizzard of protests from hordes of women to these charges, a bow in the direction of the joys of motherhood is in order here.

### The Joys of Motherhood

The phrase "joys of motherhood" is not used here in a satirical, cynical, or pejorative sense. The team of psychologists and anthropologists who commented on the heavier burden of baby care women carry in our society added in parentheses that for some this was not a burden but a joy. And it would be fatuous to deny that the rewards of having babies can be great. An infant of any species—kitten, puppy, cub—is cute and fun.[23] Human infants are the most appealing of all. We find it almost impossible not to coo or touch the baby in the carriage or backpack on the street. Or give it our finger to grasp. Watching a well-fed, healthy infant grow and develop, learn to crawl, stand, walk, reach, respond to a smile, can be the most fascinating of experiences. The joy of babies, it goes without saying, is indeed real. No one—well, hardly anyone—denies that.

But the rebelling women make a distinction between loving babies and loving motherhood. The two are far from identical. One may love babies with all one's heart, as most mothers in fact do. But one may still recognize the "hidden underside." One could love the baby much more if motherhood were structured in a way to make it more conformable to the needs of both mother and child.

Of the women who find motherhood completely fulfilling, whatever the costs, who would want nothing changed, who find all the joy it brings and none of the hidden underside, there is little to say, at least in early motherhood. Like the annals of the poor, their story is brief.[24] But not all women share their good fortune.[25]

Are we, then, perhaps dealing here with only a few disgruntled women—misfits? Are the dimensions of the dissatisfaction with the way we institutionalize motherhood trivial or frivolous? If so, there would be little point in discussing the subject at all.

### The Numbers Game

It is difficult to measure the relative proportion of women who find joy in the role of mother and those who do not. Different studies give us different clues.[26] The proportion of women who suffer the effects of the hidden underside of motherhood cannot be precisely pinpointed, for the very way we institutionalize motherhood precludes their expressing frustration even to themselves.[27] Such expression would violate one of the prescribed canons:

> Because of the societal pressures surrounding motherhood, and the mystique of the maternal instinct (joys of child care, fulfillment through others), many women are unable to pinpoint their feelings of confusion and inadequacy or are unable to feel that it is legitimate to verbalize their hesitations and problems.[28]

The proportions are, therefore, undoubtedly greater than the research findings show. But regardless of the exact number of women involved, as far as the future is concerned they must be accorded great weight. These women are leading the way. Once they have opened up the matter for scrutiny, others will follow.

### Not Good for Women

Practically all that has been written about childbirth and its aftermath has been written by men—by obstetricians, that is, or pediatricians. The message may be sympathetic; but increasingly it is felt by women to be patronizing, even insensitive. Only recently has the dysfunctional nature of early motherhood in our society come to be studied and reported on by women themselves.

And to an extent not adequately recognized before, the picture is more somber than the stereotypically gay and cheerful one to which we have been accustomed. Women find that motherhood has been romanticized and idealized; they are let down by the reality. Motherhood is "often tremendously disappointing on a work-a-day basis, in some vital way promising renewal and then often letting you down or perhaps more exactly weighting you down with the minutia of child care routine." [29]

*"The Terrible Weight of Responsibility": Anxiety.* Although from the moment the infant child is wrapped in a pink blanket it has been taken for granted by everyone that she would one day be a mother, though she has played with dolls for years, though she has cuddled live babies ever since she can remember, the female is quite unprepared for the reality she confronts with motherhood. Nothing as superficial as simple child care is involved. It is quite possible to train young women for that. Indeed, home economics colleges have been doing it for many decades. But this is not the same as preparation for the sole responsibility of a child. Responsibility puts one on the spot. It means being the person beyond whom there is no recourse, no appeal. It means being answerable oneself for whatever happens. It means being a lonely adult. Not only has the young mother been untrained for motherhood; she has been positively counter-trained for it.

Being a mother is not child's play. Niles Newton, who has researched the physiology of motherhood in detail, has contrasted cultural and biological femininity. She notes that being a mother calls for strength and power; but we have reared girls to be sweetly feminine in a watered-down facsimile of the Victorian heroine rather than to be physically strong women.

> Contrary to popular belief, women have lost status rather than gained status with the coming of the industrial revolution. When production moved out of the home, women became more dependent on their husbands' support. Women's childbearing and child-care contribution to society became depreciated as children became economic burdens and the birth rate fell. . . . These changes made feelings of insecurity, inferiority, envy, and dependence part of the accepted feminine pattern. Actions which stem from such feelings are considered culturally feminine. On the other hand, biological pressures put a premium on productiveness, activity, concerted effort, and aggressiveness in women. These biologically feminine

characteristics are often opposite from those encouraged by our society.[30]

Since in our society a woman must—at least this was so until recently—first find a man to support her, the invisible curriculum girls have suffered through, in school as elsewhere, has emphasized the importance of appealing to men and dependency has been taught as a large component of such appeal. The consequences of such a pattern of socializing girls has had wide ramifications throughout our entire society. Only in the last few years have we been re-examining the way we socialize girls and learning, much to our surprise, that while we thought we were preparing them for both motherhood and work—at least for a job before marriage—actually we have fallen between the two ideals, preparing them well for neither. We have not even been preparing them for adulthood. We have, rather, socialized them into a crippling, even child-like, dependency. Succeeding, we might add, brilliantly:

> In our early discussions it became clear that we did not really feel ourselves to be separate, independent people. The men in our lives embodied or felt they were supposed to embody, freedom and independence. The women in our lives stayed at home, needed company, and were always dependent on those near them. They embodied, or felt they should, dependency, need and connection. As we talked to each other . . . we realized that we were no longer powerless, helpless children.[31]

Since the care of babies in our society is the exclusive responsibility of the mother, any help proffered her is a gift, not an obligation on anyone's part, even the father's. Thus, all of a sudden, no matter how long they have been looking forward to motherhood, women find themselves solely responsible for the care of a human being, a responsibility they cannot slough off or share. They are face-to-face with a child who does not reward them for their efforts to please as they have been accustomed to be rewarded, who makes no concessions to their own needs. "A woman can adapt a passive dependency on a husband and still have a successful marriage, but a young mother with strong dependency needs is in for difficulty in maternal adjustment, because the role precludes such dependency." [32] Given this setting for performing the mother role, no wonder young mothers are plagued with anxiety.

*The Mystique of the Full-time Mother: Guilt.* Because of the demands we make, because we set impossibly high standards, our way of institutionalizing motherhood breeds guilt into the very fabric of a woman's character. She blames herself for every deviation from the model. "Mothers," the researchers report, "often quite freely admit feelings of guilt in regard to responsibilities; they assign their failures to emotional or personal factors in themselves. They are constantly assessing their performances in terms of some ideal standard." [33] And women reporting on their own experience corroborate the researchers' statement: "We often feel guilty, because we think our own inadequacies are the cause of our unhappiness. We rarely question whether the roles we have are realizable." [34] Hence they punish themselves, for "the chief punisher of most deviating mothers is their own conscience." [35] Anything and everything that goes wrong, or even falls slightly short of perfection is their fault. They are always apologizing for something they have done or not done. "Since the parents tend to blame themselves, and feel that others blame them . . . guilt, anxiety, and feelings of inferiority are the concomitants." [36] And the only way some can assuage their guilt is by constant dedication to the child; they permit themselves not one moment away from it. "Many women report proudly that 'no one else has ever put my children to bed' or 'no one else has ever had to feed my children.' " [37]

Along with the symbiotic relationship between mother and child there is also a built-in power struggle [38] which the Calvinists have long recognized and which our method of institutionalizing motherhood exacerbates by depriving the mother of support during the long day when she is alone with the child. For children, as the Calvinists so well understood, can be little devils as well as little angels. And the role-prescribed tender-loving-care may foster tyranny in them. The infant is imperious. Its hunger, its pain, its discomfort take precedence over everything else. Wake up! Wake up! Take care of me or else. I'll shriek or bellow until you do. No excuses. No delays. Drop whatever it is you are doing. . . . The child soon learns how useful its crying can be in controlling its environment, for the child trains its parents as well as vice versa. "Picking up the infant when he cries can . . . constitute potent reinforcement for the infant's crying." [39]

Thus not only does child care create ambivalence in the mother who, despite the annoyance she feels, nevertheless must attempt to "follow such vague maxims as . . . 'give infants as much tender loving care as they need,' " [40] but it may also spoil the child by reinforcing or rewarding "antisocial or immature responses." [41] Whether she capitulates to the infant's demands in order to quiet it or takes "a focused, disciplined role" she feels guilty. The asymmetry of this relationship is unparalleled. There is no escape. The woman and the demanding infant are in a cage together.

Nor is it much different with a small child. When two adults are left alone for any stretch of time, the first hour or so may be more or less pleasant. A certain pattern evolves according to their idiosyncrasies so that they either share evenly in the give-and-take or one takes over more than a proportionate share of the time or refuses to contribute a proportionate share. If both know there is a fixed termination to the encounter a considerable amount of asymmetry can be tolerated. But no matter how asymmetrical the relationship between two adults may be, it never approaches the asymmetry between an adult and a small child. The young mother is not prepared for it.

For perhaps an hour the woman can maintain a degree of tranquillity by centering all her attention on the child. She tells stories. She plays games. She shares toys. She can meet the child's insatiable demands for attention with moderate ease. As time passes, however, this becomes harder and harder. As she shows signs of flagging, the demands of the child become more and more insistent. In her eagerness to placate the child's demands, she has been rewarding its distressing behavior. If she is a moderately well-educated middle-class young woman who has read the books and takes her role seriously, she is vulnerable to the characteristic guilt of early motherhood.

For in attempting to appease the child her high-minded principles begin to crumble. She bribes the child with a candy bar or soft drink, worrying all the while because she knows this is not good for its teeth. The child shows no sympathy for her stress, no understanding. It perceives her mounting tensions but does not empathize with them. Instead of lowering its demands in response to these signals, it raises them. It whines, whimpers, cries. The mother's voice becomes shrill. Her muscles grow taut. She feels guilty. She should be able to pour out inexhaustible waves of patience and tolerance. She is, after all, the adult. The child is only a child. She feels guilty. What has she done wrong that makes the child so demanding, so insistent, so insatiable? She feels guilty. Where is there any help? Release? Relief? She feels guilty.

The odds were more even when the mother felt she had to break the child's will and could therefore punish with a clear conscience. Or when she was so occupied with the ordinary routine of cooking, cleaning, laundering, sewing, mending, gardening, marketing that the child did not expect much attention and the woman herself felt justified in not giving it.[42] Today, if she has nothing really pressing her—except the book she is dying to read or the music she is dying to play or the needlepoint she is dying to finish—the mother feels guilty.

The mother feels guilty not only vis-à-vis the child but also vis-à-vis the outside world. She is at the mercy of the public as well as of the child. Women are taught that they must always protect their children. But against whom? Not you and me, the outside world. When we adults are the ones being annoyed or irritated or injured by the children the mother must take our side against them. She must now attack, must punish, them. For despite all our protestations of love and concern for children, our behavior does not always shore them up. When children are on their best behavior, seen but not heard, adults can be quite fond of them. But when they act their age, our attitude can change quite remarkably. We glare at the mother of the bawling infant on the plane, train, or bus. We stare coldly at the mother of the restless child at the concert. We purse our lips at the mother of the children at the supermarket when one of them inadvertently knocks over a can of peas, though the mother is as embarrassed as anyone else.

Reared to please others, taught to appease the world, to be compliant and complacent, to maintain good relations with others, the mother now finds herself responsible for the behavior of another human being who does not as yet have her discipline, who often does things that annoy and irritate others—cries, makes a nuisance of itself. She is held hostage by the child against the outside world. Unless the outside world forces her to comply with the child's demands, it will make *their* world intolerable. So mothers are forced to protect themselves against both the child and the outside world. The child nullifies her own compliant efforts. She is held accountable for whatever the child does and the world glares at her. Now whose side is she on? If she chooses the public's side, she must punish the child; if she chooses the child's side, she must suffer the punishment of the public. In any event, guilt results.

*The Stress Toll: Noise and Fatigue.* People who see children only when they are well behaved, at rare intervals, or for only short periods of time show little concern for the stress-toll to women who have to be in the demanding company of small children for hours at a time when they are noisy, insistent, consuming, even devouring; bombarded by their crying, squabbles, the noise and disorder and whining and whimpering of small children, the constant interruptions, and all the other concomitants of child care. Including noise.

Industrial engineers have long since learned the hazards of fatigue in the factory or plant; they are now alerted to the health hazards of noise "pollution." If the biological stresses to which the mother-child relationship exposes women could be measured in the laboratory, monitored and recorded, they would be shown as enormous. A crying infant, as any sleep-starved young mother can testify, can be devastating, as can noisy play of children of any age.[43]

"It's bad enough for Asthore," one sympathetic husband notes sadly, "no new dresses, no new hats; almost never outside the house for an hour or two of change and recreation, but the noise! I hear it on the 7 to 8 A.M. shift and again on the 6 P.M. to midnight shift. She hears it—even in her sleep." [44]

And the fatigue. The high-risk hours so far as child-abuse is concerned are, not unexpectedly, the hours before and after dinner.[45] To a mother-in-law complaining about the appearance and housekeeping of a young mother of three small children, a columnist replies:

> You say this mother gives her children good care. So think what that means. Think of the feedings, the bathings, the diaper changings; the bottle washings, the bed-making. Think of the napping and play-time schedules to be woven into the daily routine, to give each baby a fair shake. Think of the endless mopping-up and picking-up, the messy hands and faces and meal-time feed spills that keep mama on the jump. Think of the always-urgent need to watch out that the kids don't invite a mortal danger in their climbing, crawling, pulling, hauling exploration of their surroundings. Think of mama's rising burden of fatigue. Think of the wear-and-tear, since the marriage began, of too much self-giving and too little rest, just in

bearing three babies in the span of four years. Top this with the relentless multiplying demands of her vital reserves, of tending the babies' growing needs.[46]

And from the mouths of the mothers themselves:

We may find ourselves, at first, with little time for even our simplest personal needs. Some of us have difficulty staying awake in social situations during the first weeks and months and find it hard to maintain involvement in outside interests. With subsequent children we often feel an inability to cope with daily household routines, finding ourselves suddenly with a family too large to manage. Often we feel that we have lost control over our lives, and dread that life will always be this way.[47]

Included among the stresses, on the basis of a questionnaire study of postpartum emotional adjustment, is lack of help from relatives or husband, especially with the longer-lasting problems: "present environmental factors . . . , such as lack of emotional support and assistance, the husband often away from home, and other relatives not available to help, were significant in cases where problems persisted for longer than six months." [48] Even from the mouth of the sympathetic, but seemingly helpless, husband of the mother of nine, the same thing. Motherhood "hasn't been a pink tea for Asthore, with her sixteen- seventeen-hour day, seven-day-week, 365-day-year—almost unrelieved. . . . [It] has meant problems . . . to be solved under relentless conditions of mental fatigue, physical weariness, spiritual—something or other. . . ." [49] She "has died to herself, for a period of a good many years. The cause of her death was an old-fashioned wedding ring. . . . Asthore was full of life, of joy, of eagerness to sing and dance and dine to music, to swim and play tennis, to pray and to read and to develop her talents." [50] Motherhood as institutionalized in our society extinguished all that. No wonder Mother hopes her daughters will not imitate her.

But Asthore had nine children! the resistant critic points out. Few women are going to have more than two or three and, as we are increasingly being told, motherhood—even if it is as stressful as these women say—takes only a small part of a woman's life. True, but long enough to break some women. They never recover.

It is not only the mothers in women's collectives, who are able to pinpoint their feelings and verbalize their protests, who make the case against our style of motherhood. A growing number of less articulate women are "voting with their feet." The increase in the number of runaway wives is startling. The head of a detective company specializing in missing persons notes that whereas in the past the ratio of runaway wives to runaway husbands among his clientele was one to three hundred, it is now one to two. "A typical runaway wife is a girl who married young and had a couple of babies not long after. And suddenly there she was with the housework and the four walls." [51] This is what motherhood as institutionalized in our society has done to women.

Plato was far more understanding. In his *Republic* motherhood was not restricted to women nor were mothers immured, unassisted, to carry the whole load themselves. "As soon as children are born, they will be taken in charge by officers appointed for the purpose, who may be men or women or both, since offices are to be shared by both sexes. The children of the better parents they will carry to the crèche to be reared in the care of nurses living apart in a certain quarter of the city. . . . These officers will also superintend the nursing of the children. They will bring the mothers to the crèche when their breasts are full, while taking every precaution that no mother shall know her own child; and if the mothers have not enough milk, they will provide wet-nurses. They will limit the time during which the mothers will suckle their children, and hand over all the hard work and sitting up at night to nurses and attendants. That will make child-bearing an easy business for the Guardians' wives." Plato may have gone overboard in one direction, but surely not in the other.

### Not Good for Children

> . . . once when she [an infant daughter] raged, I found myself stamping my foot in the kind of blind responsive rage a mother can feel when her child screams unappeased. I caught it, realized what it was. Experienced only once, it was enough to make me recognize what lies back of the desperation of a young mother, innocent of all knowledge of babies, who feels that she will never be able to cope with her baby and goes into a postpartum depression.[52]

This is Margaret Mead, one of the most civilized women in the world, speaking. She knows more about child rearing than perhaps anyone else in the world. She could cope with a raging infant. But in the setting for motherhood in our society even she was capable of "the kind of blind responsive rage a mother can feel when her child screams unappeased."

Most women, like Margaret Mead, catch themselves. At least they restrain themselves from violence. But as one psychiatrist notes, as important as actual child abuse, or more so, "is the more subtle forms which all of us witness daily on the sidewalk, in the park, or the supermarket. In such public places mothers unashamedly wallop their children, kick them, slap them, and verbally chastise them in ways that make one fear for what they must do in private. All around us there is evidence that many parents dislike their children a good deal of the time and show it in ways that result in physical or emotional harm to the child." [53] He delineates this behavior in structural terms, noting that "in the kibbutzim . . . parents could love their children more if they saw less of them, and this may very well apply equally to American parents as well." [54]

The idealization of the role of mother does not happen by chance. "In the interest of the survival of the species the mother-child relationship has to be buttressed by social regulation, [but] . . . this is often not sufficient, and . . . deficiencies have therefore to be covered up by idealization." [55] The idealization serves as an intrinsic protection for small children, a prime imperative in the maternal role. Mothers *have* to be idealized. They have to *try* to be ideal.

Mothers may from time to time laughingly refer to their small children as little monsters—there is, in fact, a literary genre specifically aimed at helping women recognize their hostilities under a benign form of humor—and although they expect us to take this as playful exasperation, they mean it more often than they admit even to themselves. For mothers must fool themselves as well as others. They are not allowed to express anything but love for their children, certainly not complaints. Complaints against motherhood would imply complaints against children, lack of love, unmotherly self-centeredness. Still they cannot always experience the prescribed emotions twenty-four hours a day. Patience is limited. They cannot by themselves, alone, absorb all the aggression from their children. "In relation to the child's insatiable demands, failures of parental response are inevitable." [56] Mothers glare and yell. "Sometimes I get so mad at that child I am afraid I'll hurt him. Isn't there something very wrong about this?" asks a moderately well-adjusted woman.[57] The time may come when the beleaguered woman slaps the child in sheer exasperation—and is shocked at her own behavior.

### Violence Against Children

Some women are, in fact, driven beyond the limits of tolerance; they lose control:

> My first son was a joy from the moment of conception on. A marvelous pregnancy. Thrilling natural childbirth. Easy nursing. He established his body balance early and we hardly lost a night of sleep. He smiled, cooed, and babbled early. He responded to me with happiness. It was a dream all the way through. Naturally I thought the second child would be just the same. I couldn't have been more wrong. A miserable pregnancy, Caesarian section, a colicky baby. He kept us awake nights for months. He cried all the time. He drove me crazy. It got so I literally hated him. No matter what I did he repaid me by more crying. His only response to anything was a yell. Nothing I did suited him. It seemed to me he was doing it on purpose. There I was, alone all day with two babies, one of them so self-centered I couldn't bear it. I finally just threw him across the room.[58]

She had *tried* to please the infant, as she had been trying to please everyone as long as she could remember. But he had not responded to her good intentions. She was not psychotic; she was not herself the product of a similar experience. She later learned to express and overcome her frustrations in Mothers Anonymous, a group consisting of other women just like her.

A similar case was helped by a similar organization, Recovery, Inc.:

> With so much being said and written these days about battered children, may I add my two cents worth? I am a mother who used to get so angry with my children I'd beat them black and blue. My 6-year-old was on drugs for a nervous condition. We were both under psychiatric care. I begged my doctor to help me be a better mother. His advice was, "Control yourself! Don't lose your temper."
>
> This went on for over a year. Then a friend told me about Recovery, Inc. Two months after I attended my first meeting I was able to control my impulses. That was three years ago and

I'm still going to meetings. I can't tell you what this organization has meant to me and to my family. .. . [59]

In these cases, "with a little bit of help," the women learn to control their blind rage. Many preliterate societies provide such support as part of the institution of motherhood. Mothers live in a setting that supplies them with support, that allows them to share their responsibilities.[60]

Not all women in our society get such help. They collapse under the weight. Their response is beyond the limits of the normal. We must be doing something—maybe many things—wrong. Such as, for example, fostering dependency in women. For there are some researchers who trace at least certain cases of child abuse to the dependency needs of mothers. One group of psychiatrists speak, for example, of "role reversal in parents," a reversal in which the child is expected to meet the mother's emotional needs rather than vice versa.[61] Another researcher reports that parents who abuse their children see the child as "capable of sensing the parent's needs and meeting them." [62] They do not see the child's needs but only their own. ". . . parents act like a needy child and expect their child to take over the role of a satisfying parent." [63] "Attacking parents look to other people for mothering besides their own mothers. Women look to husbands particularly, husbands look to wives. But if the mothering function fails in the environment, the parent quickly takes it out on the baby." [64] When the weight of all the defects—dependency, isolation, anxiety, fatigue, guilt—pile up on a woman not equipped to deal with them, we have child abuse. "What provokes child beating? An incredible sense of aloneness, worthlessness, and strangely enough, desire—desire for the child to take care of the unheeded needs of the attacker's own yesterdays. When the baby cries or when the small child doesn't yield, his caretaker cannot tolerate the feelings provoked within himself." [65]

The woman who "batters" her baby produces unspeakable revulsion in us. But only recently have we given serious research attention to it. In the first nation-wide study of all reported cases of child abuse in 1967 and 1968,[66] five sets of forces were found to be operating, only one of which—deviancy, or pathology—was clearly in the personality of the perpetrator. The other four were: environmental chance factors, environmental stress factors, disturbed intrafamily relationships, and various combinations of these sets of forces. The study's recommendations were three-fold, all dealing with structural changes: reduce violence in our society as a whole, eliminate poverty, and provide preventive or ameliora-tive services:

> . . . geared to the reduction of environmental and internal stresses on family life, and especially on mothers who carry major responsibility for the child-rearing function. Such stresses are known to precipitate incidents of physical abuse of children, and any measure that would reduce these stresses would also indirectly reduce the incidence of child abuse. Family counseling, homemaker and housekeeping services, *mothers' helpers and babysitting service, family and group day-care facilities for preschool and schoolage* children are all examples of such services. They should be available on a full coverage basis in every community to all groups in the community and not only to the rich or the very poor. Nor should such services be structured as emergency services; *they should be for normal situations,* in order to prevent emergencies. No mother should be expected to care for her children around the clock, 365 days a year. *Substitute care mechanisms should be routinely available* to offer mothers opportunities for carefree rest and recreation.[67]

We have here a genuine blue-print for at least a partial re-institu-tionalizing of motherhood in our society. There remains one major defect: it assumes that mothers still "carry major responsibility for the child-rearing function." Not, however, a defect any sensible person would cavil with at the present time.

It is sad that it has taken the suffering, even the sacrifice, of an untold number of infants and small children to alert us to the haz-ards to which motherhood in our society has subjected them. To assure for all infants and small children the tender-loving-care so essential for their normal development, some such re-structuring of motherhood as that proposed in the study quoted above is clearly imperative. We could probably do more for securing good tender-loving-care for children by guaranteeing mothers two after-noons off a week than by admonishing them for their lapses.

### Addendum

It may be noted that anything that makes it hard for mothers to supply the warmth children need may be bad not only for the children but for the social order as well. James W. Prescott and Cathy McKay, on the basis of data from 400 cultures, conclude that they "overwhelmingly support the thesis that deprivation of physical affection and body pleasure . . . throughout life but particularly during the formative periods of development (infancy, childhood and adolescence) is extraordinarily related to the prominence of warfare and interpersonal physical violence. . . . Physical affectional processes and body pleasure . . . constitute the final common pathway to understanding physical violence at the societal and individual level. Social variables, such as poverty; prejudice; mother-child households; small extended families; 'broken' families; institutionalization of children and adults; industrialization; complexity and mobility of society; social class; both parents in the work force full time; child day care centers; machismo; etc. are all considered secondary mediating variables that must be interpreted and related to the primary process variable of physical affection in meaningful human relationships. It is in this context that child abuse assumes its greatest significance and understanding as a phenomenon and which requires treatment of society and the family, as well as the individual child abuser." [68]

# CHAPTER SIX

## A Variety of Scripts

### What's A Mother To Do?

In a television commercial in the late 1960s a woman, faced with her inability to discipline her children, turned to the audience and asked, "What's a mother to do?" A good question then; a good question still. And, no doubt, a good question in the future. For mothers have to discipline their children as well as to nurture them. Our whole society is wrestling with that precise dilemma. Answering it for parents has become almost a major—even a growth—industry. For, among the vast majority of people, "child-rearing . . . is in a period of disorganization." [1]

How-to-do-it books and magazines thrive along with scholarly research reports on everything from infant care to youth alienation. We are examining in sometimes anguished detail the way our children turn out. "Permissiveness" becomes a dirty word; a great pediatrician is blamed for ruining a whole generation by advocating it and mothers are blamed for following him. Sooner or later the accusing finger always rests on mothers. No wonder they despair.

We have not yet succeeded in creating a script for the role of mother appropriate for our time. Thus at midcentury women were being given conflicting signals. On the one hand, infinite amounts of love and attention were due her children; on the other, too much of an emotional investment in her children was to be avoided. If she tried to integrate her productive and her maternal roles, she was overcome with guilt feelings for somehow or other neglecting her children. If she sacrificed her worker role she was accused by some of being overcommitted to her school-age children, or of interfering too much in the lives of older children. She was to invest most of her time in the care of her babies until they were, let us say, five or six; but she was not to have too much influence over them. She was not to permit them, especially the boys, to become too attached to her or dependent on her. Above all, she was not to become possessive; her children did not belong to her. She had no right to them. She was to keep out of their hair, make no claims on them on the basis of her emotional investment in them. Once they were grown, she was to bow out, remaining only as a friendly spectator; but she was also to remain available practically forever for help with baby-sitting or for providing financial assistance. All the while she was to socialize them. With all the emphasis on what she owed her children she was nevertheless to discipline them too. They had all the rights; she had all the obligations.

### The Extension of "Motherhood-per-Child"

Among the myriad ways in which the role of mother today is unique is its extension over time. Although child-bearing spans fewer years than formerly over a woman's total life time, in the life of each individual child it spans a longer time than it did in the past. Women used to bear more children, but each baby that survived took fewer years of her life. Since then, motherhood-per-child has increased as a result of what the nineteenth century called "the prolongation of infancy."

"Prolongation of infancy" was seen as a necessary part of social evolution because it kept the young pliable and open to learning for a longer period. The first such prolongation came in the fifteenth century when "infancy," that is, a state of dependency, was prolonged to include small children. Later on it was prolonged still further. Boys and girls remained "children" with the responsibility for their welfare still a charge on mothers, though in decreasing degrees. The nineteenth-century prolongation was extensive, as compared to the past, but of modest proportions as compared to the present. Young people were still able to assume adult responsibilities at a relatively young age. By the age of fourteen or fifteen the young person was well on his way. The Horatio Alger archetype, for example, was a young man of about fourteen or fifteen. At the turn of the century "infancy" was further prolonged to include adolescence.[2] Today at that age he is still a child. To present-day women, told that it is important for them to be there with cookies and milk when the children come home from school, fifteen seems like a very young age indeed. And now, as Kenneth Keniston has noted, we have inserted "youth" as another extension of infantilization even beyond adolescence.[3] We have prolonged "infancy" or dependence to an almost fantastic degree and extended motherhood-per-child accordingly. Today partial "infancy" may last well beyond even youth into adulthood. Mothers remain "on call" as long as they are active. Grown sons and daughters feel entitled to "depend" on them. A mother's work is, literally, never done. There is no authentic script yet to guide women in this extended role.

In our day this prolonged dependency has assumed an unanticipated quality. Young adults are kept out of the labor force; their participation in adult life is curtailed. Their life style tends toward the parasitic. The repercussions for motherhood are, of course, far-reaching. Prolonging dependence puts an increasing strain on the parent-child relationship, especially when it occurs under these increasingly stressful circumstances. Nor is the situation mollified when the script for the role of mother vis-à-vis sons and daughters in late adolescence and in youth is only in process of definition, not yet clear-cut.

## The Emergence of Childhood

If infancy is an ineluctable part of life, childhood is not. It is a relatively new conception. On the basis of iconography, especially of portraits of families and children, and on books dealing with child-rearing, Philippe Ariès has sketched for us the emergence of the idea of childhood in the fifteenth century, with appropriate notions of parenthood:

> In medieval society the idea of childhood did not exist; this is not to suggest that children were neglected, foresaken or despised. The idea of childhood is not to be confused with affection for children; it corresponds to an awareness of the particular nature of childhood, that particular nature which distinguishes the child from the adult, even the young adult. In medieval society this awareness was lacking. That is why, as soon as the child could live without the constant solicitude of his mother, his nanny or his cradle-rocker, he belonged to adult society.[4]

Children participated in traditional festivals, served as apprentices in workshops, as pages in the service of knights. A child was, for all intents and purposes, a young adult. And, for that matter, not so much younger than the adults of that society, for in a time when the span of life was relatively brief, even full-grown men and women tended to be young.

When childhood did become distinguished as a special stage of development in the fifteenth century, two quite contrasting modes of dealing with children took the place of earlier indifference, and they have, in one form or another, persisted to this day, and will, no doubt, continue into the future. One was an indulgent attitude that led to "coddling," the other was a moralizing attitude that led to stern discipline. The first tended to come from parents, the second from churchmen and moralists. Thomas More's description of the mother getting her small son off to school illustrates the contrast between her indulgence and the—male—teacher's sternness:

> When the little boy will not rise in time for her, but lies still abed and slugg, and when he is up, weepeth because he hath lien so long, fearing to be beaten at school for his late coming thither, she telleth him then that it is but early days, and he shall come time enough, and biddeth him: "Go, good son, I warrant thee, I have sent to thy master myself, take thy bread and butter with thee, thou shalt not be beaten at all.[5]

He may have been reassured enough to go to school; but he was almost certain to be beaten anyway.

At home, the child of affluent families was seen as a toy. Children were amusing and fun to play with. They were coddled, much to the annoyance of disapproving observers. Despite the numerous expressions of such disapproval by moralizing and strict disciplinarians, coddling had, by the beginning of the eighteenth century, diffused down even to the poor. "Children of the poor are particularly ill-mannered because," according to one writer in 1720, "they do just as they please, their parents paying no attention to them, even treating them in an idolatrous manner: what the children want, they want too." [6]

This indulgent attitude exasperated the moralists. "Too many parents," they admonished, "value their children only in so far as they derive pleasure and entertainment from them." [7] This would never do. Children had to be disciplined, trained, their characters developed. And this new emphasis on character meant that "the tone is sometimes grim, the emphasis being laid on strictness as opposed to the laxity and facility of contemporary manners." [8]

But the burgeoning interest in child psychology which developed in the seventeenth century tempered the strictness. People had to understand the behavior of children if they wanted to correct it. And the script did not entirely exclude tenderness:

> Familiarizing oneself with one's children, getting them to talk about all manner of things, treating them as sensible people and winning them over with sweetness, is an infallible secret for doing what one wants with them. They are young plants which need tending and watering frequently: a few words of advice offered at the right moment, a few marks of friendship and affection given now and then, touch them and bind them. A few caresses, a few little presents, a few words of cordiality and trust make an impression on their minds, and they are few in number that resist these sweet and easy methods of making them persons of honour and probity.[9]

This conflict between strict and mild discipline, between emphasis on punishment and reward, on obedience and permissiveness, on "reinforcing" and "aversive" conditioning has characterized the scripts for the role of mother ever since. Which one selects, now as then, is closely related to one's ideology or conception of the nature of human nature.

### Ideologies and Scripts for the Role of Mother:
### Calvin Versus Rousseau

Although all societies everywhere recognize socialization as intrinsic to the role of mother, they do not all agree on how to implement it. A voluminous didactic and homiletic literature telling mothers how to rear children has developed, ranging from admonitions about sparing rods to religious homilies about saving souls to scientific data about socialization and enculturation. Even within any one society some of the scripts are permissive, some are strict.

Much depends on how the child itself is viewed. Some see the child as coming direct from the hands of God, trailing clouds of glory; others see the child as already corrupted at birth with original sin. And others, equally baffled by both philosophies, alternate between them. The first have a Rousseauean ideology, the second, a Calvinist, the third, shreds of both. The first will do all they can to preserve the child's natural innocence, trying to prevent the prison walls from closing in, the chains from dragging. The second will express their love for the child by eradicating the sin, breaking its will, harsh as the process may prove to be. The third may just throw up their hands.

In the Calvinist script there is no doubt where one's sympathies lie—with the mother. The child has to be saved, his will broken, at whatever cost. Strong measures can be tolerated, even demanded in such contingencies. In Rousseauean scripts, however, we are on the side of the child. It is a poor little vulnerable innocent and the mother must protect it, again at whatever cost; she is strong, it is fragile.

Robert Sunley has summarized how the two ideologies shaped the role scripts for mothers in the United States from 1820 to 1860:

> According to the Calvinist view, the child was born depraved: "No child has ever been known since the earliest period of the world, destitute of an evil disposition—however sweet it appears." It followed that parents must vigilantly guard against the tendency of their depraved impulses; enforcing absolute obedience to adult demands could alone secure the child's salvation. Breaking the child's will meant freeing him from the hold of his evil nature. . . . The . . . school of thought advocating "gentle treatment" saw the child as having certain needs and potentialities which the parents were not to frustrate or control, but rather were to help fulfill and encourage into full development. . . . The child was a tender creature who could be harmed by the lack of nurture, kindly care, and gentle discipline.[10]

Calvin and Rousseau have fought for the minds of mothers for decades. The humanitarian movements of the nineteenth century zeroed in on exploited children and increasingly championed their side. Ellen Key hailed the twentieth century as the Century of the Child. It sounds far away and long ago. But the echoes resonate through the corridors of time. Sunley writes of the early and middle nineteenth century. He might as well have written about the twentieth. Even perhaps the twenty-first. For scripts for

95

the role of mother continue to veer from a neo-Calvinist to a neo-Rousseauean emphasis, among scientists no less than among theologians and philosophers.

## Calvin and Rousseau in Modern Guise

In the second decade of the present century, under the influence of John Holt and John Watson, mothers were instructed to impose a strict regimen on infants immediately after birth and not to deviate from it one iota. A *New Yorker* cartoon showed a young mother, bottle in hand, hovering over the infant in the crib where it lay shrieking, while she counted the minutes on her watch till feeding time. A few decades later, under the influence of Benjamin Spock, mothers were instructed to follow a self-demand schedule, feeding the infant when it called for food. The early school of thought minimized body contact between infant and mother. Later, it was recommended; for by that time the work of the Harlows on monkeys at the University of Wisconin had highlighted the importance for them of sheer physical contact with a warm body.

The contrast in points of view between the Children's Bureau 1914 edition of *Infant Care* and the 1942–45 edition may be schematized like this: [11]

| 1914 | 1942–45 |
|---|---|
| Infant has strong and dangerous impulses—auto-erotic, masturbatory, thumb-sucking; it rebels fiercely. Mother must be ceaselessly vigilant; there is a relentless battle against the sinful nature of the child. | The child is harmless; the erogenous zones are no longer a focal concern. |
| Needs and wants must be differentiated; do not pick up all the time, for this makes infant a tyrant; crying is a bad habit; playing with the child is dangerous. Mother's character must be one of strong moral devotion. | If baby cries for attention, give it to him; he'll become less demanding if you do; it is all right to play with the child, it is even healthful; motherhood is a major source of fun and enjoyment; fun is not only permissible; it is required. |

"Fun and play have assumed a new obligatory aspect," the author tells us; thus the Puritan ethic remains in making play work. By 1951 fun still prevailed but boredom now entered the picture. Fear of letting the child get the upper hand reappeared in its "unreasonable demands for attention." Now the mother was not to pick up the baby *every* time it whimpered.

Some of this 1951 "regression" appeared also in the work of Benjamin Spock, author of one of the most popular scripts for the role of mother ever written. In a Letter to the Reader of the 1957 edition of his book, he said:

> When I was writing the first edition, between 1943 and 1946, the attitude of a majority of people toward infant feeding, toilet training, and general child management was still fairly strict and inflexible. However, the need for greater understanding of children and for flexibility in their care had been made clear by educators, psychoanalysts, and pediatricians, and I was trying to encourage this. Since then a great change in attitude has occurred, and nowadays there seems to be more chance of a conscientious parent's getting into trouble with permissiveness than with strictness. So I have tried to give a more balanced view.[12]

Mothers were being let off the hook.

The pragmatic Chinese, according to one observer, seem to have come to terms with both Calvin and Rousseau. "The Chinese," she tells us, "in the handling of their children, seem to expect good behavior, cooperation, and obedience and, in general, get it. Although they clearly recognize that there is a non-cooperative, hostile, aggressive side to man [including, for example, sibling rivalry, Oedipal feelings, anger, and the like] they do not emphasize it." [13] Like B. F. Skinner, it seems, "they emphasize that side which they wish to promote." [14] With them, at least, it seems to work.

### A Projection into the Future

In 1972, Clark Vincent, a sociologist, traced trends in parent-child relations from before 1890 to the present and projected them to 1980.[15] He had more than infant care in mind. He was writing about a "caught generation," caught, that is, between a parental generation that had demanded discipline and an offspring generation that was demanding permissiveness. On the basis of his find-

97

ings he arrived at the conclusion that there had been fairly regular oscillations between strict and permissive child-rearing philosophies and that we were about at the end of a permissive period. He therefore looked to a period of restrictive parent-child practices in the near future.[16]

Whether or not Vincent's projection is correct, "permissiveness" had become a political issue in the 1970s. The President himself was calling for a halt. It it doubtful that restrictiveness, at least in the traditional form, can be revived. The props on which it rested—the acceptance of parental, especially paternal, authority—have been so severely attenuated that they cannot bear its weight.

It is true that the generation now entering parenthood, products of the high birth rate of the era of the feminine mystique, will continue to constitute a disproportionately large part of the population and thus have the weight of numbers on their side. But whether they will throw their weight in the direction of restrictiveness in relation to their children can be argued. And certainly the talk of "children's liberation" does not augur a move in the direction of restrictiveness.

There has to be at least a grain of truth in both sides of any controversy that rages so consistently and so long among so many people of great intellectual talents. The truth of the matter seems to be that human beings need both discipline and support, repression and encouragement, "bringing out" and "putting down," "aversive" as well as "reinforcing" conditioning. Overemphasis of one at the expense of the other leads to undesirable results. "The overpermissiveness with which some parents treat their children in order to reassure themselves hampers the process of social maturation no less than does neglect." [17] Most parents will doubtless continue to oscillate between the two philosophies, never completely happy with either one.

### Legal Scripts

The theory of child-rearing in our society once assigned the so-called "expressive" role to mothers and the "instrumental," including disciplinary, role to fathers, thus incorporating both the Calvinist and the Rousseauean ideology in one parental team. The law has seemed to envisage such a situation.

It is interesting to observe that although there is a considerable corpus of law and legislation dealing with the family, including parent-child relationships, there is relatively little in it about mother-child relations. Fatherhood has a large legal component; the legal rights, duties, and obligations of fathers vis-à-vis children, and vice versa, constitute a respectable part of the role script for fathers. Much of it deals with property, support, discipline, legitimacy. The common law required children to obey parents, the subordinate status of children being taken for granted. Parents were forbidden to willfully torture, torment, cruelly punish, or deprive children of food and clothing. But if a parent accidentally killed a child in the process of moderately disciplining it, that was excusable; only when the punishment was immoderate was it defined as murder or manslaughter. Since the punitive parent in such cases was more likely to be the father than the mother, the law was more likely to apply to him than to her.

Conversely, the right of the court to remove children from the custody of unfit or incompetent persons probably refers to the mother more often than to the father. What constitutes unfitness or incompetence depends on the community's definition of the maternal role. That definition has little to do with the findings of the researchers. The law often tolerates behavior vis-à-vis children that horrifies neighbors and violates every scientific finding.[18] By and large, however, mothers are conspicuous by their absence in this body of family law. Motherhood rests on custom, tradition, convention, and the mores far more than on law or legislation. And these, in turn, presumably rest on mother-love rather than on law.[19]

### Motherhood for What? Future Goals of Motherhood

A generation ago an outstanding sociologist asked, "knowledge for what?" [20] Why were we researching so assiduously? What did we hope to do with our findings? We might here ask: "Motherhood for what?" What kind of product are we asking mothers to deliver? The script for the role of mother will depend on the answer. It will depend, that is, not only on the nature of the material the mother has to work on—depraved, evil, or innocent human nature—but also on the kind of adult she is charged with producing with this material. If her society is aiming to produce God-fearing adults, then the script will call for the inculcation of fear. If it wants her to produce rugged individualists, then the script will call for the inculcation of independence. "In the child-theory based on Calvinism," for example, as Sunley notes, "methods were consciously related to the type of adult desired: a moral, honest, religious, independent individual who would take his proper place in society." [21] Conversely, if a society wants relaxed, unachieving adults, a different script will be called for.

An almost inexhaustable research literature on child-rearing practices does,[22] indeed, show that of the many possible ways of rearing children, each society, not unexpectedly, selects those that produce the kind of adult personality and character required for living in its culture. An almost vertiginous diversity prevails. And scripts change as the culture itself changes.

One of the most interesting examples of change has to do with a movement in the United States away from the development of entrepreneurial or "rugged individual" types to the development of types comfortable in bureaucratic work situations, more complaisant, more "feminine."

In the 1950s serious students of American society began to note a fundamental change, not in morals and manners so much as in basic character structure. David Riesman and his associates analyzed the effect that the increasing influence from peers as compared to parents was having on young people. Instead of a family-supplied gyroscope to keep them on course, young people had antennae to pick up cues from their peers.[23]

Miller, a psychologist, and Swanson, a sociologist, found two different kinds of parental behavior that tended to produce different kinds of characters. They related the two types to changes in the organizational styles of our economy from the entrepreneurial to the bureaucratic, from the rugged individual to organization man. Parents who were preparing their—male—children to be business men had one style—"individual-entrepreneurial"—of child-rearing; those who were preparing them for jobs with large corporations had another—"welfare-bureaucratic." [24]

The wave of the future so far as work is concerned seems to be in the direction of more "feminine" types. And there is also in process a modification of the bureaucratic form of organization which would relax its hierarchical structure and make for more individual autonomy.[25] Not the old "individuated-entrepreneurial" model nor yet the "welfare-bureaucratic" model would tend to be the pattern sought but a somewhat softened version of the first and a somewhat tougher version of the second.

### The Contribution of Scientific Research to the
### Role Script for Mothers

It was not only theology and philosophy that contributed to our thinking on the subject of the role of mother. The behavioral sciences, especially psychology and anthropology, have added their views, primarily in connection with the study of child development and child rearing. A synopsis of the direction of thinking so far in this century follows:

> Most theories of child development advanced in this century have emphasized the importance of the maternal role. [But] the specifics of what the mother should or should not do depend upon the social and cultural factors emphasized at any one time.
>
> In the first decades of the century, professional emphasis was largely on physical health, and attention was focused on safe methods of infant feeding, of hygiene and sanitation in the nursery and the kitchen, culminating in the concept of prevention of disease through routine well-baby care, and immunization schedules. Somewhat later, the scientific ordering of the environment was extended to the realm of behavior. Watson and others sought to control the psychological milieu of the nursery in order to "nurture" the type of adult deemed desirable and functional in a scientific age. Mother was seen as the first and prime promulgator of sound habits. This naive approach to the complexity of infant learning and behavior was tempered by the work of Piaget, Gesell, and others who, observing the behavior of infants and children outside the laboratory, watched their subjects "unfold" rather than become automated. These keen observers argued eloquently in favor of "nature," placing great weight on the maturing of function according to an inner genetic timetable relatively immune to the meddlesome trainer or conditioner. While they conceived of behavior in chronological terms, their commitment to the biologically determined origins of response implied the presence of individual differences, genetically dictated. Mother became the impatient watcher and waiter who read the signs of impending peace or turmoil in the nursery.
>
> Psychoanalytic insights added a dimension to biological determinism with emphasis on the social context in which behavioral and instinctual transactions were fostered and mani-

fested. From psychoanalytic theory came emphasis on the child's early experiences within the family, especially with the mother, as they through her shaped the child's concept of himself and colored the world as a comfortable or threatening and unpredictable place to be. As first developed, the infant was seen as an impressionable creature to whom things were done in more or less appropriate ways at different life stages. Sequentially unfolding, these phases were characterized by a core developmental task. The resolution of conflicting demands and wishes implicit in each phase was regarded as essential to forward movement; if the child failed to resolve the conflict, there was the possibility of becoming fixed in an earlier stage with subsequent impairment in adaptability and the possibility of later regression.

Recently, increasing importance has been given to the part played by the infant himself as a contributor to the exchange. Mother is seen as the one who comforts and gratifies, while she in turn is reassured and comforted by the responses of her child.

Resting on the understandings of each of these modes of thinking, there is emerging today an eclectic model of child development which selects relevant components from many schools of thought, no one of which can stand alone.[26]

This conclusion would be more reassuring if the scientists had more hard knowledge to offer. For, compared to the dogmatic assurance of so many of the old theological and philosophical role scripts, it is surprising how reluctant scientists themselves are to claim certainty about even simple prescriptions based on their own research.

## A Humble Science

Again and again, despite their very considerable achievements in enlarging what we do know, the scientists admit they just don't know: "the child's need to receive the emotional investment of another is exceedingly difficult to quantify"; "not enough is known about the manner in which a child relates to another person. . . ."; "probably the conflicts and crosscurrents in family day care are not the same as those in twenty-four-hour care, we have too little research to know"; "we need more precise knowledge than now exists of the relationship between specific kinds of experiences and personality, and adaptive functions and intellectual capacities"; "the question of how much tension and conflict are favorable to optimal development is an important consideration for which we have as yet no definite answer"; "we have little idea concerning minimal needs of different children. . . ."; we do not even know how to conceptualize the child's early environment; "American research has yet to clarify such elemental definitions as 'adequate' or 'inadequate' maternal care"; [27] "the so-far available data do not . . . present unequivocal evidence of the exact nature of the processes by which early life conditions are related to later development"; [28] "the general tenor of the literature of the last decade . . . seems to be one of negative findings and of skepticism regarding readily demonstrable correlations between maternal behavior and general physiological and/or psychological development." [29] Dusty answers indeed for searching mothers.

On the basis of research which they do trust, however, the scientists have come up with some help. Among the components of the maternal role script which have been specified are: adequate nourishment; a speaking social partner to provide language skills and promote interaction; an atmosphere providing reasonable consistency and repetitions, but also variety and contrast; toys and playthings; supportive and safe opportunities to move about, play, and use skills; appropriate limits and prohibitions as well as support for self-regulation and cooperative behavior.[30] "The primary adult—the mother or her surrogate—must be a source of affection, appreciation, and security." "Helping hands should be available, to be withdrawn whenever the toddler is ready to venture forth by himself." "Play . . . serves various functions. . . . [but] care must be taken not to overstimulate children." "Toddlers should not be frustrated or coerced beyond their individual tolerance." "The caretaker must be prepared for the child's repeated testing of her endurance and of the limits she sets." "Gradually, the adult has to express some disapproval which must be gauged to the child's sensitivity." "Caretakers need to recognize that although [willfulness and domination of others] make for difficulty [during the second year] they may, when patiently modified, be valuable characteristics in later life." Caretakers can help children strengthen their sense of self by appreciative comments on their appearance, bodily skills, and productions.[31] Separation from the mother in the third year "should occur not by taking the child away from the mother, but instead with her continuous assistance." "The 'good' mother or nurse responds to the baby's vocalizations from the beginning, 'talking to' him and helping the infant connect sounds with objects and actions and specific needs." "The mother-figure shares with, and evokes pleasurable responses from, the infant; she recognizes and tries to alleviate unpleasant experiences by providing comfort when the child is hurt. She tolerantly copes with crankiness, fatigue, and such irritable reaction to frustration as throwing things." "The mother-figure helps the infant and small child with his feelings." She comforts by holding, soothing, caressing, and reassuring it. "The mother also helps the toddler to 'get used to' other people, to master his fear of strangers and to begin to accept substitute caretakers.[32] With one or two exceptions the directives in this script read remarkably like those in the traditional one.

What is, then, the best way to perform the role of mother in our society today and in the future? After years of dedicated research, the only answer possible is that although we may know some of the answers we don't know all of them. It seems that except for one day in the year hardly anyone is satisfied with the way women perform their roles as mothers. To hear the complaints against them one could well conclude that anything would be better than the way we rear children today. The hue and cry about the dire results of "permissiveness" shows how dissatisfied one camp is. And the equally loud hue and cry of young people complaining that they are simply being programmed to be complacent cogs in the machine of industry show how dissatisfied another camp is.

## Does It Really Matter?

The scientists are too modest, both in their protestations of ignorance and in their claims to knowledge. Still, no matter how sure and no matter how right their contribution, there seems always to be "variance" not accounted for in their equations. Exceptions, deviances, chance, or just luck.

Open any clinical file in court or school and you find "the mother is the real problem" written in one form or another in almost every case. She may well be. But there is little documentation about the untold number of human beings who turn out very well in spite of inadequate mothers as well as human beings from homes in which mothers performed their roles in letter-perfect style who, nevertheless, come to tragic ends.

Here, for example, is Sally Carrighar whose mother hated her and wanted to get rid of her, who shuddered at her touch, almost starved her, once vented her rage in a near-murderous assault. She survived. She succeeded not only as a human being but as a student of the wilderness and interpreter of it for the rest of us. A reviewer of Sally Carrighar's last book, an autobiography, notes that the moral is that "the normal human psyche is built to take a lot of punishment. Sally Carrighar's story . . . reminds us . . . that the threat and loneliness of a distorted childhood can as plausibly lead to strength and independence as to crippling illness." [33] Conversely, there was Diane Oughton, reared in an archetypically conventional home in which both parents, so far as anyone could tell, performed their roles strictly according to the approved script. And she died in a homemade bomb factory blast.

Future research will contribute more to our knowledge, answer more questions, explain more about development, offer more help to mothers. But no script for the role will ever be able to promise all the answers. And even if we knew them, there is no guarantee that we will provide an auspicious stage for mothers to perform it on. We are far from doing so now. We have hardly even begun to diagnose the difficulty.

In the discussion so far, the role of mother has been the focus with only a nod in the direction of the role of worker. But since the role of mother is only one of women's major roles, its future cannot be understood without equal attention to their worker role as well. We cannot, as Mr. Pickwick did, write a disquisition on Chinese metaphysics by reading all about China in the encyclopedia and then all about metaphysics. We cannot write about the future of motherhood by writing separately about the role of mother and that of worker. Their integration is the heart of the matter so far as both are concerned. A brief glance, then, at the worker role of women and how it relates to the mother role is in order.

# PART FOUR

## Role Severance
## and Attrition

# Introduction

In Part Four the discussion turns from the mother role to the worker roles of women, dealing with both the work done in the home (Chapter 7) and the work done outside the home (Chapter 8).

The two worlds described in Chapter 1, the world of the home and the world of economic struggle, operated on quite different principles, one on the basis of love-and/or-duty and one on the basis of what Thomas Carlyle and Karl Marx had called a cash-nexus. Work was done by women in both worlds, but the work done in the home—motherwork and housework—differed from that done outside. Women in the home did what they did, performed the services they performed, not for pay but because it was their duty, laid down in their role script, or because they loved those they served. Since this work was not paid for it was not considered economically productive. Women in the labor force were, and are, assumed to be, like all workers, motivated by monetary payments or their equivalents in benefits of one kind or another. They receive wages and salaries. An enormous chasm yawns between these two approaches to work.

The chief "news" about the work done by women in the home has to do with the attrition it has undergone and the increasing attention being paid to ways of re-conceptualizing it. On one side there is an incipient movement to monetize it, to recognize the contribution it still makes to the economy, and to blanket it into the economy. On the other side, however, there is also a tentative definition of the conspicuous consumption engaged in by affluent housewives as a luxury that ought to be taxed.

Official recognition of the work women were doing in the labor force came in a British Royal Commission Report on Population in 1949 which recommended that "a deliberate effort should be made to devise adjustments that would render it easier for women to combine motherhood and the care of a home with outside activities." [1] President Kennedy followed suit; he established a Commission on the Status of Women in 1961. In 1956 social-science support for the two-role concept was supplied by a land-mark book on the subject by Alva Myrdal and Viola Klein.[2] Only recently has it occurred to women to ask "Why *women's* two roles?" Why should women do more of the nation's work than men? [3]

## CHAPTER SEVEN

# What Do You Mean, Work?

### So What's New?

The removal of work from the home—women's as well as men's—that came with industrialization was not entirely new. The so-called "centralized mill" (as contrasted with the scattered mill) predated the industrial revolution. But there were vast differences introduced into the nature of work by industrialization and urbanization. Some of the changes affected all workers, women as well as men. But in the present context one difference is especially relevant for women. The new system separated out the part of their work—motherwork—that related to their role as mother and the part of their work—industrial—that related to their role as worker contributing to the gross national product.

Under the cottage or scattered mill system, when spinning and weaving were part of a woman's domestic work, interspersed with gardening, cooking, child care, and whatever else she had to do, it was hard to distinguish which part of her time was being paid for when an agent came to pick up the finished cloth. Her work was all of a piece, the paid and the nonpaid. But when spinning was done in a centralized factory it was quite clear what part of her work was being paid for. "Women's work" was now bifurcated, one part becoming "gainful," that is, paid for, and one part not.[1]

### Two Historical Streams

The severance of the mother and worker roles of women, then, refers to severance of only one kind of work, not all. Much of women's work still remained in the home; it was not severed from the mother role. And it was of almost equal importance for the—then—future of motherhood.

The two kinds of work of women—outside "gainful" and household—are not unrelated. But their histories are different; their impact on motherhood has been different; the current issues they raise are different. In fact, almost everything about them is different except that they are work. Both are relevant for projecting the future of motherhood, especially at this historical moment when there is a strong effort on one hand to attract women into the labor force as a method for reducing population growth [2] and, on the other hand, a strong backlash or resistance movement on the part of some women who reject labor-force participation.[3]

The concept of work itself, wherever and by whomever done, is enormously complex. A variety of social and behavioral scientists, including psychologists, anthropologists, sociologists, economists, devote their entire professional energies to understanding it.[4] The sociological nature of work—including the so-called work ethic—ranks with the sociological nature of sex as a major puzzle for students of our society. If it is baffling in the case of men, it is doubly so in the case of women. Labor, job, career, gainful employment, labor-force participation are all encompassed in the concept of work; they are not identical concepts. All are relevant for understanding the worker role of women, gainful and non-gainful, and its relation to their mother role.

## Motherwork

With tongue in cheek a team of playful sociologists have analyzed sexual relations as "work." [5] And it is a common bromide that one must "work" at marriage in order to succeed in it. The conceptualization of motherhood in terms of work is not wholly playful nor merely figurative. Despite efforts to conceive of motherwork as "fun," [6] it is, actually, very hard work.

Motherwork has two major components. One has to do with mothering—the touching, rocking, smiling, reassuring, feeding, teaching, diaper-changing, playing with, disciplining, and all the literally countless other activities required for the emotional and physical health of infants and small children. The other has to do with the added housework caused by the addition of the infant or child, the extra amount of cleaning, cooking, laundering, and shopping entailed. The nature and the relative importance of the two components change in different stages of the child's development. When the children are small the mothering called for is direct, physical, personal, face-to-face, and extremely intense; when the children are older, it becomes more indirect. The amount of time called for is, expectedly, greater in the preschool than in the school-age years.[7] When the children are small, the physical work involves an enormous amount of housework; when they are older, it may involve part-time, outside jobs to finance their education.[8]

## The Mothering Component of Motherwork

The kind of tender-loving-care of children required of mothers or mother-surrogates is hard to come by. Sheer physical care can be purchased. But mothering in this sense is another matter. If or when mothers are not available to supply it, the outside world has few resources for providing it. Incarceration, whatever the site—hospital, "shelter," "asylum," what-have-you—may supply shelter and calories but not much more. The results are all too often disastrous and incredibly expensive.[9]

But even mothering in a less involving sense is hard to come by, such as the matter-of-fact business of performing banal activities. For despite the literal indispensability of such service it is actually, by most tests, held in low esteem. Wilma Scott Heide, for example, amply demonstrated what we really think of it.[10] She used an occupational guide designed to evaluate the status level of a wide variety of jobs with respect to three kinds of functions: people functions, data functions, and thing functions. Each occupation in this guide is assigned a three-digit weight from o to 9 according to the level of people-, data-, and thing-functions performed, the higher the index the lower the level. With respect to motherwork, the "people-function" would refer to mothering, the "thing-function" to housework. She found that neither component of motherwork was rated much above the lowest level. To illustrate the point, Ms. Heide lists some of the functions included in motherwork side-by-side with similar functions performed in the labor force with approximately equal scores:

## THE RELATIVE RANK OF MOTHERWORK AND
## COMPARABLE INDUSTRIAL WORK

| MOTHERWORK | INDUSTRIAL WORK |
|---|---|
| Foster mother, 878: "rears children in own home as members of family." | Rest room attendant, 878: "serves patrons of lavatories in stores. . . ." |
| Child care attendant, 878: ". . . house parent, special school counselor, cares for group of children housed in . . . government institution." | Parking lot attendant, 878: "parks automobiles for customers in parking lots. . . ." |
| Home health aids, 875: "cares for elderly, convalescent or handicapped persons." | Public bath maid, 878: ". . . not quite as skilled as . . . Pet Shop Attendant, 877." |
| Nursemaid, 878. | Delivery boy (newspaper carrier), 868: closer in complexity and skill level to a Mud-Mixer Helper, 887. |
| Nursery school teacher, 878: "organizes and leads activities of prekindergarten children, maintains discipline. . . ." | Marine mammal handler, 328: "signals or cues trained marine mammals. . . ." |
| Nurse, Mid-wife, 378. | Hotel clerk 368 or barber, 371. |
| Kindergartner, 878: "entertains children in nursery." | Strip-tease artist, 848 (entertains audience by . . .) |
| Nurse, practical, 878: "cares for patients and children in private homes, hospitals." | Offal man, poultry, 887: "shovels ice into chicken offal container." |

| MOTHERWORK | INDUSTRIAL WORK |
|---|---|
| Nurse, general duty, 378: "rotates among various clinical services of institution such as obstetrics, surgery, orthopedics, outpatient and admitting, pediatrics, psychology and tuberculosis. May assist with operations and deliveries." | Cosmetology, 271: cosmetologist apprentice, 271: "provides beauty services for customers." |
| Nurse, private duty, 378: "contracts independently to give nursing care. . . . administers medications (and) independent emergency measures to counteract adverse developments." | Undertaker, 168: "arranges and directs funeral services." |

She comments that "a parent or parent substitute, even a nursery school teacher (878) doesn't rate with the dog trainer (228)—job analysts having presumably observed that children are rarely or never spoken to (rated at level 6), persuaded (5), diverted (4), supervised (3), instructed (2), negotiated with (1), or mentored (0). . . . Crews of children (being 'packages' rather than people) don't need their activities to be coordinated, it seems, even in groups of 18 + . . . . It is hard to see how the judgment of 'no significant function' was arrived at" [11] for so many of the components of motherwork. She concludes laconically that the occupation "homemaker" should be reclassified and given higher ratings.

In the meanwhile, though we give lip service to the idea that motherwork is worthy, hardly anyone really believes it. Most of us agree with Philip Slater's dictum that the housewife is a nobody.[12] Mothering has "use value" but not "exchange value." The mother of young children whose admittedly indispensable activities devoted to their care leave her exhausted, does not fall into the category of worker because her activities are, by definition, not gainful.

It is not until we are faced with the problem of supplying substitutes or surrogates for mothers to perform the mothering part of motherwork, that is, when we have to "cost" child-care services, that we begin to appreciate the enormous value—this time economic or monetary or exchange value—of its contribution.[13]

The mothering component of motherwork is not, of course, limited to infants and small children. The "stroking," support, loving care, and healing which women supplied to all family members in the home according to the Victorian model remains; it is still written into the role script of all women, workers no less than mothers.[14]

## The Housework Component of Motherwork

Children add a great deal of work to housekeeping or homemaking. According to a French study in 1947, the first child adds eighteen hours of housework per week; two children, twenty-eight hours; three, thirty-nine hours.[15] A later study in the United States found that an added child requires somewhere between five and twenty extra hours of its mother's time per week, the exact figures depending on its age and birth order and on the method of computing extra hours.[16] Still another study reported that mothers of preschool children spent about fifty to sixty hours a week on household chores, the first child about doubling the amount of time spent on housework.[17] A team of economists has estimated that where there are no children, one thousand hours of housework are required a year; where there are no children under six, fifteen hundred; where there are children under six, two thousand.[18] We do not need precise figures, however, to see that the mothers of young children are perhaps the most overworked adults in our society today. And the sardonic humor of the expression "I don't work; I'm a housewife" no longer escapes us.

In spite of all the efforts of home economists over many decades to upgrade the status of the housework component of homemaking by transforming it almost into a kind of engineering or management profession,[19] it remains an occupation of low status. Wilma Heide's analysis of the status scores on typical components of housework done in the home in the Dictionary of Occupations cues us in:[20]

| FUNCTION | OCCUPATION | STATUS INDEX |
|---|---|---|
| cooking | short-order cook | 381 |
| sewing | sewing-machine operator, seamstress | 782, 884 |
| laundry | laundry operator | 884 |

| FUNCTION | OCCUPATION | STATUS INDEX |
|----------|-----------|--------------|
| ironing | mangler | 885 |
| cleaning | furniture cleaner | 887 |
| driving | chauffeur | 883 |

Housekeeping remains not only an unpaid occupation but also an occupation of low status. The two characteristics are not wholly unrelated.

Juanita Kreps is right on target when she says that failure by economists and policy makers to include the value of the services contributed in the household can have serious consequences for the social status attached to those services.

> Despite our protests that growth in income is not to be equated with improvements in welfare; that society places a high value on the services of wives in the home and in the community; that the absence of a price tag on a particular service does not render it valueless—despite these caveats, the tendency to identify one's worth with the salary he earns is a persistent one. This tendency is not peculiar to men who earn salaries; it pervades as well the thinking of women who work at unpaid jobs.[21]

Such undervaluing may lead women to make decisions about entering the labor force which are not conducive to the best allocation of resources in the economy as a whole.

### Effects of Low Status of Motherwork

It may also have a depressing effect on the homemakers' own self-concept, an effect in no way to be impatiently brushed aside or glossed over with phony reassurances of real appreciation.

No matter how much we reassure her, the homemaker knows she is *only* a housewife. Whatever we say, the proof is clear: she receives no pay for what she does. We cannot overlook or ignore the fact that in a society run on a monetary basis, in which services do not come as a matter of right—as they do in the home—in which money is required for satisfying every need, the lack of monetary payment for one's services is almost totally immobilizing. One can hardly take a step—as the young traveler learns on his first trip on his own outside the home—in the cash-nexus world without money. Mother always did these things for free.

Only those who have themselves experienced the degradation

117

of having no money can understand the humiliation countless homemakers feel when they must ask for or at least account for every penny they spend. No one needs to tell mothers that money isn't everything. They know that very well. Their own lives are a constant reminder of that fact since they serve without monetary payment. But denying that money is everything in no way denies that it is not far short of everything when she is the one who goes to the supermarket herself to shop.

### The Monetization of Motherwork

Oblique, though not direct, recognition of the monetary value of mothering has a fairly long history. At the turn of the century the Mother's Pension movement resulted in legislation in a number of states to provide support for widowed mothers so that they would not have to enter the labor force; their services in the home were judged as more valuable than their contribution to the labor force. The so-called family wage system which a number of European countries have instituted is another oblique form of such recognition; the father receives a higher wage than the nonfather, presumably to help defray the expenses of the child care supplied by the mother. If the father is to receive the same pay as the nonfather he must have the difference required to support his family made up to him.[22] The wife-and-mother is, in effect, paid albeit the pay comes through the husband. Another related form of such oblique recognition is the allowance made for dependents in grants, fellowships, scholarships, and the like. In a limited way, the law which permits a woman to deduct child-care expenses from her income for our purposes is also an oblique recognition of the economic contribution the mother makes when she cares for her children herself. More direct is a proposed law which would permit a tax allowance for the second earner in a family, almost always a wife. Despite such oblique recognition of the value of motherwork, it remains unpaid and does not therefore count as part of the economy.

Increasingly the anomaly of this position is becoming clear. The need to monetize the contribution of women in the home shows up in a number of ways. Economists have to know what its value is in order to understand how our economy works. Not knowing it introduces "a serious bias in the gross national product." [23] Industry has to know, too. Insurance companies have to know, for example, how to evaluate the contribution a woman makes so that if she is killed in an accident and the father has to hire someone else to take her place in rearing his children they can compute premiums on insurance for her. Courts have to know too, in order to adjudicate in divorce settlements. If there is a divorce instead of a death there has so far been no way to measure the contribution the wife has been making to the family by her services in the home despite the fact that "non-market income is clearly a supplement to earned income." [24] Her contribution to the joint estate has not, therefore, counted.

And increasingly, much to their own astonishment, many women are coming to learn that what they have been doing simply as part of their role as mothers has monetary value in the outside world. There seems to be a natural "law" in the world of work by which activities originally done on the basis of love-and/or-duty become "favors" and then services for which pay is expected, even professionalized. The kinds of motherwork that mothers in the home have been expected to offer as part of their role are now achieving marketable status. In a novel published in 1973 a woman discovers this surprising fact. A reviewer encapsulates the theme:

> How astonishing . . . to discover . . . that the "caring" which they [her husband and children] held in such low regard, her mother-habit which they so take for granted, is worth a great deal of money in the international civil service. There she is paid to care, and when she is done caring for one group of experts, there is another group in another hotel for another round of seminars. Her caring is a marketable skill; she is not doing anything different from what she was doing at home, but value is ascribed to it in the only way we seem to be able to ascribe value: by paying dearly for it, cash on delivery. [25]

There are, then, political, business, and personal reasons for wanting to measure the cash value of the homemaker's work.

## The Economic Value of "Consumer Maintenance"

Several economists have responded to the challenge. One has concluded that, as of 1964, about half of a family's disposable income came from the unpaid output of its members and "about 90 percent of the estimated unpaid production is in the form of housework and other types of home production." [26] Women in poor families carried a disproportionately large part of the load: "families with less than $1,000 money incomes more than tripled that income through housework and home production." [27] All that time-consuming, careful shopping for bargains, and that doing-it-herself, all that making-do, all that home cooking, freezing, canning, all that sewing and mending and patching was raising the level of family living by 200 percent. Since many housewives have small children, and hence cannot enter the labor force, they "strive to improve their standards of living (or to maintain a decent life) by increasing their non-market productive activities." [28] And the more children, the greater their contribution. "Larger families tend to have a high non-market income [contributed by the mothers] relative to disposable income." [29] Another economist concluded that, as of the late 1960s, a forty-one-year-old mother of three sons, if she had been a secretary before marriage, had a replacement value of $105,545 if she died before her last child reached the age of twenty-one.[30]

From the point of view of the gross national product, there have been in the United States, at least five attempts to compute the economic value of the work of women in the household. It has never been less than a sixth and usually at least about a quarter of the gross national income or product.[31] A British study estimated the unpaid household services in industrialized societies as amounting to 44 percent of the gross national product, an estimate reflecting, no doubt, a greater proportion contributed in poorer countries.

These estimates are made from the point of view of the positive contribution of mothers to the economy. Even more startling results are obtained when we attempt to monetize the "costs" of motherhood to her family. We reserve discussion of these results for Chapter 15.

In view of the increasing recognition of the importance of motherwork as an occupation, one economist, Carolyn Shaw Bell, has proposed a title for it, namely "consumer maintenance." It would cover the work done by homemakers in caring for the sick, the incapacitated, the elderly, and other consumers not able to take care of themselves, as well, of course, as caring for children. Or it could be called "labor-force maintenance," since, if women in the household were not keeping the work force in good condition, employers would have to do the job as, indeed, they do when there are no housewives available. In lumber camps, for example, in mining camps, remote engineering camps, or on ships and in the military, employers have to supply the services—cooking, cleaning, laundering, and nursing care—automatically supplied by housewives to the work force. When corporations send employees out on company business, they are paid extra by the day to cover the services—of chambermaid, valet, cook—supplied by housewives at home.

The logic of the times, if not, as yet, the emotions, is moving in the direction not only of the monetization of motherwork but also of actual payment for it. Compensation for the task in one form or another, in one setting or another, is seemingly the wave of the future, for increasingly the kinds of work called for in our society include the "caring" built into the mother role.[32] "Caring" not only for children but also for worker, alienated people in general, everyone, in fact, who needs mothering. Counselors of many kinds—marital, vocational, pastoral, school, parental—spring up to supply it. Motherwork of this kind becomes almost an industry in itself. Even a growth industry. In this sense it has a glorious future. And we will have to make a fairly high bid if we want to keep an adequate supply of it in the home.

## Payment for Services of Homemakers

In the early 1970s both the United States and Canada were beginning to take seriously the idea of recognizing the economic value of the work of housewives. Specifically it was being proposed that "housewives who are engaged in carrying out specified household domestic chores in their own homes, should be included as one of the occupational groups making up the active labour force; and an imputed value of the cost of specified unpaid domestic services which they provide in their own homes, should be included in the total cost of services which, together with the cost of goods make up the gross national product." [33] Among the benefits would be that housewives would then be entitled to equity in social security programs. They might even pay into such social security plans. In Canada they would also become eligible for the benefits of the adult retraining programs. There was no lack of recognition of the problems involved: how measure volume of production? how take into account the conditions under which the work is carried out? how distinguish between economic services and the "general activity of life?" Solutions were not impossible. And they were urgently needed because of "the change in the role of women in society and the emergence of older women in the labour force."

Monetary recognition of the contribution of homemakers was being urged also as a way to integrate the worker and the mother roles of women once again. By paying for it, by making it "gainful employment," its inherent status as part of the economy would be recognized and "occupation housewife" would become "occupation consumer maintenance" and be accepted as having as much legitimacy as any other. It was being suggested as at least an interim step in role integration, as a stop-gap "until cultural values— or women—change." [34]

An alternate, essentially Marxist, approach to the problem— "taking the work outside the home through child-care centers, laundry and cooking facilities, leaving only the psychological functions, and only marginal parts of these, in the home" [35]—is rejected as implying the disintegration of the family.

Who would pay for the motherwork? Replies vary: employers, government,[36] contributions by husbands to the social security fund.[37] The logic for so "paying" women for motherwork is not, actually, very new. It was recognized obliquely, as noted above, in the family wage systems of European countries whereby men with families get subsidies in their pay checks over and above the pay of workers without families. There is no intrinsic reason why the pay could not be rerouted directly to the wife rather than indirectly through her husband.

Or, conversely, the housewife could pay herself:

### AT WIT'S END: WIVES' SQUIRREL FUND

Everybody talks about giving the American housewife a salary, but no one ever does anything about it. The only positive thing our 126-hour work week has brought about within the past 10 years has been the development of the 18-hour deodorant. (We may be dumb, but we don't sweat.)

While everyone sits around haggling over our social security, our sick leaves, and our vacations, a housewife in Texas has come up with a solution. She has established a Squirrel Fund. For example, every time she fixes her own hair, she tosses $4 into the Squirrel Fund. If her cleaning lady doesn't show up, she tosses another $13 into the fund and if she alters her own clothes, she compensates the Squirrel Fund. She has become the most affluent squirrel in Texas.

During the past week, I decided to initiate a Squirrel Fund at my house. The results were rather astounding. The kids found me packing my suitcase yesterday morning. "Where are you going?" they asked. "Mama has to say good-by," I said soberly. My husband appeared with puzzlement written all over his face. "What's going on?" I shoved the list under his nose. "This is a Squirrel Fund to which I have been contributing money for every job I did that would normally be done by professionals:

Shaving the dog's rump: $8; telephone answering service for family: $15; auditioning amateur drummer who got five drums and a 6-page booklet for Christmas, $15; mediator between daughter locked in bathroom for two hours and son waiting to get in, $12; medical fees for healing infected pierced ear, $10; catering an after-hours slumber party, $25; ironing hair to straighten it, $8; plus all the usual duties of laundry, food service, chauffeuring, bookkeeping, maid service and live-in roommate.

I picked up my suitcase and turned to them. "Believe me, if it were left to me I'd like to stay. I like you. But frankly," I said turning to my husband, "I know what you make a year and the simple truth is you can't afford me." [38]

In the case of the less affluent family there is no question about the indispensability of the housewife's services. She is demonstrably indispensable. She is trebling the family's disposable income and providing services it could not afford without her. She is earning her part of the family income by her work as much as the "gainful worker" is by his.

But questions are being raised with respect to the "services" provided by women in more affluent families. Any one of them could, if asked, produce a log of her very busy day. But "shaving the dog's rump?" "Telephone answering service?" "Catering an after-hours slumber party?" Monica Boëthius, a Swedish journalist, is, in fact, asking if we can really afford the—affluent—housewife.

To John Kenneth Galbraith, the affluent housewife as lady is a crypto-servant.[39] He re-interprets her function as contributing not so much to her family as to the corporation. A full-time consumer of a wide array of goods produced by the corporation, she must run faster and faster to keep up with it. Not, in this interpretation, to prove her husband's earning power but rather to guarantee the corporation's profits.

### Housework As Luxury

Housework as we know it today is a relatively new occupation. Just as is the home as we know it. The great houses of the past had their stewards, but not humbler dwellings. The emergence of the home out of the workshop, as a place for leisure-time activities, was an important achievement in human history and is not to be denigrated. The industrial revolution which is usually viewed as taking the work of women out of the home, could just as well be viewed as moving the home out of the workshop.

> In the old days the home was in the shop or factory. The important things were the looms or the workbench and tools; the home itself was incidental. It was as though everyone lived in a little factory, for when the home was the industrial unit it was as much a small factory as a home. Most people prior to the Industrial Revolution did not have homes, in reality they lived in little workshops. The removal of its industrial functions to larger factories with power machinery meant that more of the home could be devoted to family living. The emergence of homes specialized for family life alone rather than for industrial purposes is a new phenomenon in our history. . . . Instead of thinking that industrial functions have been taken out of the home, it may be equally legitimate to think of the home as splitting off from industry and specializing in family functions.[40]

In the humble cottages of agricultural societies there was a lot of hard productive labor, but there wasn't much housework in the sense we think of it today, in the sense, that is, of property maintenance. It was only when affluence made it possible for so many people to have "nice things" in their homes that the elaboration of housework into what Veblen called conspicuous consumption developed and the practice of such consumption became a full-time job.[41]

In the case of the work of women that was performed outside of the home, the problem was, indeed, one of role severance. But in the case of the work that remained in the home, the problem was different. As technology created an industrial system that needed women more and more, it was creating a household that, even as a display of affluence, needed women less and less. So it was not so much severance of the worker from the mother role as it was attrition of the worker role in the home that affected these women.

The reaction of women to the gradual diminution of productive work within the home was diverse. One answer was, simply, to enter the labor force. Colin Clark, an economist, has pointed out that as improved household equipment increased productivity, fewer housewives were needed so that more of them could enter the labor force.[42]

Another reaction was to devote more time to the mothering aspect of motherwork. A study of the *Ladies' Home Journal* from 1886 to the present time, for example, showed that at least for middle-class women the result of the new technology in the home was likely to be a transfer of time and effort from the housework to the mothering component of motherwork. The advertisements played on the good-mother appeal. Use a washing machine and you will have more time to spend with your children. Don't leave the care of your children to uneducated, rough, vulgar servants; use our product and save time to spend with your children.[43] The modern suburban mother, this researcher reminds us, may not herself have to teach her children to read and write, spin and sew, but she does have to chauffeur them to school, classes, lessons, and social engagements; the time required for shopping, including traffic snarls and parking hassles, may be greater than the time required for old-fashioned food preparation. The household labor component of motherwork may decline as the children get to school age, but not the time a woman may invest in it. Joseph K. Folsom, a generation ago, found that "more time is spent in homemaking and family care by the city housewife and her assistants than by the farm wife and her assistants, when farm work is not counted." [44] And the city women, who had relatively little productive work to do, were reported as spending more than twice as much time proportionately in child care as women in farm homes.

### Parkinson's Law in the Home

A third reaction to the new household technology was simply to improve the standard of living. Clean clothes every day rather than every week. At first the technology may merely have compensated for the loss of the services of domestic help. At the turn of the century there was an estimated average of two servants per family of five.[45] The loss of such domestic help has had profound

125

repercussions on motherwork. Technology has only partially made up for it.

A generation ago Folsom adumbrated Parkinson's law as applied to housework. Like bureaucratic work, it increased to fill up all available time. New labor-saving equipment saved labor but not time. Since Folsom's day still more labor-saving devices and more prepared foods have been introduced so that even less physical work is left for the housewife to do. Her major contribution to the household becomes increasingly one of management. Even with higher and higher standards, however, filling up time with housework becomes harder and harder. If the young woman in early motherhood is the most burdened worker in our society the non-employed woman in middle and late motherhood is the least. Homemaking nowadays in a home without small children is no longer a full-time effort.

### Non-Work: The Housewife As Lady

The concept of the lady that arose in the nineteenth century was a concomitant of the affluence brought about by industrialization. In 1899, a wryly perceptive economist wrote a treatise on the theory of the leisure class. It contained a great deal of interesting material on the nature of work and of conquest, but it came to be known primarily for its concepts of conspicuous consumption and vicarious leisure.[46] Originally the upper class consisted of warriors who by conquest and combat could get others to do the dull productive work for them, releasing them for leisure, exploit, and consumption. When successful industrialists and financiers—the class Marx labeled the bourgeoisie—began to replace the nobility as the operative if not the symbolic upper class, they were too busy to practice that kind of leisure. Women were therefore pressed into that service; it became the function of wives and daughters to consume lavishly for them. They "performed" leisure for men to show that they did not have to work and they had also to show by their dress and toilette that they did not work. Thus a large part of the work of performing vicarious leisure consisted of conspicuous, preferably wasteful, consumption. On a lower economic level an analogous situation resulted when the fact that a wife could stay home rather than enter the labor force was taken as evidence of her husband's earning power. The Victorian "lady," sheltered from the harsh outside world, found her counterpart in the wife who did not have to "work." [47] Charlotte

Perkins Gilman, a contemporary of Veblen's, in a biting critique of the—to her—parasitical status of the non-working wife, pointed out that to the extent that a wife contributed useful labor in the household she was entitled to recompense. But the woman who was not contributing such services was simply a kept woman, paid for her sexual favors.[48] To the argument that motherhood was a full-time occupation, she replied, prove it. In her opinion women were doing a poor job as mothers, turning out adults who were tired, timid, selfish, and unprogressive. Rearing children, in fact, should become an independent profession.

Neither Veblen nor Gilman had much immediate impact on the "working mother" controversy. The "lady" remained an honorable character until well into the twentieth century.

> Economically she is supported by the toil of others; but while this is equally true of other classes of society, the oddity in her case consists in the acquiescence of those most concerned. The lady herself feels no uneasiness in her equivocal situation, and the toilers who support her do so with enthusiasm. She is not a producer; in most communities productive labour is by consent unladylike. On the other hand she is the heaviest of consumers, and theorists have not been wanting to maintain that the more she spends the better off society is. In aristocratic societies she is required for dynastic reasons to produce offspring, but in democratic societies even this demand is often waived. Under the law she is a privileged character. . . . When it is flatly put to her that she cannot become a human being and yet retain her privileges as a non-combatant, she often enough decides for etiquette.[49]

Among the wealthy, women had wet nurses and nannies to take care of infants and small children; they had staffs of household servants to run their homes; they had personal maids to take care of their persons. There was neither the child-care mothering nor the housework component of motherwork to occupy them. Even in their job of spending money they could hire social secretaries and talented people to plan the balls and other entertainments that conspicuous consumption called for. They had a function to perform and roles that prescribed how to perform them, codified in etiquette books—but no work to do. Non-work became a job.

Non-work thus acquired high status because of its association with the rich and successful. It became a desideratum for the less rich also. It gradually percolated all the way down the social ladder until the working-man's wife also achieved the non-work goal. Not, of course, to the extent that the rich did. For the working-man's wife worked in the home. Her version of the lady role took the form of bestowing an enormous amount of time and energy on merely ostentatious work around the house and abstaining from participation in the labor force outside the home.

> The leisure rendered by the wife in such cases is, of course, not a simple manifestation of idleness or indolence. It almost invariably occurs disguised under some form of work or household duties or social amenities, which prove in analysis to serve little or no ulterior end beyond showing that she does not and need not occupy herself with anything that is gainful or that is of substantial use.[50]

If a man could not afford to maintain his wife in this vicarious leisure or conspicuous consumption he was a failure.

Veblen also postulated an "instinct of workmanship" and Max Weber, a sociologist, has analyzed for us the so-called work ethic, both of which ran counter to the non-work pattern of the lady. The two patterns co-exist uneasily even today:

> This ideal [of the lady of leisure] cultivated more in the last century than in the present one, in point of fact put parasitism of women at a premium. The task of an upper-middle-class wife was chiefly to be an ornament to her husband's home and a living testimony to his wealth. Her idleness was one of the prerequisites. Up to this day, the two contrary ideals vie with each other in the columns of every woman's journal. There are on the one hand the domestic virtues with the fragrance of freshly-made bread every day, together with the statistics showing a fourteen- to sixteen-hour working day. But there are also the costly cults of the lily-white hands, of lavish entertaining, and of changing one's highly fashionable clothes oftener and oftener—the much advertised dreams of all that goes with being "well provided for," once one is married. There is a curious causal relationship (though this is not necessarily appreciated) operating in the advertising columns of modern fashion magazines. While on the one hand more and more gadgets are offered to save time and labour, more and more time-consuming beauty treatments are recommended to

keep in control a feminine figure which shows the effects of too little exercise and too much leisure.[51]

When the Swedish journalist answers her own question—Can we afford housewives?—with an unequivocal no, millions of women shudder at the implications of the question, and understandably so. They are pinioned in "golden handcuffs," victims of one of the cruelest lags in modern times. Reared in the anachronistic pattern of the Victorian model to expect upon marriage to be "taken care of" for the rest of their lives, to be called upon for nothing more than the care of a household and of children, they now find that neither of these functions is enough to fill a life, that less and less in the way of motherwork is called for.[52]

### The Other End of the Spectrum

The emergence of the home as a place for living only was an advance in many ways. Yet our experience in trying to return to it the industrial work of women to make up for its disadvantages has not been very successful. Certainly the sweat shop of the nineteenth and early twentieth century was not a solution. Nor was all the laundering and sewing that women did in their homes for pay, nor the baking nor the care of boarders and roomers.[53]

There is some talk of returning a good deal of non-manual work to the home by way of modern communication media and by the use of computers. But for a large proportion of workers, part of the reward of working consists precisely of getting away from the home. We may not be altogether sure of just how to use homes to the best advantage, but returning them to the workshop, or the workshop to them, does not figure prominently in our conception of the future.

So much, then, for the part of the work of mothers that did not move out of the home with industrialization. The part of their work that did move out of the home had a quite different history and a quite different impact on motherhood itself.

### The Continuing Option

All the decisions dealing with the role of mother are currently being complicated by the option, increasingly available, of labor-force participation, an option which used to be available only to young women of college age but one which now remains open to women for many decades thereafter. The role of gainful worker is no longer necessarily foreclosed by motherhood and an increasing proportion of mothers are also participants in the labor force. Indeed, for a considerable proportion of all mothers, labor-force participation constitutes a large component of their lives. Not only is it a release from the strains of motherhood but it is also a contribution to disposable family income. Among older mothers, labor-force participation is mainly a different kind of motherwork; it provides college for grown sons and daughters and even help in establishing themselves.

Most women in most parts of the world in most societies and in most of history have had no such options with respect to mother and worker roles. They were obliged to perform both. Increasingly in our own society they are being given such options; they may be either gainful workers or mothers; neither gainful workers nor mothers; or—increasingly—both gainful workers and mothers.

# CHAPTER EIGHT

## The Severed Roles

### So What Else Is New?

Although payment for the work of women was not new with industrialization and the factory system, what was revolutionary was that once cotton became "king" and cotton mills burgeoned, women were paid wages as individuals in their own name rather than, as in the cottage system, as family members. True, in the beginning the system of hiring whole families, women and children along with men, was carried over from the cottage to the factory system. As Karl Marx had noted, the labor of women and children was one of the first things pounced upon with the introduction of machinery. "This powerful substitute for work and workers became the immediate means for increasing the number of workers, by engaging all the members of the family, whatever their age or sex." [1]

This pattern of hiring whole families, men, women, and children, to work in the mills continued, in fact, until well into the nineteenth century. Thus "parents were forced to send their children to work as a result of low wages and because they themselves were threatened with dismissal. We read in a report on the situation in Philadelphia: 'We have known many instances where parents who are capable of giving their children a trifling education one at a time, [have been] deprived of that opportunity by their employer's threats, that if they did take one child from their employ (a short time for school), such a family must leave the employment—and we have even known these threats put into execution' . . . Workers with many children were given preference in the matter of employment. A frequent advertisement, as in the Rhode Island *Manufacturers' and Farmers' Record* of 4 May 1820, went as follows: 'Wanted, family from five to eight children capable of working in a cotton mill.' " [2] The idea that, whatever form it took, the payment of work done by women belonged to the family instead of to them persisted, in fact, until well into the twentieth century.[3]

Still the custom of paying money wages to women in their own name as individuals rather than as members of the family did finally develop and thus made possible, if not inevitable, the achievement of independence. They were "gainfully" employed, paid in the coin of the realm. The female factory worker came to be an individual, not a member of a family team or "gang."

The mother working alongside her children in the mill may be said to have lived an integrated life in the sense that both of her roles were being performed together. Her work in the factory or mill, paid for in wages, merely "replaced work freely given in the domestic circle, which was, within decent limits, carried on for the family itself." [4] But no one today would be likely to judge this pattern of role integration except in unusual circumstances a good one for either mother or child any more than anyone would judge the sweat shop a good solution to role severance.

## Woman's Place: The Reality Versus the Myth

In the pre-industrial age, women could perform an enormous amount of economic work in the home. Alexander Hamilton tells us in 1791 that "great quantities" of linen, flannel, woolen, and cotton textiles of various kinds "are made in the household way, and, in many instances, to an extent not only sufficient for the supply of the families in which they are made, but for sale, and even in some cases for exportation." [5] Still, factories were even better, for they employed families "who are willing to devote the leisure resulting from the intermissions of their ordinary pursuit to collateral labours, as a resource for multiplying their acquisitions or their employment. The husband-man himself experiences a new source of profit and support, from the increased industry of his wife and daughters; invited and stimulated by the demands of the neighbouring manufactories." [6] Noah Webster wrote that many of the poorly educated ragged children would be benefited by work in textile mills. "In 1808 the Connecticut legislature declared that Colonel Humphreys, by constructing a factory, 'had put the energies of women and children to good use.' As a reward for this, his textile factory was exempted from all taxation." [7] Women who did not respond to the call of the factories would be "doomed to idleness and its inseparable attendants, vice and guilt." [8]

They responded. In the United States in 1831, about three-fifths of all workers in the cotton manufacturing industry were women.[9] In Lowell, Massachusetts, for example, in 1833 there were 3,800 women and only 1,200 men in the industry.[10] A Committee on Education in Massachusetts wrote about factory workers as if men were not involved at all.[11] Only later was more and more work—now increasingly non-domestic, industrial, urban work—taken over by men. Although in rural areas the old love-and/or-duty pattern of work in family units remained considerably longer, it began to change also so that in time practically the whole economy came to be dominated by monetary motives.

The movement into the mill and factory of much of the work women had formerly done was pivotal to the severance of the major roles of women. It took place because factory work was much more profitable. As Albert Gallatin noted, work invested in the production of cotton and woolen goods in factories was "much more productive than if applied to the ordinary occupations of women." [12] The value in wages of the thirty-nine thousand women in the country's cotton mills was thus "so much clear gain to society." [13] Factory work was not only, therefore, a moral plus preventing idleness and vice in the women themselves, but also a great economic plus for the nation as a whole. "Woman's place was thus not in the home, according to our founders, but wherever her 'more important' work was." [14] Clearly in the mills.

The story of Lowell and the so-called "Lowell girls" is a case in point.

In 1832, Lowell was little more than a factory village. Five "corporations" were started, and the cotton mills belonging to them were building. Help was in great demand and stories were told all over the country of the new factory place, and the high wages that were offered to all classes of work-people; stories that reached the ears of mechanics' and farmers' sons and gave new life to the lonely and dependent women in distant towns and farm-houses. Into this Yankee El Dorado these needy people began to pour by the various modes of travel known to those slow old days. The stagecoach and the canal-boat came every day, always filled with new recruits for the army of useful people. . . . Young girls came from different parts of New England, and from Canada, and men were employed to collect them at so much a head, and deliver them at the factories.[15]

And the "lonely and dependent women in distant towns and farm-houses" were eager to be "collected" and delivered at the factory.

We get an inside glimpse of this great migration—great in significance if not in size by present-day standards—from Lucy Larcom, one of the "many young girls" to whom the mills were giving "the opportunity to become 'independent of home or charity'."

> I went to my first day's work in the mill with a light heart. The novelty of it made it seem easy, and it really was not hard, just to change the bobbins on the spinning-frames every three quarters of an hour or so, with half a dozen other little girls who were doing the same thing. When I came back at night, the family began to pity me for my long, tiresome day's work, but I laughed and said, "Why it is nothing but fun. It is just like play."
>
> And for a little while it was only a new amusement; I liked it better than going to school and "making believe" I was learning when I was not. . . . There were compensations for being shut in to daily toil so early. The mill itself had its lessons for us. But it was not, and could not be the right sort of life for a child, and we were happy in the knowledge that, at the longest, our employment was only to be temporary. . . .[16]

Lucy had to take time off to help her sister, to learn the domestic arts, and fulfill family obligations. When she returned to the mill, she found that she enjoyed "even the familiar, unremitting clatter of the mill, because it indicated that something was going on." She felt that she belonged to the world, that there was something for her to do in it. "Something to do; it might be very little, but still it would be my own work." Home-life had its charms, to be sure, but "when one always stays at home, [it] is necessarily narrowing. . . . To me, it was an incalculable help to find myself among so many working-girls, all of us thrown upon our own resources." The mill did, indeed, have its lessons for those young women and one was, indeed, how "to become independent of home."

Trade unions, predictably, opposed the entrance of women into the labor force. A delegate to the 1834 National Trades' Union convention complained of the way the daughters as well as the sons of farmers were being induced to go to the factories to work. A young woman might, to be sure "earn a little more in the factory than at home, but as surely [she] loses health, if not her good character, her happiness!" [17]

As industrialization spread to other industries, the nature of work in the outside world changed as much as did work in the home. More and more of it became heavy urban-type work and was taken over by men.[18] But it was not until well into the nineteenth century that women's place came to be seen as in the home rather than in the mill.[19] When men began to want the jobs women had almost monopolized in the mills and factories, Hamilton's belief that the factory rather than the home was women's place began to be challenged. The times were out of joint, wrote a man in 1829 in the *Boston Courier,* when women encroached on the exclusive dominion of men: "our sons," he concluded sarcastically "must be educated and prepared to obtain a livelihood in those dignified and more masculine professions of seamstresses, milliners, cooks, wet nurses, and chamber-maids." [20] In the next decade the National Trades' Union found the system of female labor to be "the most disgraceful [blot on the] escutcheon of the character of American freemen, and one which, if not checked by some superior cause, will entail ignorance, misery and degradation on our children to the end of time." [21] Another union man, speaking at a meeting of the Philadelphia Trades' Union, longed for the time when women could return to their place in the home; they should organize unions in the meanwhile so they could earn enough to do so. He hoped the time would come soon "when our wives no longer doomed to servile labor, will be the companions of our fireside and the instructors of our children" and that they would no longer have to do "that kind of labor which was designed for man alone to perform." [22] As late as 1875, Carroll D. Wright, Chief of the Massachusetts Bureau of Labor Statistics, was saying in his 6th Annual Report that "married women ought not to be tolerated in the mills at all . . . for it is an evil that is sapping the life of our operative population, and must sooner or later be regulated, or, more probably, stopped." [23] By 1889 women who entered the labor force were viewed as "unsexed."

Alas for these desolated men. The times remained out of joint. The blot on American character remained. "Technical and economic forces proved stronger than the warnings and yearnings of those who looked back. . . . Hence, while at the end of the century some five million women and girls were producing 'exchange values' for the market instead of 'use values' for the home, the 'sphere' of women was anomalous and confused. With some exceptions women themselves were confused no less than society at large about what they could and should be doing." [24]

It was not until the middle of the twentieth century that it finally became unequivocally clear that women were in the labor force for good—in both senses of that term, forever and for good ends—that their services were, in fact, indispensable. Only then did it become clear that they were as much part-and-parcel of the working force as men. In 1949 a Royal Commission on Population in Great Britain concluded that it would be harmful to restrict the contribution women made to the economic life of the nation, thus giving official recognition to the so-called two-role ideology. In 1961 President Kennedy also accepted the two-role ideology. In establishing a Commission on the Status of Women, he made a statement that included recognition of the necessity of making the most efficient and effective use of the skills of all persons, including women. We were back to Hamilton and Gallatin. We had, in effect, come full circle.

## Concurrent and Sequential Patterns

Today practically all women will be mothers; and almost all will also be in the labor force. Some will pursue the two roles sequentially and thus never have to face the problem of integrating them at the same time.[25] Others will pursue them concurrently, at least in certain periods of their lives and will have to face the problem of integrating them. But this will vary over time, constituting one set of problems in early motherhood when the children are preschoolers, quite another in middle motherhood when they are school age; and an altogether different set of problems in late motherhood when the children have left home. It is useful, therefore, to view the relationships between the two roles in terms of both the total life history of women and the characteristic way they interweave with one another over time.

It has taken two research streams to clarify for us this pattern of role interweaving. One, pioneered by Paul C. Glick, has had to do with the life cycle of women delineated in terms of such major demographic events as age at marriage, age at birth of first and last child, age at marriage of last child, and death of husband. The other has had to do with labor force participation. Thanks to these studies, we can now catch a glimpse not only of the extent of labor-force participation but also of the changes it has undergone in relation to motherhood, and even project trends into the future.

The idea of life as a series of stages through which one moves is a fairly old one.[26] The stages—simple or complex—themselves reflect the society in which they take place.[27] But practically all delineations of stages in the past have been based on male lives; they have not, therefore, been useful for understanding the lives of women. The few conceptualizations of the stages in the lives of women that have been delineated have been in terms of child-bearing.[28] A woman's life was divided into pre-menarchial years, child-bearing years, and post-menopausal years.[29] When women lived integrated lives so that their roles as workers and as mothers neatly intertwined, the stages in their lives could legitimately be delineated in terms of their child-bearing careers. As a child the little girl learned the domestic arts and skills from her mother, almost as an apprentice had in the past, so that by the time she became a mother herself she had acquired the work skills required to manage a household. Her work career and her maternal career were all of a piece. When the two roles were severed this was no longer the case. Now there was a hiatus between them, and the life pattern of women had to encompass both.

For statistically average women at mid-century, the story was something like this: they married at the age of twenty; they had their last child at the age of twenty-six; they were forty-eight years old when their last child was married; and they were sixty-two when they lost their husbands. The most salient point in the labor-force participation curve is, of course, the dip in the middle and late twenties, during early motherhood, when the children are preschoolers. But there is another critical point of almost equal significance in the middle thirties, during middle motherhood, when the children are of school age, from six to seventeen.

In 1957 the National Manpower Council summarized some of the changes that have already occurred so far in this century:

At the close of the last century, about half the adult women never entered paid employment. Now at least nine out of every ten women are likely to work outside the home in the course of their lives. Women who reached adulthood around the turn of the century participated in paid employment, on the average, for eleven years in the course of their lives. Those who reached adulthood just before World War II are likely, on the average, to work twenty years. Today's schoolgirls may spend twenty-five years or more in work outside the home.[30]

The figure is even higher today. Thus if a young woman of twenty remains single all during her life, she will spend 45.3 years in the labor force; if she marries but has no children, 34.9 years; if she marries and has children but does not enter the labor force until she is thirty-five, 23.8." [31] Almost a quarter of a century. An important statistic to bear in mind in thinking about the future of motherhood.

Even more interesting is the way the timing of paid work has changed in relation to marriage and motherhood. In the past practically all of the labor-force participation of women came before marriage and motherhood. Now most of it comes after marriage and even after motherhood. A variety of patterns have been delineated showing the many ways women have attempted to combine their two roles sequentially and concomitantly.[32] For the most part, although decreasingly, a sequential pattern is typical today. After a drop in labor-force participation in the child-bearing and early child-rearing years, the curve of labor-force participation rises dramatically until at the age of forty-five to fifty-four—when in the past they were already worn out with child bearing—over half of all women—still vigorous—are in the labor force; as are over a third of women with preschool children.

## Which "Instinct?" Evaluation of Worker and Mother Roles

By and large, the more education and the more family income women have, the more likely they are to rate the mother role higher than the worker role, that is, to feel that "bringing up children properly takes as much intelligence and drive as holding a top position in business or government." The large proportion (70 percent) of women in families with incomes of fifteen thousand dollars and over (as of 1972) who evaluate the mother role higher than the worker role may for that reason not be in the labor force; on the other hand, it may also be that because they are not in the labor force they evaluate what they are doing highly. Fewer young (eighteen–twenty-nine) than older women feel that "having a loving husband who is able to take care of me is much more important to me than making it on my own." [33] Still, in a sample of Chicago housewives both "worker" and "career" roles were rated at the bottom of the list so far as importance was concerned.[34] But in a national sample of women, employed mothers mentioned the worker more than the mother role as sources of feelings of importance or usefulness.[35]

The relative importance assigned to mother and worker roles varies not only among women themselves at any one time but historically over time. Early in the nineteenth century the worker role was exalted; later in that century, the mother role was preferred. Until recently if a young woman said she did not want a job, she might have been criticized as lazy, but if she said she did not want to have babies she was labeled sick. There was no contest so far as the relative importance assigned or the pressures exerted were concerned. Although some time or other during their lives about as many women will be in the labor force as will be mothers—perhaps even more—the attitudes involved toward each role are at opposite poles. For one the young woman has been coerced; [36] for the other, led mildly and without serious conviction. Judith Blake speaks of the "ruthless exclusion of structured alternatives," including careers for women which "channel motivation in the direction of goals that imply the advent and existence of children." [37] From the primer stage on, girls are taught in school that "only direst necessity drives mother to work." [38] A study of 134 elementary school books located only three working mothers portrayed.

Veblen, among others, spoke of an "instinct of workmanship," a fundamental need in human beings for the satisfactions provided by productive work well done. It was coordinate with a "parental bent." [39] Such an "instinct" in women until recently was supposed to find expression only in work in the home. If women wished to enter the labor force, the only reputable excuse was that they needed the money. Thus almost without exception, studies on why women "worked" gave this as the legitimizing reason. "Working is not a 'consumer good' for most married women: only 16.3 percent of women taking jobs in 1963 offered the reason of 'personal satisfaction,' while 61.5 percent offered a financial reason." [40]

## The "Right" to Work

Among male workers, the expression "right to work" means the right to work without having to join a labor union. Among women it means the right to work because they want to without having to face discriminatory restrictions. It is true that for most women there is, indeed, a strong component of financial need when they endure the hardships involved in combining job and motherhood. But for many, labor-force participation is an urgent emotional necessity as well.

Increasingly, recognition is being accorded to this motive, whether labeled "instinctive" or not. There is recognition of the need for what Erik Erikson calls "competence," for what R. W. White calls "effectance," and for what Heinz Hartmann refers to as ego development, all of which add up to a need felt by many women as well as men for self actualization through work. There is also recognition that such development is not incompatible with the maternal role: "a woman's highly developed ego does not mean that her sexual and maternal motivations will be less developed." [41] Indeed, denial of the right to enter the labor force may have destructive effects on women.[42] One study of sixteen working mothers concludes that there is no intrinsic conflict between the worker and the mother roles; they may even be complementary.[43] It quotes a psychiatrist to the effect that "the dichotomy would seem to be not between motherhood and career but between women who do well in both and women who do well in neither." [44]

Actually, "instinct" has had nothing to do with the labor-force participation of women: neither the maternal instinct which should have kept them out of the labor force having babies nor the instinct of workmanship which should have driven them in; neither the accolades for the worker role of Hamilton and Gallatin nor the depreciation of the worker role of union leaders and Carroll D. Wright. The demands of a burgeoning industrial economy have had much more impact.

## Supply or Demand?

Do the patterns of labor-force participation shown in the frontispiece depend on the supply of women willing to enter the labor force or on the demand for their services by the outside world?

Did women enter the labor force because they were perverse or because they were needed there? In assessing future trends it makes a difference how one answers the question. If we emphasize the supply side of the equation we will see women as autonomous individuals making decisions with respect to entering the labor force on the basis of a rational weighing of the costs and benefits and our research will concentrate on the motives of women in arriving at their decision. We will try to determine what it is that regulates the supply in terms of the psychology of women. Reasonable enough.

If we emphasize the demand side, we will study the occupational structure of the economy, assuming that if the pay offered is high enough the supply of workers will be forthcoming and women will decide to enter the labor force. Again, reasonable enough. "The evidence is just about incontrovertible . . . that the pull of a growing number of attractive job opportunities has been a prime factor in the shift of married women into the labor force." [45]

In the case of men, labor-force analysis finds this logic quite adequate. Families that need income are the ones that supply women workers; without their help, many would be in poverty. "Only 6 percent of the families with both married partners in the work force live in poverty; the corresponding proportion for families where only one spouse works is triple that figure." [46] So the answer has to be that both the demand for the services of women by the economy and the willingness of women to supply these services determine the shape of the curves in the frontispiece.

### The Demand Side

There are still those who excoriate the restlessness of married women, especially mothers, who "work" when their place is so obviously in the home and there are others who dismiss the wishes of women as of no significance and interpret the entrance of women into the labor force as a response to the demands of industry for their services. The controversy is an old one and the answer seems clearly on the demand side. Women have entered the labor force—before as well as since the industrial revolution—because that is where they have been—and still are—needed and wanted. "The sheer fact of the matter is that America's so-called 'manpower' needs would never have been met without this outpouring of married women workers." [47] No matter how strongly women may have wished to enter the labor force, it would not have been possible if the demand for their services had not been there.

So far as the future demand for the work of women in the labor force is concerned, the assessment is as follows: the occupations traditionally pursued by men are declining in importance and those traditionally followed by women—especially the service and clerical occupations—are increasing.[48] To the extent that current sex-typing of work continues to prevail, the demand for women workers can be expected to grow.[49] The demand will be particularly high—all but insatiable [50]—for clerical workers, but it will also be high for retail sales workers, hospital attendants, waitresses, nurses, telephone operators, and other "female-typed jobs." [51]

Industrial as well as occupational trends will determine the demand for women workers and here state and national policies as well as technological trends will be significant. If, for example, we aim for urban development, "female" jobs will increase relatively less than construction jobs and the demand for "women's work" will moderate; conversely, if we aim for social-welfare goals, they will increase relatively more.[52]

Population considerations will also influence the future demand for women workers. When agents scouted New England farms to recruit girls and young women for the cotton and textile mills of the booming towns early in the nineteenth century, it was market demand that sparked their activities. The mills needed the services of these young women. Today it is not only demand for the services of young women that informs policy but also demographic considerations. The idea is to attract married women into the labor force in order to motivate lower family size. In order to influence women to select labor-force participation over motherhood, working must be made worthwhile. "Women whose time is more valuable will, in general, restrict their pursuit of such time-intensive activities as child raising," [53] and turn to outside employment, as educated women, city women, and women in well-paying jobs now do.

### The Supply Side

No matter how strong might be the demands of industry for the services of women, it will be of no avail if women are not willing to respond to it. In the South, a plantation owner could increase his labor supply by buying more slaves. But in New England, a factory owner could increase his labor supply only be attracting new workers.[54]

The usual means to attract workers is money. And a good deal of the thinking about work is based on the assumption that the supply of labor is dependent on the wages offered. In the case of women, in fact, labor-force participation by wives and especially by mothers, is still justified almost entirely on the grounds of need and of the monetary income such participation supplies. But other grounds for wanting to "work" are increasingly recognized, in the case of both men and women. Labor-force analysts speak of a "propensity" to work quite aside from the monetary rewards.

In the current scene, economists see several factors at work increasing this "propensity to work" among women, ranging from changing values to technological changes:

> This increased propensity to work derives from several factors. For example, rising educational levels have had a marked influence on social values concerning the role of women in the family and workplace. These altered values have increased the supply of female labor substantially, a development which has been reinforced by the continuing introduction of goods and services which allow a housewife more free time and control over her environment.[55]

But these factors may not continue to have the same effect on the "propensity to work" of women. In the case of education, for example, Valerie Oppenheimer notes that as more women become educated they will be "overqualified" for many of the available jobs and no longer find them attractive. The rewards for entering the labor force will have to be high.

But neither money alone nor "propensity to work" tells the whole story. For labor-force participation by women does not always follow precisely the same rationale as that of men. Strictly monetary considerations do not operate the same way. "Social values concerning the role of women in the family" referred to in the passage quoted above are crucial. Indeed, the presence or absence of small children is one of the most determinative influences on female labor-force participation. Thus the supply of women workers depends on non-market as well as on market factors. "The question is whether the extent of work and the number of children are influenced by the work opportunities facing a woman" [56] or whether the number of women available for work depends on the number of children they have. That is, does demand for female workers influence the number of children they have or does the supply of women workers depend on the number of children?

### Chicken or Egg?

We know that there is a negative relationship between fertility and labor-force participation. Women who have many children are not likely to be in the labor force; women in the labor force are not likely to have many children.[57] At least this is so in America.[58] Which is cause, which effect?

Since it is impossible to perform genuinely controlled experiments to answer these questions, researchers have to manipulate statistics to tease out relationships. This they have done. They report that among women who do not control the number of births they have, having babies is what keeps them out of the labor force. But among women who do control conception, the reverse seems to be true. Labor force participation does make for fewer babies.

The researchers warn us, however, that in recent years the difference in fertility between women in the labor force and those not in it has been declining. In the 1960s women in the labor force were having almost as many babies as women not in the labor force.[59] "The rather astonishing change which is taking place in the work lives of women is that the effects of the birth of a child on work life continuity is rapidly diminishing." [60] Increasingly women work right through their pregnancies and are "then returning to work after a time lapse hardly longer than a somewhat lengthy vacation or the time their husband might require to recover from a fairly minor illness." [61] American women seem to be learning how to integrate their roles, to cope with both jobs and children, however difficult the process may be. Indeed, "the most dramatic growth in the labor force during the current decade will occur among persons twenty-five to thirty-four (particularly among young adult women in this age group)," that is, "the steepest rise in work propensity has been among women with children under three, whose labor-force participation rate increased by three-quarters, from 14.3 percent in 1960 to 26.9 percent in 1972." [62] And we can readily agree with the conclusion that "the importance of this phenomenon of increased work participation by young mothers cannot be overemphasized." [63]

## Straws in the Wind

Anyone who bases a conception of the future on statistical projections has to hedge whatever is said. Statistical projections have to be based on past experience. They cannot take into account new events, such as drastic changes in marriage and birth rates, or, perhaps equally important, social movements such as the current feminist revival.

The marriage rate is in a peculiarly hesitant phase. An upward trend began in 1963 and the greatest annual increase occurred in 1968. Still, a larger proportion of young women eighteen to twenty-four were single in 1970 than in 1960. By 1971, the marriage rate had declined by about one percent. Although it bounced back in 1972, at the beginning of 1973 it was retreating once more. Paul Glick and Arthur Nortan have come to the rescue in helping us to understand what is going on. The answer lies in the large component furnished to the marriage rate by *re*marriage rather than by first marriage. Since the late 1950s, "the trend of the first-marriage rate has continued to decline while divorce and remarriage rates rose sharply." The birth rate, which began to decline in 1957, had reached the lowest level ever observed in 1972.[64] A lowered first-marriage rate and a lowered birth rate may have quite untoward results for the future.

But whatever the statistical projections may show, if the expressed preferences of young women themselves can be viewed as straws in the wind, a high rate of labor-force participation by mothers may be anticipated. For women with a new orientation are coming on the scene and they are calling for a new look at the worker, as well as at the mother, role. They are the educated young women, more likely to be students and professionals than blue-collar workers, and therefore more likely to leave their mark on the future. Indeed, they are likely to leave their mark on the worker role sooner than on the mother role. The difference between the professional and the blue-collar women is smaller with respect to the worker than with respect to the mother role. We know that "women who intend to work for more years also plan to have fewer children, despite the fact that working women in general appear to enjoy and prize children as much as nonworkers do." [65] It is therefore worth looking at young women for future trends.

All the straws indicate that in general, despite the subtle—

though declining—denigration of career women as "deviant," [66] the wind is blowing in the direction of a life style for women that combines both work or career [67] and motherhood.

A spate of studies [68] show that the general pattern among college women for almost a quarter of a century has been one in which combining motherhood with job or career when children were of school age was approved, preferred, or planned—the questions were phrased differently in the several studies—by about half of the subjects. And about half of these women at Cornell University [69] were favorable without regard to the age of the children. At Vassar, in fact, even in the fifties, heyday of the feminine mystique, "a quarter of the students did not plan to stop working except for brief periods before and after confinement." [70]

In the last few years studies are beginning to report an increasing proportion of college women who plan to combine motherhood and career when children are of school age, rising to as high as over four-fifths of the women in some studies.[71] It was no longer even the classic old dilemma "motherhood or career" but, increasingly, "motherhood and career." Not a "career just in case" she did not marry but "a career whether or not" she married and had children.

Equally significant is the planned earlier timing of return to work after motherhood which the recent studies report. In one New England college, "between a fourth and a third of the women by 1969 and 1970, expect to work . . . when the youngest child is 4 to 6 and two to three times more women in the 1969 and 1970 graduating classes expect to work when their youngest is 2 to 4 as compared with 1967 and 1968 graduates." [72] A study at Stanford arrives at the same conclusion. A comparison of undergraduates in 1965 and 1972 shows that there has been a radical increase in the proportion who plan to work when their children are still preschoolers.[73] A life style that includes both motherhood and job or career is thus taken for granted by more and more women.

One study of college women speaks of "the contingency approach" [74] to the life that is forced on women. They can make few career decisions because so much depends on whether or not they marry. We may have to speak less and less of such "contingencies" as the integration of mother and worker roles makes each one less contingent on the other. As we learn to integrate them there will be more certainty, less dependence on chance, in arriving at both career and motherhood decisions. The career-oriented women will know that they will be resuming their careers—if, indeed, they even withdraw from them—soon after the birth of their last child. They will differ from the women with less career-salience primarily in the timing of return to work. "Young women have apparently been sold on the desirability of planning for [both motherhood] . . . *and* work, and interest in a career can no longer be attributed to a tiny, deviant minority." [75]

The preference for this mother-career life style and the continuing need for the services of women in the economy suggest increasing labor-force participation by mothers. Young women want to be in the home but they want also to be in the work force. Fewer and fewer of them want to have to forswear motherhood for careers or careers for motherhood.

Very well, one might legitimately object, these studies deal primarily with an exceptional set of women, college women, whose problems are quite different from those of other women. Women in the blue-collar world, for example, are more conservative. And so, indeed, they are. At least for the present.

### Is Working-class Traditionalism a Brake on the Future?

Cross-sectional or polling studies usually show women with lower levels of education as more conservative in their attitudes than women with more years of schooling. But this fact may merely reflect an age difference, since low levels of education are associated with age. Much of the traditionalism reported among working class women in popular polls may well be evanescent, destined to become greatly attenuated in the future. One analyst of a variety of polls and surveys concludes that:

> . . . although there is empirical support for the idea of working-class conservatism, there are indications of changes and subtleties in that traditionalism that are important in considering the possibility of future social change. . . . In entering the world, seeking employment and increasing their education women came into contact with other women, began to comprehend their social role structure—and began to seek to change it. . . . The working-class woman does predominantly define herself through her family—as someone's wife and mother. And her social relationships have been in that family network. If she works, it is because the money is needed to support her family—her income and motivation have been family-oriented.

147

She probably lives in a working-class neighborhood. . . . Historically, the sex-role divisions of working-class family life have kept her from active participation in the organization and leadership of working-class labor movements and often if she works it is in non-unionized labor. She is separated from other working-class women, as middle-class women have been; she may work with them but the major orientation is the family at home. . . . But the basis for collective action as women is there—an awareness of dissatisfaction and an increasing sympathy for certain goals in changing "woman's place." As women they have a common experience: in marriage, household maintenance, working to give economic support, childbearing and child-rearing. . . .[76]

There is, she believes no reason to assume that "working-class women are content with their current life alternatives" or that they will necessarily reject "activities geared to changing the position of women in work and family spheres of life." The future, in brief, cannot be assumed to be a replication of the present with traditional working-class orientations blocking change.

In the past, the blue-collar worker's wife, traditionally proud of her status as a housewife,[77] was comparing herself with the woman who had "to work" to keep enough food on the table because of her husband's inadequate earnings. In that context she was well off and her husband was anxious to keep her out of the labor force as proof of his adequacy as a good provider. But increasingly the blue-collar wife compares herself with the neighbor whose husband provides just as well as hers does but who has a job anyway. The second income is not necessary to set a good table or to keep a comfortable home with all the appliances. But it does make possible a better car, two television sets, even a cabin in the mountains or a boat on the lake. Or the community college for a son (if not yet for a daughter).

Of special interest is the report of one researcher who has specialized in the study of blue-collar life. "Blue-collar women," he tells us, "bitterly denounce their homey prototype, Edith Bunker, when I ask about this popular TV heroine in my research. They especially disown her Old Country passivity, naiveté, and doltishness. Working outside their homes and ethnic neighborhoods, as many do, these free-wheeling women are often aggressive, sophisticated, and mentally adroit. Long accustomed . . . to manipulating the men folk (of all ages), modern blue-collar women more often resemble (and seem to identify with) Gloria than Edith in the Bunker household." [78] And Gloria is supporting her husband.

One related point with respect to education. We know that the more education women have the more likely they are, other things being equal, to participate in the labor force and the fewer the number of children they bear. We know that, after a pause, more and more women are now going to college. Women from a working-class background will be included among them. The author just quoted speaks of "blue-collar women" as "heady with their new-found freedom from conception fears." [79]

A final, more indirectly related, fact also points in the direction of redefinition of the role of mother in the working class. It has to do with the so-called "welfare mess" of the 1960s and early 1970s. In a strange and roundabout way it was also giving us clues about the future. A host of inconsistent beliefs, tenets, convictions, and attitudes were having to be reconciled. There was the work ethic that demanded that one work for what one received. There was the stern proscription of out-of-wedlock births. There was the powerful taboo against pre- or extramarital sexual relations. There was the middle-class woman's-place-is-in-the-home ideology. There was the strong conviction that mothers should not work outside the home. There was the necessity to make provision for children whose fathers could or would not do so. . . . All these seething inconsistencies were reflected in the years of struggle for "welfare reform." And in the process a new conceptualization of motherhood was in process of being hammered out.[80]

These straws suggest that the wind is blowing in the direction of some combination of mother and worker role for a sizeable proportion of women. The young, especially the educated, women seem to prefer it that way and the need for their contribution to the labor force—clerical and service—seems to be burgeoning.

But, it is legitimate to ask, how high can the labor-force participation rate of mothers rise? Is there any limit? Will it rise to the same level as that of fathers? If so, at what level can it be supported? Is there any intrinsic reason why the rate should not go up farther than it is now?

### Are We Approaching a Ceiling?

If being a woman made no difference in labor-force participation, the proportion of women in the labor force would be the same as the proportion of men. Actually since 1900 there has been a gradual—at first extremely gradual—tendency for convergence in labor-force participation of the two sexes, the proportion of women going up and that of men, down. The rising female curve was far more spectacular than the declining male curve. In 1870 the divergence was between 86.2 percent for men and 15.5 percent for women. By 1990, according to current projections, the divergence will be less than half that size, between 78.4 percent and 45.9 percent.

The most precipitate increase in labor-force participation among women came in the 1960s, from 37.1 percent in 1960 to 42.8 percent in 1970. But the rate of increase decelerated in the early 1970s and little increase is projected for 1980 or 1990. We may, in fact, have reached some kind of limit at just under half—46 percent—by 1980. The projected increase between 1980 and 1990 is only from 45.6 to 45.9 percent.[81]

It is not likely that the male and female curves will ever meet. However minimized, there will always be some women taking time out for child bearing and for the near future, more women than men taking time out for child rearing. This is one of the answers to Henry Higgins' plaintive question, Why can't women be more like men.

The story of labor-force participation by mothers, as distinguished from women in general, is still uncertain. Some sort of ceiling seems to have been approached if not actually reached in the early 1970s. In 1971, for the first time since the early 1960s, the labor-force participation rate for married women did not increase; it went up once more in 1972, but not markedly from 52.7 to 54.9 percent. But "among the married women with children under eighteen years old, . . . 40 percent were in the labor force in 1971, the same proportion as in 1970. Both the number of mothers of children aged three to five years and their labor-force participation rates dropped somewhat." [82] In terms also of the age brackets when women are most likely to have children in the home— twenty-five to forty-four—there seems to be a limit at roughly half in the labor force, slightly less than half for the mothers of younger children and slightly more than half for the mothers of school-age children.

Whether the apparent ceiling was merely a temporary fluctuation or a permanent trend it is too early to say. Since the occupations which engage relatively large proportions of women are among those expected to grow most rapidly it seems unlikely that the slow-down could reflect a reduced demand. The demand may not be insatiable but it seems to remain high. It is possible, however, that recession has had a damping effect on the demand for women workers, causing some of them to withdraw or not to enter the labor force.

On the supply side, the slow-down, if not actual ceiling, might mean that the need of the women's families for their incomes had declined, a not very likely situation. It might mean that all the young mothers who wanted jobs now had them. Although a spate of research studies shows that more women would enter the labor force if satisfactory child-care arrangements could be made, it is just possible that about half of all mothers do not want to enter the labor force, an important consideration if true, and one with important implications for the future.[83]

Whether we have or have not reached the future, we still have not solved the problems it has brought. "Whether the recent overall stability in the number of working mothers proves temporary or extended, it is important to remember the large increase in their number during the past decade and the far-reaching social, cultural, and economic effects of this development," [84] including the need to help women integrate their two roles.

Just trying to make coherent sense out of the welter of facts and figures leaves little room for comment on the significance of these trends for women themselves. What effect does labor-force participation have on motherhood? We know that much depends on the reasons why a woman "works." If she wants to "work," remaining at home will not make her a better mother; it might even make her a worse one. If she does not want to "work," having to may also make her a worse one. If women succeed in the labor force, will their success spoil them for motherhood? Or motherhood for them? Or improve each for both? Will labor-force participation relieve some of the stresses of motherhood? The answers to these questions depend, understandably, on how high the hurdles are that we place in the way. They are high.

The Royal Commission on Population had recommended in 1949 in Britain that "a deliberate effort should be made to devise adjustments that would render it easier for women to combine motherhood and the care of a home with outside activities." And President Kennedy had asked for recommendations "for services which will enable women to continue their role as wives and mothers while making a maximum contribution to the world around them." There are probably few if any governmental commissions, presidential or congressional, whose recommendations have fallen so flat. There has been no lack of recommendations. But where are the services they recommend? Without them, some women are beginning to recognize, the two-role ideology is merely a bill of goods. Without delivery, they feel women have been had.

So much for the background. Now, the women themselves.

# PART FIVE

# Gestating
# the Future

# Introduction

Although it is now almost a quarter of a century since the British Royal Commission on Population in 1949 recommended help for women trying to integrate their homemaking and their industrial work and almost a decade and a half since President Kennedy in 1961 asked for "recommendations for services which will enable women to continue their role as wives and mothers while making a maximum contribution to the world around them" the tasks of integrating the two roles still remains a woman-by-woman responsibility. The woman has to do all the "psychological work." So here in Part Five is a brief overview of how this integration is managed among professional women and among women who, though they "work," have less commitment to the labor force. These are the women who are gestating the future. Much of the research on these women, it should be noted, presupposes the status quo. It takes for granted that the present definitions of roles and the present structure of the work world obtain. It describes how, given these circumstances, women accommodate to them. These assumptions cannot be taken for granted as permanent. In evaluating the research as a harbinger of the future, therefore, this caveat has to be borne in mind.

Most mothers in the work force have long since made their peace with the problems of integrating their two roles. They have retained all their domestic responsibilities and assumed those of the worker role as well. And all the studies comment on the resulting "overload." No one has seemed to think it unusual. Of course women were still responsible for the household, for seeing that all the chores were taken care of even if they themselves did not have to do them all. This responsibility was implicit in the two-role ideology. The services that President Kennedy called for are important and would greatly lighten the load. But there remain other aspects of integrating the mother and the worker role that would not be reached by such help. They are more personal, more subjective, more "psychological." These are the aspects looked at here.

But the future of motherhood is not entirely in the hands of these working mothers. True, they now constitute half of all mothers with school-age (but no preschool) children and therefore will enormously affect it. Though no longer "typical" there still remains the other half, the large proportion of such mothers who are not in the labor force. They include many of the women referred to in Chapter 7, affluent women in "golden cages" or "golden handcuffs." As Moms they have long been targets of enormous hostility. As victims of socialization that unfitted them for participation in the labor force—reared to expect to be "taken care of" as long as they lived—they are fighting a rear-guard action against "women's libbers" who, they believe—erroneously—are rocking their very comfortable boat. The immediate future will be a time of serious travail for women who do not wish to enter the labor force even when their children no longer need—or want—their absorbing and intimate solicitude. If they are to have the privilege of protection and shelter, the question is increasingly being raised, why shouldn't men also?

A personal addendum. Writing Chapter 11 was a difficult undertaking; it exacted great emotional costs. I wince at the diatribes against Mom. Once again the victim is blamed for being victimized. As contrasted with Mrs. Portnoy or the generation of vipers, some of the loveliest women I know are mothers who have been left without absorbing roles in mid-course. But whether in the gentle, giving version, or in the harridan version, Mom is a victim of transition and no one could view her present status, it seems to me, without compassion. And even compassion is an insult.

## CHAPTER NINE

# The Professional Mother

### What's the Question?

If the model for the role of mother inherited from the Victorian past was designed for a love-and/or-duty world that ran on totally different principles from those of the outside occupational world, and if the two worlds were, therefore, so different, is it really possible for women to participate in both of them? Different personality characteristics are associated with the work world and the home, with industrial work and motherwork; competitiveness is called for in one, nurturance in the other. Can both kinds be combined in the same woman? Won't success in role integration be at the expense of the nurturant qualities of women? Talcott Parsons had thought so; the only way to solve this problem, he said, was "by making sure that . . . only one member of the . . . conjugal family plays a full competitive role in the occupational system. This member is the husband and father." [1]

Professional mothers, on the basis of their own experience, were asking a different question and arriving at a different answer. Instead of asking "can a woman quite successfully integrate both career and traditional endeavors?" they were asking, might not a woman, albeit subject to severe "role strains," "even find herself enjoying the increased variety and the personal flexibility such a life style necessarily entails?" [2] For, as a matter of fact, they concluded, it was a myth that one could be only either non-competitive and dependent to fit the mother role or the opposite, only competitive and non-dependent to fit the professional role. One did not have to be trapped by that myth, and many women were not. "One wonders if to some extent the married professionals' capacity to integrate what on the surface are discrepant characteristics rests not so much on their uniqueness but rather reflects the fact that in actuality these characteristics are really not discrepant and can very comfortably coexist." [3] Roles, not women, were stereotyped; structures, not women, were rigid. Women themselves were multi-dimensional. They could be competent *and* nurturant both at home and at the office.

### "Comfortable Coexistence"

It is not coming to terms with "discrepant characteristics" in her own personality that constitutes the "psychological work" of the career mother. That is no problem at all. She can be both nurturant and competent. She may even enjoy the change of pace her two roles call for if or when it is called for. The matter is not quite so simple, though. There are "discrepant characteristics" called for in the two worlds. Women are protected from the discrepancy, however, by having the anti-nurturant characteristics socialized out of their personalities.

All women are socialized into the nurturant or "stroking" function.[4] That is, they are reared to build up those around them. It is required of all women in whatever role they perform. And this "stroking" function is, indeed, antithetical to the macho qualities required for success in the work world, that is, the harsh, driving, competitive qualities needed for the top positions. Being non-aggressive—at least not offensively aggressive [5]—and pleasing do disqualify women for the kinds of careers that demand a harsh, no-holds-barred, win-at-any-cost approach. So much has to be conceded. But mothers are no more disadvantaged in this respect than other women.

To the extent that women are disqualified for the top positions, Talcott Parsons' analysis has validity. People driven by the macho compulsion to win, to make it, to reach the top, are not likely to have the qualities that make for successful motherhood. And, in a study of top tycoons some years ago, they were not averse to admitting that they preferred their work to their families.[6] This discrepancy between machismo and motherwork is not, of course, absolute. We have also the stereotype of the harsh, driving father who is nevertheless putty in the hands of an adored daughter. But for the most part, the gist of the Parsons analysis holds up. The dedicated careerist, male or female, in the competitive occupations is not likely to be a warm and loving parent. The relevant point here is, however, that few mothers are likely to be in these macho-type occupations.

Most are in professions in which the nurturant characteristics bred into them are assets rather than disqualifying liabilities. Or, if they are, indeed, in the macho professions they are in subordinate positions. For these positions they are well prepared. They can be competent, rational, efficient without any sacrifice of the "feminine" qualities of nurturance. Screen and stage may portray the successful career woman as the harsh macho type. Not many are.

If, however, women have been disqualified for the top—fighting, competing—jobs, they have been extremely well qualified for the second spot, the competent and efficient assistant or secretary or associate who runs the shop and who may, behind the scenes, also determine policy—discreetly. In fact, one of the patronizingly chauvinistic sops thrown to these women is for the top man to admit to everyone that it is his secretary or assistant who really takes care of things while he drums up business on the golf course. It is clearly not impossible to be rational, clear-thinking, competent, and efficient as well as "stroking."

This is no more impossible at home than at the office. Home economics colleges had for decades increasingly defined homemaking in managerial if not engineering terms. And successful professional mothers all report that such skills are basic to integrating their roles. Few have been as explicit in laying out the process as a French woman, mother of four boys and fabulously successful as a journalist. By applying business-management concepts to her home she has found it quite feasible to integrate her roles. (Incidentally, labeling what the homemaker does with business-stamped names immediately upgrades them.) And to dispel any idea that applying business principles to the home would be destructive of the nurturance that should diffuse that sanctuary, the husband reported that he loved it:

> . . . I learned, while a chill crept up my spine, that my home was a business, both a transformation industry and den of office workers at the same time. . . . I discovered that our household political system allowed for a participatory form of government. . . . Until now I had nursed the illusion that my vocabulary [planning, brain-storming, group dynamics, etc.] could not be adapted to our private world. . . . [It would

make home a hell. But] if I had succeeded in descending into hell without noticing it, and even in doing so voluntarily, I realized on reflection that it was probably because there is no hell, or, in any case, hell is not where I thought it was.[7]

The major difficulty in this talented woman's success in integrating her two roles from a feminist viewpoint is that she alone is the one who must achieve this integration.

Millions of mothers have demonstrated that they could be both nurturant and competent. The sexes are not really all that specialized, permitting only one set of virtues and strengths per sex. Mothers could apply their competencies as effectively in the home as in the office and vice versa. If the sexes were indeed as specialized as the stereotypes imply, it would be impossible to integrate the two roles. Actually they are not. The discrepancies that challenge the professional mother are not in her personal characteristics; they are in the structural demands of the roles.

### Discrepant Role Demands

How is it that a father can live so successfully in both worlds? That's easy. After struggling hard all day long at the office—fighting, competing, "making it"—he returns home where he is met by his children with his slippers (figuratively) and his wife with a cocktail, for he is now entitled to be pampered and coddled all evening. He has been working all day; she, as everyone knows, has obviously not. He may do a few male-type jobs around the yard but after that he is free to watch football for hours. He can relax. He has provided, and fulfilled his role. At work he is also protected from the demands of his family. In some bureaucracies wives are specifically instructed not to call their husbands at the office; the company owns all the man's working time.[8] Not to mention family time as well, on occasion. And if he brings work home that work takes precedence over everything else. A man can be a professional and a parent—of sorts—more easily than a woman can. Little is required of him in the family; his contribution is not demanding.

Only recently has it occurred to us to note the anomaly of speaking of women's two roles but not men's. Why must women integrate roles made structurally "discrepant" but men not have to?

It is a commonplace that assuming a professional career in no way emancipates a woman from responsibility for the home. She retains all of her domestic obligations. Even though a husband may help—as increasingly he does—it is still her responsibility to see that he *can* help, to see that the work for him is all laid out, to see that it is made ready for him to do. He doesn't have to see what has to be done, often the hardest part of the job. For although the physical labor that is required in the home may not be onerous—as, increasingly, it is not—the planning, management, supervision, and overseeing of all the chores is.

Because the questioning of the two-role definition of the professional mother's life is so new, the answers are not yet forthcoming. Meanwhile there is an increasing research literature on the dual-career or two-career family to show us how the career mother does deal with "role strain." "Although from a structural point of view a considerable degree of role strain is inevitable between the woman's 'professional' and 'home' roles. . . . it is capable of being managed through the use of a number of techniques through which women are able to subjectively control any structurally-induced role strains." [9]

A major technique has to do with "establishing a salient role in their particular role constellation." And this salient role is that of mother. "For example, if a conflict situation occurs between family demands and career responsibilities (e.g., the baby sitter does not show up, a child is sick, there is a parent-teacher meeting, etc.), the family demands are first on the list of the woman's priorities." A second technique is role segregation or "compartmentalization." Thus, "as much as possible the wife tries to keep her home role distant and separate from her professional role. . . . Very few female respondents [in this study] brought work home with them, although their husbands frequently did." [10] And, finally, a third technique used by the successful mothers was compromise. "The wife is careful to control the extent of her career involvement to fit in with a number of factors, including the attitude of her husband toward her profession, demands placed on the wife by her husband's profession, the ages of the children, the wife's personal philosophy on the role of the mother, and the amount of sheer physical and psychic energy she has to withstand the demands of her two roles. When one or more of these factors is out of kilter, the wife makes the necessary adjustment to manage role strain. She generally expects little and asks nothing of the family to better enable her to adjust family and career demands." [11] No wonder that "overload" is universally reported in all studies of career mothers.

Important as these "tension management techniques" may be for dealing with "role strains," they pale into insignificance compared with the basic rule, Choose the right husband.

## Husbands

There are few sociological "laws" better supported in the research literature than the "law of husband cooperation" in connection with careers for mothers. All the studies show that integrating a domestic and a professional role depends on the cooperation of one's husband. Without it, all else is impossible. The road is just too rough. And if there is positive opposition, the game is up, as any number of Hollywood careers can testify. All of the successful career mothers have done the right thing: they have selected men who could accept successful wives, for "given the married professionals' desire to integrate both traditional feminine and serious occupational goals and the reality of the current social structure, these women must find husbands who are eager or at least willing to accommodate themselves to the challenges they will face." [12]

So in all the studies the women say things like "the choice of a husband is very important in making a career possible—if you don't have a husband that supports you and is interested in your work, you can't survive," "you've got to have a *very* understanding husband," and "this really is the secret—to be careful who you marry." [13] Or, from another researcher, "the attitudes of the fathers are of major importance." [14] There is unanimous corroboration of this "law" in all studies of working mothers, non-professional as well as professional.

What kind of husbands are the right kind? In a Michigan study, "the married professionals' husbands tended to be in less power- and production-oriented, less traditionally masculine professions and also to be more egalitarian both in values and in actual role behavior at home." [15] They tended to be in the more reflective, intellectually oriented, academic-scientific occupations. They were apparently, secure enough in their own masculinity not to be threatened. They even helped with the household chores. [16]

One of the interesting things we are learning about men—or they are learning about themselves—is that they can take a good deal more than they once thought they could. They can take career wives, for example. Even more, successful career wives. And like it. "My fiancé says he could not live with me if he thought I was stagnating," says one young woman.[17] "My husband's attitudes are ideal for my working," says another. "He is proud of my accomplishments." [18] "My husband is proud of my position and believes my outside contacts make me a more interesting wife." [19] The professional wife may, in brief, add luster to the husband's own success, and be fun also. The women did not, therefore, have to fight machismo. But they did have to reciprocate.

For what husbands cannot take, at least not yet, are wives who are as successful as they are. And certainly they are far from being able to accept career wives who are more successful than they are. To this extent women must still ransom male sexuality. It is no longer necessary for women to give up careers in order to do this; but they must give up success greater than their husbands'. "Virtually the only way to be a real man in our society is to have an adequate job and earn a living. . . . The essential problem seems to be that there is a compulsive element in our pattern of masculinity which covers over an undue and unfortunate type of dependence on women." [20]

It is extremely difficult for women, usually so secure in their own sexuality, to understand the insecurity of men. It is true, as George Gilder says, that "women rarely appreciate the significance of the absence of an extended sexual identity in men. Women take their sexuality for granted, when they are aware of it at all, and assume that were it not for some cultural peculiarity, some unfortunate wrinkle in the social fabric, men too might enjoy such deep-seated sexual authenticity." This sexual insecurity puts men at a great disadvantage. "The man must be made equal by the culture; he must be given a way to make himself equal." [21] And this way is by discriminating in his favor in the work world.

Successful career mothers have long since recognized this situation. And they have therefore conformed to the second sociological "law" for successful role integration, the "two-steps-behind" law. Or, perhaps it should be called the Longfellow "law," for it was celebrated in its pristine form in one of his poems.

> I'm sorry that I spelled the word,
> I hate to go above you,
> Because, the brown eyes lower fell,
> Because, you see, I love you.

Not only must career mothers select men for husbands who can tolerate their talents, but they must also be sure to bolster the men's own self-esteem. His security must be safeguarded.

This the women could do easily for they genuinely believed their husbands to be superior. "While the married professional is certainly psychologically freer than most women to seek personal distinction, . . . she does so only on constraint, given the implicit permission of a significant man in her life space. She is free to do her very best only because she is convinced that her husband can do still better." [22] The researcher allows a moment of doubt, but only a moment: "there is no question but that the married professionals are either married to remarkable men or choose to or need to see them as a kind of Superman of the intelligentsia. They speak of their husbands as achievers, as remarkably intelligent, brilliant, creative, talented, sensitive men who can do anything." They put their husbands on a "pedestal higher than they could ever reach." [23] In this way they have no fear of success.

Corroborating this study was another one on two-career families. "He's considered one of the best people in his field and it's just, you know, a very secure position. . . . I'm just a regular, ordinary sort of college teacher." [24] It isn't necessarily easy in every case, as the dentist husband of a physician in another study commented on her questionnaire "the major problem with which intelligent and educated women must contend is vain and pretentious men." [25]

By refusing to compete with their husbands these women assure their security. "Several women said there was no sense of competition because the husband was ahead. One woman explained: 'there's no competition at all . . . .[my husband's position is] nothing I could compete with.' " [26] The researcher concludes that "at some subconscious level these people defined their situation in non-competitive terms." Thus, says one wife: "we identify very much with each other, and we look upon our work as joint work. That is, we will be in competition together against some other person, not in competition with each other." [27]

When neither a wife's acceptance of inferiority or a non-competitive definition of the situation succeeded in coping with competitive feelings, "the most commonly used technique for coping with feelings of competition was avoidance. . . . They ceased discussing the aspect of the work that gave them difficulty, they ceased doing joint work, or they ceased attending jointly social gatherings where the wife was apt to receive more attention." [28]

Another study also corroborates the importance of protecting the husband from competition.[29] It found that marriages in which the woman's career was viewed as merely an avocation or hobby, not as serious as the husband's, experienced relatively few psychological problems. When the wife's income was a serious contribution to the family, so that the husband was not clearly the breadwinner, problems increased. And when the wife's income was greater than the husband's and family reliance on it substantial, there were serious marital dislocations. In several cases the wives would have been willing to cut down on their own earnings rather than surpass their husbands.[30]

At least for the present, role integration is handicapped, though by no means foreclosed, by structural patterns. It by no means guarantees egalitarianism. For most marriages it may, in fact, still depend on non-egalitarianism.

It is one thing to pick a cooperative husband. Children are another matter. They are not so easy to choose. They have not read the books or heard the arguments. If a prime requisite for success for the professional mother is protection of the husband it is, on the other hand, mastering the feelings of guilt with regard to the children. Women who enjoy what they are doing have to pay for their satisfactions; they may not admit that their satisfactions are purchased at the expense of their children's welfare. Actually, they aren't, but more than factual evidence is needed in dealing with psychological demands.

### Children

Professional mothers are no more invulnerable than other mothers to guilt feelings. In their case feelings of guilt may even be enhanced. Until recently the anti-career attitude of the public put the professional mother and her children on the spot. If her children showed even the normal mishaps of development, the accusing finger was pointed at her. And, further, the fact that she liked her career added to her vulnerability; her success had to mean that her children suffered.

One reported way to deal with potential guilt feelings was to note how awful a mother the woman would be if she had to stay home with her children all the time. "I told myself—and still tell myself—that if I had stayed home and not done what I did, I would have been one of those bloody awful martyred mothers who sat around all the rest of her life seeing her children as the cross to which she has been nailed. There is nothing more awful than that, and that is the way I would have felt.[31] The converse of this has also been reported, that the woman enjoys her children more because she does not have to be with them all day long. "I find that I enjoy the children a lot more because I am working. I don't feel confined with them like I did with the first child." [32] Or, "if I felt the children were being harmed, this would be the one thing that would keep me from working. I do feel, however, that my being away from the children part of the time makes me enjoy being with them all the more." [33]

Allied to this method of dealing with potential guilt feelings was one that stated that the woman felt she was a better mother precisely because she had a career. Whatever the research literature may say about the effect on children of working mothers, the professionally employed women see their work as making *"them* better mothers than they otherwise would have been." [34] An often reported reason for considering themselves better mothers because they had careers was that the children were protected from over-involvement by the mother. "I am a better mother because I work and can expend my energies on something other than the over-mothering of my children." [35] The career mothers did not want to live through their children, as did so many other mothers.[36] One woman who had mended her ways reported that in her first marriage she had thought motherhood-career had to be an either-or thing. As a result she had "over invested in my child." [37] Now she had learned better; she could be a better mother because of her professional career.

From the clinical couch comes a case illustrating a situation in which a woman could only become a mother if or when she also had a career. Helene Deutsch gives us the story of a woman, suicidal in her youth, who many years after analysis, now a mother, had become an outstanding physicist. Before therapy she had been unable to reconcile her feminine infantilism or dependency with her desire for motherhood; but after analysis she was able to restructure her ego in order to handle the difficulty. "Her capacity for accomplishments in her work could now be used as a defensive power toward the infantile form of her femininity, the masochistic part of which was not and could not be mastered completely in analysis. A glance at her postanalytic life shows that she was able to take the role of a wife and mother only when she felt secure in the other role, that of an active career woman. To her, femininity was and is the degradation to the passive, slavish role of her mother. She can accept the reality of her marriage and her motherhood only on her own terms: by opposing defensively her femininity with work and intellectual life." [38] Without attributing bizarre family backgrounds to them, we can all recognize women like this one. They are perfectly normal; we do not have to "explain" them. They are good and happy mothers as long as they do not have to be mothers exclusively, as long as they can continue in their professions. Deprived of these satisfactions, the demands of motherhood become intolerable to them.

Career mothers also handle their susceptibility to guilt feelings by means of the way they conceive of their role as mothers. "Despite the married professional's potential susceptibility to guilt and self-recrimination with regard to how their careers might affect their children, these women maintain a very positive attitude toward work . . . [while holding] firmly to an ideology of child rearing that not only allows but supports their career commitments." [39] The working mother, as distinguished from the career mother, has relatively little psychological work to do to integrate her roles. She is still doing motherwork, only of a different kind; her job at the typist's pool is just part of her job as mother; she is earning the money to help with the children's needs. [40] The career mother requires a slightly more sophisticated approach. She cannot say that her earnings are needed for her children's essentials. It is not the money she earns but her attitude toward work and her ideology of child rearing that help integrate the roles.

The conception the women had of the mother role was reflected in the qualities they considered important in their children. Professional mothers in one study, for example, tended to emphasize the importance of independence and discipline, non-professional women, of protectiveness and empathy, suggesting a less sentimental if not more tough-minded approach. [41] They are equally "good" mothers but by differing criteria. Both act according to the way they define the child's best interests. In both cases, the child's best interests are seen to coincide with the mother's. In projective tests, the stories dealing with mother-child relations told by the professional mothers struck the researcher "as somewhat more matter-of-fact, distant or intellectualized, more measured and even self-conscious in tone, at times approaching a kind of dry tongue-in-cheek as they view motherhood both very personally from an inside seat and from a more remote perspective, a shifting in focus that may mirror their own daily moves in and out of the role." [42] The role of mother, according to the implied conception disclosed in these stories, should not be so all-encompassing as to preclude an objective perspective.

The professional mothers' conception of their role did not even remotely follow the Victorian model. "In her relations, she is not at all self-sacrificing. . . . she is even somewhat wary of compromises." [43] In discussing the impact of child rearing on a woman's life, the professional mother in this study hardly mentioned self-sacrifice. "That is not to say that the married professionals unrealistically romanticize maternity; they don't lose sight of the hard work and demands children place on a mother. But they almost never respond by joyfully picking up the yoke and extolling the virtues of self-sacrifice." [44] If they did not permit their maternal commitments to interfere with their professional ones, neither did they permit their professional commitments to have deleterious effects on their performance of the maternal role. This nice balance of commitments was "not a rejection or separation from parental values but rather an internalization and further development of them." [45]

The allocation of time plays an especially important part in the career mother's conception of her role. A great deal is made of the quality rather than the amount of time spent with children. Mothers make a point of devoting their undivided attention to their children in the limited amount of time they have. One way to manage, they reported, is to be meticulous in scheduling time. "I try to keep the hours from 4:00 to 6:00 open for the family," "I'm available from 2:30 until my daughter goes to bed," and "from 6:00 until the time the children go to sleep, which is 9:00 or later, I'm a full-time mother." [46] "I spend more actual time with my children than my non-working neighbors who are very active in volunteer work." [47] If anything has to be given up for lack of time it is not child-related activities. Different women give up different activities: they may be social life, the creative arts, gardening, leisure-time reading, a smoothly-run house, or community involvement.

Amusing—to observers if not always to participants—consequences may ensue when the role-segregation policy cannot be implemented, when, for example, a woman must be both professional and mother at the same time, i.e. at the company or department picnic where families are invited. The children are privileged to make demands on her that her subordinates on the job are not. They can put her in a ridiculous position vis-à-vis her employees or subordinates. The next time she discusses their work with them they will remember her buttoning up the panties of a four-year-old little boy. Or, more seriously, when professional colleagues drop by at home and the children naggingly insist on priority of attention and she feels she owes it to them to read to them as usual but still must firm up the agenda for tomorrow morning's critical meeting with the men on a site visit from Washington, her situation can be untenable. Some bear the anomaly with resignation—they are accustomed to role anomalies, to the uncertainty people feel about which role takes priority, wife or professional—and some actually enjoy the in-and-out pattern of their lives. The children of high-powered women have no such uncertainty about their mothers. They do not even know that their mothers are special. They run to her at the office just as they do at home, as though she were just any mother. Doesn't *every*one's mother have an office with lots of people around?

Some professional mothers make a point of *not* segregating their roles. They take their children with them on trips, to conferences, to committee meetings. Often to the annoyance of their colleagues who, if they are sympathetic, pretend to ignore the annoying intrusion of the children, and if they are not, avoid contact with the women altogether.

These, it must be emphasized, are not rejecting mothers. No one who has watched the serious concern they show for their children can accuse them of neglect. They find as much pleasure as other women in motherhood, if not more. They have read the books but are not cowed by them. They believe they are better mothers when they have relief from fulltime attention to their children and they think it is better for their children as well. Without their work they could become resentful, sullen, angry, depressed.

The prime requisite for successful role integration is, then, protecting the husband in his role and overcoming feelings of guilt with respect to the children. They were summarized succinctly by one informant with whom, we are assured, all the others would have heartily agreed:

I think it is perfectly possible to combine a profession and marriage—as long as you have these basic premises: as long as the man is not threatened by the woman's capabilities and achievements; as long as he sees it as adding to his stature and not as diminishing it; as long as a woman has worked out her own role as a mother; and as long as she is not ambivalent about her roles. If a woman feels secure about leaving her children with a housekeeper and feels she is a better mother because of it, there is nothing intrinsically difficult about it.[48]

### Momism in Reverse

One of the hazards the professional mother is less susceptible to than is the non-employed mother is the hazard of over-involvement with her children. This can be a not inconsiderable plus.[49] Unfriendly critics might say that the way career mothers define their role as mother may simply be a way of making a virtue of necessity. They do not have the time to become over-involved.

Still, one important rule for integrating the two roles remains giving priority to the children. And all the professional mothers profess adherence to it. Well and good. The question does arise, however, when does this priority cease to be required. Does it go on forever? If not, when does it end? When they are small, children come to expect first claim on their mothers, career or no career. How long may they legitimately continue to make this claim? How about the claim on father? Now, that's different. Here, for example, are grown children—daughters in these cases— who resent it if their mothers do not set aside professional obligations in their favor.

The daughter of a professional woman asks her mother to meet her plane when she comes home from college for a visit. It so happens that the mother has a professional obligation at that particular time and cannot comply; she says she will pay for a taxicab. The daughter accuses her of not meeting her maternal obligations, of not having her priorities in order. When the mother asks if the father had given the same reason—professional obligations—for not meeting the plane, would she have given the same reply? No, of course not. That's different. Or still another young woman who had "deserted"—her mother's term—her mother by marrying out of the family's faith and leaving the country, calls on her mother to stay with her for several weeks when her baby arrives. The mother replies she would be glad to come for a weekend when she could get off because she did want to see the baby but she could not leave her job at that particular time. She would, however, be glad to pay for the services of a nurse. The daughter accuses her mother of trying to buy her off. Never a word about the father.

Far more serious was the case of the woman almost destroyed by the demands of her daughter. In her late forties, Mary Stone had just declared her independence from bondage to her daughter's needs. She had bought a Jaguar. Money that had been mortgaged for years to care for the problem-plagued daughter was now being re-channeled into the new car. The mother was exhilarated but frightened by what she had done. The daughter, who had been a source of family distress for no less than ten years, had reached the age of eighteen. She had been in and out of schools and treatment centers and clinics for several years and had left home, ultimately, just a year ago. Now she was pregnant, unmarried, living with a friend on welfare. Mary Stone, a proud woman, was able for the first time to say finally, Enough. She was still not free enough, though, to accept the situation openly, and she sought the shelter of secrecy from the world at large. Despite years of anguish, despite years invested in family therapy that might well have been invested in furthering her own professional training, despite bills that used up incredible amounts of money, she still felt guilt, shame, and humiliation. Her husband suffered too, but not in his professional self-esteem. His share in the burden of guilt was lighter. For the professional mother more than the professional father bears the onus of parental failure. Any defect, any failure, any short-fall is attributed to her career, and she is punished for it. There may not be much choice between demanding mothers and demanding children. So far we have heard less about the first than the second. For the present, the scale weighs heavily against the Mom.

## Rewards and Challenges

Having paid the price of admission, the rewards for the professional mothers are great. Not the least of them is a high level of self-esteem. Professional mothers are almost blatantly pleased with themselves and the lives they live. They have the best of all worlds. "The married professional woman is basically satisfied with life the way she lives it. Among the women we interviewed, most found being a wife and a mother very satisfying and taking precedence over their professional lives. . . . They seem quite satisfied with their lot." [50] And other studies corroborate these happy findings:

> Active and self-assured, she maintains a complex personal integration based on a high level of energy and the experience of work and mastery as pleasurable and intrinsically gratifying rather than extrinsically motivated or externally compelled. She works not because she has to or feels she ought to but because she wants to and very much enjoys what she does. . . . Working regularly provides her with a solid day-by-day framework that encourages productivity and consequently enhances her esteem.[51]

These women seem to be gestating a future that bodes well for motherhood.

Yet they are being challenged today on two sides. On one, women who find homemaking completely rewarding are becoming increasingly vocal in their resentment for the kudos heaped on the professional mother [52] and, on the other, feminists are challenging the structural hurdles these women are forced to jump, hurdles which mean that only the most vigorous and hardy can make the grade. Why should it be true that "the 'difficulties of combining the career (sic) of marriage and motherhood with a career as a scholar and teacher' will be beyond the physical and mental energies of all but the 'exceptional woman' (but never, of course, of men, who are presumed to spend no time at all being husbands, and fathers)." [53] For it does seem to be true that the selective processes involved are more drastic among mothers than fathers.[54] Even the most successful admit that the course can be rough:

> These married professional women, while relatively unswerving in their occupational commitment, do make it clear that they have chosen a difficult albeit an extremely rewarding life for themselves. They seem intensely involved with and gratified by both work and family commitments, although they are sometimes assailed by doubts about their competence on both fronts. Finally, they are quite open about how hard it sometimes seems and how pressed for time they feel. While they do not seem overwhelmed and by no means seem willing to give up their role, one senses their fervent wish that things would somehow change to make life more manageable for

women who refuse to forego either achievement strivings or the joys and tribulations of womanhood complete with marriage and children.[55]

It is the acceptance of this high price that feminists object to, the acceptance of less than equality in their marriages, the acceptance of the entire bill for the social costs of motherhood. There is, thus, creeping into the literature a defensiveness of their alleged Aunt Tabbyism.

> Despite cries from radical feminists for the complete "emancipation" of women, most of our respondents showed no real desire for such emancipation. Their assertion is strong that, in light of our contemporary social structure, the family must come first for a woman. Call them Aunt Tabbys if you will, but they seem quite satisfied with their lot.[56]

The operant words are "in light of our contemporary social structure."

The feminists are not challenging the basic rule for the professional mother, namely that the family must come first. They are asking why it should not come first for fathers too. Why are not men's two roles equally relevant? They are challenging the two-role concept which has been accepted without challenge for a generation. When the two-role concept had been recognized at mid-century it had, in fact, been viewed as an advance in thinking about women.[57] President Kennedy had embraced it; the report of his Commission on the Status of Women had embraced it. Today feminists are repudiating some of its basic assumptions:

> [One] fundamental assumption of the Report was that, notwithstanding women's dual role, every obstacle to their full participation in society must be removed. Today's feminists would argue that in fact these two assumptions are contradictory: the barriers against women's *full* participation in society cannot be removed until and unless men (and society at large) share equally with women the responsibilities of homemaking and child rearing.[58]

### Men's Two Roles: The Expansion of Fatherhood

Quite aside from the feminist argument there has been a growing recognition that children deserve more time and attention from their fathers, that the removal of the father from the home by industrialization and urbanization was as serious as the removal of the mother. As one newspaper columnist put it, "for the past year or so, like goose feathers floating from ripped pillows, small weightless bits of news have been in the air that tell us something about the state of American fatherhood." [59] He cites the cases of Joe Garagiola, Weeb Ewbank, and Alan King, all of whom have gone on record as wanting to put more time into their obligations as fathers. But these men are only "goose feathers floating from ripped pillows, small weightless bits of news," news precisely because they are so unusual. "Many other American fathers have their optic nerves trained to greater visions; their obligations to their children are much less important than their obligations of time and energy to the company, a cause or some vague goal about 'getting ahead in the world.' These fathers sing all the right notes about loving their children, but it is often love at a distance. In between is a space that the children see all too well, and may want to close. But they can't because their fathers are absent most of the time." [60]

Other information suggests that industry itself is being offered advice on how to help top executives deal with the problems of fatherhood. They are to be helped to integrate *their* father and professional roles. Research Institute of America, Inc., is now offering—at $3.00 a month—a periodical, *Personal Report,* which will provide executives with "some insight in dealing with children who are lax with their studies. . . . ideas on how to deal with children who you feel have dating problems. . . . approaches to use with youngsters who downgrade the 'establishment' they claim you belong to. . . . plus general knowledge on drugs and other 'hang-ups' some youngsters claim as 'doing their thing'—until it gets out of hand." Mothers have been asking fathers to provide this kind of help for a long time. But *Personal Report* does not have the family in mind. It promises to provide executives with "novel ways to get understanding from family members when you must spend long hours at the office . . . or miss an occasional family function." The job still takes precedence. Women will be justified in looking this gift horse in the mouth and counting every single tooth. It comes from a profit-making corporation selling its no-holds-barred services to executives to help them "increase productivity and profits by improving interpersonal skills." [61] It is peddled to executives not as a way to back mothers up but as a way to get mothers off their backs in as acceptable a way as possible. It is certainly a far cry from what young women have in mind.

However helpful the husband may be and however successful the "tension-management" devices used, it is still true that, like wives in general, the professional mother makes the accommodations that have to be made to assure a well-run household. Young women now entering the scene want more than merely supportive husbands. They want fatherhood itself expanded. The sharing of the provider role by the mother is felt to call for a sharing of the parental role by the father in the child-care and socializing function.[62]

Many of the younger fathers see nothing untoward in this idea. In the cooperative child-care arrangements set up by the younger, less affluent members of a professional association at their annual meetings, a lively bunch of small children had a wonderful time under the casual, not-too-watchful eyes of men and women volunteers. At the official child-care facility set up by the association itself upon the urgent request of a women's caucus, one child of an affluent family played forlornly by herself with elegant toys under the watchful eyes of an expensive baby-sitter. A number of morals could be drawn from this cautionary tale. The most relevant one here is that among younger, if not older, men there is acceptance of the fact that fatherhood has its responsibilities too.

Role sharing [63] does not, of course, mean role reversal; it does not mean that the mother takes over the provider role exclusively and the father the child-care role. Nor is role sharing the same as mere helping. A considerable number of fathers are willing to help their wives. They will give an infant a bottle; they will even change a diaper. They will carry the baby in its shoulder pack. They will baby-sit several evenings a week. But these contributions—not to be undervalued as helping wives to bear their load— are not the same as role sharing, not the same as sharing responsibility, and it is the responsibilities of the mother role that make integrating it with the worker role so difficult. Just helping, which does not relieve the mother of any of her responsibilities, is therefore not enough. A helper can relieve the mother but can also renege or cop out or not show up or withdraw the help. Making sure the service is performed can be as wearing as performing it oneself. And being held responsible for its actual performance is the hardest part of all. It is the working mother rather than the father who is called when an emergency arises. Thus even though a mother may be practicing her profession in the hospital or at the bar, she is also performing the work of assuming responsibility for whatever it is that is happening at home. True role sharing would mean that the working father was as responsible as the working mother for seeing that what needed doing was getting done.

In some modern relationships, the details of role sharing are incorporated in a contract and this seems to be a wave of the future. Although the idea of marriage contracts is a fairly old one, for the most part they have had to do with property [64] or with legal rights.[65] In the current contracts it is the division of responsibilities that is dealt with. One example that has invited a considerable amount of attention is that of the Shulman's which appeared in a popular women's magazine in 1971.[66] The first part stated the principles on which the contract was based, including the following: the work that brings in more money is not for that reason more valuable; each partner has equal right to her/his own time, work, value, choices; both parents must share all responsibility for the care of children and home; and deviation from a 50–50 sharing may call for periodic or occasional revision of the schedule. So far as that particular marriage was concerned, the success was unequivocal. It changed the lives of both partners and improved the quality of all their family relationships. "One day, after it had been in effect for only four months our daughter said to my husband, 'you know, Daddy, I used to love Mommy more than you, but now I love you both the same.' "After a month or two the contract was put away in a drawer, no longer necessary.

The popularity of this idea is attested to by the fact that his-and-her work-charts for fifty-two weeks are now available as gifts: for ten dollars you can get B-H Silk Screen Design to make up a pad of fifty-two sheets of brown butcher paper imprinted with black ink. For each week there is a list of chores—bed, garbage, cooking, car, bills, shopping, laundry, heavy cleaning, light cleaning, plants-and-pet-care—and a column for him and one for her.[67] Child-care could be added.

There are, of course, many ways to design a role-sharing plan. It does not have to be on a 50–50 basis. If there are clear-cut preferences by each partner for one role or the other, there is little difficulty for the couples themselves. Difficulties arise from the community when or if there is a reversed role preference. Problems arise for the partners themselves when both prefer or reject the same role. In such cases, it would seem that justice requires both to share both the preferred and the rejected role according to some principle that takes into account the relative strength of each one's preferences.

The benefits for both father and child have been recognized by observers who have long bemoaned the isolation of men from their children. But little has been done to facilitate participation by the father. Sweden is farthest along in attempts to implement this line of thought.[68]

But it is the benefits for the woman attempting to integrate her roles that are most appealing. For her it looks utopian:

> The cooperation of men and women in their marriages and in their work would probably be the most Utopian solution of all. If the society at large could break free of the rigid form of the working day and kick the habit of hiring only full-time workers, many families could manage two careers and family life with a minimum of outside help. . . . The husband's sharing of all tasks on an informal shift system allowed the women to work. Women finally entering the mainstream of American life might be the beginning of a transformation of work in our society into a more meaningful, individualized activity.[69]

### Dissenting Voices: The Specter of Androgyny

There is no intrinsic reason why the worker and the mother roles of women cannot be integrated without "de-sexing" the women or "feminizing" their work. Still there is resistance to the idea of shared roles, the one way that is most auspicious for integrating women's two roles. A judge's dictum that "fathers don't make good mothers" headlines a newspaper story of a California case in which a father asked for the custody of his children in a divorce case. The father's request was denied.[70] A New York lawyer is quoted as saying that "there is an enormous bias in favor of the mother. . . . Judges can't imagine a man regularly diapering a baby." [71]

Nor, apparently, can a great many other people. Bruno Bettelheim, for example, is of the opinion that:

> . . . parents should not be the same either in their personality or in the roles they play. They provide the pool of resources from which the child chooses those things he wishes to integrate and internalize into himself. If the complementation of the parents is right, it makes for the right tensions, challenges,

and authority to provide the child with a wide range of choices which, when combined with his own genetic endowment, emerge in a unique personality. If the complementation is not right, if the tensions and challenges are destructive, or if they do not exist, then the child will emerge without a well-defined personality or with a destructive one.[72]

Clinicians come up with horrendous conclusions about the "right" and "wrong" complementation. One team of psychiatrists, for example, reported dire results when parents shared roles. They divided the ninety-six families in their study into four categories: "the balanced family [42 percent] . . . in which the husband took responsibility for at least 18 percent of the tasks and shared at least another 15 percent with his wife. . . . The sharing family [36 percent] . . . in which the father's participation was almost entirely on a sharing level; a family was placed in this category if the father took responsibility for less than 18 percent of the tasks and shared more than 15 percent of them; usually these fathers took responsibility for about 12 percent and shared over 33 percent of the tasks; the distinctive mark of this type of family was lack of role differentiation, or role confusion. . . . The traditional family [16 percent] . . . in which the father participated in almost no household tasks; he took responsibility for less than 18 percent and shared less than 15 percent of the tasks, ordinarily . . . about 16 percent and . . . 10 percent. . . . The unconventional family [7 percent] . . . in which the father did as much as the mother, or more. . . . they may have reversed the traditional roles." [73]

In line with the documentable male bias of clinicians,[74] these researchers found horrendous results for children in all but the balanced families. The worst off were children in unconventional families; all of them were disturbed. Next worst off were those in the traditional family; two-thirds were disturbed. But even in the sharing family over half were disturbed. In fairness to the authors it should be noted that they were modest in their claims for the validity of their measures of emotional health. They themselves raise questions "about the degree to which the study validates its criteria of emotional health." [75] They therefore made no claims of validity and restricted themselves to gross evaluations of emotional health and illness.

We see in these dissenting voices the myth of family structure that lingers in our thinking about the roles of fathers and mothers.

It reflects, however unclearly, the nostalgic image of the Victorian model. Here we have the stern but just father, symbol of strength and power, the disciplinarian, the one who supplies strength and firmness to the family. And his "opposite," the tender, ever-loving mother to whom mercy is more important than justice, the nurturer, the tender healer of hurts and so on and on. To blur these differences can only be deleterious to the child.

### The Vision of Androgyny

In direct opposition to those who see androgyny as a sinister specter are those who see it as a goal to be aspired to. "An androgynous conception of sex role means that each sex will cultivate some of the characteristics usually associated with the other in traditional sex role definitions." [76] Our fear of androgyny results from the way we conceive of the sexes. We think of them as opposites and any change must therefore automatically constitute a reversal.

We have fallen into a basic error. If one sex is aggressive, the other must be passive; if one is B the other must be A. Since every desirable quality in either sex must, according to this view, imply its opposite—an undesirable quality—in the other, we begin with stereotypes. We mutilate personalities trying to make them fit these stereotypes. We insist that each sex specialize in only one set of virtues. Rather than seek complete, wholesome, non-mutilated personalities that can have both "masculine" and "feminine" virtues—be just and merciful as the occasion demands or be stern and gentle, be healer and disciplinarian—we assign one set of virtues exclusively to the father and another exclusively to the mother. They must complement rather than supplement one another, be opposites rather than merely different. A "supplement" adds something to supply a deficit: perhaps the father is not stern enough or even absent; the "opposite sex" or complementary theory makes no provision for the mother's supplying the deficit; she may not be stern. The mother is not tender enough; the stereotype does not permit the father to make up for this deficit; he may not be tender.

Far more realistic than the stereotype-blinded California judge was the Virginia court which made a year-old infant the ward of a divorced physician, a forty-one-year-old father of a daughter of twelve. He had kept one of his patients, an ailing infant alive all her life and now, when the parents were divorced and no longer able to bear the responsibility, he was taking over. He has "maids and babysitters I specially trained to care for her. I used to take her to work once in a while. I had a folding playpen in my office. I just do it because I do it. You never know, but I feel if she stays with me she'll grow up and go to college and get married and hopefully by then we'll have a cure. I hope I don't prove myself wrong. I'd die of heartbreak." [77] Aspersions on his masculinity anyone?

Actually we do not accept the fallacy of the "opposite sex" conceptualization. In a moving picture, *Sounder,* that achieved award-winning status in 1973 the black father was tender and gentle with his family, as well as aggressive enough to steal to feed them; the mother was strong and aggressive in behalf of her children and her imprisoned husband, as well as tender and gentle with them. Their different bodies in no way precluded their being both tender and strong. There was no loss of stature as human beings in either case. Nor were the children disturbed in the sense of lacking in mental or emotional strength. We admired them all. The family had the "right tensions, challenges, and authority" that Bettelheim calls for.

The popularity of this film reveals a longing in the public for just such heroes and heroines, for men and women who do not specialize in just one set of virtues but who, instead, encompass many. We want fathers who can be gentle and tender; we want mothers who can be strong and aggressive. And these are the kinds we are going to get. The California judge who declared that fathers did not make good mothers is fighting a rear-guard action. The trend of the times seems to be against him. Some of our best mothers will be fathers in the future, as, indeed, many already are.

In almost two-fifths of contested divorce cases, custody is given to fathers, for "recent cultural changes in American society have weakened the stereotype of the woman as the homemaker and the man as the provider." [78] And two sociologists looking into the future of sex characteristics foresee a "softening of gender identity lines" which will have the effect of rendering men "more capable of responding positively to changes in women's roles as they occur." [79] It will be easier and easier for professional women to find the kinds of husbands they need to help them integrate their mother and their worker roles and the husbands will contribute more than mere financial support.

The gifted mothers who pursue professional careers represent only a relatively small proportion of all working mothers who are gestating the future. Far more are simply mothers who have jobs. For them the worker role can be easily assimilated to the mother role; as earners they can do more for their children than as home-bodies.

## CHAPTER TEN

# The Working Mother

## Mothers with Jobs

Although professional mothers constitute only about a fifth of all working mothers,[1] they have attracted a disproportionate amount of research attention. Mothers with jobs are different from career mothers in many respects. Among the former at least two types are usually distinguished, one type being "female heads of households," [2] especially the subsidized working mothers on welfare rolls and, more especially, the black mothers on welfare rolls. The issues they raise are fundamental and crucial and have enormous relevance for the future of motherhood. In fact, these women are having as much impact on our thinking about motherhood as are the career women.[3] The other type would be the mothers with jobs. They are part of that great non-homogeneous population that we usually bracket together as "the middle class," or as "middle America." Some of them verge close to the career-woman category, others to the lower class. Only the delineation of overall trends is aimed at here, certainly not detailed precision. The mothers with jobs are for the most part relatively conservative in their conceptions of the mother role and in their family relationships in general. But even in this respect they are changing. These women are important not as harbingers of the future but as illustrations of how the future is creeping up on us.

These mothers are probably in clerical and sales occupations.[4] Many are from ethnic backgrounds, being perhaps only a generation or two away from the immigrant generation. Although they themselves are likely to be white-collar workers—about a third, in fact, are in clerical positions—they may be married to blue-collar workers, and they have a little more schooling, at least through high-school, than their husbands. They read such periodicals as *Redbook, McCall's, Ladies' Home Journal,* movie and confessional magazines.[5] They are the women we meet in the advertisements on television. In fact, the advertisements themselves change as the women change. Although these mothers are conservative, they are no more immune to the temper of the times than are the career mothers or the welfare mothers.

### "Identity Crisis"

There is something both snobbish and jarring in the inappropriateness of so much of the theorizing on female development. Somehow or other the girls who were to become mothers with jobs have escaped the analysts' scalpel. Their "identity crises" have gone unreported. There was an implicit assumption that perhaps they had none. The course of their life was so clearly marked out for them that there was no occasion for a crisis.

When Erik Erikson studied the development of women he saw their achievement of "identity" in terms of their relations to men. He saw women only as mothers and female development in terms of dependency. He said that the identity of women is achieved when they commit themselves to the future father of their children. "The stage of life crucial for the emergence of an integrated female identity is the step from youth to maturity, the stage when the young woman, whatever her work career, relinquishes the care received from the parental family in order to commit herself to the love of a stranger and to the care to be given to his and her offspring." [6] She transfers her dependency from her parents to her husband, not only psychological dependency but also economic dependency. "Much of a young woman's identity is already defined in her kind of attractiveness and in the selective nature of her search for the man (or men) by whom she wishes to be sought." [7] Finis. Room was later made for the college woman; she was given a "moratorium" so that she could look around the world during four years of college. Career women could indulge in having identity crises. But most women had their identities prescribed for them. The core problem of female identity was a "biological, psychological, and ethical commitment to take care of human infancy." [8]

But "identity crises" are contagious. Lest, therefore, it be supposed that only educated or sophisticated women undergo such crises, the case of a reader of *True Love*, whose readership is presumably made up of working-class women, usually reported as traditional in orientation, is presented to show that even these women were not immune to such crises.

> Today's woman thinks and knows she has a right to her own thoughts. She knows she has a right to her own pursuits and endeavors. She knows she has a right to self-realize. She knows motherhood is not all bliss, and that to be a better mother she needs to be a well-rounded person. . . . She does not feel guilty for wanting to enjoy her life, to enjoy sex, to enjoy the pursuit of womanhood toward personhood. . . . She's confused about her level of aspiration. . . . Motherhood's not always as clean and sweet as the ads show. . . . Her husband doesn't know what she's talking about. She can get a job, return to school (avoid the issue), and/or begin to self-fulfill. No matter what she chooses, it'll mean changes. She's not prepared for the real world. But then the real world is unprepared for her reality. . . . She has trouble making decisions on her own authority and following through on them with security. . . . She's reacting the way anyone does when *he* realizes how much *he's* let *himself* be had. . . . She would have a great cultural weight lifted from her shoulders if some qualified "male-business-habituated" female authority would come along to tell her that all the subtle truths she feels about being a woman, and subtly denies herself, are really true.[9]

At the present time quite a few "male-business-habituated" females are, in fact, telling her that the truths she feels about being a woman are valid. The point is that even traditional women in middle America are having "identity crises." The old scripts for the role of mother are no longer as clear-cut as they once were.

The script forbade taking a job while the children were still preschoolers. But room was increasingly being made for mothers with school-age children to take jobs. In one study of fifty-eight blue-collar marriages, researched in the late fifties the change was already notable:

> The majority of the men and women interviewed believed that the wife's place is "in the home," but this generally held view obscures the great distance that they have traveled from

the traditional attitude. The questions that in the past aroused indignation—"Should a married woman work?" or "Should a mother of teenagers work?"—are now discussed calmly. The current debate about the employment of wives centers on the children, and it is the working mother of younger children who is attacked.[10]

The old shibboleths were being eroded: "if a woman has very young children and goes to work, then that's for bread and butter and people might feel sorry for her. But if the children are older, say in the fifth grade or so, and she works part-time, they know it is just for the extras, and that's nothing against her husband." [11]

As long as the discussion of labor-force participation applied primarily to unmarried women, it touched the matter of motherhood only tangentially. When the discussion turned to working wives, it quickly approached effects on motherhood. By the late 1960s, for quite extraneous reasons related to mothers on welfare rolls as well as to the new feminist movement, the discussion had turned to working mothers.[12] Presently, though popular polls still show the persistence of the woman's-place-is-in-the-home ideology, women themselves are "voting with their feet," middle-American mothers along with the others.

By the time the ratio between working and non-working women in middle motherhood—the period when their younger children were of school age—approached equality, the temper of the discussion of woman's place began to change drastically. Until then the balance had favored the women who remained out of the labor force. By the late 1960s the balance was beginning to tip.[13] Now women who did not enter the labor force began to feel that they were on the defensive.

> Prejudices against employing married women, although still persisting in some quarters, are on the wane, and the practice of going out to work, at least part-time, has become so widespread among women in their thirties and forties, irrespective of social class, that those who fail to do so now almost have to give an explanation for staying at home.[14]

And some women who had no desire to enter the labor force felt guilty if they did not do so to add to the family income,[15] especially since they were reported to be much in demand. "Mothers whose children have reached school age or are in their teens, constitute a labour force whose incorporation into the labour market would be a distinct benefit to society. The measurable costs in the form of retraining and part-time work seem small in comparison. Measures are being taken to stimulate labour market participation by this group." [16] Such pressures are not easy to resist and increasing numbers did take jobs.

It is easier for the mother with a job to integrate her two roles than it is for the career mother. In fact, the worker role tends to be primarily an extension of the mother role.[17] "If asked why they work, there is a good chance they would say that they are supplementing family income, to provide their children with a college education, or to help buy or furnish a new home, or to pay for an additional car." [18] Or even perhaps to help a son get established in his career or in marriage. There is little psychological turmoil. The working mother has little if any sense of guilt; [19] after all, she is working for the sake of her family as mothers have done from time immemorial. The kind of work she does in the labor force is not coveted by men; she is no one's competitor; she is needed in the offices, hospitals, and restaurants. She is therefore in an easier psychological spot than the career woman, who speaks a different language. More remarkably, she has better mental health even than the housewives who remain at home.[20]

This does not mean that she is necessarily in an easier physical spot. By no means. Very few concessions are made to the double load she carries, for of course she is still responsible for the household. Still, many women are willing to undertake the extra load. There are many incentives, reasons, rationalizations, justifications, or causes that are inferred or explicitly stated to explain their willingness.

## Job As Surrogate for Child Care

Labor-force participation is sometimes motivated by a need to fill the void left by the diminishing demands of child-care. In the era of the feminine mystique it had been found that women were having all those fourth, fifth, and sixth babies precisely in order to fill the void in their lives left when the last child entered school. Jobs do serve as child surrogates for some women.[21] Such a motivation may be viewed as "self expression" by default. It was recognition of this fact that led to the more or less deliberate use of positive work psychology by antinatalists to forestall more babies at this critical juncture. Encouraging mothers to enter the labor force had once been seen as a way to get a cheap labor supply; it was now viewed as a profitable way to achieve a lowered birth rate.

### Money

So strong has been the bias in the past against female employment outside the home for any other reason than the monetary that the only acceptable one for taking a job has been remuneration. Thus researchers who have accumulated a sizeable literature on why women work always pay their respects to money as a major motive. If women are obliged for any reason to support themselves, that would excuse their going to work, as would the fact that their husbands could not supply a good enough income. Also if a woman had dependents she was responsible for, here too working was acceptable. But any woman living with a husband who had an income capable of supporting her at even a modest level was not supposed to take a job.

But the money she earned was to expand the family income; it was certainly not for personal frivolities. Some of the monetary reasons given by mothers for entering the labor force have been: a drop in the husband's income, payment of family debts, payment for credit purchases, hospital bills. Sometimes the monetary "need" expanded dramatically to include dancing or music lessons for children, or personal travel, or putting them through college. All these reasons were justifiable because these expenses were for family welfare. "Pin money" was sometimes given as a reason. Since mothers who worked partly because they wanted to be in the mainstream, to achieve at least a modicum of independence, to escape the isolation of the household, were so disapproved of, these reasons tended not to show up in the research. Mothers hesitated to admit them to the researchers.

But times are changing. Need for money may have been the most respectable reason for mothers to give the researchers when asked to explain why they were in the labor force. But increasingly other reasons are becoming respectable.

### Good for Husbands

In the Victorian model, a working wife was a symbol of male failure. No self-respecting husband would tolerate having his wife "work" because that would reflect on him. That old pattern of thought is now in process of attrition and will certainly not continue long into the future. A Harris Poll taken in 1971 reported more married men (41 percent) than married women (38 percent), more working-class than upper-middle class women to be enthusiastic for women's liberation.[22] Little by little it was becoming clear that the income contributed to the family by women in the labor force was liberating to husbands. And there was no disgrace or humiliation associated with it. Men who have wives who can contribute to family income have more options; they can support longer periods of unemployment.

> The worker who loses his job will not feel the pressure to get work immediately if his unemployment compensation can be supplemented by his wife's earnings. The worker facing a cutback in overtime may be less eager to moonlight if his wife can bring in additional income from part-time work. In fact, over the past two years the duration of unemployment among married men has averaged significantly longer than among single men; and the percentage of married men who have remained unemployed for over fifteen weeks has consistently exceeded the figure for single men. Clearly, the family can withstand economic hardship, despite unemployment for the "breadwinner," by means of the earnings of working wives.[23]

The situation differs from the past when the working wife reflected the failure of her husband; the present day employment of women spares him humiliation.

It does even more. The man who wishes to change his job or even his career, feels freer to do so when there is a wife's income to back him up. "Working women have enabled men to drop in and out of the labor force when . . . educational opportunity presents itself or seems reasonable to pursue." [24] If the increased education improves the husband's earning power, it facilitates upward mobility.

In recent years a new twist has appeared. The worker role, though still oriented toward the husband, has a different slant. A woman writes in a Reader's Exchange in a metropolitan newspaper that developing an identity of her own by taking a job "will allow her husband to develop interests he has of his own, without suffering guilt." [25] A wife's dependencies, psychological in this instance, could become a bore to her husband, a burden. Entering the labor force was a way of releasing him from it. A popular journal reaffirms this point of view. "If years of marriage have nar-

rowed your interests . . . maybe it's time to get a part-time job.
. . . Develop another side of yourself. You'll be less dependent on
your husband." [26]

The mother with a job is relieved of the "two-steps-behind"
rule. Though she is more likely than her husband to be a high-
school graduate, more likely than he to be in a white-collar job,
there is little chance that she will ever surpass him occupa-
tionally. Or, if in the same occupation, little chance she will receive equal pay. Among men in sales work, almost half have wives
in clerical occupations, and most of them are not secretaries, stenographers, or typists. Among skilled workers, a third have wives
in clerical occupations, again not secretaries, stenographers, or
typists; and a fifth have wives in unskilled jobs. True, a quarter of
the unskilled and service workers have wives in clerical jobs and
there could conceivably be superiority in status for wives in these
families; but superiority in pay is not likely. Even women with
college degrees average lower earnings than men with only
high school educations. [27]

We take time out here to insert the underlying justification for
the "two-steps-behind" rule. It appears that the increasing participation of women in the labor force still has terrifying implications
for some men. One gloomily foresees Armageddon.

### A Terrifying Future

It is vital here to understand the sexual role of money. Particularly in relatively poor communities, a woman with more
money than the men around her tends to demoralise them.
Undermining their usefulness as providers, she weakens their
connections with the community and promotes a reliance
upon other, anti-social ways of confirming their masculinity:
the priapic modes of hunting and fighting. A society of relatively wealthy and independent women will be a society of
sexually and economically predatory males, or a society of
narcotized drones who have abandoned sexuality entirely.

A male's money, on the other hand, is socially affirmative. If
the man is unmarried, a much higher proportion of his money
than a woman's will be spent on the opposite sex. His money
gives him the wherewithal to undertake long-term sexual ini-
tiative. It gives him an incentive to submit to female sexual
patterns, for he knows he will retain the important role of
provider. His sexual impulses can assume a civilizing, not a
subversive, form.

The women's movement argues that most women work because they *need* the money. That is precisely the point, and these women must be permitted to earn it. . . . But men also need the money—and need an increment above the woman's pay—for unfortunately nonrational uses: for the "luxury" spending on women that is necessary if men are to establish and support families. The more men who are induced to serve as providers, the fewer women who will be left to support children alone.

Nothing is so important to the sexual constitution as the creation and maintenance of families. And since the role of the male as principal provider is a crucial prop for the family, the society must support it one way or the other. Today, however, the burdens of childbearing no longer prevent women from performing the provider role; and if day care becomes widely available, it will be possible for a matriarchal social pattern to emerge. Under such conditions, however, the men will inevitably bolt. And this development, an entirely feasible one, would probably require the simultaneous emergence of a police state to supervise the undisciplined men and a child care state to manage the children. Thus will the costs of sexual job equality be passed on to the public in vastly increased taxes. The present sexual constitution is cheaper. . . . At this point, therefore, any serious governmental campaign for equal pay for equal work would be destructive.[28]

One wonders who and where are all these castrating working women. Egalitarianism, let alone superiority, is a long way off.

### Good for Children

Another new twist to the working mother situation is the reversal of attitudes from one that deplored her labor-force participation as having a deleterious effect on her children to one that urges labor-force participation as having a benign effect on them.[29]

Among the replies evoked by a question on the subject of part-time employment in a Reader's Exchange was one that advised women to consider more than the merely monetary factor: "a woman might not think it worth the effort to work [part-time] and pay most of her salary for household help, but perhaps she ought to look forward to the day when her children leave home to lead lives of their own. . . . A job outside the home will help a woman develop her own identity." [30] And then, in true mother-role style, the author demonstrates that developing her own identity is good for her family also, for it "will help her children gain their eventual freedom more easily." [31] In a time when the dangers of over-involvement in children were highlighted, outside work would help de-fuse the role. "Thus part-time employment may help the mother of an adolescent to move from the role of protector and nurturer to that of independence trainer, thus enabling both mother and child to adapt more easily to this period of transition before the child leaves the family for adult status." [32]

Actually there is little clear-cut evidence one way or the other about the way working mothers handle adolescence in their children. For some mothers working may be a way to escape responsibility for the adolescents. Excusing them from exerting control over them. One study found this reaction especially characteristic of women with high power motivation. "An employed woman might feel that she could have controlled her child had she been home. This realization might make her feel guilty about working but less defensive about her lack of influence." [33] Employed mothers with high achievement drive found a great deal of satisfaction in their maternal role when the children were of school age but not when they were adolescent. [34] The researchers conclude that when the worker role does not hamper performance of the maternal role, outside employment enhances the mother's satisfaction with it. [35]

Although the employment of mothers of adolescents does not show demonstrably harmful effects on boys, there is one shred of evidence that bears scrutiny. In the past when mothers worked and added to family income, the family could afford to live in neighborhoods that protected children from temptations to delinquency. But in a study made a decade ago there did seem to be a relationship between the employment of mothers and delinquency in the case of at least middle-class young men. [36] Sons of employed mothers are more likely than sons of non-employed mothers to disagree with their mothers over hair, clothing, and religion, and to disagree more seriously. [37] It could be argued that participating in delinquent acts and disagreeing with mothers had a positive aspect, implying that the adolescent was breaking loose, achieving autonomy, and that the more conforming behavior of the sons of mothers not employed implied too great input from the mother in holding them back. For the non-working mother, the role of mother may come to include that of policeman and probation officer. This interpretation would be in line with the thinking of those who, like Edgar Friedenberg, see mothers as over-involved, investing too much control in adolescent children and thus fostering a sick, sticky dependency that hampers development.

Labor-force participation by mothers, in these instances, has been rationalized as being not in their own behalf but in behalf of husbands and children. The worker role has been interpreted as, in fact, contributing to the welfare of the family. The mother who works relieves her husband of the entire weight of family financial needs and avoids the over-involvement in her children which is destructive to them. The worker and the mother role are thus assimilated, the first becoming, in effect, a component of the second.

## Self-fulfillment? No

Comments made by housewives in one study "indicate a definition of outside employment not as a source of self-expression, but as an imposition brought about by a shortage of money." They might like to relieve their husbands from having to work so hard, bur certainly they would not work for anything as trivial as self-fulfillment.[38]

Still, even personal satisfactions are now admitted. "Apart from money, the working wives" in blue-collar marriages "mentioned other rewards of working: the enjoyment of social life on the job, the pleasures of workmanship, the bracing effect of having to get dressed up in the morning, some relief from constant association with young children, and 'having something interesting to tell my husband.' " [39] In a family therapy experiment sponsored by the National Institute of Health, it was found that most of the mothers who took part in the experiment went to work or back to school. The therapist explained that "the women discovered they could exist as separate individuals in their own right; they no longer need to live only for their husbands and children." [40] Surely a derogation of the role of mother? Surely not a wholesome development? Quite the reverse. It proved to be a plus because, having discovered their own potential and restored their own self-esteem, they no longer projected on to their families the dislike they had felt for themselves. But this, too, is rationalized as being a plus for the family, and not trivial self-fulfillment. As in the case of the career woman, the emphasis is now less and less on the deviancy of the woman's performance of the role of mother and more on its positive aspects.

In seeing their jobs as part of their family obligations, working mothers do not differ basically from fathers who also see their work as part of their family obligations. The difference is that it has not until now been written into the scenario for the mother role that labor-force participation was part of that role. The working mother is engaged in a "try-out" of a new script. Unlike the father, she still incorporates responsibility for the home. It is precisely this dilemma that calls for help in integrating the two roles.

The absence of guilt and the success in the "psychological work" of assimilating her two roles have benign effects on working mothers. In a national survey of mental health as measured in terms of symptoms of psychological distress, women in the labor force showed up better than housewives.[41] And taking a job is apparently a contagious step. "Contacts with working women arouse longings for a job in some homemakers." [42]

### The "Mature" Woman in the Labor Force: The Mothers of Adults

Sooner or later sons and daughters marry or leave home to find their own way. Although the responsibilities retained by women in this stage of late motherhood for their grown sons and daughters may be greatly attenuated—reduced officially if not psychologically—the worker role may still remain, in effect, an adjunct to the mother role.

As startling as anything else in the recent history of women is the phenomenal increase in the labor-force participation of women whom the tactful researchers label "mature." In 1970, more than half—54.0 percent—of all women between the ages of forty-five and fifty-four were in the labor force—proportionately as many as of women aged twenty to twenty-four. And by 1990 the proportion is projected to be even higher, 58.0 percent.[43] It is hard to think of these women as the harassed and harassing, depressed and depressing interfering mothers-in-law of the stereotypes. The chances are high that the woman we purchased goods from this morning or the women doing clerical work in the offices we enter every day are in this period of late motherhood; they are certainly not the harridans of the media.

Even among women fifty-five to sixty-four years of age the increase in labor-force participation has been phenomenal, rising from 18 percent in 1940 to 43 percent in 1970 and projected to be

46 percent in 1990.[44] Again, it is hard to reconcile these women with the stereotype of the devouring, interfering mother-in-law or the demanding Mom.

The more modernized of these "mature" women constitute almost a brand new sex.[45] If they have not been in the labor force till now, they stream back into the schools and colleges, along with younger women, in continuing education programs to prepare themselves for the new "careers" now proliferating so profusely. They assume more and more leadership activities in communities. Some achieve "consciousness" and become Gray Panthers. We have not yet grasped the significance for the future of the emergence, as part of the structure of modern society, of a group as substantial as are ethnic groups, the middle class, or other sizeable building blocks needed by social analysts for interpreting society.

A study done in the 1950s found "no relationships significantly differentiating full-time employed mothers and full-time housewives when their children were adults. This would suggest that for this older group the role of work does not have much bearing on the role of motherhood. It seems obvious that only in special instances would a job for a mother of an adult present any interferences or difficulties in the functions that are required of her as a mother." [46] Actually, the employed mother may have a benign effect on her grown children's lives. It is probably the income of the "mature" mother in the labor force that makes it possible for parents to help young couples just starting out. One of the most interesting findings of recent research on kinship ties is that such financial help is, in fact, available from parents for many young families. It may also be the added income that makes possible a more comfortable nursing home for the working woman's own mother, for at this stage of a woman's life roles may be reversed and the daughter now has the responsibility for her own mother's care.

Unfortunately we do not have much hard research on these women vis-à-vis their sisters not in the labor force. We can only make inferences from the research about women who become roleless in these years. We know that they tend to succumb to the empty-nest syndrome, go into severe depression, become Moms or the distressing mothers-in-law of folk cliché.

We know from fragments and snatches of evidence what, at least up to now, depriving people of work does to them. It is said—no doubt apocryphally, though no less "true" for all that—that the ancient Chinese absorbed wave after wave of invaders by smothering them with service, depriving them of any useful work and thus precipitating their decadence. We see in our country what depriving Indian men of their work has done to them. We know how often retirement or deprivation of work has a deteriorating effect on workers, and we know the even more serious effects which unemployment has. We are beginning to see also how damaging it was, despite our good intentions, to deprive young men and women of the opportunity to work by our child-labor and compulsory schooling laws. Students of the direction industrial society is taking express concern with respect to the leisure time that "threatens" us in the future. Or, at least, some of us.

If the career mother is presaging the future, closely followed by the working mother with a job, the remaining half of mothers of school-age children, who are not in the labor force, are—some of them in any event—fighting a rear-guard action to preserve the status quo with a few of them even waging an aggressive campaign against the future.

# CHAPTER ELEVEN

## The Other Half

### Role Attrition

Although the proportion of mothers of school-age children who are not in the labor force is shrinking, it remains considerable and even by 1990 it will still be at least 40 percent.[1] So any account of future trends must still include these non-working mothers. The situation these women confront is not, like that of the women who enter the labor force, one of role integration but of role attrition. As children enter school and grow up the responsibilities of the mother role become attenuated so that by the time the children reach adolescence, the direct, personal care requirements have been reduced to a minimum and the amount of work called for in the home declines. If early motherhood combines the worst ways to institutionalize the role of mothers, middle, and especially late, motherhood for some women can be the best of all possible worlds. They are relieved of the most onerous aspects of the role of mother. And they have the option of entering or remaining out of the labor force.

Although all of the women in this half have opted—have been obliged—to remain housewives, they do not all define their roles in the same way nor do they all have the same degree of commitment. Some teeter and may—like some women in the labor force—reverse themselves. Some champ at the bit; some settle for the "just a housewife" position in a sweetly passive manner. Some have surrogate careers as volunteers in a church or community agency and lead serenely untroubled service-filled lives. They have no identity problems. And some, finding their privileged status challenged, lash out aggressively in a many-pronged back-lash including, at one extreme, lobbying against state confirmation of the Equal Rights Amendment, and at the other, enrollment in church-sponsored courses on Fascinating Womanhood.

### Mom: Stranded on the Beach

The term "retirement" turns up quite often in discussions of modern motherhood. Sometimes the term is used resentfully, sometimes cheerfully. For some women, as is also true among some men, it precipitates depression; other women, again like some men, greet it with liberated cries of joy. When motherhood lasted practically a—rather short—lifetime, or at least until a woman was worn out, the post-motherhood period of her life was not a matter of much concern. Today when many women are "re-tired" from the one engrossing role of their lives, motherhood, at an early and vigorous age or when, at any rate, the role of mother becomes greatly attenuated, the situation is quite different. The character-type pejoratively labelled "Mom" may result.

The peculiar hostility, and even passionate hatred, "Mom" has inspired is hard for women to understand. She is, according to one student, without precedent in mythology and folklore. "It is," he tells us, "a stunning fact . . . that we find for her, in all of my-thology and folklore, and in all literature . . . over a hundred years old, no precedent. She is . . . truly a new phenomenon." [2] This student, a psychiatrist, interprets Mom in terms of her over-in-volvement in her children, especially her sons. "In all previous cultures, whether matriarchal or patriarchal, the boy at a certain age, formally and ritualistically passed out of mother's hands and into the pedagogical authority of men." [3] Our society makes no pro-vision for such emancipation from the mother. And she, with no other engrossing role, clings to the one role that has so far vali-dated her life. Permitted few involvements outside the home, she has made an enormous investment in her children. She needs them far more than they need her.

If she wins in her attempt to salvage the relationship in which she has invested so much of herself, there are ineradicable scars. If the child wins its independence, she retains only what the child chooses to give; if the child loses, he or she is crippled for the rest of his or her life, tied irretrievably to a mother who no longer mothers or supports but only weighs heavily. We read from time to time of powerful old matriarchs who dominate children and the children's children. But they are few and far between. Usually their "power" turns out to be only an indulgent charade played out by children to flatter, or is—in cases where the mother controls wealth—sheer sycophancy.

### Transitional Mothers: "Arrested Moms," "Late Bloomers," "Late Starters"

Many of the mothers who are not in the labor force are in transition from the status of housewife to the status of professional, for while some cling to the role of mother even when their children no longer need dedicated care and become Moms, others, reading the message on the wall, try to roll with the punch, face the changes, and work with rather than against the tide. They include the women who are now streaming back into the colleges, institutes, and universities hoping either to complete interrupted college courses or prepare for new professional careers in the future. Among the many experimental programs for women now in process is one proposal—singled out merely as an example—for Women's Centers for Change which would cater to four groups of women. One consists of working women; another, the so-called "new students" who are low-income, high-achieving ethnic women; traditional college women; and, most relevant here, women who have passed normal college age, who "by the time they have reached thirty-five, have sent their youngest child to school and face at least thirty remaining productive years." [4] At such institutes professional training will be available at any time, there will be no age restrictions, no credentialism. The hurdles which have served as barriers for women wishing to resume their professional preparation when their mother-role obligations have become attenuated will be removed and the path cleared for the next stage in their development.

The fact that only passing attention can be paid here to these new trends should in no way be taken as underestimating their part in the future of motherhood. These women emerge from the tunnel primed to pick up where they left off. They are extraordinary in almost every way, a delight to teach, a challenge to educational systems of whatever kind. Watch them. The mere existence of schools designed precisely for them is going to have a genuine impact on the way girls and women conceive of motherhood in the future.

### Conflicted Housewife

Some of the mothers not in the labor force, or preparing to enter it, wish they were. Here is one:

> I have spent the last two years rationalizing all the problems away. I have joined committees that meet during the three hours the children are now in school. I have used up countless hours sewing clothes I don't need and probably will never wear, but it fills the time. I read endlessly, can even recite from memory the ingredients on the "King Vitaman" box. I take an occasional day off and haunt the museums, art galleries, movie theaters. I am, as they say, "up on things."
>
> But let me tell you, I'm lost. And I was probably lost . . . long before I ever agreed to give up my career plans. . . . I am definitely *not* one of the Pepsi generation, or the liberated generation; I belong, most certainly, to the last of the schlepp generation—two years too old for the pill, the Peace Corps, real liberation.
>
> I don't know what the answers are. If I did, I wouldn't find myself wondering, in near-terror, what to do with myself on days when both my children are invited to friends' houses after school on the same day, and being furious that I have allowed myself to be lured into this trap; that I've let my life become so circumscribed that I have nothing to do some days. What I do know is that there will have to be major changes in the way we all live before anything changes. . . . The women of my generation were not prepared for life. The realities of existence were not part of our training and education. We're not equipped to function in the lives we live.[5]

This cacophony of misery has a strange ring. A few years earlier the author had been happily engaged in a part-time job, enjoying both her work and her motherhood. Then, at her husband's insistence, the family had moved to a different city where his, but not her, career opportunities were better. Because our society expects women to live where their husbands live, they went. Pursuing her work became impossible. She rejected the housewife, if not the maternal, identity. She was miserable.

There are other women who, like her, are "not prepared for life." They are emotionally and psychologically unprepared to leave the protection of the home to enter the labor force, so they really do not have that option. The early leaders of the women's liberation movement did not address themselves to these women knowing that as yet there was no alternative they could offer them.[6] The kinds of jobs available to these women were in no way an improvement on their present status. Unexpectedly, however, their message was heard. Consciousness was raised. Housewives began to reassess their positions. They re-evaluated their marriages, their relations with their children, their position in the community. No longer housebound, no longer responsible for small children, they were beginning to wonder just who they were anyway. They saw themselves as having the worst of all worlds.

There are others, however, who are traditional housewives from conventional home backgrounds and they do not want anything changed. They, too, are conflicted, though in a different way. They do not want to enter the labor force, they want to remain home, sheltered and protected. But they feel defensive, put down, denigrated by the emphasis on autonomy among the avant garde. This conflicted housewife, as reported in one study, was, point for point, the mirror image of the professional career woman.

## Point Counterpoint

These homemakers, to begin with, had selected men quite different from those the professional women had chosen. Their husbands tended to be in the high-status, power-and-performance-oriented, "masculine" professions such as medicine, law, engineering, big business, and finance. They shared their wives' traditional values. They did not want to share the child-care role nor did their wives want them to. But, interestingly, these husbands were more receptive than were the homemakers themselves to the idea of their wives' working.[7]

One of the best things these women found in their marriages was "feeling emotionally and/or financially secure in being cared for and needed. They value their husbands as protectors on whom they can depend and in turn feel themselves both needed and cared for." Security and a feeling of being needed also loomed large.

They felt the best thing about motherhood was the joy of being needed; the worst, the anxiety, guilt, and feelings of inadequacy it generated. They did not wish they had more children; some even wished they had fewer. They reflected the Victorian model of the role of mother to an almost incredible extent. Duty, self-sacrifice, martyrdom showed up prominently in their conceptualization of their role:

> Most of the homemakers emphasize a kind of martyrdom or at least self-sacrifice in describing the impact children have on a woman's life. They speak virtuously of such things as how you must subordinate yourself and put the children first, how they are your purpose in life and you are subject to their demands. . . . They focus on duty and responsibility, on what a woman must and should do.[8]

The mother of school-age children has many problems to contend with if she is in the labor force; over-investment in the children is not, however, likely to be one of them. But the woman whose identity is almost wholly that of a mother may suffer, figuratively speaking, "withdrawal symptoms" when the demands of the role of mother taper off and all but vanish. The woman who found fulfillment when her children were small begins to face a phasing out during middle motherhood. If she continues to invest herself fully in her children, living vicariously through them, she may continue to achieve fulfillment in such make-work as chauffeuring her children to dancing school, athletic events, and other activities. She sews, knits, embroiders clothes for her daughter, and provides refreshments for the boys or girls who drop in to listen to the records in the family room. So far as she is concerned motherwork is still a full-time and rewarding occupation. The homemakers seemed to the researcher to be over-involved with their children.[9]

As contrasted with professional mothers, the homemakers "were more emotionally reactive and labile, responding with both more intense gratification and more sadness and depression to the experience of motherhood as it is tapped by these [TAT] pictures. Very much preoccupied with child-rearing, they seem almost naively unselfconscious and open in responding to the joys and tragedies of motherhood." [10] They felt that careers interfered with relationships with children and they handled their "fear of success" by "bowing out of the competition." [11]

Although these mothers tended to view marriage as restrictive or burdensome or demanding, few felt unhappy with their marriages. "This finding," the researcher notes, "serves as a reminder that the homemakers are getting pretty much what they have been brought up to expect from marriage. They do not subjectively experience the described restrictions, burdens or demands as negative." [12]

The homemakers projected a positive image, smiling, cheerful, unassuming, self-deprecating, unthreatening. One describes herself, the researcher reports, as "very conventional, dependent and not at all competitive. Her personality style is built on muting of self assertion and aggression and affirmation of love, nurturance and self-sacrifice. Fearful of attenuating family relationships, she avoids employment. Motherhood is her focal life role and she derives a sense of purpose and vitality as well as some vicarious achievement satisfaction from her large family." The lovely homes in the beautiful suburbs across the country are presided over by women just like this one.

Yet although these women present a seemingly self-fulfilled exterior, their replies on projective tests showed that they were actually experiencing "considerable psychic turmoil, a depressed sense of emotional well-being and low self-esteem." They do not feel attractive to men nor "competent at anything, even child care and the social graces, let alone work and intellectual functioning." They feel "somewhat lonely and isolated . . . uncertain and on the sidelines." Though their lives are working out as expected, they still feel "an inexplicable sense of failure and disappointment, of having been left behind." [13]

A suburban woman who returned to her profession after a divorce sketches the situation of her former associates from the unintentional outpourings inadvertently overheard:

> Every two or three weeks I indulge myself with a visit to the masseuse at the country club not too far from my home. I drive in and park my car among all the Cadillacs, Buicks, and Lincolns and walk along the tennis courts, swimming pool, golf links, and patio where the women are playing, gossiping, card-playing, all of them svelte, elegant, plastic, coiffed to perfection. Completely idyllic. Here is, truly, the dream come true. I enter the masseuse's parlor and lie down on the table in my separate little booth. Next to me, separated by the curtain, there is always a woman pouring out her heart to the masseuse. Her husband is playing around with a young chick. She has just discovered that her son is a hustler. That her daughter has left college and is living in a commune, heaven

only knows where. That she is lonely. . . . I know exactly how they feel. I had been one of them.[14]

Sôme, like this woman, do think seriously of returning to work. But the researcher quoted earlier has doubts about the feasibility of such a course for most of them; the consequences of failure might be traumatic.

> Given her basic personality, style, and current unsettled con-
> dition, and especially if the contemplated return to work falls
> through, we can not help but worry about the onset of depres-
> sive episodes in this typically self-sacrificing, aggression-
> denying homemaker as she moves further along into middle
> age. Expecting her children somehow to fulfill her, bitter dis-
> appointment and considerable anger may result as the chil-
> dren inevitably head off to college and lives of their own,
> perhaps keeping in touch only with an occasional phone call
> or letter. It is not surprising that involutional melancholia is
> so common among middle-aged, middle class women and un-
> fortunately the homemaker seems already a vulnerable push-
> over to just such difficulties.[15]

The researcher's pessimistic prognosis for this seemingly well-positioned woman may appear excessively grim, but it is worth noting that the highest suicide rate in the country occurs among women in the most affluent area, northwest Washington and Chevy Chase, Maryland.

It is for women like them that the medical journals advertise their tranquilizers:

> M.A. (fine arts) . . . PTA (President-elect) . . . a life currently
> centered around home and children with too little time to pur-
> sue a vocation for which she has spent many years in training.
> . . . A situation that may bespeak continuous frustration and
> stress; a perfect framework for her to translate the functional
> symptoms of psychic tension into major problems. For this
> kind of patient—with no demonstrable pathology yet repeated
> complaints—consider the distinctive properties of——[a tran-
> quilizer].[16]

The most infuriating aspect of the situation for many of these women is not boredom or frustration but the fact that, regardless of what the researcher may say, they *are* happy. It's true that their self-esteem is badly battered. The constant assault on them, in fact, is the major fly in the ointment so far as they are concerned. The one thing that could make them happier would be the disappearance of all those successful and happy "career mothers." It is their existence that bugs them. It makes them feel denigrated. It is not a matter of sour grapes. They do not want to be career mothers themselves; they do not envy career mothers. They like their life as it is. They do not resent their "golden handcuffs." It annoys them that others do not see it the same way they do. Because the career mothers are no longer apologetic, it seems to the homemakers that they are gloating. Here is how one woman sees it:

> I am an intelligent person and my role for the next 10 or so years is to bring these children up straight and strong. I'm sick and tired of being put down as leading a mundane life by people like you. . . . You . . . have not been living in a realistic world of school age children of today. Their by-word is "love" and they have to have it from those that brought them into this life and not from a day-care center!! I will exclude the mothers who work to keep a family together financially. I am angry at the women who opt for a career and children to the detriment of the children—they are selfish and we are headed into a generation of extremely insecure people as a result. . . . My hurt is that the awakening of women (Women's Lib is a trite phrase) will be destroyed by selfish females who reproduce for the sake of reproduction. A "career" is basically money earned and money spent. Children are an investment in the future of this world. I look to my investment as the only one that counts—enlightened, secure, loved people to take forward what has been given to them in an hour-by-hour of guidance.

> P.S. My husband is with me all the way. WE raise children. (Personal letter).

To these genuinely committed mothers, it is the presence of the career mothers at the PTA meeting that explains the "only" in the "only a housewife" response she gives when introduced to guests. She doesn't want a career herself. And feels put down because others do.

The career mothers, far from gloating, are serenely unaware of the sagging self-esteem of the happy housewives all around them.

But the picture is not so gloomy for all non-employed mothers in middle motherhood. Some find surrogate careers in voluntary work in the community.

### Voluntarism As Surrogate Career

A very old, as well as current, reply to the question, what are women to do with their lives once motherhood has ceased to be a major preoccupation is: do volunteer work in the community.

The voluntary organization has an old and honorable history in our country. Even De Tocqueville, over a hundred years ago, commented upon it. These organizations fulfilled a need that could not be met by the government; they demonstrated, by their simple existence, the glories of democracy. (Some countries forbade them, fearing the threat of such potential for power.) Some of the work in these organizations was and is high-level; it approximates paid professional work including research and report writing and complex administrative tasks. Indeed, the trend has been increasingly for it to become *paid* professional work.

But there is also another kind of volunteer work that emphasizes love, tenderness, compassion, the simple desire to help. It is essentially an expansion of the mother role; the woman extends her mothering to persons outside her family who need such ministrations. It permits a major commitment to the home but also a commitment, of varying degree and extent, to an outside activity—church related, school related, community related. Such a commitment may supply much of the satisfaction that the woman in the labor force receives from job or career. It does not, of course, supply income and hence a modicum of autonomy, as does job or career.

> The Literacy Council needs volunteers who are interested in helping illiterate adults learn to read. This is one-to-one volunteer work and can be most rewarding. You need not be a professional teacher to help teach adults to read. The Literacy Council needs willing workers who want to help illiterate adults lead fuller lives. And you need not give up other interests or volunteer activities to take on this kind of job. As a Literacy Council volunteer, you would meet with your student-friend at a church or library convenient to both of you, once or twice a week. Workshops for volunteers will be held. . . .[17]

There will be no lack of women who will respond to this appeal. For a great many of the women who seek satisfying surrogate careers as volunteers have great stores of the qualities specified for mothers in the Victorian model. They are, indeed, loving, gentle, patient, giving people. They are, indeed, eager to serve, to help, to do all the things that the archetypal mother was assigned to do. And they do, indeed, make important contributions to those they help. Individually or as members of church groups they bring food and clothing to poor families in a simple, direct, personal, uncluttered manner. Or they supply tender loving care to infants in a hospital or to elderly inmates in a nursing home, or simple attention to the sick, the deprived, the unfortunate, the needy just anywhere.[18] Or they become teachers' aides, tutors, den mothers, or girl scout leaders, or teach illiterates to lead fuller lives.

Among women of the more affluent classes the voluntary effort may take the form of sponsorship of art exhibits, symphony orchestras, museums, hospitals, and other good works. If the woman is not affluent enough to sponsor such expensive community projects herself, she may sit on boards or make her contribution in the form of volunteer services in agencies of one kind or another. Membership in non-professional social welfare organizations among women is growing at the rate of one percent a year, which is small as compared to a rate of increase of 9.4 percent in membership in sports and recreational groups but large as compared to the losses reported for membership in old-fashioned fraternal, ethnic, and hereditary groups.[19]

The arguments leveled against voluntarism by the National Organization for Women include one to the effect that it threatens jobs needed by other women or at least lowers the pay for such jobs. "I could always get a volunteer to do your job" says the exploitative employer. Voluntarism is sometimes condescending and patronizing so that, on the other side there is the stigma allegedly attached to the recipient.

In an attempt to upgrade the status of the volunteer, Ellen Straus has made a *Call for Action* with a program that believes that workers should: be covered by insurance, be given out-of-pocket expenses, be given written agreements stating rights and responsibilities, be given tax deductions for time donated, be in the social security system, have a guild or union.

## What's So Wrong about Leisure?

If not back to school, or voluntarism, or a job, what *is* there? Well, of course, there's always bridge, the country club, the sewing circle, the theater, museums, galleries, sports, whatever you can afford. Enjoy the leisure now possible.

But all by ourselves? Without men?

Leisure is as complex a concept as work itself, as puzzling, theoretically, to economists as it is to moralists. On the moral side there is the whole weight of the puritan ethic, the conviction that the devil finds mischief for idle hands. When Hamilton and Gallatin, among others, argued for employing women in the mills, one support they invoked was that it would protect women from vice and idleness. When feminists became too vehement, however, in their championing of "women's two roles," they were put on the defensive. They replied that it was not work for work's sake they urged but a fairer sharing of work itself:

> Some . . . may object that our attitude to life, and to women's life in particular, is too utilitarian. Why are you trying . . . to press-gang women into jobs? Why this puritanical attitude towards work as the soul's salvation? Would it not be better to preserve, as long as possible, the vestiges of a leisured group, or at least a category of people who are able to arrange things in their own time, to do the many odd and unremunerative jobs that need doing, and to enjoy what is really worth-while in life, friendships and books and art?
>
> To [these questions] we would like to say two things: Firstly, our modern economy cannot afford, nor can our democratic ideology tolerate, the existence of a large section of the population living by the efforts of others. Whether we like it or not, the leisured class has passed into history, together with the coach-and-four, the home-brewed ale, and other symbols of the "good old times." The gentleman of leisure, who spent his time travelling, educating himself, and enjoying the good things in life has disappeared, and the lady of leisure is bound to follow. With changed technical means our social aims, too, have altered. If we want to live in a fairly just, fairly rational society; if we want the living standard of our population to improve and its children to be educated; if we want to free old age from the anxieties of dire poverty—we shall all have to contribute according to our best ability.
>
> Secondly, far from preaching a gospel of hard work, we hope

for increased leisure so that more people may have a share in the
"good life." Leisure must, however, be understood in its true
function: as a period of rest and re-creation within a full life.

We, too, . . . want to live in a world in which people are, first
of all, human beings and not only "good citizens." We, too,
abhor the ant-hill State in which the value of a person is assessed
only in terms of his, or her, share in the fulfillment of a pre-
determined plan of production. We hold that a life of nothing but
work would be too dull to be worth living.

It is for this reason that we have become convinced that a
fairer re-distribution of work and leisure between the sexes is
necessary. . . .[20]

And another researcher notes that in addition to the financial limita-
tions to the elaboration of "homemaker, clubwoman, and leisured
role possible by a non-working wife" there is, for many Americans
"something rather distasteful about the notion that women should
lead a life significantly devoted to play or even 'good works' while
their husbands are under constant economic pressure to provide the
suitable setting for such conspicuous leisure."[21] The moral argument the feminists were making was not that leisure was in and of
itself an evil thing but that making it a privilege for only women
was. They wanted men to share it.

Economists are still struggling with the best way to conceptualize
leisure. For the way it is conceptualized makes a difference in the
way we think about it. Defensible if we look at it one way, not so, if
we look at it another way.

If we think of our economy as a system for producing as many
goods and services as it can, as efficiently as possible, then the
nonemployment of women is a cost to the total economy. And,
difficult as it may be, this cost can be toted up and a bill rendered. But
if leisure is viewed as a consumer good, then there is no more reason
to deny it to those who prefer it to other consumer goods than there is
to deny any other consumer choice. People are entitled to "buy"
leisure and pay for it in the form of earnings they forego by not
working. A Canadian economist puts it this way:

women are consumers . . . and . . . any measurement of their
welfare must take into consideration not only the income from
their labour but also the emotional gains offered by leisure or
unpaid activities. To the extent that the absence of women
from the labour market is voluntary and reflects a preference

for leisure and activities within the home, it is difficult to claim that these decisions reduce in any way the welfare of the Canadian people.[22]

Still, the feminists might ask, why not permit men "the emotional gains offered by leisure"?

The old economic argument that women were performing the important function of consumption was also coming in for attack. The absurdity of vicarious leisure and conspicuous consumption was becoming evident to everyone. The man who had enjoyed the envy of his peers for his ability to shower jewels and mink coats on his wife came to look rather puerile and the woman who made a career of displaying them, rather trivial. Columnists were beginning to poke malicious fun at them. One called them an "endangered species."

> The New York Zoological Society recently got a number of rich women to donate to it all their fur coats and alligator bags, for an exhibit on how unspeakable it was for them ever to have had such possessions. Thus, in one stroke, the society accomplished what generations of revolutionaries and muggers have dreamed of: taking the upper classes' pretty things away from them, making them apologize in the process.
>
> In this case, it was done by a committee headed by Mrs. Vincent Astor and concerned with the lifestyle problems of endangered species. Chief among these is a problem which the animals and the committee members have in common: a tendency to find themselves in Fifth Avenue specialty shops all the time.
>
> But Mrs. Astor and her friends have apparently not yet come to the realization that they may also be an endangered species. The time may come when a genuine, recognizable, in-the-wild rich woman will no longer exist for the public to watch and enjoy. The rich woman's natural environment is being eroded. . . . Obviously, we must act now to preserve this way of life before it is too late. . . . We have an obligation to see that "these quaint little creatures" are not allowed to become victims of our increasing civilization.[23]

It is bad enough to be laughed at. But it becomes really serious when your pocketbook is hit. The coup de grace, figuratively speaking, for the—affluent—homemaker was delivered when proposals began to appear that she and the services, if any, that she provided be taxed as a luxury. She or her husband would thus have to pay for the privileged spot she enjoyed. Why not? Her leisure was as much a luxury as any other. "In effect, the proposed change would implicitly tax the extra leisure and extra production of household goods and services enjoyed by one-earner, relative to two-earner families." [24] A *very* far cry from "woman's place is in the home"! As far back as Hamilton and Gallatin, in fact.

## A Turning Tide

There had been a long-standing conflict between women who preferred the sheltered protection of conventional marriage and those—pejoratively called "career women"—who wished to participate freely in the outside world. Mothers who left the home to take jobs unless they had to were unwomanly. It was the dependent, feminine, home-centered housewife who received the accolade. She had no qualms about remaining in the home. She certainly did not have to defend herself. The apologia for the woman's-place-is-in-the-home ideology rested solidly on high-level moral, theological, and even scientific, grounds. The housewife was carrying out God's design which clearly called for her to remain in the home. And so long as the woman's-place-is-in-the-home ideology had unquestioned authority, the sheltered homebody did not have to bolster her position. There were others to do this for her. In the nineteenth century and early twentieth, many of the most serious opponents of the women's movement had been conventionally married women, secure in their dependence on their husbands. As late as mid-century, career women were still the "bad guys" to them, "castrating females," deviants. Housewives consistently devalued them.[25]

As, indeed, did scientists. A spate of psychological research had consistently found career-oriented college women to be deviant, off beat, not quite normal. "The very term 'career woman' suggested pretentiousness or hard-boiled insensitivity and rejection of femininity." [26] The woman whose primary choice was a career was seen as a victim of childhood trauma:

> the girl who aims for a career is likely to be frustrated and dissatisfied with herself as a person. . . . She is less well adjusted than those who are content to become housewives. Not only is [she] likely to have a poor self-concept, but she also probably lacks a close relationship with her family. . . . There

is still the possibility that a career orientation among girls grows out of personal dissatisfactions, so that the career becomes a frustration outlet.[27]

The researchers found that the best-adjusted college women were the underachievers who were not preparing for careers but for a "healthy integration" of feminine role and intellectual aspirations. As more and more women did combine career and motherhood, grudging recognition was accorded them. At least they were tolerated.

By 1964 it was being recognized that although college women might expect to have both family and interesting work, they would, of course, put family first. "To summarize, what the 1950s and 1960s consolidated was the idea of the woman who, though married and the mother of children, might still work as the family required it, or on a second-priority basis, to fulfill herself and contribute to society." [28] Research on employed mothers had shown that the employment of mothers was not such an important factor in child-rearing as had been supposed.[29] But, of course, these women would not resent the inequality in the work world that resulted from their motherhood.

In the late sixties and early seventies, there was a new twist. A tide was turning in favor of the career woman. Now the research was beginning to show that the career women were not even casualties of unhappy home backgrounds. On the contrary, they were positive, effective persons with a strong desire to use their capabilities and to be helpful to others. So completely were the tables turned, in fact, that one longitudinal study of college women found it was the young woman who was *not* planning a career who was on the deviant side. "It looks as though the woman who has either no plan or who is non-career-oriented at the time of college graduation is more likely to be our low-striving, introverted, perhaps not so well-adjusted person . . . somewhat withdrawn and more than a bit demoralized." [30] And so far as low self-esteem—formerly attributed to the career-oriented woman—was concerned, it was now being reported in the non-career rather than in the career woman.

Still another four-year study that had followed a group of women through college from 1954 to 1968 found little support for the interpretation of the career-oriented women as deviant; it found a better interpretation in the concept of "enrichment." In this view, "a career is not a solution to personal conflict [as previous research had implied] but a positive choice growing out of differential learning situations and influences from important reference groups." From this study, so far from looking like the sad sacks of earlier research, "the career aspirers emerge as emancipated women, equalitarian in outlook about domestic life. They expect to marry and have children as do their classmates, but they feel at least partly expendable from child-rearing chores. They expect husbands to share the household tasks including child-care, cooking, cleaning. In that sense they are 'modern' rather than 'traditional' in sex role conceptions." [31] (The operant phrases to note are "expendable from child-rearing chores" and "expect husbands to share." This was the generation challenging the successful professional mothers described earlier.) [32]

So far from discouraging the career aspirations of college women, the reverse, as a result of the turning tide, was being advocated. One researcher concludes that "we cannot in good conscience raise girls to seek their primary personal fulfillment through the experience of motherhood. . . . If bright women seek no other sources of gratification in addition to marriage and maternity, self esteem eventually drops and loneliness and uncertainty plague her." [33] Difficult as it might be to integrate the worker and mother roles, ultimately it would prove preferable to relying entirely on the mother role for lifelong satisfactions. Momism, among other calamities, was one possible outcome of placing all one's eggs in one basket.

There were reverberations from this re-evaluation of careers; a new perspective on combining them with motherhood resulted. The old arguments against the employment of mothers began to suffer attrition as increasingly it became recognized that women did, indeed, have a right, even an obligation, to participate in the labor force. Not only unmarried women but wives also, and even mothers. Finally, so far from simply defending the right of women who wished to have careers to have them, old ideologies were being actively challenged. Even as they related to the middle- and working-class mothers whose non-employment took the form merely of proving their husband's success in the provider role. Non-employed mothers were losing the ideological support that guaranteed them shelter and protection as long as they lived simply because they were women, mothers of men's children.

## Backlash

Housewives began to complain that they were being put on the defensive, that there was so much acceptance, approval, even honoring of career and working women that they were made to feel denigrated if they did not also enter the labor force. The right *not* to have to do so was being threatened, so it seemed to them, by feminists. It became an issue. Didn't the feminists know they were upsetting the applecart? A backlash against "women's libbers" began.

Arguments that it had seemed better to leave unarticulated in the past when there had been moralists, theologians, and even scientists to argue their case, now came to be verbalized. A "holier-than-thou" flavor no longer characterized their statement of the case but rather a "more-sensible-than-thou" flavor: There are rich rewards in the traditional role; it is a bargain whatever the price; women really have it made; "women's libbers" are rocking a very comfortable boat; "unless we stop making equality noises, men might wake up and realize what they have been missing"; "God help us then!" [34]

The feminists did, indeed, know what the rewards of the traditional role had been. But they added them up to a different total. The Fall, 1972, issue of *The American Scholar*, journal of the Phi Beta Kappa Society, carried the discussion of a panel of top-flight women achievers in reply to the question, "if we win, what will we lose?" In it, Lillian Hellman, echoing Charlotte Gilman, an early twentieth-century feminist, noted that "the upper-class lady, or the middle-class lady, has made out very well as the weaker and the more fragile of the pair, husband and wife. . . . There is still a good living and a great many mink coats to be earned by pretense. Respectable whoredom. Marx wrote about it. I think it's been quite deliberately done by women and quite deliberately kept alive." [35] And the women who made a good living by traditional life styles were not likely to welcome changed role conceptions. Carolyn Heilbrun commented on the "envy of these 'unvigorous' women" and noted that it had become apparent to her "early in life how miserable they were." [36]

It did seem to sheltered housewives that the "women's libbers" were out to coerce everyone into the labor force, to impose a new kind of servitude:

I'm not a member of any women's organization, but I am concerned about women's rights. I'm very concerned because of the terrible name the women's liberation movement has among the common men, and, worse, the common women. From personal experience . . . it seems the majority of the people see the women's rights groups as composed of screaming, wild women who want to force women to work and who see homemakers as useless. . . . I personally know women who are "sure" that women's "liberationists" are . . . for putting all pre-school children in day-care centers so their mothers will be able to work (whether they want to work or not).[37]

The charge that feminists were attempting to foist on women the same kind of careerism that men were beginning to reject was already an old one. Alva Myrdal and Viola Klein in the passage quoted above had felt called upon to defend themselves for their emphasis on outside work for women. But, despite their passionate apologia, it was not the "women's libbers" who were trying to get all women into the labor force, willy nilly. They had early on recognized that the "happy housewife" was not to be disturbed. She had made her peace with her lot and since she had no alternatives, there was no point in raising her consciousness. It would only cause anxiety since as yet the feminist movement could not supply decent alternatives. Certainly a poorly paid menial job was no big deal. In early 1969 a young "women's libber" had stated the situation clearly:

Don't tell these women that going to work is emancipation. They'll laugh in your face. It's just another slavery, served concurrently. And not entirely honorable, at that, because what was wrong with her that she couldn't get a husband who could support her?

To tell these women that they are as good as their men, to tell them to free themselves from their oppression and to take charge of their own destinies, to tell them they are being weak and parasitic, existing in a degraded state, is to make them feel inexplicably slapped in the face: they will not understand what you are talking about or what could make you want to attack them that way.

Since to free themselves is out of the question within the current givens of the situation, your exhortations only accuse them once again of inadequacy. . . .

So don't talk to these women unless you can find something to say that is so obviously true and revolutionary that it cuts through all that conditioning and all that helplessness. And don't tell them to go out and work because only if you're educated, able and ambitious can you hope to get a job you might enjoy. . . .

She is not liberatable until the conditions that hold her in slavery are alleviated, until liberation comes to appear feasible and respectable. . . .[38]

The name of the motherhood game was to be options, with no special kudos for any special option whether housewife or career. The housewife who complained that she was denigrated should not expect rewards for a choice when it excused her from the hardships that others could not avoid. The woman with grown children—herself still young and vigorous—who expected homage merely for staying home was asking the unreasonable. As, indeed, was the career woman who expected homage for doing her thing.

The current scene may look, as it does to Edmund Dahlström, like a battle "between 'housewives' and 'working women.'"[39] But that glosses the situation.

It is not, as the anti-feminists say, the career women who are trying to get all mothers into the labor force. It is not achieving women who make careers not only respectable but desirable and who thus implicitly put them on the spot. It is, rather, those who seek to limit the rate of population growth who play up careers for women. These policy makers are the ones who are searching for ways and means to entice women out of the home, into the labor force, as, hopefully, an effective way to discourage motherhood.

### And the Future? Polls

Can the women who are trying to preserve the status quo retain their position as a sheltered leisure class? Can they be given the option of remaining out of the labor force? Is there a future for the "kept woman"? Or, once more, as Monica Boëthius, the Swedish journalist put it, can we continue to be able to afford the housewife? To help find the answer, several clues are available. One is a Harris poll conducted in 1971 and 1972 which asked whether the respondents favored or opposed efforts to strengthen or change women's status in society. For both men and women the proportion favoring such changes increased, among men by 11 percent, among women by 20 percent. In 1972, half of both sexes favored such efforts. Married women favoring change increased by 21 percent, married men, by 15 percent; young women, by 22 percent; young men by 15 percent. College-educated women favoring change increased by 30 percent, college-educated men, by 27 percent.

In 1972, fewer young women than older women agreed that "having a loving husband who is able to take care of me is much more important to me than making it on my own." Fewer young than older women believed "my life is much easier than a man's since I don't have to worry about earning a steady income." Fewer young than older women agreed that "to be really active in politics, women have to neglect their husbands and children." Fewer young than older women agreed that "women should take care of running their homes and leave running the country up to men." Inexorably, women were moving away from the traditional position.[40]

It is projected that by 1990 55.2 percent of women thirty-five to forty-four years of age will be in the labor force, amost 10 per cent more than in 1970, as will 58.0 per cent of women forty-five to fifty-four years of age—a small increase from the 54.0 percent in 1970, but still significant. Not all of these women will necessarily be mothers; but a very substantial proportion will be. For the remainder of this century at least half of all women with school-age children will probably be in the labor force.

### The Future: The Equal Rights Amendment and Motherhood

Since the history of women has yet to be written, what seems new today may be merely a replay of an old record that historical researchers will soon uncover for us. What is in process now is a seemingly new kind of class conflict, different from the Marxian version. Not female brawling and lady-like cat fights, which are old stuff, long familiar in film and tale. It is a conflict between the women fighting to preserve old privileges and those fighting to achieve new ones. The issues center around the Equal Rights Amendment. The proposed amendment is simple: equality of rights shall not be denied or abridged by the United States or by any State on account of sex.[41] Who can be against it? Quite a few women, it soon appeared.

The women who are for the amendment are strong, competent

women who felt they were being held back in their careers by a wide variety of restrictions based on sex. The general feeling was that such restrictions—whether couched in protective legislation for women or in openly discriminatory practices—would be outlawed by the amendment. A number of other non-work-related restrictions (jury duty, for example) and inequalities, (punishment for the same offenses) will, it is hoped, also be removed.

The women dealing with the impact of the amendment on the work world were on fairly safe ground. They could handle the objections to the amendment usually raised. Protective legislation had been exploitative legislation; it had "protected" women from well-paying jobs but not from the lowest menial jobs. (Further, the Civil Rights Act of 1964 had taken precedence over most state protective laws.) They hoped that the amendment's most important achievement would be the reorientation of thinking about sex and sex roles, in the work world as well as at home. To say, as the amendment did, that distinctions could not be made on the basis of sex is not the same as saying that they could not be made on other grounds. Individual differences in size, or weight, or skill, or talent, or a host of other relevant—repeat, relevant—grounds would remain legitimate bases for distinctions. And so also would function. A person, regardless of sex, who could not lift fifty pounds without damage would not be eligible for a job that called for the ability to lift fifty pounds and that would be legitimate and sustainable in a court of law. A person, man or woman, with rough hands, a frightening voice, and a foul breath would not be eligible for a job in a day-care center involving the handling of infants. Any set of qualifications that could be shown to be relevant for any job would still be permitted as criteria and persons, male or female, without such qualifications, could be barred from that job. But just being male would not be enough to get a job; having the qualifications of the job to a higher degree than the female applicant would be. All this was in line with the Civil Rights Act of 1964. In general, the issues centering in the worker role were not very hot ones.

It was the home-related issues that rallied the protesting women to oppose the amendment. In truth, no one could really anticipate what all the ramifications of the amendment might prove to be. There are always unanticipated consequences—benign or sinister—of any kind of legislation. But there were women who feared the worst, as there were who hoped for the best. If restric-

tions against women would be removed, so, too would many restrictions against men said the women who leaned heavily on men
for protection and support. For example, men would not have to
pay alimony, added a lot of bitterly resentful women left stranded
in their middle years. Nor would men be forced to support their
wives and children, they alleged. Whatever benefits the professional women might gain, the non-working family women would
lose, and badly.

Much of what the home-oriented women feared they would be
losing with the amendment was, in actuality, only a mirage. It was
true, for example, that the common law held husbands responsible
for the support of their wives and a large corpus of state legislation
shored this up. In reality it was practically impossible to enforce
these laws as long as a husband and wife were living together,
since the courts were extremely unwilling to intrude upon a marriage so long as it remained intact. And even if the husband left
his wife, securing for her the support legally due her was in many
cases all but impossible. The right to support had never been that
secure, with or without an amendment. Even after divorce, child-
support, let alone alimony, was a sometime thing in a large proportion of cases. After a few years, a woman could forget it.

The home-oriented women were pursuing a faultless, if terrible,
logic. They knew intuitively that, reality or mirage, the idea behind the common law, behind alimony, was something powerful,
something they could not afford to lose. It may have become a
myth. The amendment may not have been an immediate threat to
any of them. They might themselves have been quite secure in
the protection of their husbands. But they could not afford to see
the protection built into the myth endangered for any woman. A
host of amenities also rested on that myth. It entitled women to
numerous prerogatives and privileges, such as having doors
opened for them, cigarettes lighted, chairs held, street-crossings
guided, and other gallantries, all perhaps trivial in themselves.
But if one began to unravel the fabric even at the corner, the
whole thing came undone. It led to questions like, do women
have the right to be supported all through their lives just because
they are women?

As mentioned before, there is no doubt that many women in
middle motherhood, whose children are schoolage or older, are
victims of a cruel transition. They are terribly vulnerable. They
have been crippled. They were reared to fit well into a social sys-

tem which provided that, once married, they would be "taken care of" the rest of their lives. Now that system was being drastically shaken up, leaving them high and dry, at the mercy of, they thought, husbands, whose protection they needed against a harsh outside world for which they were unprepared. Women who had built their lives around motherhood, resting securely on the solid common-law underpinnings, could not afford to let them crumble.

To make function, not sex, the criterion for allocating privileges and prerogatives is a legitimate goal. There is, however, a major fly in the ointment. Child bearing remains exclusively female. It cannot be judged on its merits as between spouses; there is no way to assign it on the basis of the relative qualifications of men or women. No court, with or without the amendment, can decree that the husband rather than the wife in any specific marriage is better qualified to bear the children. Women must bear all the costs of motherhood.

In our long and painful struggle to reconcile the worker and the mother roles of women we have arrived at this point, then, a point at which women's worker role is to be freed from the restrictions imposed by sex but not from those imposed by motherhood. The costs of bearing children can in no way be mitigated by the amendment. But that is another story.[42]

### The Equal Rights Amendment and Motherhood

Virginia J. Cyrus has excerpted statements from an article in the April, 1971 issue of the *Yale Law Review* attempting to show how the ERA would affect the position of women. Among them are the following which refer to motherhood.*

The present legal structure of domestic relations represents the incorporation into law of social and religious views of the proper roles for men and women with respect to family life. Changing social attitudes and economic experiences are already breaking down these rigid stereotypes. The ERA, continuing this trend, would prohibit dictating different roles for men and women within the family on the basis of their sex. Most of the legal changes required by the Amendment would leave couples free to allocate privileges and responsibilities

---

* The present citation is from a Report to the President, The Citizens' Advisory Council on the Status of Women, *Women in 1972* (Govt. Printing Office, 1973), pp.36 ff.

between themselves according to their own individual preferences and capacities.

The Amendment would only prohibit the states from requiring that a child's last name be the same as his or her father's, or from requiring that a child's last name be the same as his or her mother's.

The ERA would prohibit both statutory and common law presumptions about which parent was the proper guardian based on the sex of the parent. Given present social realities and subconscious values of judges, mothers would undoubtedly continue to be awarded custody in the preponderance of situations, but the . . . law would no longer weight the balance in this direction.

In all states husbands are primarily liable for the support of their wives and children, although the details of this liability and the possible defenses vary. . . . The child-support sections of the criminal nonsupport laws would continue to be valid under the ERA in any jurisdiction where they apply equally to mothers and fathers. However, the sections of the laws dealing with interspousal duty of support could not be sustained where only the male is liable for support. . . . With regard to civil enforcement of support laws, courts could take a more flexible approach. The ERA would bar a state from imposing greater liability for support on a husband than on a wife merely because of his sex. However, a court could equalize the civil law by extending the duty of support to women. With regard to child support this is already the rule in Iowa, where father and mother are under the same legal duty to support the children. Alarmists claim that the ERA would change the institution of the family as we know it by weakening the husband's duty of marital support in an ongoing marriage. This concern is based on a misunderstanding of the role laws about support actually play. Many courts flatly refuse to enter a support decree when the husband and wife are living together. In most such cases the husband, as head of the family, is free to determine how much or how little of his property his wife and children will receive.

Similarly the laws could provide support payments for a parent with custody of a young child who stays at home to care for that child, so long as there was no legal presumption that the parent granted custody should be the mother. In short, as long as the law was written in terms of parental function, marital contribution, and ability to pay, rather than the sex of the spouse, it would not violate the ERA.

. . . a rule allowing workers to take sick leave when any member of their household was sick would be an appropriate functional classification. Unlike a rule allowing such leave only to mothers, which denies parents the opportunity to choose which of them will stay home, the functional rule is neutral, allowing workers to choose whether they wish to follow traditional sex-roles or share child rearing and other familial responsibilities. A system of functional classification may thus be utilized in ways which achieve important social objectives without discriminating against individuals on account of their sex.

There are several permissible alternatives to . . . military deferment provisions under the ERA. Deferment might be extended to women, so that neither parent in a family with children would be drafted. Alternatively, the section could provide that one, but not both, of the parents would be deferred. For example, whichever parent was called first might be eligible for service; the remaining parent, male or female, would be deferred. A third possibility would be to grant a deferment to the individual in the couple who is responsible for child care. The couple could decide which one was going to perform this function, and the other member would be liable for service. In a one-parent household Congress would probably defer the parent.

# PART SIX

## Technologies, Politics, and Economics of Motherhood

# Introduction

F. Scott Fitzgerald once said that if a student sleeping in an economics class were ever awakened by a professor's unexpected question, all he had to say was "supply and demand." In an analogous way, all one has to say in reply to many sociological questions is "technology." This is true in reply even to questions about motherhood, for technology has shaped the nature of motherhood in the past and will be equally influential in the future.

Technology is not a homogeneous monolith that operates all of a piece. Some technologies are familiar, having to do with physical things such as machines, engineering, electric and nuclear power and the like, which gave us factories and railroads and air transportation. Some are biological, like the domestication of plants and animals, which gave us agriculture and husbandry. More recently we have developed medical technologies that promise control not only over conception but also over heredity and prenatal defects. Even chemical technologies now give us drugs that affect our moods and behavior; and some, the psychological technologies, influence our minds and emotions. Technologies thus affect the quality as well as the quantity of motherhood. Organizational technologies—the corporation with its bureaucratic structure is one well-researched example—in an indirect way have also influenced motherhood. Some technologies are political, taking the form of laws, legislation, administrative rulings, legal rules; some are economic, providing ways of using the productive capacity for the encouragement or discouragement of specific goals, a technology which Kenneth Boulding, an economist, has called the "grants system."

If necessity is indeed the mother of invention, the reverse proposition is equally tenable. The inventions now called for by necessity include a wide gamut of technological innovations such as: architectural designs for homes to reduce isolation while preserving privacy; better contraception; non-coercive ways to affect family size; optimal ways to supply child care; and ways to pay for it. Buckminster Fuller has taught us that it is more effective to deal with problems by way of technology than by trying to change human beings. Thus, we can probably better improve motherhood by technology than by trying to change mothers. One way would be to apply to motherhood in our society what the six-culture study of motherhood taught us was the best way to institutionalize it.

Technology does not operate in a vacuum. It operates in an ideological ambience. When that technology was agricultural and the ideology pronatalist, familism tended to prevail and women were valued more as mothers than as workers; there was no severance of their roles. When, as now, technology is industrialized and ideology is becoming antinatalist, women's worker role is coming to be favored. But it is well to remind ourselves that behind the roles, however structured, there are women.

Sometimes, as the research presented in Part Six suggests, we are likely to forget that fact. In all the discussions, one hardly catches a glimpse of the women themselves. Technology should not be denigrated. But what there should be more of is "technogyny," technology at the service of women.

## CHAPTER TWELVE

# Physical and
# Social Technologies

### Technologies Make Mother's Habitat
### More Pleasant

We know from the six-culture study, previously quoted, that living arrangements affect motherhood, with both crowding and isolation having a negative effect. Decent housing makes good motherhood possible, poor housing, almost impossible. As Ariès reminds us "there has to be a certain amount of space or family life is impossible." [1] Without space, the members tend to disperse. And the disposition of that space itself makes a difference. The style of motherhood in a court, as among the Rajputs of India, is different from the style on a lonely ranch on the western plains; motherhood on a traffic-clogged street is different from motherhood in an Appalachian hollow. Space in a high-rise building has a different effect on motherhood than does space in a garden apartment. Families are more "real" when their members can spend a considerable amount of time in one another's presence, or at least remain within sight or sound of one another.

The home itself, architecturally, economically, and sociologically a product par excellence of technology, has been the beneficiary or the victim of enough of that technology to transform it several times in the last four or five centuries. Before the fifteenth century, the hovels of the poor, in town or country, consisted of only a room or two. "They were obviously shelters for sleeping and sometimes (not always) eating. These little houses fulfilled no social function. They could not even serve as homes for families. . . . We may conclude that these poor, badly housed people felt a commonplace love for little children . . . but were ignorant of the more complex and more modern forms of the concept of the family. It is certain that the young must have left at a very early age these single rooms which we would call hovels, either to move into other hovels—two brothers together, or husband and wife—or to live as apprentices, servants or clerks in the big houses of the local notabilities." [2] Certainly not very auspicious circumstances for the practice of motherhood.

It was not until the fifteenth century that the places where people lived started to become more or less comfortable. Technological innovations rendered them even agreeable. The idea began to arise that the home might actually be a pleasant place in which to spend time.

> The inventions and changes of the fifteenth century made indoor life less barren and more agreeable. . . . Domestic comfort began to enter the homes even of the poor. They began to provide their cottages with chimneys. The use of window glass spread and pillows appeared on the beds of the common people. The new conditions made real family life possible. The home became the center of pleasurable activities.[3]

The home was no longer a place to escape from when work was done. Domestic pleasures were becoming feasible for all classes. The tavern remained, to be sure, a powerful competitor and magnet for the lower classes and riotous communal entertainment was still appealing to them. Until well into the eighteenth century, gentlemen still had their coffee houses where they smoked, dined, wrote letters, discussed politics and literature, and got drunk. But it was increasingly possible for the home to compete with outside pleasures. A manual for gentlemen in 1778 urged them not to think "domestic pleasures, cares, and duties, beneath their notice." [4] Improvements in lighting and in heating, in conveniences and in sanitation, in architecture and in design all contributed to making the home a more attractive stage for family relationships among those who could afford them. By the time industrialization began to sever mother and worker roles, the cottages of even the humbler classes were already quite attractive, and the homes of the more affluent classes remain to this day models of domestic beauty.

## Technologies Distance Infants from
## Mother's Body

There was a continued increase in consumer goods in the nineteenth century. They not only served to make mother's habitat more comfortable, but also to modify her relations with her children. Household appliances made it possible for mothers to spend more time with them.[5] But consumer goods also modified motherwork in a more intimate and personal way. Even an artifact as simple as the nursing bottle and nipple had the effect of relieving at least middle-class mothers from the necessity of breast feeding, as upper-class women had been by the wet nurse in the past. The baby carriage gave mothers more mobility. Canned baby food, disposable diapers, even the lowly safety pin made their humble contributions to the reduction of motherwork. Some of the new products of technology, however, increased rather than diminished motherwork. A century ago when floors were bare and furnishings few, toilet-training could be relaxed without threatening family property. With the advent of carpets, children had to be kept clean. And the increased number of appliances that had to be protected from children—as well as, of course, vice versa—also added to motherwork.

Some years ago a psychiatrist tried to explain the differences in mental health between 1870 and 1930.[6] He included, among a wide variety of hygienic and psychological variables, a number of simple physical devices. In another book, I have summarized them in terms of the three c's:

In general, one might summarize these changes in terms of "the three c's—carriages, carpets, and cans"—the net effect of which was to separate the child from contact with his mother's body. Carriages took the baby out of the shawl for transportation purposes. Carpets symbolized abundance in the form of more expensive household furnishings which demand protection against the child's depredations, so that much of the content of the relationship between a small child and his mother came to have reference to training "not to touch." And, finally, canned baby food, . . . tended to put the child in front of the mother rather than next to her in feeding.[7]

## Technology Supplies Instant
## Child-Care Facilities

Outside as well as inside the home technology is supplying consumer goods that have an impact on motherhood and, perhaps, replace older, more personal ways of doing things. For a long time young mothers have striven to provide cooperative child-care facilities for their children with very little help. Seeing a service that needed to be supplied, two young women in Cambridge, Massachusetts, set up an information exchange to help them overcome such hurdles as: lack of self-confidence, money, staffing, finding a place. They provided advice, catalogs, floor plans, sample budgets, licensing requirements, and staffing guidelines.

Now here comes technology. The General Learning Corporation, for example, began to market a "line" of do-it-yourself child-care-center kits called "Adaptispace units." It also offered a program for training day-care personnel. Thus anyone could just contract with the Corporation "to pick a center site, furnish it, fill it with materials, train the teachers, and then turn the key over to the sponsor." It did not as yet include tender-loving-care in its "line." Just an oversight no doubt that would soon be remedied. But in the meanwhile the Cambridge women were offering a very special item: "lots of reassurance." [8]

Who knows? The time may not be too far off when a mother will contract with General Learning Corporation, or some other, to supply all the toys, teachers, and treatments that her child will need. Nanny used to do it. Why not General Learning Corporation?

As important as the technologies creating consumer goods which transformed hovels into homes and moved infants away from their mothers' bodies, were the technologies of production that transferred the very nature of human relationships, between men and women, husbands and wives, parents and children, masters and servants—in fact, among everyone

## Technology Takes Work Out of the Home

One need not be a Marxist to interpret the history of motherhood in terms of the history of the production of material goods. A thorough-going survey of the way these technologies have affected how the role of mother is institutionalized would have to begin in prehistory, before agriculture and settled communities. But the crucial technological changes so far as modern motherhood is concerned began in the late eighteenth century when the factory system first began to separate family and work, or at least to accelerate that separation.

The mechanics, engineers, and scientists of the eighteenth century who put the wherewithal for improving spinning, weaving, mining, and farming at the disposal of headstrong men, and the theorists who guided the policy makers, had no idea what the consequences of industrialization were going to be for motherhood; neither did the machinists who hitched the internal combustion machine to the carriage, nor Henry Ford who made it profitable to do so—no one had any idea what the consequences of the resulting suburbanization was going to have on the institution of motherhood.

Fathers were not the first to move out of the home to work in factories [9] but, over time, more and more fathers than mothers did so, thus turning over an ever larger share of parental care to women. This made a difference in motherhood. When men, as they had done in preindustrial societies or, later, in rural areas, had assumed a considerable part in the rearing of children, especially of sons, force and fear had been a major factor in child rearing. The powerful father-image loomed large in the minds of children. The whip (itself a technological device, like the teacher's ruler) was not an unknown instrument. But:

> . . . when women took over the socialization of children, the process was transformed from manipulation by threat of force to manipulation by seduction, enticement, and guilt. Brutal physical punishment—and even spanking and slapping—have become almost extinct among the middle classes. . . . Mothers today shape the development of the child by assuming love and trust . . . and demanding guilt. The changed style of child-rearing has had specific consequences for the character formation of people in the highly industrialized countries. The emphasis has shifted from external behavior to internal motives.[10]

There is more to the story. Not only did industrialization have the effect of giving mothers an increased portion of the job of socializing children, but the urbanization which accompanied it—including suburbanization—also complicated the picture by moving the work of the father farther and farther away from the family at home.

The new technologies in agriculture, in transportation, and in communication that accompanied the new industrial order not only made the growth of cities possible—in fact, inevitable—but also had the effect of vastly increasing the spatial separation of the father from the mother left at home struggling with child rearing, for despite the greater concentration of settlement in cities, individual households themselves became more and more isolated and removed from work sites.

The kinds of relationships that were possible in small villages or towns, in which children knew where fathers were and could even accompany them to work, were quite different from those in large cities where fathers just disappeared every morning into distant limbos. There was probably less difference between preliterate village life and preindustrial rural life than between preindustrial life and urban life today.

Cities widened the scope of the necessity for child protection. They encroached on the areas of safety for children till there seemed to be few remaining places in which children could be left unguarded, few places where the children could play without supervision. Traffic is a constant threat outdoors and even indoors danger lurks everywhere in the guise of electric appliances and household necessities on closet shelves in both the kitchen and bathroom. Overseeing children becomes an ever-expanding occupation, not only to keep them amused, but actually out of harm. High-rise apartments, according to Constantinos A. Doxiadis, "work against man himself, especially against children." [11] Family life becomes separated from the community life and from nature down below.[12] Children have to wait until mother can take them to the play area, if, indeed, there is any. Without free space in which to find their own proper business, children must appeal to mother: "what should we do now? " Older children just disappear from sight.

The transporation technology that made suburbia possible has not eased the problems of motherhood. It did, originally at least, provide space. What could be better for children than the quasi-rural pattern, a pattern of individual houses on wide lots with green lawns surrounded by yards? How could suburbia have anything but a benign influence? So far as small children are con-

cerned, suburban living may indeed be benign. But it is not necessarily so for their mothers, who must spend a large part of their day
in a mobile prison toting children, groceries, adolescents, and
husbands hither and yon. The same is true for wives of blue-collar
workers who are more dependent than middle-class women on
family and friends left behind in the old neighborhood. "Life in
suburbia may be viewed by the wives as beneficial for the children. . . . However, when these benefits are at the cost of giving
up meaningful and integrative personal relations resulting in an
increased sense of isolation, they may question whether the 'advantages' are worth the price." [13] Once more mother pays the—
emotional—bill.

Suburban life does not seem to be benign for adolescents either.
Jack Cohen, an architect responsible for a great deal of the suburban housing development in the most affluent county in the country, pronounces it a failure for them. In an interview he is quoted
as saying:

> "People [in the suburban developments] were cut off from
> the community services they needed." Long stretches of road-
> ways were needed to reach separate houses. Mass transpor-
> tation became inefficient, and people became dependent on
> the automobile, even to do their casual visiting. Still the sub-
> urbs grew. . . . And now an entire suburban-grown genera-
> tion has come of age—without . . . a sense of self-sufficiency.
> "There were no facilities available to them on their own.
> Their mothers had to enroll them in dance school or music
> lessons—and then drive them there." This lack of self-suf-
> ficiency and . . . the "dull monotony of the suburban environ-
> ment" were key preconditions of the so-called drug culture.
> "I don't think any of us were aware of this" at the time, the
> 1950s and early 1960s.[14]

Taking pot-shots at suburbia has become such a cheap and easy
gambit that it seems unfair to add this to the charges against it. Yet
no account of motherhood today can ignore the impact suburbia
has on it. The outward migration from the cities began with the
best of intentions. All the values embedded in the dream that un-
derlay it had quite understandable and benign origins. In the nineteenth century, protection of the home from the powerful forces
that were creating the cities, which no one had had any experi-

ence living in, was important. The home *was* a sanctuary. No one had dreamed that instead, one day it would become a prison however placid and beautiful its setting.

Suburbia depends almost completely on the automobile.[15] We have based an entire life style on it. Any reduction in the supply of fuel required to power the automobile would leave millions of women stranded in the suburban developments. Now, in the 1970s, the automobile's place is being challenged from many angles: environmental, economic, sociological. Curtailment of the use of the private car is actually being proposed and even legislated. If successful, it could increase the isolation of the housebound homemaker, whether father or mother, immured in the suburban ghetto. It will call on planners to reverse the processes that have distanced work from family so drastically. And that, precisely, is what planners have been trying to do for some time.

### Technology to the Rescue?

The catalog of complaints against the setting in which motherhood had to be performed did not pass unnoticed. Consulting agencies began to turn the researchers toward them. They looked, they studied, they examined and, like the complaining mothers, they agreed: something was wrong. "Basic to every other reform, whether educational, health service, penal, family, or whatnot, are issues of where and how Americans shall live. Here, in a most telling way, the floundering of a ship without a rudder scuttles the nation's (enormous latent) potential." [16]

The floundering resulted from the unplanned suburban housing developments that had proliferated after World War II. The queen's garden became ever more luxurious, ever more elegant, ever more comfortable. An analysis of the advertisements for condominiums and houses in these developments offers us clues with respect to the trends in life styles for at least the immediate future. It is a future that replicates the past. The new developments are setting in concrete—literally—the mold for at least a generation. The result includes superb provision for physical and material facilities but relatively little provision for the relief of housebound young mothers. Such amenities as wall-to-wall carpeting, central air conditioning, self-defrosting refrigerators, eye-level ovens, are standard. (Saunas and bidets are mentioned in some.) Indoor recreation is a standard provision in the form of family or recreation rooms; but outdoor recreation is also featured prominently: golf courses, swimming pools, bicycle paths, walking trails. A major feature of location is driving time to major traffic routes or urban facilities, as well as walking distance to shopping malls and schools. Fun is emphasized as much as luxury. Ominously, security is also a selling point. Featured appeals are to the upwardly mobile young, with room for growing families and association with affluent neighbors.

As long as the present stock of housing survives—and, because new houses preserve the life style of the old ones, this will be a long time—the site on which motherwork is performed will remain pretty much as it is today. While many young women are looking for ways to live more cooperatively, there is little provision for such a life style in suburbia. Both privacy and community recreation are highlighted, but architectural designs that facilitate cooperation are notable by their absence. Young women themselves could not jump this hurdle. Again, as Buckminster Fuller reminds us, we have to provide the environment if we wish to change the behavior of people. Not until the architects have designed the setting that makes it possible for families to cooperate while at the same time retaining their coveted privacy will young women find ways to practice the life style so many of them now crave. Architecture and community non-planning constitute great roadblocks so far as physical isolation is concerned. But the isolation that cuts mothers off is social as well as physical.

The newer thinking takes account of the need to provide physical facilities to overcome the built-in isolation of the young mother. Thus a young architect—female, it so happens—has this to say on the subject:

> . . . neighborhood child-care facilities might make a particularly good New Town center-of-focus. From a sociological perspective, it would help mothers meet one another and make new friends, as well as help free them for new role activities; from a psychological perspective, it would demonstrate the high value in which children and (professionally-aided) child-rearing were held in the New Town. From a community-building perspective, it would be available for evening seminars on issues in child-rearing, as well as general purpose settlement-house programs. In all, its "message" would complement the New Town in every way.[17]

235

### Technology's Task

Thus an old idea, revived in the late sixties and early seventies, proposed a solution in the form of so-called New Towns, (thoroughly planned self-contained new cities of 100,000 or so on approximately 10,000 acres of previously unused land). A host of economic, political, and social arguments were invoked to justify the development of such new towns against the powerful opposition of tract developers, big-city mayors, minority-group spokesmen, "Old City romantics," and financiers. Still, enough experiments have been and are being made to give us hints with respect to the future such new towns portend. Mixed with the positives were enough negatives to give thoughtful people pause, including a syndrome called "New Town Blues." And who suffered this syndrome?

> To begin with, the phenomena, "New Town Blues," clearly warrant comment. Many early residents apparently suffer from a syndrome first identified in England in 1959. Its symptoms include discontent among younger residents, who miss cosmopolitan amenities, and depression among housewives, who complain of feeling cut off from the world. Cutting across the symptoms is a common sense of disequilibrium where time is concerned: it is hard to acknowledge that when left more time and energy to be, you come up short. Time comes to weigh heavy on the hands of those unfamiliar with it; strangeness breeds (self) contempt and more ambivalence than humanly comfortable.[18]

Children and teenagers also had problems, the children suffering from feeling "isolated, regimented, and bored" in towns seen as "concrete fortresses of cleanliness, order, and boredom"; the teenagers suffering from a restlessness which disturbed the adult world. And children were, of course, the responsibility of mother who had to deal with the child's problems as well as with her own. (Among the more sterile ideas was one that sought to bring a bit of adventure in the form of chaos back to the children, the so-called "junk" playgrounds, "rich in castoff building materials; children are free to construct, destruct, and reconstruct their own playhouses, forts, space stations, castles, and the like."[19] We are reminded of William James's comments on Chautauqua: Oh, for a bit of disorder!)

Not one of the several new towns attacked the automobile head-on. But one planned for Fairfax County, Virginia, did. Its brochure spelled out its idea:

New Franconia contributes greatly to the freedom of the individual by eliminating the real need for a car as a primary means of transportation. Unique to this model town is a pollution-free monorail-like transporter providing 24-hour service to any point in the New Franconia network within eight minutes. Operating much like an elevator, this silent electric system will stop inside buildings to pick up passengers for a swift, toll-free ride throughout the community. Each neighborhood in New Franconia has a stop within a few hundred feet of residences. A connecting Metro station on the outskirts of Franconia will carry residents to points throughout the Metropolitan Washington, D.C. area, while shops on the mobility system also connect with Virginia's shuttle and express busses. A heliport on the east end of the project rounds out the transportation requirements of those who elect to live in New Franconia without a car.

Also indicative of the orientation of this plan was provision for day care centers:

Through day care centers and "tot lots" in every neighborhood of the new town, a mother will be afforded the freedom to pursue her own interests outside the home—to work, take classes, become involved in civic and governmental affairs—while her children are given the opportunity to relate to other adults.

And, again, an attack on the separation of work from home: "virtually every man and woman who lives in New Franconia will be able to work in the new town's architecturally stimulating employment center. Jobs of every description will be available to New Franconia's residents and neighbors. The mobility system and day care centers offer freedom of movement never before achieved in a self-contained environment." Provision is also made for the carless teenager and the elderly in the form of recreational facilities. Shopping facilities, education, and utilities are provided as a matter of course as all tract developments do; but it is the additional recognition given to ecology in eliminating the need for automobiles that makes this new town a brave new world indeed.

Little by little we are inching our way to undoing the damage done to motherhood by the industrial revolution of the eighteenth and nineteenth centuries and the urbanization that accompanied it, hopefully not by way of regressing to all the disabilities motherhood suffered in those preindustrial agricultural days. It is not regression that is called for but a new design. And not until planning begins with mothers and builds to their specifications, including a wide variety of options, will we be successful.

A major difficulty is that we really cannot instruct the planners. We have not worked out the social angles. When young mothers are asked what kinds of living arrangements they would like they come up with ideas still limited by what already exists. One group suggests taking over a whole floor in an apartment building and using one apartment in common; a sort of cooperative "affinity family" arrangement. Another group thinks in terms of adjacent houses on a city block. Another would like a housing development centered around their children's school. Another would like a large "extended family" consisting of congenial people of all ages not necessarily related by blood but by common ideas. Another dreams in terms of several families sharing several acres of green countryside.

Given four or five congenial families who knew what they wanted, an architect could easily come up with a design to provide it. And if these families were to remain unchanged and immobile over time, this might be a solution for them. But if the families changed, as families inevitably must, the arrangements might not suit other families, they might be too idiosyncratic to pass marketability tests. Once the original families have used up the design, so to speak, it would become disposable. We might, in time, standardize a wide variety of designs so that any three families could adapt to them, as families now have to adapt to what they find in the existing market.[20]

## Communication Technologies and Motherhood

The telephone plays a large part in family relations today. Women in late motherhood depend on it to maintain contacts with sons and daughters and vice versa. In addition to television, which serves as a baby sitter, there now looms large the prospect of telecommunication, which will make it possible in time for everyone to have his or her own private channel and thus be in a position to communicate with any other individual, seeing as well as hearing the other person any time, anywhere.[21] If such telecommunication becomes a reality, mothers and their sons and daughters may maintain relationships over time and distances which now prohibit them. The sons and daughters in the North will no longer be able to excuse their lack of contact with their parents in the South, and loosening family ties will become more difficult.

The prospect might seem horrendous to some. Sons or daughters might bemoan their mother's perpetual "interference." And mothers, on their side, might groan, "Will I *never* be free of their demands?" The prospect may be delightful to others. It would make it possible for lonely old women who do not wish to participate actively in the lives of their sons and daughters, to watch them rather than the soap operas that are now their daily fare. And the anxious daughter could feel reassured that mother is really OK if she could see her over the telecommunication network. Indeed, telecommunication would seem to be the ideal medium for mother-son or mother-daughter contacts in a great many families. In the meanwhile, many mothers, sons, and daughters would settle for just good telephone connections.

As a service for housebound young mothers, Catherine Chilman of the University of Wisconsin has proposed to the State Department of Health and Social Services that there be established a "mother's hot line." When the overwhelmed mother could no longer bear the stresses around her she could send out an SOS and there would be instant help available to take over until she could resume the load. Or someone could take care of the baby while she took Jimmy to the doctor or could take Jimmy to the doctor for her. This is, in effect, a way to put technology—the telephone in this case—to use in supplying, within vocal reach, the help once available to the mother in the neighborhood.

The growing salience of communication and computer technologies in all kinds of production has led some observers to believe that a great deal of work could now be returned to the home. There has not been much evidence, in the conventional world, as yet of a return of work to the home; the work experience by women in the home has not been all that auspicious as the history of sweatshops in the late nineteenth and early twentieth centuries shows. Such home workers tended to be exploitable, without protection. True, many in the counterculture have returned to crafts such as pottery and jewelry making but the movement has not yet burgeoned. Now, however, come new technologies that make possible a wholly new concept. In Seattle a system was established by which one could pick up a telephone in one's own home and program a variety of services: to pay bills, be reminded of birthdays, appointments, and other obligations, order products. Such a gadget certainly has enormous possibilities. It does bring closer the time when a large part of the clerical work and even some of the services can be performed in the home. But will this device really catch on? Women who do editorial work, typing of manuscripts, and other fairly high-level work at home, find it boring. They want out. But for some women, it may be ideal. It would certainly help reintegrate her mother and her work roles.

## Social Technologies and Motherhood

Not all technologies have to do with physical inventions. Sociologists speak of social inventions, including innovations in organization. Among the scores of such innovations, one of the most important, according to some observers, is the bureaucratic form of organization which has come to predominate in both government and industry. The effects have been far-reaching, touching many aspects of our lives—even family life, including parenthood.

The so-called permissiveness that, in the sixties and early seventies, came in for so much criticism, has been shown to be related, through a round-about path, to this style of organization. It may seem very far-fetched to postulate, a technological influence on motherhood in the rise of bureaucracy. Still, two serious researchers, one a psychologist and one a sociologist, did claim to find such an influence. On the basis of 575 interviews in Detroit in 1953 they found that the practice of parenthood was indeed affected by the kind of work the father did. If he were an entrepreneur ("rugged individualist"), one set of values was inculcated in children; if he were employed in a highly organized industry ("welfare bureaucracy"), quite a different one was inculcated. The authors themselves took a benign attitude toward bureaucracy. And they saw that in homes of bureaucratic workers was produced the kind of person demanded by it. They hypothesized that "children reared in welfare-bureaucratic homes will be encouraged to be accommodative, to allow their impulses some spontaneous expression, and to seek direction from the organizational programs in which they participate." By way of contrast, they hypothesized that "children reared in individuated and entrepreneurial homes will be encouraged to be highly rational, to exercise great self-control, to be self-reliant, and to assume an active, manipulative stance toward their environment." Their expectations were borne out. Mothers in entrepreneurial homes did in fact tend to emphasize strong self-control in rearing their children; and mothers in bureaucratic homes did tend to emphasize "a more accommodative and adjustive way of life." [22]

Since this study was made there has emerged a strong reaction against the bureaucratic form of organization. It was seen as producing alienation among workers with resulting "poor mental health, poor motivation, alcoholism, drug abuse, and social dissatisfaction among workers." Whatever the parents in bureaucratic families were aiming at in their child-rearing practices, a seemingly large segment of their sons and daughters were rebelling against the impact of bureaucracies on their lives. A wide variety of remedies were being suggested "to meet the problems of work alienation, including more flexible hours of work, reduced working days, profit sharing, additional responsibility for workers, job rotation, *worker participation in the decision-making process with regard to the nature and content of his job,* redesign of jobs and production patterns, *autonomous work groups,* and additional opportunity for education, training, and advancement." [23]

New forms of organization were being called for by quite a different trend—the occupational changes taking place as a result of technological changes. They were calling for socializing young people in the direction of stereotypically "female" qualities. We are, in fact, being told that the United States is now going through an occupational shift as momentous and profound as any in the past, "recalling the movement of peasants into factories during the Industrial Revolution." [24] This shift results from the disappearance of some specialized functions and the rise of new ones. Quite new—traditionally female—kinds of talents and skills are increasingly being called for in these new jobs.

> In perhaps twenty or thirty years, feminine virtues will be diffused through the society, because women . . . will have begun to lose their defined occupational role. Men adjusting to the new kinds of work will incorporate characteristics that were previously defined as female virtues, partly because they will want to . . . but also because economic conditions will require it. Women will incorporate virtues previously defined as male, due to their industrial involvement and independence. The result will be a greater richness in the

human character. We will find independence coupled with yieldingness and compromise, thrust coupled with tenderness, adventure and experiment coupled with stability, decision-making and responsibility coupled with guilt.[25]

Only as many women will choose motherhood as, say, men will choose engineering. Mothers, as suggested by the nonmotherhood movement, will be a mere specialty group in the United States.

This state of affairs will not result from the activity of women so much as from the economic results of technological change. "Women must be 'liberated' to enjoy the fruits of other occupations, whether they want to be or not." For, in view of technological changes now in process, "motherhood must undergo a drastic revision." [26] As David B. Lynn, a psychologist notes, if the women's liberation movement had not arisen spontaneously it would have had to be invented.[27]

## CHAPTER THIRTEEN

# Medical, Pharmacological, and Psychological Technologies

## Whose Selection?

Human heredity was established in its more-or-less present form not less than ten thousand years ago. It has changed only very slowly, if at all, since then. Mutations have occurred and selective breeding, non-purposive as well as purposive, has produced different strains and changes in pigmentation, size, immunities, and susceptibilities. We have lost most of our fur, and some organs, notably the appendix, have become vestigial. Imaginative interpreters of anthropological research predict other physical changes in the future. Some picture our bald-headed descendents as having massive skulls housing enlarged brains atop shrunken, puny, little bodies allowed to degenerate for lack of use.

In the nineteenth century, human beings began to repudiate the idea of allowing natural selection to decide our future heredity; they felt they'd rather do it themselves. They wanted humans to decide their own futures by means of deliberate, conscious, rational breeding by a process called eugenics. Today we are going even further. We are beginning to tinker with the stuff of heredity itself.

Until now we have had to make do with the bodies and brains with which our species began history. For all intents and purposes, certainly so far as reproduction is concerned, human heredity has been a constant. Although reproduction still involves, as it always has, conception, gestation, birth, and lactation, we are, nevertheless, closer and closer to new ways of doing it, with incalculable implications for the future of motherhood.

## A Severing Effect

Anything that improves the health and longevity of women, anything that gives them control over conception, anything that takes reproduction out of the hands of divinity and gives women more say in the matter, anything that lowers the demand by industry or government for a large number of babies will facilitate the severing of the mother and worker roles. The biological technologies have had all these effects. They have thus had profound and continuing effects on motherhood.

They have made it possible for more and more infants to survive, thus reducing the necessity for large numbers of pregnancies in order to ensure surviving sons and daughters; better maternal care has helped more and more women survive childbirth, cutting down the number of motherless children and stepmothers; and improved health and sanitation have extended the life span for both men and women so that fewer women are now left to rear children as widowed mothers. The net result of such medical technologies has been a rate of population growth greater than the earth can safely accommodate. There has been a consequent call for moderation, which means less motherhood.

Only passing reference needs to be made to improved contraception techniques. New and more acceptable forms are constantly being sought and taught, so that there has been a decline in the rate of unwanted child bearing.[1] Voluntary sterilization, the most reliable of all forms of birth control, showed a dramatic increase between 1965 and 1970. Although overall it was chosen by only 16 percent of all the couples in one sample, it was the most popular method among couples in which the wife was thirty years of age or older. Husbands and wives underwent such sterilization in about equal numbers.[2] Contraceptive technology is important because it makes voluntary motherhood possible for more and more women. It guarantees that all babies born are not only wanted but planned.

## Medical Technologies and the New Sex

Medicine has not only extended the life expectancy of women, it has also created youthful bodies to go along nowadays with the added years. It has extended the lives of women far beyond the years of active motherwork thus releasing them for other roles. Indeed, one of the most startling developments of recent times is the headlong rush of many of these women into the labor force. Medicine has, in effect, created a new age category, for just as childhood emerged in the fifteenth century, adolescence at the beginning of the twentieth, and youth at midcentury, so, too, has a new generation of women—products of medical technology—appeared on the scene today. These women do not fit any of the old stereotypes. They announce, with as much surprise and incredulity as they expect to find in their listeners, that they are *grand*mothers! And in the near future they will be *great*-grandmothers, for the four-generation family is almost inevitable.

Traditionally the image of the grandmother has been one of a benign little old lady delightedly serving roast turkey and pumpkin pie to a large family. It has now become common to speak of glamorous grandmothers. As, indeed, many of them, still only in their late forties or fifties, are. Motherhood will not be a sufficient role for an increasing number of these lively women. Here is what they are like:

> Something new has been added in recent years. A genuinely new biological subsex has been added to the human stock of sexes. A new kind of woman. She is the result of cultural forces, technological as well as normative, and of advances in medicine, nutrition, and health care, especially obstetrical. She was not designed and shaped for a specific function, as some other manufactured subsexes were. She was, in fact, an unanticipated consequence of modern science.
>
> In the past when we spoke of "the new woman" we were likely to be thinking of women with new ideas and attitudes, new aspirations and new conceptions of themselves and of their relations to the world. But the new women today are new in a quite different way. Not in the sense that they are young, for they are not; they may be in their fifties and even, in some rare cases, their sixties. They are new in the sense that women like them have never existed on this planet until now. Their very existence is a brand-new human and therefore social phenomenon—as a whole generation, that is; there have always been such individuals.
>
> A demographic revolution has extended sexuality into later years than in the past. The menopause comes later now than it used to. Not only do women live longer than preceding generations did; they also retain their youth and even beauty much

longer. And those who do not do so naturally can be helped to do so by the new hormonal therapy.

If they were new only in this demographic sense they would not necessarily be new sociologically. They would just be more of the same—old women in larger numbers than before. And in fact, not all of these surviving women really are new. Many still are the same old kind of women as in the past. But some are genuinely new.[3]

It is, however, at the other end of the age gradient, among young women, that medical technologies are having their most important impact on the future of motherhood. Medical technologies are giving us more and more control over reproduction. And here we approach the very core of the matter. "More than any other modern technology, the research into new modes of human reproduction now going on in thousands of biological and medical laboratories around the world . . . strikes at the very heart of human society because it cuts to the quick of the human family."[4] True, indeed, for step-by-step, from insemination to the predetermining of the sex of the child, technology is extending our control over reproduction until, theoretically at least, it could become as impersonal as animal breeding.

### Three Levels of Intervention

There are three levels at which science and technology can interfere to affect, if not control, reproduction. One occurs at the moment of birth when some defects of metabolism can be diagnosed and treated. A second level pushes back the point of intervention to the prenatal stage. Here, by means of "amniocentesis" or "fetoscopy," diagnoses of defects may be made in utero and, if indicated, termination of the pregnancy undertaken. The third level pushes the intervention back even further, to the pre-parental, even pre-marital, level. It is based on knowledge about the laws of heredity or, where these do not apply, to statistical analysis of known cases of certain defects. This kind of intervention has a fairly long history in the form of eugenics, so-called, or "good breeding," of both a positive and a negative kind, that is, "breeding in" good traits and "breeding out" bad ones. What is new, however, is the possibility of active modification of genetic defects rather than mere accommodation to them after they appear. Anything that can improve the health of children and reduce the occurrence of defects among them has a liberating effect on mothers, freeing them from the all-encompassing demands that illness and defects make on them.

### The First Level

For at least one inherited metabolic defect—phenylketonuria, or PKU—treatment initiated immediately upon birth and continued until maturity can prevent severe retardation. Other defects can also be pinpointed as inherited and in some states, as in Maryland, all newborn infants must be screened for such genetic metabolic disorders. Even though we have no way of correcting it, except by way of environmental control, questions are being raised with respect to testing males for the presence of the extra Y chromosome which, at least in some cases allegedly leads to aggressiveness and antisocial behavior.

It is not, however, the scientific aspects of intervention that concern us here but the impact it may have on mothers, which varies widely. Sometimes the defect is so gross that there would seem to be little to warrant salvaging. In one case, for example, it was 'an infant born without eyes or any recognizable brain tissue, with severe abnormality of the abdominal wall." [5] Surely no candidate for heroic (and expensive) measures. Still, "the distraught family pleaded with the doctor to do something for the infant. They needed badly to be assured that everything possible was being done so they could have no regrets later. 'Grief and disappointment can be accepted in time, but guilt is impossible to handle.' So the infant was operated on . . . and died later in the day as expected." [6] The family thanked the physician. "They informed me that the family was reunited after their grief and was able to accept the death." [7] One can only imagine the relief a mother would experience when honorably released from a lifelong martyrdom to the care of a vegetating blob of tissue. In another case, on the other hand, the parents refused consent for therapeutic surgery on a mongoloid child "on the grounds it would be unfair to their normal child to bring a retarded infant into the home. They added that, even if the child had lived, they never would have accepted him." [8] So the child lay in its crib in a dark corner of the hospital, starving to death. Again, one can only imagine the anguish of the mother waiting for the end. It took 15 days.[9]

Thus the emotional demands made on mothers become enormously complex as new scientific knowledge increases our understanding of genetics and technologies give us control over defects. Although science and technology do a great deal to make motherhood easier and safer than in the past, at the same time, by giving women more decisions to make, they can also make it harder, emotionally though not physically. When God made all the decisions, women had no choice but to accept them. If an Act of God gave you a defective child you learned to live with perpetual grief. But there was little guilt or spiritual laceration. Now, however, that science and technology tell mothers they do not have to accept that fate, the Act of God is transformed into an act of her own. The decisions she may have to make can be harrowing.

They must have great strength to make decisions: Whether or not to bear children at all if there are defective genes in either her or her husband's heredity; whether or not to have an abortion if prenatal examination shows the presence of disease or defect; and whether or not to permit heroic measures to save an infant with defective metabolism. The intellectual, as well as the emotional, demands also become complex, for not everyone can easily comprehend the information supplied by the scientists.[10]

### The Second Level

Some defects can now be detected before the infant is born, especially the ones that have structural or metabolic effects on the fetus. The best known are Tay-Sachs syndrome and Down's syndrome, better known as mongolism. These diseases cannot as yet be treated; the intervention, if any, must take the form of abortion.

### The Third Level

So long as knowledge of genetics was incomplete, technology unsophisticated, and control a matter of selective mating rather than more complex intervention, the impact on motherhood was mild and received only relatively desultory attention. True, several jurisdictions did try to impose rules requiring sterilization for certain kinds of criminals, for women who bore more than a minimum number of children outside of marriage, and so on. But this remained a minor matter until technology placed within our reach much that once seemed fanciful, not necessarily in the form of pills or surgery but in the form of knowledge.

What modern science does is to provide information on which men and women can base their decisions about parenthood. It can determine for them what chances there are for a genetic defect in their family to show up in their children. "Supported by Mendelian genetics, the notions of dominant and recessive autosomal or x-linked modes of inheritance, the counselor can often provide specific information about recurrence risks." [11] In cases where genetic defects do not follow Mendelian laws, the scientist "must rely upon empirical statistics of risk . . . derived from studying the incidence of a disease in many families. From these observations the counselor can provide the clients with approximations of the recurrence risk of a specific disease." [12] When neither Mendelian ratios nor statistical estimates are available, the scientist must admit his ignorance.

The most widely publicized illness that can now be "predicted" from family histories is sickle-cell anemia. Another is hemophilia, popularized because of its incidence in the royal houses of Europe. Such "predictions" refine old attempts to avoid traits that "run in families." What is new today is better determination of the existence of the genetic defect without having to wait for it to show itself in living victims and, of far greater complexity, the ability to do something about the problem by means of artificial insemination, inovulation, and "genetic engineering."

The first of these techniques, artificial insemination, is the best known. If it is determined, for example, that the husband carries a defective gene, it is now possible to fertilize the wife's ovum with the sperm of a donor. One estimate places the number of babies resulting from such artificial insemination to be about twenty thousand per year as of 1958. About a fifth of such inseminations survive, so that attempted inseminations may be as many as one hundred thousand. Another estimate places attempts at five hundred thousand and births at one million.[13]

The second technique, "inovulation" is not fully developed. Among animals it is now possible to remove an embryo from the uterus of one—genetically—superior cow and replace it in the uterus of another, genetically inferior, animal. Thus a genetic "super-mother" can produce a much larger number of superior calves than if she had to gestate them herself. The technicians can go a step further to relieve the superior female even of conceiving. Her ovaries can be transplanted. With human beings this is not yet possible, only probable. Two researchers in England, Dr. Robert G. Edwards and Dr. Patrick C. Steptoe, have, in fact, reportedly conceived a human embryo in vitro in their laboratory.[14] Thus, in the future, if it is the wife rather than the husband who has the genetic defect, an ovum from another woman could conceivably be transferred to her body to be fertilized by her own husband and gestated in her body. She would then give birth to a child to whose genetic composition she would have contributed nothing at all.

This technology is a two-way street. A woman with normal genetic constitution might wish to contribute to the genetic heritage of a child but not be bothered with gestating it. She might have an ovum from her body transplanted to the body of another woman, fertilized there, and gestated by the other woman, sparing the genetic mother the nine months of pregnancy.

In the Biblical story, Hagar bore Abraham a son because Sarah was barren. Modern technology could have managed it better and spared Ishmael his sad fate. The Shah of Persia divorced a beloved wife because she bore him no sons. Modern technology could have spared her this misfortune. But modern technology can also de-humanize reproduction. Perhaps the most important effect of these reproductive technologies will be the de-sacralization of motherhood, the dispelling of its *mythos*. The major impact may be on our thinking, on our conceptualization of motherhood. Reproduction will no longer be a proof of either maleness or femaleness. Anyone can do it. All that is needed is a skillful medical technician.

A third kind of preparental intervention takes the form of so-called genetic engineering. The time is coming when defective genes can be altered rather than by-passed.[15] Already such genetic engineering is becoming feasible on laboratory subjects. The chromosomes in the sperm may be modified to produce animals with desired qualities. With animals the problems are fairly simple because the genetic engineer knows precisely what he wants to achieve, which chromosome bearing what quality he wants to change. The matter is not nearly so simple in the case of human beings. With respect to genes carrying defects the question would be relatively simple. But what about other genes, normal in all respects, but not carrying the traits the parents want? Like, for example, sex? One of the future possibilities of genetic engineering will be precisely control of the sex of offspring. What, it is often asked, would be the consequences? We know that overall there seems to be a preference for boys. If couples have three girls the chances are more likely that they will "try" for a boy than that they will "try" for a girl after a "run" of boys. (Still, girls are more in demand for adoption.) If sex does become controllable, a market-type situation may well result. If there are "too many" boys being born, there would tend to be a demand for more girls, and vice versa. We know that males, at all ages from conception on, are less viable than females—the sex ratio at conception has been estimated to be one hundred fifty males to one hundred females and known to be about 104–105 males to 100 females at birth [16]—so that parents would doubtless opt for boys in enough cases to ensure the survival of at least a minimum number of sons.

One scientist asks whether we are mature enough to handle so much power over human heredity. "Will future parents demand that all their firstborn offspring be white, blond, blue-eyed males, just because technology is available to make it so? Or will we insist that gene therapy only be employed for a defined and limited group of diseases?" [17]

I have enough confidence in women to answer that they will show good judgment in handling this question. It is doubtful that black mothers would order white children or white women, black. Or that blue eyes would be ordered more than brown. There is no reason to suppose that decisions would be trivial or frivolous.

What limited research we do have shows, in fact, that women are remarkably conscientious about their maternal responsibilities. In one study of twenty-five women who had experienced amniocentesis, extraordinary awareness was shown.

> For most of the twenty-five couples . . . (all of whom had already had one damaged child) undertaking amniocentesis was . . . an experiment to get a healthy child. One of the mothers early in the study reflected on this and said, "These days you have a choice about having a healthy baby.". . . When, as in three cases, the experiment ended in failure, all of the women elected to be sterilized. When asked why not the husband, one woman replied, "It's my fault, why should he have to pay for it?" This self-imposed sense of genetic responsibility and guilt appeared to be markedly impressed on all of the female members of the pregnancy partnership.[18]

Even with artificial insemination or inovulation and fetal transplants, however, and even with genetic engineering, a female body—the supplier of the ovum or some other woman—must still have the fetus implanted in her womb, gestate it for nine months, and give birth to it in the old-fashioned way. But modern technologies may, in the future, free women from even this contribution to the reproductive process. The ultimate step is taken when women can be dispensed with entirely, when subhuman animals or artificial mechanical wombs can gestate the fertilized eggs.

This is not quite the ultimate step. For now we are told that it is possible to achieve sexual pleasure by direct electrical stimulation of the brain in a far more efficient manner than by the usual old-fashioned dependence on the other sex.[19] Ovum and sperm can meet one another in vitro and go about their business without bothering to involve either the male or the female who are now free to engage in prolonged orgies with their electrical stimulators.

### "Genethics"

The moral, or individual, not to mention the ethical, or societal problems generated by these technologies are overwhelming. "The questions being raised are questions almost totally beyond the comprehension of traditional patterns of thought simply because they present us with possibilities that clearly forebode a major revolution in human society." [20] What effect for example, will the new technologies have on the traditional monogamous family? "Certainly, the use of mercenary mothers and their possible prevalence in the coming generation raises serious questions about the exclusivity of the couple marriage." [21] With the appearance of surrogate mothers, will we evolve toward a broader conception of the family circle? "The classic meaning of terms like mother, father, parent, and our whole conception of motherhood takes on new meaning." [22] We will have to distinguish between genetic mother, donor mother, natal mother and social—not to mention mechanical—mother. Will inovulation make for a stronger mother-child relationship than will simple postnatal adoption? Will the woman undergoing abortion give permission to have it transplanted to a woman eager for a child of her own? And "who is the natal mother when a subhuman foster mother carries the child to birth? A cow? How would you explain that your grandchild has a simian natal mother?" [23]

The game becomes mind-boggling when the question turns to the child's response to a bovine or simian surrogate "mother"; "would he [the fetus] recognize the substitution and subconsciously react, biologically, hormonally, or biochemically, to the foreign womb? How is his human body and mind likely to accommodate itself to the hormonal differences of nine months in the womb of an animal of another species? Postnatally, how might the child react? Would he look with pride on his nine-month prenatal life grazing in the backyard as being a mark of distinction, sophistication, and aristocracy, or might he come to resent his mother who put him out to pasture while she played gourmet cook and cultured hostess, lover and intellectual companion to his father?" [24] We can only agree that these questions do, as the author admits, "sound absurd, grotesque, hideous, and downright repulsive." [25] (And male-oriented.)

They are, however, being taken seriously. A new discipline known as "genethics" is taking shape to examine the moral and ethical aspects of genetic and reproductive decisions. Suppose, as an easy starter, that an unborn child is genetically defective—has Down's syndrome, let us say, or Tay-Sachs disease, or hemophilia—or some other defect which, though not necessarily genetic or lethal, is a serious handicap, costly to parents. The moral issue here is fairly clear and there is, in fact, a consensus that such a pregnancy should be terminated.[26]

The problem becomes more complicated once an infant with a treatable genetic defect is born. It can be salvaged, as, for example, in the case of PKU. Retardation is avoided and the child grows up to become a normal adult. But its genetic constitution is unchanged. It can still become the father or mother of a defective child. Genethics asks what will be the effect of the survival of such carriers on the gene pool of any population? "In the case of PKU, treatment is not only enlarging the number of carriers in the genetic pool, it is effectively creating a new disease." [27]

Also in the case of PKU, what about the normal woman who is a carrier of the defective gene that produces it? Does she have a "right" to become a mother who can transmit the defect to her own children? Dr. Neil A. Holtzman put the question this way: "these women with [successfully treated] PKU have themselves been afforded the benefit of having had a normal life without retardation. In exchange for that, can we [not] ask their families, or can they [not] ask themselves, to forego the right to have children? That's an individual decision which they must make for themselves." [28] The issue is by no means new. It is only sharper now that we have more precise knowledge about defects which in the past we only suspected "ran in families." Diabetes resembles PKU in the parameters of the problem: it is diagnosable and treatable so that the individual can live a normal life but remains a possible carrier of the defect. Less clear-cut as yet are the genetic factors in other illnesses including cancer and especially the mental illnesses for which neither early diagnosis nor treatment is available. Illustrative of one such defect which, while diagnosable, remains untreatable, is the chromosomal anomaly consisting of an extra Y or male chromosome in some men referred to above. Men with this defect show up relatively more frequently among the emotionally disturbed and/or those in penal institutions than they do in the general population. They tend to be more aggressive or antisocial in their behavior and to have abnormal neurological patterns. The problem here is not the eugenic one of preserving the "unfit" because sterility tends to accompany this defect. But what should be done with them? Would the mother who was told that her son had this defect "unconsciously tend to expect, and thus facilitate, the tendency to anti-social behavior that may be associated with the gene?" [29] Or, since we know that anti-social children tend to come from troubled families, should the mother be requested, or even required, to surrender the child so that he could be reared in an environment that "could perhaps channel his aggressiveness better?" [30] Who would have the right to make this demand?

As yet answers are not forthcoming for the treatment of many diagnosable defects. It is the lag between diagnosis and treatment that confounds the genethicist. It is true that "medicine has come a long way since the days when doctors performed autopsy after autopsy, searching for the 'inherited' brain lesions they believed caused insanity, epilepsy, sexual excesses, and criminal behavior. The time is approaching when it will be possible to locate and alter the defective gene which causes a given abnormality. As scientists understand more about DNA, which makes up the basis of all genetic material, perhaps another nucleotide, or a virus, or a nucleus from a normal cell, could be substituted for the faulty one, thus permanently curing the affliction." [31] Until that time arrives, however, mothers are left with the emotional trauma of making profound decisions with respect to child bearing. A new profession of genetic counseling is emerging to help them.

### Genetic Counseling

Genetic counseling is a medical service which differs from traditional medical practice. Some counselors retain the old doctor-patient concept and feel called upon to advise; others see their function as simply one of conveying to the patient all the information available for the decisions called for. The first type might, for example, go beyond merely stating risks; he might also "suggest how patients should use the information he gives them. . . . He may discuss in detail the psychological consequences of an abnormal child [as though she didn't know!], or the economic burden of genetic abnormality. He may also point out to the parents the impact on the family of a defective child. . . . All of these are important factors in conveying the meaning of genetic risks to parents and undoubtedly have an impact on the parents' decisions about future reproductive behavior." [32] The second type of counselor is more hesitant, especially in the case of defects still incompletely understood, such as the XYY anomaly. Further, the way the counselor makes the statement of any specific risk may influence the patient's interpretation. If in any specific case the risk of an abnormal child is 1 in 4, should it be viewed as high or low? Should it be stated in that form or in the form that the chances for a normal birth are 3 in 4? [33] It might make a difference in the patient's decision. For genetic counselors must think of "the wide range of psychological effects brought into play when a person is informed that he or she is the carrier of defective genes, or when a family is informed its newborn is defective?" [34] The counselor has to balance these psychological effects against the need to help families make informed decisions.

The future of motherhood will depend to some extent on the reproductive decisions made after counseling. Until more research shows us who seeks genetic counseling, it is difficult to assess what its effect will be on their decisions. In at least one study, of cystic fibrosis, it is found that "degree of risk significantly affects parental decisions to reproduce or not." But "other factors operate as well." [35] We know that religion makes a difference in the acceptance of defective children, Catholic mothers being more accepting than non-Catholic mothers. Does religion operate in a similar way in reproductive decisions at the pre-parental or fetal levels? How about cultural values aside from religion? Do they shape decisions involving risk-taking? Some parents "may so desire a child of their own that they will risk disease and its attendant problems. . . . Studies are needed . . . on parental desires regarding the health of their children." [36]

### How Widely Sought?

For the present at least, new recourses for dealing with reproduction—artificial insemination, artificial inovulation, surrogate wombs, genetic engineering—are not widely sought, or is their availability well known.[37] But the rapidity with which the contraceptive pills were accepted when they became known suggests that the acceptance of more radical interventions in reproduction may prove to be accepted more rapidly than present attitudes indicate.

As of now, according to a Harris poll published in June, 1969, the public tends to accept some of the less drastic forms of reproductive technology, including both psychiatric and hormonal treatment for infertility, and even including artificial insemination with a husband's sperm. But "the more a new method appears as a threat to the family tradition, the more widely it is . . . rejected." [38] There is, however, an interesting and strange anomaly. Anything that tends to change the mother's traditional role is rejected by both sexes; but women seemed "much more willing to change than men. . . . In every question the women were significantly more open to change than were the men.[39] Since women are the ones most directly concerned with reproduction, their views are likely to carry much more weight in terms of our future direction than are the views of men." And, as in the case of so many other trends adumbrating the future, "the greatest degree of acceptance was expressed by the younger generation and by the better educated segments." [40] In general, natural methods of reproduction are overwhelmingly and quite expectably preferred: "most people still consider natural parenthood by the legitimate social parents to be the most desirable state. Use of artificial means of reproduction, except when they benefit the health of the mother, is not favored by any significant segment of the population." [41]

Nevertheless, despite the lack of enthusiasm by women, inch by inch the technicians plow on. We hear from time to time about male womb envy, the envy men feel of women's procreative powers. Cronus, as a prototypical example, swallowed all of his children except Zeus who was spared by a ruse of his mother, Rhea. When grown, Zeus with Earth's help forced Cronus to disgorge them all.[42] As good an imitation of birth as he, without female equipment, could manage. If the technologists succeed will they do better than Cronus? Will they wrest woman's unique capacity away from her? Will it become their job instead of hers to procreate? Will hers become simply one of supplying an ovum or two from time to time?

Human mothers may slough all this research off as too farfetched to have immediate application to them. But technologies have a way of creeping up on us and practical application may, in fact, be not too far off. All these miraculous technologies and more may be possible. But for most men and women they are not likely soon to supplant the old-fashioned way of achieving either sexual satisfaction or motherhood. I believe women will continue to perform sexual and gestating functions well into the future, hopefully, of course, at their own discretion.

### Technology's Task

In addition to the personal questions raised for parents, the reproductive technologies available today raise once more all the old ethical questions dealing with society as a whole raised in the original nineteenth-century eugenics movement. One of the arguments against the nineteenth-century vision was that there was no person or group who should be given the right to decide what kind of human being to strive for. What kind of character or personality should we ask them to work toward? How much consensus could we arrive at? It was asked, even if there were consensus, what right does any one generation have to determine the composition of the genetic pool for future generations? Some things could be taken for granted. We should eliminate so far as possible the destructive illnesses and defects.

But even here there are those who raise questions. Would mothers lay down the same specifications as business men? bureaucrats? priests? ministers and rabbis? politicians? generals or admirals? professors? Would they be stricter or more lenient? Would they be willing to permit more defects in the genetic pool than bureaucrats? Would their desire for babies be so strong that they would willingly undertake the chance of defect? Some have argued that taking care of defective children performs a sanctifying function for their caretakers. And families with children suffering from Down's syndrome report that the presence of these gentle, loving members is in fact a positive influence in their families.[43] But in these cases the defects were unpredicted. Would mothers deliberately bear them if they had a choice not to? Far more likely that unwillingness to assume the burdens of mother-hood in such cases would lead them to insist on abortion. It has taken a long time grudgingly to accord to women even this much control of their bodies. They are not likely soon to surrender it.

On a more positive note, then, there is one thing we can say with some assurance about the future of motherhood. There will be fewer mothers of children with defects which are amenable to fetal or neonatal treatment. There will be fewer mothers suffering from the "chronic sorrow" reported in mothers of mentally defective children. The loss of children to fetal illnesses will virtually disappear. The source of a great deal of maternal grief will thus be removed. To this extent motherhood will, as a result of genetic technology, be a happier experience in the future than it is at the present.

In addition to the medical and genetic engineering technologies which affect reproduction there are also chemical or phar-macological technologies that affect mothering itself, such, for ex-ample, as mood- and behavior-modifying drugs. They seem to be emerging as possible influences on the future of motherhood.

### Pharmacological Technologies: Surrogates for Motherwork?

In 1932, a book appeared in Warsaw in which an imaginary confrontation between East and West resulted in complete victory for the East, a victory won by the use of so-called Murti-Bing hap-piness pills.

> Murti-Bing was a Mongolian philosopher who had succeeded in producing an organic means of transporting a "philosophy of life." This Murti-Bing "philosophy of life," which consti-tuted the strength of the Sino-Mongolian army, was contained in pills in an extremely condensed form. A man who used these pills changed completely. He became serene and happy. The problems he had struggled with until then sud-denly appeared to be superficial and unimportant. He smiled indulgently at those who continued to worry about them. Most affected were all questions pertaining to unsolvable on-tological difficulties. A man who swallowed Murti-Bing pills became impervious to any metaphysical concerns. The ex-cesses into which art falls when people vainly seek in form the wherewithal to appease their spiritual hunger were but outmoded stupidities for him. He no longer considered the

approach of the Sino-Mongolian army as a tragedy for his own civilization. He lived in the midst of his compatriots like a healthy individual surrounded by madmen. More and more people took the Murti-Bing cure, and their resultant calm contrasted sharply with the nervousness of their environment.[44]

Mothers have not had access to Murti-Bing pills, but they have relied on similar pharmacological technologies for a long time.

Many years ago, in cities of South America and India, I saw women carrying narcotized infants in their arms as they went begging in the streets. More recently I have seen an infant given a slug of whisky at Shannon airport as the family settled down for a long transatlantic flight. Even in our own country there was a time when giving children paregoric, an opiate, was an acceptable practice. It was, in effect, a substitute for tender-loving-care from exhausted mothers. It stopped the infant's crying. Its use as a tranquilizer is now interdicted.

But pharmacological technology is synthesizing new drugs all the time. Some are mood-controlling chemicals. Some are behavior-controlling drugs. Hyper-activity in children can be controlled by them. Distraught mothers are given prescriptions for their children; schools administer them. Concern has been expressed that the legitimate use of such drugs may be extended until they become simply a way to veil mismanagement of children.

Antibiotics spare mothers the all-night bedside vigil. Jeanne Binstock makes the laconic observation that "instead of endurance, patience, fortitude, and tenderness—the traditional virtues of women in all previous historical periods—we have contraception and penicillin." [45]

It is, finally, not the children only who are tranquilized, the mothers are too. The television advertisement shows distraught women how to deal with noisy sons and daughters. Take a pill. Or how to be an "incredible mother." Easy. Take iron.

More than mere tranquilization may be in store for women. Recent research on prenatal development has revealed the interesting fact that the primordial fetal stuff is female. In order for even the genetically male fetus to become masculinized it must be exposed to the male hormone, androgen. Normally its genetic heredity will see to it that this androgen is supplied and the masculinization will take place to produce a male. Such androgenization is not provided for in female heredity to the same extent, so the genetically female fetus does not develop male characteristics.

But sometimes accidents occur. In one set of cases genetically female fetuses were exposed prenatally to more than a normal amount of androgen. They were followed in their development for several years by psychologists and were reported to be more active, daring, adventuresome, and tomboyish than other girls their age. They tended to be less "maternal" also, not especially attracted by dolls or playing house.[46] If such changes in "maternalness" can, indeed, be shown to result from androgenization, a logical anti-natalist corollary would be that women who have high maternal drives could have them damped down by deliberate androgenization.

Alice Rossi has suggested that young women who are active in the feminist movement today may be women with naturally high androgen levels.[47] So, also, may career women be. If this should prove to be the case, prescribing androgens to women might have not only the effect of reducing "infant hunger" but also of increasing career or work motivations. Instead of using drugs to tranquilize women, they could be used to energize them for active nonmaternal roles. This is an almost ideal solution for the subjective aspects of role integration. As yet, of course, this solution is only fanciful.

## Psychological Technologies and Motherhood

Fear of having our minds controlled by malevolent outsiders has an ancient history. The evil eye, hypnotism, brain-washing, have been bugabears among a wide variety of people, and not without reason. For many years concern has been expressed that a great deal of the psychological research on conditioning was being applied for the exploitation rather than for the benefit of human beings. Advertisers and propagandists were hiring the scientists to show them how to manipulate buyers and voters. A generation ago Bertrand Russell was expressing misgivings at the uses being made of psychological research for purposes of control. Like Julian Huxley and George Orwell he anticipated a fearful future in which scientific techniques would be used to manipulate us at will. Despite Arthur Koestler's conclusion that human behavior is too complex for the kind of tinkering successful with pigeons, the nightmare described by Huxley and Orwell still haunts the minds of many people; they fear the uses which the newly developing skills will give to power-seekers.

In the 1970s there were proliferations of psychological techniques for treatment of many kinds of problems, including family problems. Mothers were being taught how to use new skills in dealing with child rearing.[48] Today there is scarcely a book on child care that does not recommend some form of psychological technique for shaping the child's mind or character. Play therapy, reward systems, a whole gamut of scientific skills is invoked. In contrast to older approaches to child rearing which insisted that the cause of behavior had to be understood before it could be changed, the "behavior modification" school, based primarily on reinforcing desired responses, states that behavior is controlled by its consequences, so that rewards are the key to control. The new technology shows how to practice such control, including record-keeping, selection of appropriate rewards, avoidance of accidental conditions, and the like. It alerts parents to ways in which they inadvertently reward undesirable behavior, as when they reward and encourage the child to scream by picking it up.

To those who express concern at the burgeoning "behavior modification" movement—which has not yet decided who is qualified to use the techniques or how to use them ethically—the answer given is that control is always being practiced anyway. Why not let those with benign motives in on it?

> Most behaviorists would add that behavior mod itself is neutral. It is not. Behavior mod tries to make behavior a science, and employs a technology for its change. Presumably, a change for the better. But it is in the nature of technology to create more technology to meet its needs. It is in the nature of technology to change its user.
>
> A gun is a tool, just like behavior mod. The gunowner's fist has grown the ability to strike instantly at a distance. The owner is changed by this growth. Behavior mod extends our ability to manipulate others. It will be used well. It will be used badly. But whatever else, the technological society is closer.[49]

It is true that mothers have taken seriously all kinds of techniques, from John Watson's original behaviorism reflected in early Children's Bureau publications on the subject to the tender-loving-care orthodoxy which called, in effect, for rewarding anything the child did by ever-loving attention. And some, no doubt, are also applying behavior modifying techniques. But there is a safeguard. Children learn. And before you can say B. F. Skinner, they are using behavior modification on their parents. For, we are learning, children train their parents as well as parents their children.

Another psychological technology presently enjoying some success is called Parent Effectiveness Training, "the no-lose program for raising responsible children," which is neither permissive nor authoritarian. Begun in 1963 by Thomas Gordon, a clinical psychologist in Pasadena, it now has two thousand qualified instructors in the United States giving a twenty-four-hour course, usually sponsored by churches, community centers, and colleges. Unlike behavior modification, the emphasis here is on understanding, on communication, on active listening. Role-playing constitutes an important learning tool. One mother reports:

> In the months since I completed Parent Effectiveness Training, I've found a new sense of awareness creeping into all of my relationships which often tells me more about myself than others. I no longer feel guilty about everything that goes wrong, nor responsible for everything that goes right. I am not afraid of drowning when I wade into a difficult situation. I know I can find my way through. In slowing down to listen, my ears and eyes have grown rich in the joys of motherhood. . . . The course has forced me to examine many of my own values, . . . induced me to relax my thinking on many things, and taught me to accept almost everything except intolerance. The honesty that has resulted between my children and myself hasn't always been easy to take. It took practice to be able not to overreact to their attacks on my values; or to accept their refusals of some of my "I" messages. . . .[50]

Moving farther away from the recipe-book methodology we find still another rapidly growing approach to motherwork, this one based on the work of Alfred Adler, especially as propagated by Rudolph Dreikurs. Discussion groups for parents and teachers are organized into Individual Psychology Associations, many affiliated with the American Society of Adlerian Psychology.

> The generation gap, the increasing anti-social behavior of our youth, plus the dissatisfaction with our schools—all indicate

the obsolescence of traditional methods of child rearing. The growing awareness of the need to establish democratic rather than authoritarian practices in our homes and schools has not been met with appropriate skills and action. We need to learn new principles of raising children that will foster the inner motivation of the child to develop fully, to cooperate, to be courageous, to respect himself and others, and to take on his share of responsibility. Such methods exist and have been proven effective, both in the home and school, based upon the dynamic psychology of Alfred Adler and Rudolf Dreikurs.

As opposed to punishment, we teach logical consequences; instead of reward, we emphasize encouragement; instead of analyzing causes from the past, we deal with the purposes of behavior in the present.

The purpose of Individual Psychology Association is to promote improved relationships between individuals—especially adults and children—emphasizing ways of preventing typical troublesome situations from developing into more serious behavior problems.[51]


Whatever the techniques taught in these several approaches, the most important implication is that they are, in effect, re-writing the "scientific" script for the role of mother. And the most relevant consequence in the present context is that they relax the demands on mothers and thus render at least some aspects of role integration more attainable.

Less relevant but worth at least a nod is the work now being done on the transmission of learned behavior from one organism to another. Such vicarious learning is not to be expected in the near future, but is probably in the cards in the distant future. In the case of mice, for example, responses learned by one set of animals were "acquired" by another set of animals when the bits of the brains of the mice that had learned the response were injected into the untrained animals. By analyzing the chemicals involved in such transfer of learned behavior, the hope of the experimenters is to be able to "crack the memory code." [52] Presumably the time could come when mothers could learn all about child care from a bottle of pills and children could learn French the same way. The pain associated with learning could thus be obviated. The anguish of mothers who bemoan the fact that their children cannot profit by their own experience could be assuaged. The mother could just offer a smidgeon of her own brain to be injected into her children's and, presto, they would remember her past, unfortunately now irrelevant. But *profit* from it? There has to be a better way.[53]

### Choices

Our exploding technology of human reproduction . . . brings us to a critical threshold in human history which can thrust us, men and women, into a new and fuller plane of personalization where we become more human, more personal, more male, and more female. But it can also cast us into the asexual impersonal world of assembly-line-produced, thought-controlled, genetically engineered ghosts of men and women. The choice is ours.[54]

But, some people ask, is it? Do we really have a choice?

For there are some who argue that we really do not have a choice, that technology has its own élan, its own inertia, its own dynamic, its own thrust, its own inevitability; they conclude therefore that we have little control over it, that if a thing is possible, it will be done.

Others argue the opposite point of view. We can control technology, we can subject it to moral constraints. There are many ways in which any technology can be used and the social "support system" in which it is embedded makes a difference. We can, for example, "have a social system that emphasizes the private use of the automobile" and thus encourages it by highways, parking facilities, and similar prerogatives; or we can have a social support system that judges twenty feet of street space too much for a single individual and thus refuses to support private uses of automobiles. We can, further, learn to assess the costs of all kinds of technologies, as we are now learning the social costs assessable to the automobile in the form of air pollution. "The sources of our predicament [vis-à-vis technology] is not the 'imperatives' of technology but a lack of decision mechanisms for choosing the kinds of technology and social support patterns we want." [55] For as technology allows God fewer and fewer Acts, motherhood itself becomes increasingly a matter of political as well as of individual decisions.

# CHAPTER FOURTEEN

## The Politics of Motherhood

### "Technology and Social Support Systems"

Technologies can tell us how to do things. But we have to decide first what we want to do, by no means an easy task. We don't always know, or agree. Disagreement means issues. Issues mean politics. Politics mean ethics. Ethics in the sense of reflecting an *ethos*, "the prevalent tone or sentiment of a people or community." We have become increasingly sensitive since the *ethos* of the Nazis permitted them to practice genocide on a mammoth scale, invoke racism to desecrate motherhood, corrupt parent-child relationships. The uses to which technologies were put alerted us to the importance of keeping them under the strictest control. The issues raised then keep cropping up all the time in discussions of abortion, genetic counseling, genetic engineering, and a host of other matters relating to motherhood, as the issues raised at Nuremberg keep cropping up in more abstract areas. What kind of social support system do we want? To what uses do we want technologies to be put?

Of the many issues, three are selected for extended comment here. First, the quantity and the quality of population; second, the politicization of sex; and finally the control of the socialization process. All deal directly or indirectly with the revolution now in process which will determine the future of motherhood.

### Population Policy Versus Motherhood

It is a great leap from motherhood to "population policy" so it is understandable that the woman struggling to juggle all her obligations to nursery and school has time for only a puzzled "who, me?" when terms like "pronatalism" and "antinatalism" are used. Are they talking about *her?*

Yes, they are. About her vulnerability to all the forces in her world, formal and informal, public and private, organized and unorganized, official and unofficial, that influence her decisions about the number of children she will have.[1]

The discussion of population policy and the discussion of motherhood take place in totally different intellectual atmospheres. A great deal of the thinking and research on motherhood has been done by women;[2] almost all of the thinking on population policy, by men.

Until technology gave women better control over conception, policy dealt with "population" and it was taken for granted that women would comply with whatever the policy-makers prescribed. The women didn't. One of the most interesting lessons of the past has, in fact, been how resistant the birth rate has been to political pressures. Whether policy was "pronatalist"—designed to encourage women to have babies—or "antinatalist"—designed to moderate the number of babies they had—the birth rate has followed its own course. Over the decades since records have been kept, the long-term trend has been toward fewer children. When women expected to lose half of the children they bore, they bore a great many. But as the loss of infants declined, they had fewer. True, the number of children born in any one year fluctuated with good times and bad, going down in times of depression and up in times of prosperity, and also with times of war and peace. Still, the number of children women bear has been declining quite independently of what congresses and commissars may have told women to do.

Sometimes policy makers wanted women to bear lots of babies. Militarists argued that the country needed a large supply of soldiers. Industrialists argued that the country needed a large supply of cheap labor. Even in the twentieth century arguments of this kind were still being used. In pre-war Germany, for example, it was argued that since surrounding countries—Italy, for example, and Poland—were out-breeding Germany, its safety was endangered. Women must therefore be encouraged to have more babies. Girls were told not to worry about marriage; the state would provide. Indeed, retreats were established to provide premarital and neonatal services for young women who had—

Nordic—babies out of wedlock. In many countries incentives of one kind or another—subsidies, sharing of costs, tax benefits, free services, rent concessions—were offered to women to stimulate motherhood. Medals, badges, honors were awarded to women who bore large numbers of babies until a truly fertile woman could have a chestful of medals as colorful as a general's. Hitler offered to be godfather to the seventh son of any woman. To achieve this honor, a woman would have to bear about fourteen children.

Strange as it may seem, however, nothing seemed to influence the resistant women. For a while it looked as though Hitler had succeeded in raising the birth rate. For it did, in fact, go up when he came to power. But when the scientists got to work on the statistics they found that the only policy that had had a demonstrable effect was the prohibition of abortion.[3]

The resistance of the birth rate to political controls—in this case to limit it—is illustrated in the Third World today where one of the stubbornest problems policy makers face in stimulating national development is how to get women to limit the number of children they bear. Hardly any program they dream up has the desired effect of definitively curbing the birth rate. Some theorists speak of "baby hunger" as part of the explanation, a "hunger" that policy cannot touch.

The experience in our own country in the 1930s is another puzzling example of how subtle and surprisingly independent of seemingly related forces are the forces that influence women to have or not have children. At the very bottom of the great depression when no one knew that the economic indicators were beginning to turn up, the birth rate began to rise. It was not a cheerful time; it was not a hopeful time; it was not a buoyant time; it was not a confident time. It was not a time when women could look forward to a good world in which to rear children. But there it was, an upturn in the birth rate. Women were beginning to have babies again.

In fact the coincidence was so surprising that at least one student, Maurice Hexter, argued that it was the rise in the birth rate that led to the rise in the economic curves rather than, as most thought, the other way around.[4] And advocates of growth continue to argue as though a growing population is good for business. Whichever is cause and whichever effect can be argued persuasively and endlessly. Either way the strange phenomenon of the great depression illustrates the point made here: the autonomy of the birth rate. And when we speak of birth rates we are, of course, talking about mothers.

One last example has to do with the era of the feminine mystique, caught in the top curve of the frontispiece chart. All of a sudden after World War II women began to have more babies—fourth, fifth, sixth babies. Then, in 1957, the birth rate turned down dramatically. The era of large families ended as mysteriously as it had begun, even before environmentalism had become a factor. The fourth, fifth, and sixth babies just faded away. Even, in fact, third babies. Women had simply changed their minds, but no one really knew why.

It was not until the late 1960s that motherhood became a serious political issue in our country. Like so many other issues, it came not in clear-cut, carefully thought-through form but in a murky conglomerate of ecology, environmental protection, and a "welfare mess." It took an "antinatalist" slant. The problem posed was how to stop women from having so many babies. Ecologists frightened us with images of millions suffocating for lack of oxygen and hostile reformers with images of women—especially black women—having babies in order to remain on welfare rolls. The first group directed their attack against middle-class women, the second, against welfare women.

### Policy Ambiguity

For the most part, American policy with respect to motherhood, whether deliberate or inadvertent—and usually it was inadvertent—has tended to be ambiguous. On one side it has been pronatalist, as expressed in Title V of the Social Security Act, which encouraged women to remain home to take care of children; but on the other side it has been antinatalist, as in the several acts that encouraged women to enter the labor force.[5]

All-in-all, some argue, the balance has been pronatalist. "Government policies have reinforced the pro-natalist influences of the general society and have partially offset the economic disadvantages of children through such provisions as: high taxes on single individuals, tax deductions for children, provision of public housing and public assistance only for families with children, encouragement of single-family suburban housing of special advantage to families with many children, and so on."[6] In addition they point to a varied and extensive array of federally supported facilities, personnel, and services for the care of children, ranging from a

1962 amendment to the Social Security Act authorizing grants to state public welfare agencies for day care services to the authorization of funds—by HEW, HUD, and Model Cities agencies—for day-care facility construction.[7]

True, much of this legislation had to do with easing the mother's load by helping in cases of mental or physical handicap, emotional disturbance, poor family relationships, and inadequate living conditions "which do not provide a place for play or adult supervision after school." [8] But the ambiguity shows up here too. Much of it was aimed also at encouraging the employment of mothers.

In the second half of the twentieth century there was increasing, almost militant, pressure to reverse pronatalism and replace it with a clear-cut antinatalist policy. Or at least to reduce the pronatalist pressures. For, as Judith Blake Davis pointed out, what was needed as much as an aggressive antinatalism was merely a reduction of all the pressures operating on women to want to have babies. If they could be relaxed or totally eliminated, little more would be needed.

> The existence of such pronatalist policies becomes apparent when we recall that, among human beings, population replacement would not occur at all were it not for the complex social organization and system of incentives that encourage mating, pregnancy, and the care, support, and rearing of children. . . . Antinatalist policies will not necessarily involve the introduction of coercive measures. In fact, just the opposite is the case. Many of these new policies will entail *lifting* of pressures *to* reproduce, rather than an *imposition* of pressures *not* to do so.[9]

Until we make up our minds, the technologies required to achieve our goals are secondary. Do we want to pursue a pro- or an antinatalist policy? Do we want to encourage or discourage motherhood? Should we or should we not ease the mother's load? Should we or should we not encourage labor-force participation by mothers? Which role is more encouraged by child-care or child-development centers, the mother or the worker role? If we help mothers bear their load will the effect be to have more babies or to enter the labor force? Does labor-force participation really have an antinatalist effect? The answers still evade us. Impressive research can be invoked to support opposite points of view. We are wrestling with a violent reorientation of a sacrosanct—till now—ethos. The new ethos will profoundly affect the future of motherhood.

## Quality As Well As Quantity As a Political Issue: The Old Eugenics

In the nineteenth century a Frenchman proposed that the genetically best young women be recruited solely for breeding purposes, to be supported and taken care of by the state while they produced offspring by mating with the genetically best men that could be found. A counterpart to this positive eugenics was one that aimed to prevent the unfit from reproducing their kind. Both positive and negative eugenics remained more or less a fantasy until the time of Hitler under whom they began to take on an ominous reality. Under his racial policy, anyone, so long as she was properly Nordic, should be encouraged to bear children, regardless of marital status. The unfit were to be eliminated by Draconian measures. Hitler found technological answers to his problems. His engineers created the hardware to exterminate millions of people, if not elegantly, at least with relative dispatch. Not yet available were the technologies now available for reproduction control; if they had been, he would doubtless have used them.

In 1970, the President's Task Force on the Mentally Handicapped had recommended that there be increased availability of birth-control measures, including voluntary sterilization. Such provision is easier to recommend than to implement. In 1973, eighteen women on welfare rolls were told by a physician that he would not deliver their babies unless they submitted to sterilization.[10] These women were not mentally handicapped and most were probably quite willing, even eager, to comply. But one who was not willing reported this precondition and a great brouhaha resulted.

In the indignant debate, little was said about the feelings of the other women. Did the mother of twelve children really want any more? Did the mothers of even five? The outrage was more about the attitude of the physician than about the fate of the women themselves. In another state the reason given by the less well-educated women for resisting sterilization was not that it interfered with reproduction—they had had enough of that as it was—but that, so they had been told, it interfered with sexual pleasure. And even on that score they were themselves willing to forego the sexual pleasure if it relieved them of motherhood as well. It was the men who feared the mythic loss of sexual responsiveness in the sterilized women.

So long as the coercion was a matter of pressure by the obstetrician alone it was not, strictly speaking, a political issue. It was a case in Alabama that rendered the issue a political one. There it was charged that two girls, fourteen and twelve, were sterilized by a Federally funded agency without the consent of their parents. In the course of the court case, the Department of Health, Education, and Welfare and the Office of Economic Opportunity were asked to stop using Federal money for sterilization until new standards and guidelines were formulated. Such standards were to include, though not be limited to, medical and psychological counseling and surgery.[11]

### New Problems

The ethical and political questions raised in the old eugenics seem relatively simple as compared to those raised in the new eugenics, and expectably so in view of the greater sophistication of the technologies now at our disposal. In the old "survival of the fittest" argument against the care of the "unfit" the fallacy lay in the definition of "unfit" which was often simply in terms of success or failure in a harsh economic system. The poor and the dependent were unfit almost by definition. Nowadays we can in some cases predict certain kinds of unfitness at birth, as in the case of retardation caused by PKU. The question now takes on a strangely hard-nosed aspect, for "economic constraints often shape and dictate important decisions concerning the use of medical knowledge." The question is not should we protect them by treatment but is it worth the cost? Is it, for example, economically worthwhile to require neonatal screening for PKU when so few actual cases are found? In Massachusetts, for example, only eight cases a year are identified as having this defect. The screening program costs $175,000. Is this expenditure justified?

The answer is, even on strictly economic—let alone humanitarian—grounds, yes. For "if these children were not identified and treated, the cost to the state would be approximately $150,000 to $200,000 per lifetime for each child." [12] In general, the economic costs of genetic defects depend on the age of onset, the duration, and the nature of the defect. (In general also, prevention by way of genetic counseling or abortion is more economical than treatment.)

In the last third of the twentieth century "genethics" was calling for new thinking and new policies. Now that quantity of births was no longer a problem, the quality aspects of the population could receive more attention. "Human life is so abundant . . . we should opt for a higher quality of life. . . . Since man (sic!) has to limit his (sic!) birthrate in any case, it would be reasonable to avoid the birth of defectives by prenatal screening and selective abortion, if this can be done in a voluntary and socially acceptable way." [13]

Supposing such "genetic screening" became mandatory everywhere, before, during, or after pregnancy, what then? What are the ethical rules that should guide us if we find defects? Suppose counseling does not deter the mother? Does everyone have the right to reproduce? Should the mother have the right to make the decision whether or not to abort the defective fetus? Suppose she wants the child? And if not, who has the right to decide?

Does the community? In Pennsylvania, parents of a child with hemophilia are now asking the state to share the $22,000 per year treatment of his illness costs. Once the child is born we have little choice other than to sustain it.[14] But if the community must share the expense of rearing children, as in the case now of renal dialysis, will it willingly pay for the expensive treatment if the mother knowingly bore it? Says one scientist, "if a family has a major risk of bearing children with major genetic deficiencies, it is not only a tragedy for the individual and family, but society may have to shoulder a major share of the medical and social cost. If a family should choose to ignore the risk, can society take upon itself the right to limit the number of children such a family might bear? Prenatal detection tests or appropriate preventive treatment become public health measures analogous to the right of a community to restrict the movement of an individual with smallpox. Genetic diseases are not contagious, but they are transmissible. What should we do?" [15]

Why, change the genes, obviously. Genetic engineering makes such a possibility increasingly possible. But it does not remove the ethical questions. It just moves them farther back. What right does the community have to require genetic engineering on defective genes?

### The Politics of Abortion

The case of abortion is almost archetypical of the kinds of moral and ethical and political throes through which we must pass on our way to a new biological ethos. The Oxford dictionary gives, among others, two contradictory definitions for the word "throe," that is, the pain and the struggle of childbirth and the agony of death. The term may be too dramatic, not to say melodramatic, as applied to abortion. But it is right on target. It is not too strong a term to apply to the struggle of two conceptualizations of women—one as basically a bearer of children with no rights of her own and one as basically a human being with rights to the uses made of her body—now in process. Abortion in and of itself is important enough; but as symbolic of an underlying issue it is doubly so.

Abortion was held *not* to be a way to limit motherhood by a substantial part of the public.[16] Even those who favored legalized abortion viewed it less as a standard form of birth control than as a legitimate last resort when contraception had failed or when there had been rape or incest. It came, therefore, as a shocking surprise to most people when abortion surfaced as a national issue in the political campaign of 1972, actually debated by the platform committees of both parties. The issue was obviously far more than population control.

Abortion, like infanticide and abandonment of infants, has had an ancient if not necessarily always an honorable history. It is a mark of our cultural parochialism that we think replenishing the earth has always and everywhere been a major human preoccupation. Not so. Infanticide has long since passed away as a respectable pratice in most societies, though it still remains, disguised or sub rosa, even in our own society today.[17] But abortion has a different history.

At the beginning of the century William Graham Sumner, a sociologist, sketched the use of abortion as a form of population control in preliterate societies showing the relationship between personal behavior and custom. In pastoral-nomadic life, children were much wanted and in the horde rearing them was not much of a burden. With agriculture and the emergence of narrower family bonds, children came to be felt as a burden.

Children add to the weight of the struggle for existence of their parents. The relation of parent to child is one of sacrifice. The interest of children and parents are antagonistic. The fact that there are, or may be, compensations does not affect the primary relation between the two. It may well be believed that, if procreation had not been put under the dominion of a great passion, it would have been caused to cease by the burdens it entails. Abortion and infanticide are especially interesting because they show how early in the history of civilization the burden of children became so heavy that parents began to shirk it, and also because they show the rise of a population policy, which is one of the most important programmes of practical expediency which any society ever can adopt. . . .

At a very early time in the history of human society . . . the evils of overpopulation were perceived as facts, and policies were instinctively adopted to protect the adults. The facts caused pain, and the acts resolved upon to avoid it were very summary, and were adopted with very little reasoning. Abortion and infanticide protected the society, unless its situation with respect to neighbors was such that war and pestilence kept down the numbers and made children valuable for war. . . . When practiced by man (sic!), and through a long time . . . they are no longer individual acts of resistance to pain [but accepted folkways].[18]

In 1972 it was not abortion as a means of population control that became the issue—no one seriously argued that point—but rather abortion as a right of women to control their own bodies, specifically in the context of making decisions about undertaking motherhood themselves. The right to make the decision to become a mother—or, rather, not to become a mother—was merely the last of the long succession of rights women had been fighting for. It was as a right, then, not as a population policy—it was admittedly a very poor second to proper contraception—that abortion became a political issue.

The anguish modern societies experience when confronted with issues closely tied to emotion showed itself in the conventions of both political parties.[19] In the Democratic Party convention abortion was kept from the floor for discussion as a plank in the platform despite the urgent efforts of women who felt strongly about it. A similar fight took place at the Republican Party convention.[20] Abortion was discussed for three days in a subcommittee of the

Republican platform committee and twice in the full Committee. In the case of both parties, it was only political expediency that kept abortion from becoming a plank in the platforms of either party. In the more remote parts of the country it was still shocking to have abortion discussed so openly. Proponents were not discouraged. Next time around the public would be readier. As an issue it might remain schismatic, even among women, for some time, but it would not stay down. In a decade we would wonder what all the fighting was about. . . .

There was no need to have worried. It did not take four years. In a stunning decision, the Supreme Court in January, 1973, struck down all restrictive abortion laws. No new rights were granted to women in the reasoning on which the decision rested. It was their right to privacy, not their right to control their bodies, that the decision was protecting.

If the Supreme Court decision really has settled the matter, the future of abortion would be certain. Abortion on demand would become fixed policy from this time. But for a considerable segment of the population, especially older people, it is not yet a settled issue. There is a movement to amend the constitution so as to forbid abortion, and some states began to retreat from previously liberalized positions. The issue of abortion will become attenuated to insignificance only when infallible contraception becomes feasible for all women so that there will no longer be need for it. The right of women to control their bodies has not yet been fully granted.

## The Politicizing of Sex

We introduce here parenthetically a factor of serious, if tangential, relevance for the future of motherhood, namely the movement begun in the late 1960s by a group of feminists to politicize a wide array of issues that had never been publicized before. Why did these feminists insist on embarrassing everyone, including political leaders, and antagonizing so many people?

There was method in their seeming madness. Until now there had been enormous reluctance to bring into public view anything that had to do, however remotely, with the private lives of women. This was true not only for abortion but also for rape. Rape, too, was being publicized to an extent never dreamed of before. Conferences were being held on the subject, articles and books written about it. Much to the embarrassment of millions of people, women were talking about the victims of rape as much as about the rapists themselves. Women who had never before dared to report rape were now daring to do so. The reported rates zoomed.

The result of the past policy of silence, if not the intent, was to hide women qua women from public life. The issues that were important to them, including abortion, rape, prostitution, were not worthy of the public's attention. It was not good form to talk about them. Women were thus obliterated as the serious concern of policy makers. Let the church concern itself with the problems of women, but not the state.

Now women were learning that so long as each individual viewed her own problems as secret, private, and unique, she had no power to deal with them. This fact put her at a disadvantage vis-à-vis men in any sexual encounter. The fact that any such encounter could result in conception and hence unwanted motherhood put women at an enormous disadvantage. The men could always go away, leaving the women to face the consequences alone. Singly, one by one, women were relentlessly disadvantaged. That was how it had always been, certainly as long as any kind of functional organization among them was impossible.

Feminists sought to create a new atmosphere in which the position of women in their many roles could be examined. No longer was any aspect of any role to be interpreted by men. Feminists were saying: we want to be protected against the superior physical strength of men that makes rape possible; we want access to contraceptive services regardless of age or marital status or parental consent; we want control over our bodies; we want the exploitation of prostitutes exposed.

There was, understandably, tremendous public resistance to the strategy of politicizing women's issues. Even thinking about them let alone discussing them in the media, violated many of the taboos the public held sacred. But bringing out all the little secrets of the individual confrontations of the sexes was a powerful strategy, however unpalatable to many. Here was consciousness raising on a national level. It could not help but reverberate on the future of motherhood.

## The Banality of Motherhood

The politics of motherhood does not end with the birth or non-birth of babies, for policy has to do not only with the number and normality of children women bear but also with control over the way the children, once borne, are reared. Responsibility for the health, protection, and—most especially—education or socialization, even indoctrination, of children also involves political issues. Child rearing as well as child bearing has political overtones.

No matter how much women engaged in child care may differ among themselves as human beings, they are all engaged—the brilliant as well as the dull—in banal activities. Hannah Arendt has alerted us to the banality of evil. Enormous crimes may be carried through by bureaucrats at their desks signing documents and answering telephone calls. And so, also, can goodness be utterly banal. Generations of children are protected, sheltered, nourished, and socialized into human beings by the banal activities of diaper-changing, dish-washing, bandaging, and swing-pushing.

## Beyond Banality: The Politics of Child Rearing

Theologians in the West have always looked beyond the banality of motherhood. They "knew" clearly the part played by mothers in the great battle between Good and Evil. The prophets could see the urgency of the proper training of the child in keeping the Covenant with Yawhah, and the Jewish mother's part was never minimized. The Church Fathers, once they came to terms with marriage,[21] could see the importance of the human mother in the salvation of the human race, one by one, and her part was never minimized. The Jesuits asked for the child only during the first seven years. After that it made little difference; they had shaped him, he was forever locked into the vise they had forged. Philosophers in the seventeenth century could also see beyond the banality. Coustel told thinking men they must overcome the repugnance which children aroused in them. "If one considers the child's exterior, which is nothing but weakness and infirmity of either body or mind, it cannot be denied that there is no apparent reason for holding it in high esteem. But one changes one's opinion if one looks into the future and acts in the light of Faith," for then one sees, not the insignificant child but rather "the good magistrate," "the good priest," "the good lord." [22]

One of the oldest battles in history had to do with control of the child. And this "battle for the babies" [23] remains one of the most relentless in totalitarian societies.[24] The Nazis fought a mortal combat with families for control of the children. One of the first fronts in the Russian revolution was in this battle: "among the Soviet communists it was a foregone conclusion that parenthood was a declining occupation that was to be replaced by social rearing." [25] In the words of one woman, "We must rescue these children from the nefarious influence of family life. In other words we must nationalize them. They will be taught the ABCs of communism and later become true communists. Our task now is to oblige the mother to give her children to us—to the Soviet State." [26] And, from an admittedly hostile reporter, the Grand Duchess, Marie, Princess Pontiantine, we learn that "for the purpose of bringing them [the children] up in the 'spirit of communism,' they are taken from their parents before they can speak and placed in so-called 'children's palaces.' Thus in Tulsa [USSR], seven thousand children under the age of ten were recently taken from their families. The parents who protested against such aggression were arrested. Many of the unfortunate mothers became insane, others committed suicide." [27]

Actually, subsequent events did not bear out the assumptions on which the original policy was based. The death rate among infants in state care became so alarming that the Department of Motherhood and Infancy of the Commissariat of Health in 1924 concluded that health was more important than principles of social training. The program had failed "because funds were lacking, because methods had not been worked out to organize it, and because the population was not ready for it." [28] Fifty years later a watered down "social training" was reported by a sympathetic observer.[29] Not a new Soviet Man, but a compliant and cooperative citizen was the objective. The child was still being shaped to be a future member of Soviet society. It was socialized to work cooperatively for superordinate goals.

In the People's Republic of China, control of child care centers for political purposes became a critical issue during the Cultural Revolution when control was taken over by the Communist Party.[30] In the nursery today a major goal is political: to keep children healthy and strong so they will become good productive workers when they are older. Later they attempt "to fashion a human being who will put the needs of the society before his own, who will identify with those in the society who do the menial labor, who will integrate intellectual labor and physical labor, and who will be motivated by altruism rather than by self interest. They start with the child in the nursing room and, using a variety of techniques and skills, attempt by the time he is seven years old to inculcate him with these values." [31] All this because they realize that "the education of children is important to the success of the party and to the consolidation of the proletarian dictatorship." [32] Governments do not spend their time on banalities.

It is sensitivity to these political and ideological implications of control that leads mothers in this country to insist that whatever plans are drawn up for child care and no matter how they are financed, the parents must be the ones who control them. They reject the idea of subjecting their children to centers or nursery schools or preschools operated by anyone with biases they find objectionable. No matter who pays the bill—community, private franchisers, industrial management—they believe parents should control them. The Day Care and Child Development Council of America, Inc., agrees. Says its Associate Director, "we believe that any child care is, at best, barren and probably destructive to children and families when it fails to provide for the basic right-responsibility of parents for the lives of their children." [33]

Still, the political issues of child rearing in this country deal less with control than with financial support.[34] Feeding and diapering babies may be banal activities; but decisions about who does them, how and where, are not banal. Any more than is motherhood itself.

## The Throes of Revolution

It is staggering to us, reared in the tradition of the Victorian script for mothers and aware of no other, that in Finland in the 1960s it was being argued that "every mother is entitled . . . to a free choice as to whether she wants to care for her child herself or have someone else do it," [35] and that it would be argued, further, that if she chose to care for the child herself she should be paid for the service. Or that child care would become a political issue even in our own country. That, in fact, for the first time in American history a President's Economic Report would, in 1973, include a whole section devoted to child care.[36] But so it was, as, in fact, it was all over the industrial world, for all modern nations were struggling to redefine the mother's role, to re-institutionalize motherhood, to come to terms with the bifurcation of women's lives which modern conditions produced. The problems of motherhood were as pressing in communist as in capitalist countries. The revolution they were all dealing with was far more profound than anything as relatively superficial as systems of government or economic organization. They were all trying to find out what was the most appropriate form of family for industrialized societies, for the integration of the mother and the worker roles is more than a psychological accommodation with which each woman must come to terms within herself as an individual. It is also a structural accommodation. It calls for policy decisions about both roles. The dimensions of the issue were only beginning to become visible in the 1960s.

Even in the United States, who would have imagined a decade ago, that motherhood would be a national issue in the early 1970s? But, under the guise of welfare legislation proposals it had, indeed, become just that. And in the process of debating that legislation a revolution long gestating became articulated and the issues clarified. It was almost irrelevant that the debate centered about day care. The latent issue was far more profound.

### Cracks in the Structure

It is when a system breaks down that we begin to notice much that we took for granted before. When there are no husbands to supply child support the cracks in the system become visible. The true revolution in motherhood is taking place among "female-headed households." Here we are faced with the basic issue: what do we *really* want women to do? If we have to choose between having them perform the child-care role or having them perform the worker role, which do we opt for? The answer slowly emerging is: the worker role. And once this decision is accepted it cannot be limited to welfare women. Once an ideology has developed for one segment of the population it is hard to prevent its spread to others. If the tender loving care of the welfare mother is expendable vis-à-vis her children, so is it for other women. And that makes a difference. If women have to enter the labor force because there is no man to support their children we are admitting that labor-force participation is not antithetical to motherwork.

We may hem and haw and say that labor-force participation is only the lesser of two evils. But the principle remains: a woman must take a job to support her children. The motivation back of this about-face on motherhood is murky; the rhetoric is filled with racial overtones; the rationale is pervaded by evocative sexual allusions. But the net result is still a changing institution of motherhood.

### The Politics of Day Care

The painful throes involved in coming to terms with the modern world were illustrated both in the Executive and the Legislative branches of our government in the 1970s. In 1969, President Nixon, in a message establishing the Office of Child Development, said:

> So critical is the matter of early growth that we must make a national commitment to provide all American children an opportunity for healthy and stimulating development during the first five years of life.[37]

Three years later, in December, 1971, he was saying in a veto message on the Comprehensive Child Development Bill:

> Neither the immediate *need* nor the desirability of a national child-development program of this character has been demonstrated. . . . For the federal government to plunge headlong financially into supporting child development would commit the vast moral authority of the national government to the side of communal approaches to child-rearing over against the family-centered approach.[38]

There was strong difference of opinion between the two major political parties. In the 1972 presidential campaign the Democratic platform included a strong endorsement of a comprehensive day-care system, federally funded, available to women of all income levels. This outraged the Republicans. President Nixon had already vetoed a bill to provide such a system, with stern warnings that it would undercut the family. The original Republican platform emphatically opposed "all proposals to place the federal government in the day-care business." But Republican women would not accept this position. The final statement said:

> We believe the primary responsibility for the care and upbringing of the child lies with the family. However, we recognize that economic and other reasons often require that parents seek assistance in the care of their children.* To meet this need, we favor the development of voluntary public and

---

*Actually a larger proportion of children with college-educated mothers were enrolled in preschools than were children of less educated women.

private comprehensive day-care centers which would be federally assisted but locally controlled, with the requirement that those participating pay their fair share of the costs according to their ability. We oppose ill-considered proposals incapable of being administered effectively, which would heavily engage the federal government in this area.

The economic reasons recognized by conservatives as legitimizing day-care centers referred to the women on welfare. It was legitimate to provide day-care centers for their children so the women themselves could enter the labor force and get workfare, not welfare. But conservatives are often quite revolutionary in their efforts to preserve a status quo. The policy maker who, for example, is most insistent that woman's place is in the home when he opposes any legislation that makes it easier for women to pursue full-time careers is also most insistent that day-care centers be provided for the children of women who have no husbands to support them and their children, so they can participate in the labor force. Keep middle-class women, like their own wives, at home, and force women from welfare rolls into the labor force.

At the turn of the century the prevailing consensus among policy makers was that a woman was worth more taking care of her children in the home than she was in the labor force. The movement known then as Mothers' Pensions developed to provide income for widowed women so that they would not be obliged to leave their homes to enter the labor force. States began to incorporate the idea into their legislative programs. The idea of providing income for fatherless families still prevailed in the 1930s when it was incorporated into the Social Security Act of 1935 as provision for Aid to Dependent Children, which was simply recognition of the same principle.[39] The idea was taken for granted that these children would be the sons and daughters of widowed women or of disabled men. It shored up a conception of the world in which there was a natural specialization of functions: Fathers were providers, mothers homemakers. If there was no father to provide, then either private charity or the community must do so.

A generation later, however, more and more of the beneficiaries were the children of unmarried or deserted women, even children borne by women already being supported by welfare funds. The fathers were not necessarily deceased or disabled but, in many cases, just missing. This made an enormous difference to policy makers. An almost complete reversal in ideology now occurred. The motto became workfare, not welfare. Women were to go to work, even mothers of small children, if care for them could be provided. Not the children but the mothers drew the policy makers' attention. And anger. Providing for children became secondary to punishing fathers by way of mothers and children.

The emotion invested in this attack revealed a powerful animus. No more of this subsidization of immorality. Women who bore children whose fathers would not support them would have to go to work to support the children themselves. In the policy of workfare there was no intention of extending the same underlying philosophy to women of their own class. For the woman who worked because it was important to her, for whatever reason, there was to be no provision for child care. The place of women whose husbands were living with them was still in the home. And now the child was a matter of great solicitude.

Little did the legislators realize they could not write a new script for welfare mothers and retain the old script for their own wives and daughters. Such a dichotomy could not survive. In their blow for workfare, the legislators were striking a blow against the old script for the role of mother, further severing the mother and the worker roles.

There were ten bills introduced in the 92nd Congress that, one way or other, indirectly or directly, included child-care provisions. These bills highlight the process by which the role of mother was being redefined. The bills ranged in outlook from the traditional, old-fashioned child-welfare philosophy all the way up to the modern women's and children's rights orientation. The objective of the women's and children's rights orientation "would be to provide real choices and options for mothers and children." Programs would be available for all women. They would "offer the mother the right to pursue work or interests other than twenty-four-hour mothering, and at the same time meet a child's need to have relationships with other children and adults. According to this point of view the modern family is a small, isolated, and alienated unit within society consisting of mothers who spend most of their time behind chain-link fences cut off from the rest of society, and children who are forced to grow up in female ghettos. It is an argument for human growth and mental health." [40] It will take a considerable amount of time for men and women beyond the age of thirty to digest all the implications of this conception of the role of mother.

Patrick Daniel Moynihan attempted in the early 1970s to re-conceptualize the whole issue of "workfare vs. welfare." He saw the policy of making payments to mothers of small children not as welfare, with all the stigma attached to that status, but as a return to the policy embodied in the early mothers' pension ideology. It was a payment, in effect, for the services these women were performing. Their motherwork was essential and should not be defined out of existence by viewing payment for it as welfare. The arguments in its favor were couched in terms of the right of every family to a minimum income and a variety of techniques were proposed for implementing this, including the so-called negative income tax.

## Young People Adumbrate the Future

As usual, young people find it easier to accept the newer trends. And it is their view of motherhood that adumbrates the future better than current debates. Among the resolutions passed at the White House Conference on Youth in 1971 was one to the effect that "Congress address itself to the needs for economic security for the family, including: (1) high quality child care centers . . . available through public funds with the dual purpose of enriching child development and freeing parents for development of their own potential; (2) [to] a parent in a single-headed family . . . the choice of going to work or staying home to care for his or her children; in a two-parent home the non-breadwinner . . . the same choice. . . ." [41] The conferees did add that "individual freedoms are limited by the responsibility of child-rearing" but they did not specify that this responsibility was a one-sex obligation. Policy makers might debate fine points. But the young people saw clearly that once the principle was accepted that the worker role took precedence over the role of mother among some women, it could no longer be denied among other women.

Surveying the infant- and child-care services provided or being experimented with throughout the industrialized world is like watching a giant stirring, slowly, awkwardly, hesitantly, even reluctantly. A small group, fully aware of what is happening in the last third of the century, are trying to persuade reluctant traditionalists that the old roles just don't fit any more, that merely tinkering with the script won't do, that living in today's and tomorrow's world calls for conceptions of child care and development quite different from those of the past.

As soon as motherhood becomes a political issue it becomes also an economic issue. For who is to bear the costs of motherhood, the individual family or the community?

# CHAPTER FIFTEEN

## The Economics of Motherhood

### Children As Investment and As Consumer Goods

There was a time when children constituted an accepted form of investment insurance. Parents took care of their children when they were young and children, in turn, took care of their parents when they were old. Logical, reasonable, sensible. But in a modern industrial society that is no longer the way it is done. We lay it all out in a "social" rather than in a "family" security system so that although each generation does, in fact, support the generation ahead of it, the bookkeeping is so complicated that it is hard to understand how any particular son or daughter is supporting any specific parent. It is not a direct, personal parent-child but an inter-generational relationship. So in any one family, although sons and daughters do often contribute to the care of elderly parents, children can no longer be viewed as an investment. At the present time, in fact, many parents are still contributing to the support of young adult sons and daughters.

Children have also been viewed as a kind of consumer goods. "Most married couples believe that children will afford them psychological satisfactions for which they are willing to pay." [1] The young husband and working wife ask themselves when they can "afford" to have children, and how many they can "afford." Should she give up her job now; should she wait until they have the car paid for? In the 1950s people were deciding to spend money on having the fourth, fifth, and sixth child rather than to spend it on other things such as boats, trips, or third cars. Women "indulged" in motherhood instead of in other consumer activities.

Children had, to use the economist's term, greater "utility" for them than other ways of disposing of income. Proponents of the child-free family emphasize this aspect of motherhood, playing up the satisfactions one can buy with money not spent on children.[2]

The idea of thinking of motherhood in these economic terms is repugnant to many people. Children an investment, consumer goods? Oh, no! Still, however conceptualized, people have always recognized that whether children were viewed as duty, Acts of God, investment, or as pleasurable consumer goods, there were costs associated with them. Both the "investment" and the "consumer-goods" conceptualizations are anachronistic today. But that does not mean that there is no economic aspect to motherhood, to the economy as a whole, as well as to women themselves. The costs may be paid willingly or reluctantly; they are no less real in either case.

### Costs and Prices

Economists make a distinction between cost and price. The two may coincide but they do not have to. The cost of anything includes the material, time, effort, and energy invested in producing it. All goods and services may thus be said to have a cost. But that does not necessarily mean there is also a price attached to them. They may be "priceless," in two ways: (1) the owner will not exchange them for any amount or (2) no one will pay the producer anything at all for them. For price involves an exchange.

Ordinarily children are priceless in both of these ways. There is a Talmudic saying to the effect that a parent will take nothing in exchange for his child, but neither will he pay anything at all for someone else's.[3]

Costs may be of many kinds. Some are monetary; some are emotional; some are both. Some are direct; some indirect.[4] Some—labelled "opportunity costs"—consist of what you have to give up in order to get what you want. If, for example, you take a trip you will lose the money you would be earning if you remained on the job. When figuring out the cost of taking the trip, the lost pay has to be included.

Prices may be paid in many ways. They may be paid "in kind," or in some form of barter, as when young mothers exchange baby-sitting services, hour for hour. But in our day and age practically all are paid in money. For although children themselves may be priceless, the services required to rear them are not. Increasingly child care is becoming a purchasable service with a—monetary—price tag. And one of the most puzzling accounting assignments today has to do with "costing" child-care services in order to determine what price has to be paid to produce them. Child care is, in effect, becoming an "industry."

## Monetary Costs of Children to the Family

The obvious monetary costs to the family of children have not been traditionally assessed to mothers; under the common law they have been the father's obligation. The extent of this kind of cost has been a matter of both practical and research interest for some time.[5] The precise amount has varied according to time, according to standards, and according to definitions. As of 1969, the Institute of Life Insurance estimated that it cost a middle-income family $23,000 to $25,000 to rear a child to the age of eighteen. College added $12,000 to $15,000 more. The Commission on Population Growth and the American Future found that the first child had a direct "undiscounted" cost of about $40,000. If the opportunity costs for the average woman were included, the figure soared to $98,000; each additional child cost $48,000.[6] (Table 15/1.) An other approach to the "costing" of children concluded that for middle-income families and below, the cost of rearing a child to the age of eighteen amounted to two and one-half times the average annual income of the family wage earners, wife as well as husband. "So, if the family income is $8,000 a year, it will cost about $20,000 to raise a child to age eighteen." [7] College is extra. Another way of seeing the situation leads to the conclusion that the total cost of two children over twenty years is five years' salary. "So to raise two children you must spend 25 percent of your earnings. Over a period of twenty years you must live only 75 percent as well as you would if you had no children." [8] All these estimates of monetary costs include such obvious standard items as rent, food, clothing, normal medical care,[9] recreation, transportation, and the like. (Transportation deserves a parenthetical aside. It is taken for granted in middle-class suburban families that of course a teenager must have his own car; otherwise he is like a restless, caged animal. Thus almost all families—80 percent—with at least one child fifteen years of age or over, have a second car.) [10] The more sophisticated "costing" approaches have included, in addition, the earnings of children sacrificed if they continue their education beyond a given age instead of entering the labor force.

### Monetary Costs to Women

Attention is increasingly being paid to the incomes women would earn in the time devoted to child bearing and child rearing if they were in the labor force earning money instead of staying at home.[11]

### THE TOTAL COST OF A CHILD, 1969 *

| | DISCOUNTED | UNDISCOUNTED† |
|---|---|---|
| Cost of giving birth | $ 1,534 | $ 1,534 |
| Cost of raising child | 17,576 | 32,830 |
| Cost of a college education | 1,244 | 5,560 |
| Total direct cost | 20,354 | 39,924 |
| Opportunity costs for the average woman‡ | 39,273 | 58,437 |
| Total costs of a first child | $59,627 | $98,361 |

* Population and the American Future, The Report of the Commission on Population Growth and the American Future (Washington: Government Printing Office, 1972, p. 81). The source is from *Costs of Children*, prepared for the Commission, 1972, by Ritchie H. Reed and Susan McIntosh.

† Discounted and undiscounted costs—spending $1,000 today costs more than spending $1,000 over a ten-year period because of the nine years of potential interest on the latter. This fact is allowed for in the discounted figures by assuming interest earned on money not spent in the first year. True costs are not accurately reflected in the undiscounted estimates, for these are simply accumulations of total outlays without regard to the year in which they must be made.

‡ Depending on the educational background of the mother, the opportunity costs (earnings foregone by not working) could be higher or lower.

This "cost" varies, obviously, according to the level of her marketable skills and talents. Time spent taking care of infants and small children could, theoretically at least, be spent writing briefs or operating on patients or designing buildings or, more likely, typing letters.[12] The earnings a woman gives up in order to take care of her children constitute the opportunity costs that are increasingly being incorporated into the concept of the monetary costs of children.

In addition, women are increasingly contributing in a more direct way to paying the monetary costs of children. Carolyn Shaw Bell, for example, calls our attention to this fact when she reminds us that "nobody knows the number of married women whose earnings provide money for their children's college fees, or for their education in specialized areas." [13] Indeed, there are many young men and women who would not be in college at all without the contribution to the family exchequer made by the mother's earnings in middle and late motherhood. Usually payment to baby sitter or nurse for child care also comes out of the mother's income.

Recently, attention has been paid to the monetary cost to women of the years in early motherhood when they drop out of the labor force to take care of their children. This has been understood in terms of the effect such dropping out has on her earnings when she returns to the labor force. Opportunity costs are increasingly coming to be seen as including more than the loss of earnings when she is engaged in child care, they also include the reduced value of her skills lost during this period. There has been not only an attrition of her skills but also a de-grading of her professional knowledge, for a very fast pace is necessary to keep up with any occupation these days. An absence of even a few years can render one's knowledge obsolete. Vacant spaces appear in the woman's work history when she applies for a position. All these intangibles militate against her when she looks for employment after a several years' absence.[14] She has, further, not been accumulating experience useful for improved earnings: "the lack of continuity in women's attachment to the labor force means that they will not have accumulated as much experience as men at a given age. The relatively steeper rise of men's income with age has been attributed to their greater accumulation of experience, of 'human capital' acquired on the job." [15] Women have not accumulated this kind of "human capital," however valuable the kind they have been accumulating might be in other contexts.[16]

## Some Non-monetary Costs of Motherhood

Sacrifice is an intrinsic component of what Kenneth Boulding has called the non-market "grants economy," or "integry," the part of our society that does not operate on exchange principles. It has always been an intrinsic component in the traditional script for the role of mother. She sacrificed her body while gestating the infant, a fact recognized in the folk saying that each child "cost" a tooth. The Catholic Church taught that if there had to be a choice between an infant and its mother, the mother was to be sacrificed. If there was a shortage of food, the mother surrendered part or all of her share to feed her children. If there was not enough of anything, in fact, the mother yielded to the needs of her children. Scrimping and saving for the children was part of the script.

Relatively few women in our society have to sacrifice food and basic survival needs for their children. But there are other costs even today. The wear-and-tear on the mother's body involved in motherwork cannot be ignored. The guilt-stress-fatigue syndrome which so many young women feel is very real.[17] Now that research is revealing some of the lethal consequences that are possible when this syndrome is allowed to become exacerbated, we can no longer sweep it under the rug. It has been one of the most unappreciated costs of motherhood by all concerned—husbands, public health officials, even the medical profession. If this had not been so, provision would long since have been made for the relief of house-bound young women in the vulnerable years of early motherhood.

Even for women to whom motherhood provides the supreme form of self-fulfillment, to whom none of the investment of herself has seemed like a cost, let alone a sacrifice, there are different costs. She only pays them later. All she can do is choose when and how to pay them. If she invests herself completely in the role of mother, the cost will be exacted when her children cease to need her in her middle years. If she wishes to retain selfhood beyond the early years of all-engrossing motherhood, she has to moderate her investment in it during her earlier years. She may, if forewarned, thus pay the costs earlier in the form of less intense investment in her small children and greater investment in ties with the outside world. She may also have fewer children, a cost of considerable size to some women.

True, it is harder than one thinks for the young woman to make such decisions. Radiant and engrossed in the care of infant and small child, she can see little beyond the satisfying present. She sees only more such fulfilling years stretching ahead of her, years busily engaged in meeting the needs of her brood. Talk of other commitments (job or career) chill her. She feels threatened by it. And the more threatened she feels, the more she fills her days with loving services for her children.

Still, inexorably, the bill comes due. The "empty nest" becomes a grim reality. And a respectable corpus of research documents the fact that Mrs. Portnoy's complaint is far more serious than her son's.[18]

## Quasi-Monetary Costs of Motherhood

There are some costs of motherhood that cannot be categorized as either monetary or non-monetary but which, nevertheless, are costs. We know, for example, that potential as well as actual motherhood is a major rationalization for discriminating against women workers. If at all possible, they are not hired in the first place for fear they will drop out to have babies; they are not given expensive training for fear they will not use it when they have children; they are not given high-level positions because their maternal responsibilities will compete with corporate responsibilities. We can't afford to educate women because they won't be able to practice when they become mothers. If accepted, they are discouraged. "In graduate school I took my final exam in my ninth month of pregnancy. Every month some man was saying, 'you won't make it.' The faculty was saying, 'it goes to prove we wasted our money by giving you a fellowship.' " [19]

All these costs—monetary, non-monetary, quasi-monetary—are assessed against women themselves. But some of them may also be viewed as costs to the economy as a whole. What looks like a consumer good from one angle can also be made to look like a factor of production from another, either a luxury or a cost.

## Some Costs of Motherhood to the Economy

Using a tough-minded approach, the time and energy spent on child care can be counted, or "accounted," as time and energy withheld from the labor force and therefore from "real" economic productivity, real, that is, in the sense of being worthy of inclusion in the gross national product (at least until child care comes to be counted as productive in this sense).

According to Stewart Garfinkle, the first baby "costs" about ten years of labor-force participation, the second, three additional years, the third, only two more. These costs, incidentally, seem to be declining as the difference in number of children between women in and not in the labor force declines; women take little more time off for babies than the average amount of time men take off for other reasons.[20] Analogously, the costs to professional women of having children in terms of achievement may also be viewed as costs to the economy in terms of the services they would have contributed if they had not had children.[21]

A novel twist to the cost-accounting of motherhood has been given by those working for population control. They tell us that if women limit themselves to two children rather than three, the average family income in our country could be as much as 15 percent higher.[22] That is, the "cost" of having the third child to the economy in terms of the productivity of the economy is very considerable. And a Swedish economist, Per Holmberg, has concluded that if women were as productive and gainfully employed as men, the standard of living would be improved by about a third.[23] Carolyn Shaw Bell notes also that "as economists agree to recognize education as one type of investment in human capital, they might well acknowledge a major source of funds for this investment to be the earnings of married women." [24] To the extent that the earnings of women in middle and late motherhood contribute to the college education and professional training of sons and daughters they are contributing to human capital, and *not* contributing is a cost.

The concept of costs can be applied to the environment as well as to the economy. The idea is sometimes presented that if the Smiths are well enough off to afford ten children, why not? The implication is that the Smiths pay the entire cost of rearing their children. Quite aside from the taxes they pay for the services supplied by the community to school, protect, and serve other needs of children, they use up a considerable part of our natural resources; they are a charge on the environment. Indeed, among the wealthy, the share per individual is greater than among others, for they consume more than less affluent families. The costs of the children of wealthy families are not all financial nor are they all borne by the parents.

### Motherwork or Other Work?

Basically, from the economic point of view, the costs of motherhood have to do with the relative value of a woman's time. Is it worth more invested in the production of subsistence, marketable goods and services, or in child care? Or in some other activity or non-activity?

In preliterate societies, we remind ourselves again, there is no choice. The adult woman is worth more in the production of food than in simple child care. Older siblings or co-wives or sisters or grandmothers can tend to the children. A scanning of the situation around the world in the 1960s showed that in all except New England, adult women turn the care of small children over to others who are less productive so that they can work in the fields or gardens.[25] Taking care of children is absolutely essential, necessary, indispensable, of course, like all the services that women perform in the home. But of little worth in terms of material goods in a market.

The relatively greater importance of productive work as compared with motherwork was recognized in western societies until recently. Under the domestic system of organizing industry, adult women were not excused from productive labor—spinning, weaving, gardening, sewing—in order to take care of children. Nor were they excused in rural communities. Alexander Hamilton and Albert Gallatin, we remind ourselves, found women's place to be in the mill.[26] The productive work of adult women, in brief, has taken priority over or at least been accorded equal status with mere child care. Usually women have done both. It is only within the recent past and in affluent societies that it has even been argued that women should spend all their time taking care of children. Even if only a hand-full of household chores remains in the home, it is argued by some that child care should be the woman's full-time preoccupation.

Whether or not an adult woman's time is worth more taking care of children than in the labor force depends on the kind of alternative child care that is being contemplated and the kind of work the woman can do. If the child-care requirements are minimal and high quality care is available and the woman is capable of well-paid work, the economic—if not the psychological and sociological—aspects of the matter are clear-cut. If the kind of child care contemplated is minimal and the kind of work the woman is capable of is not well paid, the situation is clear-cut but reversed. Working out the economic angles is far from a simple task even if one ignores all other—psychological—considerations.

And even after they have been worked out, the accounting problems remain. How, for example, do you "cost" child care? How do you decide what the price should be when it is transformed into a marketable commodity? We are still in a provisional, tentative, trial-and-error stage when we try to appraise the monetary worth or value of services that have never before been appraised. It staggers us to read of "costing" child-care services in counting-house terminology; to have a market value placed upon the love and care we know small children need; to have a top-flight management consulting firm drawing up reports on "costs-per-child-hour," counting "two part-time children as one full-time equivalent child," figuring "full-time equivalency on a per-hour basis," and tabulating "marginal cost by quality of care." [27] We have been learning that "shifting from a non-monetized to a monetized service is always confusing," [28] increasingly so as more and more human services have moved from the home to the marketplace. It is exceptionally confusing "as our society slowly turns toward paid child care." [29] We are overwhelmed by the price we have to pay for the services we have always taken for granted.

### To Market, To Market . . .

All societies are riddled with paradoxes. One of the most striking in our own is the situation in which an admittedly salient function, motherwork, is worth practically nothing. It pays very poorly so that it is difficult to attract high level personnel. All plans for providing auxiliary or surrogate persons to provide child care run up against the obstacle of finding and training and motivating people to do it, in addition to paying them. For the truth of the matter is that motherwork—taking care of the psychological as well as the physical needs of infants and small children—is, as the disenchanted young women put it, "shit work." "The intrinsic significance and value of early maternal child care seems implicitly devalued. . . . Cultural trends . . . seem myopically to disavow, if not deprecate, the typical child caretaker, the much discussed and abused mother" [30] or, for that matter, anyone else who performs the function.

Price becomes a major issue when the problem is how much one has to pay for alternatives to maternal child-care. Now we are not in the world of love-and/or-duty but in a conventional market situation. Child-care has a price. Money has to be paid for it. There is an exchange, not a "grant" or a sacrifice, situation.

And the price is high:

> . . . for many people who have not yet come in contact with organized, full time day care, and know only informal arrangements, it can at first be hard to believe the apparently high costs of organized center care. The legislator who says "A good mother is priceless," may derive his understanding of

child care values from his own childhood when aunts, mothers and grandmothers were not paid in cash, or a domestic servant was paid very low wages. Such a legislator may feel child care shouldn't really cost much.[31]

Actually, like any other service this one varies in price per child according to quality, kind, and amount of service, purchased from $1,245 for minimal level care to $2,320 for a desirable level for group care. Costs may go up as high as $3,000 to $4,000 for full-time quality group care.[32] For family day care, from $1,423 to $2,373.[33]

Simply to illustrate the complexities involved in "costing" child care, some of the problems faced are presented here. How extensive is the service to be? All day? How much in the way of donations and volunteer service can be counted on? [34] How much for start-up costs? Recurrent costs? What provision should be made for inflation in salaries? (Staff costs constitute 70 to 80 percent of day care costs.) How measure quality? (At present, in the absence of measures of social and emotional development, a staff-child ratio is used.) [35] The average staff salary across the nation reported in one study was just above the poverty level. Most workers were paid below it.[36]

### Picking Up the Tab

A wide variety of ways of paying for group child care and a variety of sources characterize the current scene: government, industry, parents, volunteers are all involved.

Although the Women's Bureau had been reporting on the female labor force, including mothers, for many years, it was not until 1973 that the President's Economic Report took official note of child care among their "special problems." And, understandably, it was concerned primarily with the question "whether the Government should pay for part or all of the cost of child care." In the 92nd Congress, federal contribution to child-care programs became a major concern, and for the first time serious attention had to be paid to the costs involved in the several provisions suggested in the ten bills dealing, one way or another, with child care. For the first time technical accounting problems had to be confronted, concepts had to be defined, new ways of viewing old relationships had to be adjusted to. In most parts of the world, child care is subsidized by the state and the same is expected by some advocates in this country. A very substantial part of the estimated thirty billion dollar bill for across-the-board child care for preschoolers was expected to be paid by the federal, state, or local government.

Industry's share of the bill is taken for granted in China; and in the USSR, crèches and day care are also provided by industry quite as a matter of course. In this country, however, industry has been less involved. But some experience is available. Gwen Morgan has been concerned with the provision of child care in the Cambridge, Massachusetts, area and has observed the part such industries as Kaiser and Polaroid have played. She reports that industry and parents alone cannot afford to pay the entire cost of child care. The community has to share it. As, in some cases, do universities, churches, colleges, and all of the other special "communities" that constitute a local community.

She reports on an experiment that began at Kaiser Industries in which both the company and the parents contributed. When the company had to retrench, it could no longer bear the financial weight of the program. The management of the Center was then taken over by a board—including parent representatives—whose function it was to allocate the available space in the Center. The several industries and agencies in the area then asked for "slots" for the children they would like to have accommodated.

> The KLH industrial company reserves X number of slots . . . and pays for them. MIT, Polaroid, and a small company in the neighborhood, Advent, also reserve and pay for blocks of spaces. The Welfare Department sends a number of children on contract. Each of the sending agencies pays full cost for the day care on a per child basis, and this is later adjusted on the basis of the sliding fees which are collected. The Board of the Center is therefore in the business of selling slots, planning on the basis of these reserved slots, with the available funds from the sending agencies.[37]

Gwen Morgan recommends government incentives to industry in the form of tax exemptions or subsidies to encourage day care programs.[38]

Volunteers, anachronistic as it may seem, pick up a considerable chunk of the child-care tab. Planners give formal recognition to this fact. One team suggests that "one possibility is to build on the experience of 25 percent 'funding' in kind, now used by the centers and systems surveyed by Abt Associates. Extending such a system means determinedly locating child care centers in high schools, near old age homes, near universities, and other sources of able volunteers. Conscientious objectors, delinquents, retarded adults, the handicapped, rehabilitating patients and prisoners, and home based retirees are other groups who might contribute much to child care." [39] Locating production facilities near to the raw material is an old economic law.

Government, industry, volunteers. . . . But when all is said and done, it is usually the mother who pays. Certainly middle and upper-middle class women usually bear the monetary costs of child care. A common form of child care is the cooperative center or nursery school. These are organized by the mothers themselves and each parent, father as well as mother, is called upon to contribute services. In order to facilitate such organization, a Child Care Resource Center was set up as part of the Cambridge Policy Studies in 1971. Even instant day-care centers are now becoming available; General Learning Corporation could supply ready-made equipment already packaged. [40]

One wonders what all the shouting is about when it was reported by the Women's Bureau in 1973 that only 3 percent of children were cared for at a center or group facility. [41] The commonest arrangements were still make-shift. The major forms were: care in the child's own home by some family member; care by neighbor, relative, or friend or babysitter [42] in her home. [43] All presuppose the continuation of the present isolated household, the present life style. In addition, cooperative households are beginning to experiment with other arrangements, mothers taking turns in caring for one another's children or one mother specializing in the care of all the children. And, of course, communes are also beginning to have to face the problems of child care as well. [44]

### Some Afterthoughts

Two almost antithetical views of the assessment of the costs of motherhood coexist side by side. One view concentrates on the individual women who bear children. Motherhood is no one's business but their own. Let them make their own provision for the costs involved. True, the child is an expensive charge on the community's resources also because, however much one emphasizes the private nature of motherhood, children do have to be provided for. The other view sees children not as the private concerns of the women who bear them but as "resources" for the future, as, in effect, a public charge.

The British, we are told, were shocked into this point of view when the contrast between the pale millhands from Birmingham at Dunkirk were contrasted with the glowingly healthy Nazi soldiers. They were galvanized then into an acceptance of their responsibility for their children. A similar shock struck the United States during World War II when it was found that 40 percent of the young men 21 to 35 were physically unfit or fit for at best only limited military service.[45] From this point of view mothers are merely temporary caretakers, rather like "employees." Health care, schools, and similar services are public investments in the future. The child is expected to bring in a handsome return. As, indeed, he did, for Hitler.

In the United States the other view has tended to prevail. It sees the child as the private property of the parents alone, profits and losses, benefits and costs, are solely the concern of the owners, the parents who are to assume all the costs. It rejects interference by the state. This view is in line with the "pattern" of our culture.

The concept "patterns of culture" implies that there is a "strain for consistency" in a culture, a common *leitmotiv* that runs through all its components, including family, work, leisure, what-have-you. The same thread shows up in all parts of the fabric. If a society is characterized by an emphasis on rugged individualism, individualism will show up in all its institutions. If it is characterized by an emphasis on the importance of the general welfare, constraints will show up in all its institutions. (There is a saying in Austria contrasting two patterns, represented respectively by England and Germany. In England one may do anything not specifically forbidden; in Germany, one may not do anything unless specifically permitted.) In our society the balance has been in the direction of individualism; slowly and inexorably, however, we may be moving in the direction of more emphasis on the social order.

It makes a difference in assessing costs which of these views prevails. If motherhood is a personal, private, individual matter, if women themselves make the decisions whether or not to have children, whether or not to enter the labor force, it is up to them to pay the costs—personal, career, or whatever—involved. If the other view prevails, motherhood is seen as too important a societal institution to leave the entire cost to be borne by the women themselves.

There is an advantage for those who hold the rugged-individual view in convincing women that they need motherhood in order to achieve fulfillment.[46] If motherhood is self-fulfilling, then it is its own reward and women may legitimately be required to pay for it, whatever form the costs may take. If, on the other hand, the idea that prevails is that motherhood is a national concern, the costs must be shared.

The joker is that some of the costs of motherhood cannot be shared. They cannot be "passed on." Long after all the other issues relating to sex roles have been resolved this one will remain. Bearing children is one role specialization that cannot be shared. The question shifts from one of economics to one of justice.

## The Quality of Justice

What *is* justice in a case like this? The question is no easier to answer today than it was when a cynical judge asked it two millennia ago. Theories, yes. Cultural patterns, yes. But clear-cut answers, no.

There are some who base their conception of justice on Nature. If a thing is natural it is right. Justice requires us to follow its "dictates." This is, in effect, the position apotheosized in Social Darwinism. But there are others who believe just the reverse: Justice requires us to correct Nature. As applied to motherhood, the first point of view sees it as eminently fair that all the costs of motherhood in both mother and worker roles be borne by women; the second sees it as unfair. The first sees many of the costs as, in fact, unsharable. They are intrinsic in Nature. And that ends the matter.

A sociologist early in the century, Lester Frank Ward, propounded the thesis that the artificial was better than the natural. The conservative school of philosophy holds that justice consists in following nature; the liberal, in correcting it.

> The picture of the social order and the natural order that underlies the classical conception is not that the social order properly corrects the arbitrary, and rationally unintelligible, distribution of natural advantages but rather that the social order properly reflects the hallowed distinctions of degree, status, and role that

are perceptible in the natural order, which itself has a harmonious structure pleasing to the Creator. The social order is sick and liable to violence, total disorder, and death when it no longer reflects, as in a mirror, the due subordinations and separations of degree that nature everywhere requires. Examples would be the subordination of female to male, of children to parents, of subject to monarch, of the layman to the priest, and so on. These subordinations, and many like them, represent natural law. . . The liberal conception of justice . . . opposes the designed and invented moral order to the blind causality of the natural order, the moralized and socialized citizen to the natural man.[47]

To say, therefore, that biology—here viewed as the costs of motherhood—is destiny does not, according to the liberal conception of justice, mean that it is fair to make women bear its entire cost. The fact that reproduction is natural is not the same as saying that there is nothing that can be done about mitigating its costs. To accept the biology-is-destiny view in this context in a fatalistic way is the same as accepting the Social Darwinian thesis that it is the destiny of the weak to be exploited, of the strong to dominate. We do not permit that philosophy to prevail without at least trying to mitigate its implementation. The quality of justice is no more strained than the quality of mercy. We invent social protections for the disadvantaged. A similar stance is called for in the case of motherhood. To the extent that reproduction—*not*, be it noted, sex per se—puts women at a disadvantage, societal compensation for such a disadvantage is fair and legitimate.

Beyond reproduction, biology is no longer destiny. It is true that a very special kind of care is needed by infants and small children, a kind of care extremely difficult to secure on a market basis. It may thus be granted that ordinarily the mother, who has no out—until fathers are willing to share the role with her—is the most feasible person to supply it. So far so good. But is it fair to ask her to pay all the costs involved in professional or career setbacks resulting from the years she is obliged to withdraw from active participation in the labor force? A "fairness doctrine" calls for a redress for these intrinsic—as yet—disabilities of motherhood. If, that is, the exigencies of motherhood require a different work history for women than for men, for example, compensation for this time out—whatever form such compensation might take—is clearly called for. Instead of refusing her entrance into the professional school because she is going to have children some day, the dean will simply draw up a different schedule for the young woman. No sweat. Of course we can manage that. It's all provided for. How about Plan Y?

An interesting insight. Here is a case where sharing costs greatly reduces them for all concerned. Not, of course, a matter of role integration made easy. Just easier.

# PART SEVEN

# What to Do About the Future of Motherhood

# Introduction

### "Motherhood"

. . . I am sick and tired of reading that housewives and mothers feel they lead relatively useless and unexciting lives —that they daydream only about the past or far-away future. . . . What is the purpose of reporting on all this insecurity, unhappiness, uselessness? Since these people you write about don't seem to be able to find ways to combine family life with other worthwhile activities, why don't you as a community-minded newspaper do a positive article suggesting what these women can do? You've identified and described the problem many times—please help us do something about it! (Letter to *The Washington Post,* May 25, 1973.)

### The Classic Approach

The classic approach to the dilemmas and quandaries of women caught in the cross currents of our—or other—times has been a simple "grin-and-bear-it" prescription. Get control of yourself. Come to terms with your divinely ordained status. Use religion, yoga, meditation, tranquilizers, therapy, encounter groups, what-have-you. An enormous industry is at work to reconcile these dilemmas, and for some it succeeds.

Others, following Buckminster Fuller's principle that instead of trying to change the human nature of women, limited in the energy, emotional concern, and attention available, argue that we should change the structure in which motherhood operates. Mollify the setting. Since the circumstances we set up for the performance of the role of mother render it virtually impossible for anyone to do it well, change the circumstances. Here is the way one psychiatrist sees the situation:

> . . . parents in America have been browbeaten into a state of perplexity and confusion which has left them both guilty and frightened. It is time that we stopped telling them that they have done terrible things to their children or that they have failed to do other absolutely essential things *for* their children. Rather than berate them for not having talents they were not born with, rather than ask the impossible from them in terms of changing their most basic feelings, attitudes, and values, we should begin to admit what is obviously the truth—that almost every parent in existence is trying to be a good parent. The mother or father who *consciously* is out to destroy or harm a child is a very rare one. A mother in the course of a postpartum psychosis can develop a murderous hostility toward her infant, and a father can become so infuriated by a squalling baby that he is driven to inflict physical harm, but such attitudes are part of an illness or an uncontrollable rage and cannot be considered the parents' natural or normal behavior. Every parent vacillates to some degree in [her or] his feelings toward [her or] his child just as [she or] he does toward every other person who is important to [her or] him.

> Parents cannot be constantly loving to their children, nor can they be totally consistent in administering discipline. Yet so much of the child-rearing literature from advice columns in the daily newspaper to professional manuals seems to assume that every parent is capable of being superhuman in this respect. . . .[1]

But what, exactly, does changing the structure really mean?

### Changing the Structure: Reform or Revolution?

In this revolution, as in any other, there are those who say reform the status quo, change it only enough to meet the problem, and there are those who say, no, we have to start from a different set of premises. One, accepting the two-role ideology, starts with the way things are and tries to devise ways to help women integrate their roles; the other, rejecting the status quo, starts with experimental communities or communes and tries to re-define roles.

The reform approach, if we accept the research findings of the psychologists and anthropologists, would include, among other things: relieving mothers of the entire responsibility for child care and child rearing; more support from relatives, including fathers; less exclusive specialization of mothers in child care; less isolation of the mother; a wide array of services of many kinds—medical, educational, psychological. The revolutionary approach, if we accept the psychiatrist's analysis of the situation, would involve a total re-structuring of parental roles:

> Rather than try to bend parents into some kind of unnatural shape, perhaps it would be better to provide more opportunities for children to find consistent and understanding attitudes from individuals less harassed and less split in their allegiances and affection than parents must be. Perhaps parents need less criticism and more help. Blaming them for their problem children and asking them to beef up their output of love as a cure for their children's problems may not be as effective a solution as relieving them of some of the burden of child care by developing alternatives to traditional family living. Such alternatives would bring the children under the care of people both inclined and trained to provide what is needed for healthy emotional growth.[2]

In the reform approach, traditional tenets of motherhood still prevail. It begins where we are now. The revolutionary approach involves change in total life styles which, in one fell swoop, attack all the structural dysfunctions for women at once. Actually, as it happens, the reform approach often ends up as far more revolutionary, the total-change approach often as far more traditional, not to say regressive.

A sobering thought for both revolutionaries and reformers: one begins with seemingly simple suggestions for, let us say, child care; one ends, finally, with questions about "our notions of all property." Two psychologists have asked some thought-provoking questions:

> As society undertakes more and more child-rearing functions, could children continue to be identified as the property of parents? If children are not to be identified as the property of particular persons, need the matings which produced them be considered permanent? If not, what living arrangements will maximize both security and freedom of choice—not just for

once, but always? With freedom of choice, what will be the prevalence of monogamy and its alternatives, homosexual union and its alternatives, communal families, and combinations of these and other forms of social-sexual co-existence? Will our notions of all property have to change?" [3]

With no expectation of finding answers to these questions, we begin with a brief overview of motherhood in communal life styles.

# CHAPTER SIXTEEN

## Experimental Communities

### Low Profile

Revolutionary rationales for tampering with motherhood may vary from one that views it as liberating women from the shackles of its obligations to one that views child care and child rearing as too important to leave to mothers. It is, therefore, quite surprising to find how little serious attention is paid to motherhood in reports on the numerous, presumably revolutionary, experimental or intentional communities today. A survey of the communal movement as of April, 1971, for example, reported a wide variety—sixteen kinds—of communes, but there is scarcely a word about motherhood; [1] the theoretical attention devoted to it falls far short of the attention directed toward other problems. A brief glance is given to child care or mother-child relationships, but in-depth studies are yet to appear.[2] Actually, children are not welcome. They cost too much.

The true costs of children stand out with brutal clarity in the communes. When a group of, let us say, ten to fifteen people are struggling to maintain themselves at even a subsistence level on a poorly equipped farm, the time required to take care of children is a real drain on the labor force. Thus, notices of new communities sometimes specify that they "are looking for people without children," because they cannot afford dependents. And one bitter woman named Sandy, cries out desperately against the rejection of children:

Right now, I feel very, very discouraged and depressed. Maybe things are better out West, but I would like to be near

Eugene [her husband], so I've been searching and searching back East for the kind of communal situation Julian [her baby] and I would fit into. . . . If I had a penny for every commune-hip community that Julian and I aren't welcome to join, well, I'd have almost 50 cents!

Other mothers out there will know exactly what I mean if you have ever tried to fend for yourself and your children alone. It's weird and sad, but I have actually had more sympathy from the *bourgeois* community than from the *hip* community. The hip people have come across "No vacancies" ("Sorry, we're all snugly settled here, and we haven't got time to listen to *your* problems. Tough shit!") or else "No babies at all"—("Sorry, how would you work? You can't expect *us* to look after Julian! Horrors! We have our own things to do! And don't expect us to turn our hi-fis down at 8:30, just to let the baby sleep! We believe in total *freedom*, and babies are just a bother!")

All too often, hip people come across as a bunch of selfish pigs. I hate to say that, but it's depressingly true—at least in my experience. From free schools—no babies allowed?? Ye gods! Even from a highly publicized hip, political, non-profit, supposedly (but not actually) libertarian project—"We can't be bothered with children." Maybe all too many hip communities are havens for too many "adult babies" who see other children as competition—but I won't get psychoanalytic.[3]

Hardboiled and heartless as it looks to the rejected mother, from the side of the commune the rejection makes economic, if not reform, sense. The struggling commune cannot afford too many dependents, that is, members who do not contribute their share to the work load. Even at Twin Oaks, a model of communitarian zeal, rules for selecting new members specify that not more than a fourth of them should be dependents, including little children. "Per capita income on the farm may be very low the first few years, and too great a number of dependents may cause you to go under." [4] The costs of motherhood to women and to the economy in "ordinary" communities stand out in bold relief in the commune.

Another commune, Springtree, consisting of twelve adults and eight children of elementary school age, is also concerned about the costs, this time of schooling. "Adult labor is scarce and they are concerned about how much time 'school' will take." [5] In communes that do not support themselves by their own efforts—as in the anarchist communes on the West Coast—there is no such rejection of mothers with children. Such children bring in income. In fact, "these women are often very acceptable to communes as new members. They are likely to be seen as potentially less disruptive to ongoing commune life than a single man; they are likely to be seen as more dependable and stable than a single man; and these women provide a fairly stable source of income through the welfare payments that many of them receive." [6]

There is, in fact, great diversity among the experiments so far as motherhood is concerned, varying from simple sharing of mother-work among women to complex plural mothering. As yet the whole movement is too new to subsume the patterns of motherhood under any clear-cut classification or encapsulate them in neat tables and charts. Until we have more painstaking (and, I fear in some cases, pain-generating) research, much of the material dealing with these experiments and blueprints has to be in the form of personal documents and experience. Still, at least a glance in their direction is called for to see what, if anything, we can learn from them about the future of motherhood.

### The Gamut

The variety of conceptualizations of motherhood in communes, communities, and experimental households is as great as, if not greater than, it is in the establishmentarian world. At one extreme there is, for example, the so-called Religious Society of Families in which reproduction is by "preadoption" and at the other extreme, the Biblical conceptualization of the Bruderhof, whose founder, Eberhard Arnold, wrote that "woman's task is to be loving and motherly, dedicated to preserve, protect, and keep pure the circle of those who are close to her; to train, foster, and to cherish them. . . . If it should be given to us to affirm woman's tasks and not wish for her the work of administration and direction, then our common life will be a happy one." [7] And, from all reports, their common life is a happy one.

Here they are, the two extremes, first the Religious Society of Families and then the Bruderhof.

### RELIGIOUS SOCIETY OF FAMILIES

Religious Society of Families is a disciplined neo-monastic religious society for the prevention of bionomic cruelty to the planet and genetic cruelty to posterity. Emphasis is on decom-

mercialized land-use, homesteading, solar power, decentral-
ization of production and authority, recycling materials, population control, and survival of mankind and other wildlife.
Unique features include eugenics practice requiring members
to forego reproduction in the earlier barbarian tradition. Scientific humanism is the theological gist. Nominal monogamy
is the sexual gist. Land available; members needed. Serious,
sincere inquiries cordially invited.

Germinal material of the human race is common property
regardless of who is carrying it. Everyone has the right to use
the genetic information of all others in the creation of children.

Birth and conception are never brought about by coitus.
Recreational and procreative sex are totally separated. All accidental pregnancies are aborted. Children are conceived by
bringing gametes together artificially and implanting the
fertilized egg in the womb of the second mother who is pre-
adopting the child. Cloning, parthenogenesis, and such forms
of deliberate twinning are taboo, because they deny the child
his right to a unique personality.

Marriage is redefined as license to create two children; not
more, not less. . . .[8]

And, at the other extreme, The Bruderhof, Society of Brothers.
Including women.

## WOODCREST COMMUNITY

Woodcrest is the oldest [1954] and largest of the three Bruderhof communities. Located on a wooded, ninety-five-acre tract
near Rifton, New York, it is comprised of nearly 300 members.
. . . Located away from the surrounding towns, Woodcrest
has the advantage of seclusion without being severely isolated. . . . From my observations. . , it seemed that
about one half of the members were in their fifties or over.
Most of the Bruderhof's income is derived from the manufacture of *Community Playthings*. . . . In the communitarian's life "there can be no seeking for idyllic human sociability or leisurely comfort. No kind of satisfaction of romantic
desires, or of egoistical longing for personal happiness. . . .

The community's view towards masculine and feminine
roles is very traditional. There is a strict dichotomy of jobs between the two sexes: the men do all the strenuous, traditionally masculine work; the women do the less physically
taxing, traditionally feminine work. In the men's area is the

shop. . . , maintenance, bindery work, and dish washing (since it involves carrying heavy loads of dishes and is therefore properly a man's job); in the women's area is cooking, sewing and mending, and cleaning, in addition to child-care, which is primarily handled by women. Community schooling is a job of both sexes. These roles are extremely strict; any deviation is considered improper. . . .

The family is a very important part of community life at the Bruderhof. Almost everyone is expected to get married and raise a family. Marriage is an important ceremony. . . . Time is always reserved in the evening for the entire family to be together, even though the children and parents may be separated the rest of the day. This time forms one of the most important parts of a member's day.

Until the age of six months, babies stay with the mother during the day; from this age on they are cared for *in small groups of their peers*. Through the eighth grade the children attend a community school, where they learn standard subjects from accredited teachers. . . .[9]

The emphasis is added in the above passage in order to call attention to the fact that in this community, so traditional and conservative in its over-all sex-role structure, infants from the age of six months on are no longer, apparently, the sole responsibility of their mothers. The are cared for in "groups of their peers." For those who see proposals for similar plans in the outside society as attacks on the family, the success of the Bruderhof system must be perplexing.

Between these extremes there is a wide array of models. One is currently in progress in New England. According to a psychiatrist, this is how motherhood is institutionalized there:

Children who come to the Brotherhood of the Spirit or are born there are identified as affiliated with their mother, and her word is final when it comes to making important decisions such as going out of the commune for a visit or calling a doctor in case of illness. If the child's father is known and if he is married to the mother or committed to her, he is included in the decision-making process. Except for these times of crisis the responsibility for care and entertainment of the children is equally shared by *all members* of the Brotherhood. Those who enjoy children the most end up by doing most of the work involved in caring for them. The youngsters gravitate toward those adults who appeal to them at any particular moment. They soon learn who will tell them a story, who will play a game, who will listen, and who will make them laugh. They seek out the individual who will satisfy their need of the moment. But they do not just run loose. Much thought and careful planning are put into providing a program for the children during non-school hours. Playrooms, outside work, and recreational projects are supervised by the adults so that the children are rarely bored.

One of the mothers told me of her enormous relief after joining the Brotherhood because she can at last travel without taking her son with her. He did not like riding in automobiles, but before, if she went without him, he cried constantly. There had been no one that she could leave him with who could console him. Now she can travel without the burden of his company or the burden of her own guilt because she knows he is happy with other children his own age and the adult caretakers in the commune.

The children of the Brotherhood attend the local elementary and high schools and fit in well with the family-reared children there. Recently a comprehensive study was done of the physical and intellectual health of all the students in one of these schools. . . . The Brotherhood children were in better physical condition and showed academic performance levels in relation to intellectual potential considerably higher than the others. School officials reported that there were no disciplinary problems among the commune children.

Not all parents are suited to commune life, but some of the principles of communal child rearing may well be compatible with the life-style of the average American family. Sharing of responsibility for care and entertainment with many individuals does not need to rob the child of his identity as a son or daughter of two specific individuals, nor does it seem to mean that the child suffers from feelings of resentment and hostility because he yearns for more contact with his natural parents. Instead most children seem to thrive in an environment where many adults are interested in them and they are not dependent on the mood of only two for an appropriate response to their needs of the moment. . . .

Recognition of the fact that motherhood should not be considered a full-time job and that women equally with men should be able to lead productive lives without interruption . . . brings with it a responsibility to plan a way for the child-rearing chores to be accomplished out of the home by trained individuals who choose their occupation as a life-long career.

Such people and the organizations where they work could bring better care to our children, as well as more freedom for both mothers and fathers to develop their individual talents unhampered by inhibiting responsibilities toward their offspring.[10]

Among the six adults at Omega House, the children "are the responsibility of their parents, but most other adults will help too." The parents wish the children to have "better human qualities and to abhor violence." [11]

One writer, citing the Kibbutz and Hutterite experience, concludes that separating children from their parents is a good thing. "Adults, especially women, do not have to have their lives revolve around their children; with someone else to take good care of them, the mother and father are free to pursue their own interests and still see their children every day for several hours. The children learn to cooperate, and from the beginning have a sense of group identity like they will have when they become adults." [12] But another writer, on the basis of experience in two communal houses, finds differences in child-rearing practices among the irritations: "different persons had different ideas as to how Evelyn (the three-year-old) should be raised. Bob and I wanted to pinpoint and modify the child's behavior. Sally, [the mother] thought behavior modification was 'too mechanical' and the key thing, with a child, was to 'be spontaneous.' " [13]

## The Children

Thus at one end of the continuum are the conservative religious communities with their rigidly defined sex roles and authoritarian styles of parenting and at the other, the radical libertarian theories—if not practices—of child rearing in the anarchist communes of the West Coast. Even in some of the conservative non-religious communes, despite the privileges accorded children, the parents "want to keep direct control over their children. They believe in the right of a family to raise its children as it sees fit, and without interference from the state." [14] They make strict rules for their children. Two observers report that "one notable trait among both parents and children is a certain rigidity of attitude, possibly a reaction to the permissiveness of the 1950s," [15] an apparent validation of Clark Vincent's projection of a decline in permissiveness.[16] A brave old world.

But at the other end of the continuum we have Bennett Berger's observations concerning motherhood in the thirty-eight anarchist communes he and his associates studied in Northern California. Among these communes, infants and "knee babies" are cared for by their mothers who have primary responsibility for them. Fathers may or may not cooperate; there is no pressure on them to do so. It is optional for him, not for the mother. When the children are two to four, they "belong" to the commune in the sense that their care is now shared by other mothers with small children. The child remains a child only until about the age of four when its status changes and maternal responsibility becomes attenuated. The child becomes a person in his own right, worthy of love and respect but not necessarily of attention. Children address their parents by their first names and are seen as the equals of adults.[17] (In one commune they have set up their own separate residence.) "It is assumed that by this age [four], children are old enough to do things for themselves, and hence parents and other adults refuse to fetch and tote for them. . . . Further, it is assumed that children of such age are old enough to do something useful for others, and hence parents and other adults in the household will frequently send young children on errands." [18] Along with these responsibilities go also the privileges of general membership in the commune: access to marijuana, sex play, aggressive play or hassles; chioce of work and television.[19]

The theory that informs child rearing is that the parental role is one of setting an example rather than one of paternalism, authoritarianism, didacticism, or exhortation. Parents attempt to let the child grow naturally to become an autonomous and free adult. Children are to work out their own fate. The children's experience is not "fateful or self-implicating for adults." [20] The child's behavior does not "reflect" on the parents; they are not responsible for it. All this, be it noted, is as yet very tentative inasmuch as most of the children in the communes studied were still under six.

Bennett Berger makes the cogent and perceptive point that "communal ideologies tend to be elaborated by men." [21] They are not willing to sacrifice their mobility and the theory of communal child rearing frees them from the parental responsibility that might interfere with it. They achieve "a freedom that is itself legitimated in part by the view of children as autonomous." [22] He notes also that in these rural communes it may be quite feasible to permit a great deal of autonomy to children. But the benefits are inadvertent rather than the result of the legitimizing theory.

Under the guise, then, of liberating the child, members have liberated themselves. The same theory that sees the child as, in effect, the innocent noble savage justifies a laissez-faire policy with respect to it. Berger also adds the interesting comment that it is the welfare check the mother receives for the child's support that contributes to the existence of the commune. "Behind all this child-equality lies one important contextual fact: they bring in a lot of the money that supports anarchist communes; an unrelated woman-with-child is the modal nuclear unit; there is a sense in which the kids objectively support these communes by the ADC their very existence brings in." [23]

To the questions, are the children happy and healthy? Will they also rebel in due course? Since there is not as yet any reliable information, "one can say just about anything one wishes to suit one's prejudices." [24] But to the question, are the children neglected, an interesting reply is offered. Compared with the child-centered model of the middle class, yes, these children may be said to be neglected. But the researchers are skeptical of the wholesomeness of that model with its prolongation of dependency. The communes reverse this tendency; they abolish adolescence: ". . . often by age thirteen the youngsters are carrying a full share of the physical and emotional load." [25] If, the researchers conclude, the communal treatment does nothing more than abolish adolescence, "it may have been worthwhile after all." [26]

With this theory practiced in the communes, it is understandable that a Newsletter published by a High School Information Center can proclaim a fifteen-point Platform which includes such items as:

> We believe that the nuclear family is not in the best interests of humanity. Young people are now considered possessions— to be molded in the image of their parents. This is intolerable. The only solution lies in communal extended families where children can grow in the company of many peers and with the influence of many adults. Then they will begin to learn the co-operation of community rather than the oppression of ownership. Until healthy communal families are a reality, Youth Communities, run by their residents, must be established for

317

young people whose present conditions of life force them to become cultural refugees.[27]

These are among the sons and daughters sitting across the table from suburban mothers in countless homes all over the country. Or escaping to communes like those in Northern California.

All this from the point of view of the men. The mothers have not found the practices of child rearing in communes auspicious. Here, according to one of them, is what is wrong.

### KIDS IN COMMUNES

Having lived in communes with many other adults, I would like to say that it is potentially the best arrangement in which to raise children: best for parents, other adults, and children alike. I have to admit, dismally, that in most cases I've seen, because of the attitudes of many of the adults concerned, it is one of the worst.

Children need privacy, quiet and a sense of order to cope with the rapid physical, mental and emotional changes occurring within them. This is difficult to provide in a house with many adults, but it is essential to the child's development as an individual. All too often though, with numerous adult trips and chaos happening around them, they feel lost and confused and their confusion comes out in destructive ways—crying jags, running around, making lots of noise and destroying things.

Children need to be treated with love, understanding, and respect as growing individuals with decided personalities and temperaments of their own. They need individual attention that is not superficial, and they want to feel pride in their achievements and be acknowledged for them. Even if the communards are tuned into the kids, you'll inevitably have problems with some of your friends treating them like inconvenient housepets, giving them superficial attention when they're feeling benevolent, or when the child does something irritating. If children are ignored and are greeted with "That's nice, dear," when they show you something they've done that they're proud of, they will [stop one and continue the other]; they do things like kicking the baby or peeing in someone's shoe because they *really* get noticed.

Children need to feel identification with a group of people—the family or collective—especially for the first few years. This can only be achieved if the group is fairly constant and people are not forever splitting for Montreal or San Francisco or wherever every couple of weeks. In that case the child is surrounded by a bunch of strangers and never gets to know any of them.

Children must be allowed to assert themselves and make many decisions for themselves. This is most a problem for the communal child who is not yet talking. Unless everyone in the commune knows the child well enough to understand when he/she mumbles something, he/she is likely to be trampled by well-meaning adults who think they know better.

Since you are so much bigger, louder and have so much power over the child's life, you must be very careful not to lay your trips on her, or expect him to necessarily get off on your trips. A sensitive, excitable small child will not benefit from being taken to a long, loud rock concert no matter how much her/his parents dig it. He experiences things so intensely that she'll likely suffer from sensory overload and scream from fatigue and frustration. The same goes for other adult trips —blowing dope in the kid's face is extremely unfair until he/she gets old enough to ask for it; the same goes for booze, extreme food trips, loud parties with her/him in the room and taking him/her places you want to go, where he/she is not going to have a good time. For instance, we made the mistake of taking two small ones on the Unemployed March to Victoria last week. It took them (and us) two days to recuperate from being cooped up on crowded buses and ferries for hours at a time and being dragged around from place to place. Next time we'll leave them home and a good time will be guaranteed for all.[28]

The whole commune scene—especially in the drug culture— looks quite different from the perspective of the women.

## WOMEN

One of the things that surprised me is that there are probably more peak-out women than men. I would have thought that the man would be the one to abandon the responsibility of raising and tending the family, and all of that. But women with children, and sometimes without, seem to feel the emptiness and sterility of their life-patterns at least as intolerably as men do, and look for alternatives. For many women, the commune is the only real option available if they want to have children, but don't want to be locked into a couple relationship. . . . It's easier for them to be creative in such a situation than if they were stuck in an apartment, and had to hold a regular job. Most things done in communes are done together in groups; there are a lot of people around to help remove the prison of the home in which so many women are trapped.[29]

They may escape the prison of the home. But there are other kinds of prisons. Even in the new communes, motherwork remains very much like motherwork in suburbia. Thus, for example, a 4½-year-old girl "goes everywhere with her mother, . . . is never spanked. When she is being a nuisance, her mother gives her things to do or fends her off with seemingly infinite patience." [30] Mothers' practice of carrying children with them everywhere, even when hitch-hiking, makes it hard to wean them away from their mothers. And, like mothers from time immemorial, these mothers defend their children against their fathers. When Tor, aged twelve, for example, retreats into silence and crying, his mother defends him but his father objects. "You're always doing that. You talk about community and then you jump in like a mother-hen when one of your kids is involved." "I have a right to do that if I feel like it," she shouts back.[31]

It is interesting to note that it is often only in defense of their children that many of the extremely passively-dependent women show any aggression. The young women attracted to at least some of the communes, especially those in the drug culture, are extraordinarily passive and dependent. According to one study of the drug culture in an East Coast urban setting, they "drifted in a passive way into a dependent relationship with a boy." [32] They were "remarkably undemanding, seemingly unresentful, and tractable to their partners' whims." [33] As soon, however, as they became mothers their behavior changed. They supplied physical care and nurture to their children and, in addition, even became capable of aggression: "though these girls could not demand for themselves they could certainly demand for their children." [34] They tended to be more affectionate with the men than with the babies. As mothers: "only once, when it appeared that Edsel might have abused the baby, did we see Maryann become enraged and protective of her infant"; [35] two girls "felt trapped by marriage and children and were passive and somewhat indifferent to their husbands and in their care of the children"; [36] "as a mother Ruth Ann seemed conscientious but remote and nonresponsive. With the child as with her husband she was resentful of demands while at the same time being very demanding herself"; [37] "warm but firm with the babies and at the same time fiercely protective of them, Carla could and did suppress her rage with Eric's inadequacies as provider and partner; in fact a row culminating in the necessity for five stitches in her scalp found her accepting even this, but his inability to provide the necessary immunizations roused her to an abusive rage. Her sense of responsibility for the children was the prime motivating factor in her leaving Eric. . . ." [38]

The researchers note that far from representing a counter-culture, the young women in these particular communes were caricaturing the conventional culture: "for the girls were more compliant, more masochistic, more submissive, and less autonomous than their parent culture or even than usual adolescent rebellion, a rebellion, then, that was more apparent than real." [39] They concluded that this caricature "reflects the position that the parent culture is imposing on women and represents a put-down of them as fully functioning members of that culture." [40] They see this as a polar opposite to the attempts of radical women to achieve integration on a basis of equality.[41] It is hard not to agree, however sympathetic one might be with these self-selected victims of a world they never made, a world they can neither live in or escape from. In any event, theirs is not a very positive way to work through to a role script for either a conventional or a counter culture. There is not much to be learned about the future of motherhood from women who are themselves so inadequate for coping with the modern world.

In the anarchist communes of the West Coast, the mothers are not dependent on the child's father, for "the state is a much better provider than most men who are available to her. And an infant to care for provides more meaning and security in her life than most men could." [42] They are welcome in the rural communes for the income they bring with them. They are willing therefore—according to the male researchers—to have the children resulting from even casual sexual contacts. Their status is that of "person," as that of men is of "human being." [43]

Rather, however, than reflecting an egalitarian ethos, this policy performs the latent function of liberating parents from the responsibilities intrinsic to the status of parenthood. But, of course, not really in the case of women. Like young mothers everywhere, the young women in communes protest against the burdens of child care from which, unlike the fathers, they cannot escape. "What I wanted was a *baby;* but a *kid,* that's something else." [44] They have not committed themselves beyond the period of infancy; they are not ready to settle down; they are not willing to sacrifice their own search for identity to the care of children. But they do. They may dream of an ideal lover or a permanent partner, but they do not really expect one. They compensate in the *image* of a communal group, all "working, playing, loving, rapping, 'hanging out.'" [45]

Some survive, some even triumph:

> Oh, it was beautiful to be the earth mother. It was middle America in the year 1966 and the crossroads were Haight and Ashbury and many of us women were pregnant. . . . We walked the streets like queens . . . the world was at our feet . . . our minds and bodies pregnant with the widsom of life and love . . . the sacred vessels of our men's desires, the harbingers of the new world to come. . . .
>
> So it went our world along its separate (?) course . . . symbolically independent . . . but the summer of love came and with it the babies . . . reality strode heavy into our lives . . . babies in all their full bloom with wild cries that didn't fit earth mother and Lady Madonna images. Our hip brothers forgot us . . . it's hard to be a queen after childbirth.
>
> Bodies refuse their previous refinements . . . they make demands on any woman . . . so does the child. Most of the brothers skipped out . . . it didn't matter . . . we were strong and undaunted still. Love would suffice . . . our lives were independent . . . we did not need what our mothers had—security—material comfort—fathers for our children . . . we were a new culture . . . no ties or binds on anyone . . . but then the babies began to grow as they do . . . the men came and went . . . the scenes came and went . . . the summer of love wore its way out . . . the winter that followed became a horror of great middle mirror America . . . so some of us began to move . . . many of the sisters married their love brothers . . . . we moved away to make new lives in the unknown places of our great land . . . but everywhere we went reality strode heavy into our lives . . . the men kept walking out . . . the children kept growing.
>
> The enchantment wore off—our relationships deteriorated—the communes could not survive on leathercraft, bead stringing, and love—none of it was pure enough—true enough—no trip was "right" enough—the men kept splitting—the children kept growing—we kept finding ourselves alone with the children—children of the men who made our world. Flower children—suddenly defoliated.

Six years later those children stare at us finding lives defined by the only image that stands by them—their mothers' . . . women who have, in time, grown strong . . . who finally are rising . . . Standing up from years in the kitchens and nurseries of mirror America—undaunted and strong—still in contact with our feelings, we rise with wings at last—wings of rage and pity and freedom . . . crying tears with feelings that are still in contact with the earth and stars . . . but Powerful with the blood of our bodies and the sweat of our labors. We find our true alliances with our mothers and all our sisters—the wave is building, growing, gathering strength . . . our wild children grow strong with us . . . great middle mirror America lies exposed . . . our fathers and our flower children's fathers—two images blended into one reflection in the looking glass of alternate America.[46]

The Women's Liberation Movement was finally reaching "mirror America," the counter-culture. Men having failed them, the women were now looking to one another for support in their motherhood.

### Sisterhood and Motherhood

In the July–August, 1972, issue of *Work Force,* Lois Haas inserted an advertisement for a libertarian community, "living communally with women with school age children. . . . The collective would help other women of all ages and life conditions by offering them asylum, by gathering information about available resources to help women free themselves, and encouraging the creation of women's collectives. It would also help with child care while women get a new life together. . . . I have a house and eight acres of land on which to creat the collective. Where are my sisters?" [47]

Sandy, quoted above, was one of the sisters who responded by letters, phone calls, and visits. She had cried out earlier "does anyone out there—parents or non-parents—have any advice? Does anyone want to get together and try to *form* a family??? A big, mutually supporting, mutually consciousness-raising, loving family—that's what I dream of. That's what this 'movement' *should* be about. . . . The movement is *nothing* if it is not life style—and life style is *nothing* if it has no room for children, and yes, also for our elderly parents. Please—let's get together!" [48]

Sandy and Lois found one another. Lois reports:

It was thanks to Lois Haas' ad . . . that Sandy stopped being depressed and started doing something. . . .

We can help all women. I have by now many letters, most of them from women with infants or small children, who say they turned to the Movement for help and got none, even felt somewhat despised for having borne children. So it's time we realize there *is* no movement for all practical purposes, and make one ourselves. Let's get moving. I have learned a lot. First of all, I once said that I wanted to offer asylum to women while they got new lives together, but I now realize the impossibility of taking women in for a short time, when there is no place for them to go at the end of that limited time. Eight acres can support only a few. What this means is that, before risking blowing the whole thing thru overextension, there should be a *national network* of places, information, whatever.

Women with small children need communal living, to avoid the system where roles invariably get crystallized at childbirth (man-woman roles). Women with small children need to share child care so that all have some time to be creative.

I also have met many women who have said "No kids—now that my kids have grown up, I don't want to be a part of a commune with kids." People should be free to say that, without guilt. I know it hurt me to meet these women when I was so needy. I thought, "If women won't help me, who will?" The answer is: *other women (or women and men) with exactly the same needs!* Men who are really trying can't be wasted—can't be turned out.[49]

A call went out for a meeting at the sand boxes in Union Square Park. No report as yet on the sequel.

There was no loss of faith in the communal ideal among more conventional women. At its best they found many pluses in it. For children, for example, it provided more "friends of all ages and exposure to many people's different trips (it's too bad old people aren't included)"; it prevented "shyness and super-dependency on one or two people"; it lessened "the damaging effect of bad mistakes made by the parents or others because there are more people with whom the child has secure relationships." [50] And for adults, it gave "many their first exposure to children," it offered a "feeling of true family to those who've been floating around transient for a while and are feeling lonely and somewhat alienated," it shared "the work load, so everyone is much freer and less burdened by it," it underlined "the double standard for women; in other words, if only the women look after the kids and wash the diapers, the guys are full of shit about being communal," it made it "possible for women to support each other in demanding their rights and equal sharing of responsibilities," it removed "financial pressures from the parents by sharing food, housing costs, and baby equipment," and it permitted "proper post-natal pampering of mothers with new babies." [51]

And, in contrast to the drug-culture communes, East and West, these goals were in process of becoming realized in at least some urban communes. These communes are "home and family-centered, but in a collective sense. They are more reformist as opposed to revolutionary, and consist of people working in urban institutions who look and act very conventional, compared to hippies," according to Rosabeth Moss Kanter, who has done a considerable amount of research on urban communes.[52] Her studies show that old sex-role stereotypes are, in fact, altered, that the weight of the maternal role is, in fact, lightened. But they also show that sex-role segregation, modified as it is, remains. Mothers retain major responsibility for child care.[53]

Equally challenging so far as the role of mother is concerned is the experience of a rural commune, Twin Oaks.

## Twin Oaks

Twin Oaks is the paradigm of communes and communities, the model upon which many others fashion themselves. It is ideological in the sense that it was founded to practice the principles of aversive conditioning and reinforcement propounded by B. F. Skinner in his book *Walden Two*, including child rearing as well as of interpersonal relations. Right from the start, therefore, a great deal of thinking had to be invested in the best way to institutionalize motherhood. It is significant, it seems to me, that Twin Oaks was led in its pioneering years by a woman. In fact, a mother.

During the earliest years, the experience with children was discouraging.[54] Over the first five years there were nine children. Four belonged to one member and created no special problems. The others, however, raised issues concerning where to invest authority for decisions about education and training and sometimes child-raising policy. The care of children was seen as work as legitimate as any other kind and therefore it was put under the labor credit system; a person could select it like any other kind of work. One woman did most of it but others shared. One child learned, as any bright child might, soon to play one adult off against another and, expectably, became spoiled, a nuisance instead of a pleasure. Adults no longer volunteered to take care of him as part of their work load. He and his mother left after a few weeks.

Another child, a year and a half old, was taken care of by eight adults, including the father and mother, in two-hour shifts. But the Child Manager could not stand up to the father, nor could anyone else. After several months these parents also decided to leave. But even for the time remaining before they left there was resentment among the caretakers, since the time devoted to the child's care which, it seemed to them, was wasteful of labor, was needed in other projects. "So we continued to throw away fourteen hours a day on caring for a child who didn't belong to us, and we resented every hour of it." They decided not to take any more children until facilities were available. The community needed time to get on its feet economically "without the drain of nonproducers."

When one woman became pregnant she "shyly asked whether we felt we could afford to have a child." It was agreeable to the community but not to the father; he concurred only because having the child was the price she was demanding for remaining in the community. The family situation was tense and after a stormy period the mother left with the child. The mother of another of the children, a seven-year-old, did not object to sharing authority with the community but she wished it would exercise authority. Everything was left to her.

In 1969, as a result of these experiences, the community clamped down. No more children until the children's house was ready and there was some assurance of permanence in keeping the child. The failures to date had not been due to people so much as to the difficulty of supporting small children when the community could hardly support itself. "Pioneers in community child care must, I think, be people who have a heavy investment in the theory. . . . Our next set of parents have to be people who are committed communitarians *first*." [55]

By 1972 Twin Oaks felt it could finally afford children. Four women asked permission to become mothers. One changed her mind. The other three became pregnant. Here we pick up the story of motherhood at Twin Oaks:

## CHILD MEETINGS IN EARNEST

In about four months there will be a baby here at Twin Oaks, and it is about time we got ourselves together and decided what to do with it. The child meetings we have had heretofore have been concerned with very general things—what goals to aim toward, and general outlines of ways to achieve them. Now it is time to discuss newborn infant care and very specific techniques of handling children in a communal setup.

We have agreed that we need a core of dedicated people who care for the babies consistently. But how big can that core be, and how long should their shifts be? Also, what shall we call them?

The naming problem again! We considered the obvious ones. "Nurses" carries connotations of sickness to some members, as well as of femininity, so we discarded it. We talked for a while about "Mothers." After all, we have sweet-potato mothers and dining-room mothers, and concrete mothers. Why not child mothers? They would of course be of both sexes. Ultimately we decided against calling the child-care people "mothers," also. Some people felt that the word should have no feminine connotations. Others simply wanted to avoid the confusion.

There is no really good word in English. Everything we could think of sounded either too precious or too institutional.

In Israel a child-care person is called a "metapalet" (attendant). We would have adopted this word with relief, but we felt it was too long. Solution: shorten it. We achieved a rapid consensus on "meta." Joe tells us that this abbreviation would make no sense in Hebrew, since "tpl" is the root and "me" is only a prefix, but this does not trouble us. We checked it out for double meanings and found nothing terribly objectionable. It sounds enough like "mother" to invite puns, but puns are the staff of life at Twin Oaks.

The Greek meaning of "meta" which appears in English words like metaphysics is "beyond." We don't mind that either. It reminds us of "beyond freedom and dignity."

Next question: How many metas can we use? We did a survey a short time ago to find out how many people were interested in committing themselves to child care. The list was far too long. Some of us feel that ten people is an absolute maximum in this area. Others thought we could perhaps use more, or that we ought to have fewer. We left the matter for future decision, to be made at the conclusion of our initial training sessions. Anyone interested may participate in the training.

What will the training consist of? That is the topic for next week's meeting. Presumably it will combine the theoretical and the practical; how to bathe a baby; how to extinguish an undesirable behavior; what are the expected normal behaviors of the newborn? How to tell when a baby is sick? Etc., etc.

At this point we are finding it easy to come to agreement on child-care issues. It is true that we have not yet decided whether or not to circumcise though we have discussed the issue three times. But we all know that none of us cares a great deal whether we do or not, and that once the decision is made, we will all be content with it. Spirits are high, and the months we have spent in theoretical discussions have given us confidence in each other.[56]

The first baby under the new regimen was born in the spring.

## METAS AND MAYA

Maya is now over two months old, and seems to be thoroughly enjoying the life of a communal baby. Of course, right now he is our only baby, and so has the sole attention of fifty parents. The day he came home from the hospital, he was looked at by everyone and held by many. By now he's been cuddled at least a couple of times by almost everyone.

There are currently eight people who are metas, and these are the people whom Maya is with most constantly. In any given week, perhaps six of these people will care for him, (there are always a few metas either sick or on vacation) and this means each of them gets five or six four-hour child-care shifts a week.

On a typical day, I arrive at the nursery at 7 AM, where all is quiet. Maya generally wakens within the hour for a feeding and goes back to sleep. Later he awakens again and I dress him, play with him, and look out the window with him. Then back in the aircrib for a quick nap, usually, before his next feeding. Jeffrey arrives at 11, and cares for Maya till 3, changing him, loving him and every few days, giving him a bath. From 3 to 7, Bree or Eve would come on, and sing to him or take him outside for a while. Carole has the 7–11 PM shift during which Maya generally settles down. Around 11, Maya is fed, and unlike other feedings (which are by demand), he is wakened for this one. We're trying to eliminate the middle-of-the-night feeding, and feeding him for sure at this hour makes it likely he'll sleep longer through the night.

Leah stays on the night shift, since she shares her room with the nursery, and since she is breast feeding Maya. (When Thrush is born, Maya will move to Juniper, where a separate room is set up as a nursery until the children's building is finished. Then other metas may begin to take the night shift. Leah does not stay up during this shift, of course, but is there to wake up when Maya needs to be fed.

With a system of more than one person taking care of the baby, it is important that we have good communication and trust among metas. We meet once or twice a week to discuss how things are going in the nursery, and to give each other feedback and discuss feelings. If we can keep the air clear between metas, then that can't get in the way of our being close to the children. Last week for instance, we talked about the twinges of possessiveness each of us has felt, and how we can deal with such feelings.

We also, of course, discuss more objective things, such as whether we can increase the amount of time he is happy when he's awake by systematically giving him more attention when he's awake and happy than awake and fussing. We're concerned, too, about the number of germs Maya gets exposed to. He has just gotten over a cold, and there really seems no way in community to isolate any individual from colds. They do go around, and we always know it too late. But we take what precautions we can. The first thing a meta does when co feels a cold coming on is to give co's meta shifts to other metas.

In the next months, the meta shifts will be busier with two babies to care for. Now metas often have time to do other things (such as writing Leaves articles) while Maya sleeps.[57]

The love, the affection, the concern, the joy that surround the infant parallels the response a happy family feels anywhere when the child is welcome. This child will not lack the perquisites of wholesome childhood. In the atmosphere of this nursery one brushes aside the qualms that nag at one's conscience. B. F. Skinner tells us that "one great source of wisdom is now about to be tapped: Twin Oaks is ready to raise children. If the lives of those children are properly managed, lessons will be learned of extraordinary value to the community and to us all." [58] What a weight to place on the shoulder of these infants! Unless they are protected from the media they will be vulnerable to the same hazards as those of other children reared in the public view—children of moving picture stars, professors, ministers, political leaders—who have to bear the weight of parental achievement.[59]

Another question: will these babies be content to remain their whole lives in the gentle cocoon of Twin Oaks? Won't they be seduced by the media? Won't they want to see the wide world? Will they be able to function in it? There is a great deal more to motherhood—whether practiced by mothers or by communities—than air cribs and reinforcement. The venturesome and courageous young people at Twin Oaks are very well aware of this. The odds in my opinion are more than even that they will profit well from their experience. And so will we.

### Wave of the Future?

And what can we learn from these communities? Not until motherhood becomes the focus of careful research in a wide variety of experimental situations, urban as well as rural, will there be much we can learn about its future from their experience. So far from representing the wave of the future, some of the communities hark back to the nineteenth-century rural past. Especially among religious communes sex roles are clearly delineated and motherwork is the exclusive prerogative of women. Conventional definitions of the mother's role prevail although provision is often made for more cooperation among women so that help is made available to share the responsibility as well as the work of child care. Those that are rural are too far out of line with at least the present and immediate future to serve as models for urban life. Some attract members who are too alienated from the mainstream to be interested in changing it. But some, especially those who follow the pattern developing at Twin Oaks, have a great deal to teach us about the future of motherhood. Hopefully we can learn it without too great cost to the children themselves. Actually there may be more genuinely revolutionary potential in women like those of the Boston collective who face up squarely to the structural defects with respect to motherhood in our society and lay out plans for getting rid of them.

Still, to the incredulous who see no possibility that these experiments can contribute to the restructuring of motherhood in our society, the only reasonable reply seems to be: Didn't we feel the same way about the counter culture in the 1960s? Long hair on men and sideburns are as acceptable today as the crewcut of yesterday. They are only superficial indices of more subtle changes in our view of the world. The serious popular journals are now publishing in subdued prose many of the ideas published in more flamboyant prose in the female mimeographed communication network of the 1960s. It would be a mistake to sell short the lessons we can learn from the experiments, from failures as well as from successes.

Although I do not share to the same extent as the author does the enthusiasm in the following passage, I think we should be grateful for the willingness of the experimenters to risk so much anguish for the sake of trying new paths. I am not willing myself to do it. I'm glad some are.

> The commune movement has opened a new and wide range of alternative life-styles and offers another frontier to those who have the courage for adventure. It is the test tube for the growth of a new type of social relatedness, for the development of an organization having a structure that appears, disappears, and reappears as it chooses and as it is needed. Communes may well serve as a laboratory for the study of the processes involved in the regeneration of our social institutions. They have become the symbol of man's [sic] new freedom to explore alternative life styles and to develop deep and fulfilling human relationships through the rebirth and extension of our capacity for familiar togetherness.[60]

My hope is that women as well as men will profit by these alternative life styles.

So much, then, for the revolutionary approach for providing the help called for by the desperate woman quoted earlier. For women it has equivocal possibilities: It can, like the little girl with the curl, be very, very good; or it can be horrid. When we turn from this approach to the more pedestrian reform route, we enter a totally different atmosphere. Pedestrian, to be sure; but potentially perhaps more revolutionary than the communal approach.

# CHAPTER SEVENTEEN

## Revolution via Reform

### Which Horn of the Dilemma: Do We Have a Choice?

Theoretically there are two ways to reform the mother-worker situation. The worker role could be eliminated; or the mother role could be minimized for most women and eliminated for some. In actuality, though, both ways are impossible.

Even without the ERA, if a woman wants to work, she cannot be denied employment because she has small children; the Civil Rights Act of 1964 has been found by the Supreme Court to forbid such action. Persuasion is not likely to make her reject a job or likely to make industry willing to forego her services. So there will always be working mothers. Neither, for that matter, can we legislate motherhood out of existence for normal women. This approach has not, like the first one, been tried and tested in the courts. But the furor created in the summer of 1973, when an administrative ruling made it possible for a Mississippi agency to sterilize two young women, one retarded, shows how far off that test is likely to be. Communes might be able to eliminate the role of mother by fiat, but the outside world cannot.

Nevertheless, both approaches to reform—via motherhood and via the labor force—are being launched on the first stage of the political process—widespread public debate—first among an avant garde and then, presumably, among the men and women on the street.

### Force Versus a Voluntary Approach to the Reduction of Motherhood

Evidence from women themselves has shown that, left alone, they are not as enthusiastic about motherhood as the sometimes hysterical antinatalists implied. In line with this way of viewing the situation, in a message on population to Congress, President Nixon had asked in 1969, "how can we better assist American families so that they will have no more children than they wish to have?" He noted that increasing population "needlessly adds to the burdens placed on all our resources." He appointed a Commission to look into the matter. It produced a report on Population and the American Future that constitutes a basis for thinking about policy with respect to motherhood.[1]

Still, though women left on their own seemed to be satisfied with a moderate family size, a reduction below even the relatively modest number of children they preferred, about two or three,[2] was called for by ecological trends. So the problem now was how to get women to *not* have babies rather than how to get them to *have* babies.

Some, though not many, people were willing to advocate coercion or force in limiting the birth rate. A variety of administrative, legal, sociological, economic technologies were called for. Some of the techniques for applying such force were novel, ingenious, and technologically, if not politically, sophisticated. They included: licensing parenthood, demanding proof of eligibility for parenthood, distributing ration cards for babies that could be exchanged, or sold to couples who wanted more than their allotted number. Enforcement could be implemented by the use of mass infertility drugs, either by way of compulsory innoculation or by way of the water supply. If people wanted babies they would then apply for a counteracting fertility drug. One writer gives a eugenic slant, killing two birds—quality as well as quantity—with one stone. Policy should be selective, requiring prospective parents to prove their qualifications. Although he decries the use of force, he predicts that "it is going to be necessary to force people to limit family size."[3] He hopes, however, that other methods of control will foreclose this necessity. He suggests that people be rewarded for sterilization.[4] "Our society," he concludes, "can afford to spend several thousand dollars to persuade each person who is unqualified for parenthood to remain childless."[5]

From the point of view of our political traditions, voluntary family restriction is far more congenial than coercion, however applied:

> It is always easier to insist that "there ought to be a law" and to think you've solved the problem with a "you must" or "you can't" than to eschew coercion and go through the tedium of adopting practical programs to change what is . . . to what should be.
>
> It is for civil libertarians to recognize what needs to be done to avert a totalitarian pattern of laws as to human reproduction. Unless and until it is clear that voluntary measures, legally and factually available (which they never have been), won't and can't eliminate the threat of overpopulation, government coercion and compulsion are contraindicated.
>
> It is for civil libertarians to acknowledge that while the state must more and more assume the responsibility for the physical and material well-being of its citizens because our interdependent mass production economy demands this as the price of its functioning and our survival, the state must stay out of the moral and spiritual aspects of their lives. . . .
>
> Yes, indeed, the state should act to make real freedom of choice possible. It should do everything from repealing repressive laws, to encouraging research in contraceptive and abortificient technology, to ensuring effective delivery of services on a voluntary basis to all segments of our population to waging educational campaigns.
>
> If we pursue these objectives, we should be able to take a long step in the direction of solving the population problem without resorting to compulsory measures which would strike at the roots of one of our basic freedoms: the right of free choice in matters of human reproduction—no less basic because it has so recently been recognized and acknowledged.[6]

Another argument against coercion is the fact that it is counterproductive: "coercion inevitably engenders hostility and resistance, which tend to grow in a cumulative fashion over time. Eventually, some threshold is passed and resistance is sufficient to interrupt, and possibly frustrate, the measures being pursued. In short, coercion is not a dependable method, and non-coercive approaches can be preferred in terms of their relative efficacy." [7] Education in population affairs—in schools, in public debate—including consciousness-raising with respect to the pronatalist co-

ercion exerted by informal pressures, is the preferred technique.[8]
On the basis of past attempts to control motherhood by way of
legislative programs, this approach—whether coercive or voluntary in method—does not seem very hopeful. Women, as we have
noted, make their decisions about motherhood on quite different
bases. They have proved resistant to all kinds of political pressures.

Another approach to the problem is not so direct; it works by
way of attractive alternatives to motherhood.

### Carrots

Since coercion or fiat is as yet out of the question, the way to get
women to have fewer babies is to make them *want* fewer. They
should be shown that they are paying dearly for "buying" children. "The problem, therefore, is compounded of how to persuade
couples to act more in their own economic self-interest and that of
their children; how to assist them in obtaining more psychological
satisfactions from sources other than large families; and how to
replace the outworn and now inimical tradition of the large family
with a new 'instant tradition' of smaller families." [9]

In the nineteenth century it was argued that the higher education of women had untoward effect on their reproductive capacity.
It was clear from the statistics that educated women had fewer
babies than other women. Moral: if you want women to bear children, keep them out of the schools and colleges. And, conversely,
if you want them not to bear children, encourage them to remain
in school and go to college. While it is still true that college-
educated women bear fewer children than less well-educated
women, the differential is declining and, in any event, the difference can be quite well explained in terms of age at marriage
and at birth of first child, rather than in terms of education per se.

"Many parents—primarily mothers—seek large families as a
psychic defense against lack of interesting employment, lack of a
sense of belonging to a satisfying social group, or lack of other
forms of self-realization." [10] We must, therefore, supply interesting
employment and other forms of self-realization. It follows that
"the more satisfying the employment opportunities which women
have, the less likely they are to want large families." [11] It is, indeed, demonstrable that wherever in the world women are in the
labor force the birth rate is lower among them than among women
who are not.[12] There is no question that it would be hard to make

all the adjustments needed to accommodate women in the labor force, but there is, according to advocates, no more promising approach, especially if the emphasis was "on opportunities for women of childbearing age." [13]

Even the most tradition-minded had to admit that the jobs-for-women strategy was better than licensing and rationing parenthood or enforced sterilization after the second or third child. Or better than tax penalties or concessions.

But here, as in the case of education, the differential in births between women in and women not in the labor force was declining.[14] "Women . . . were learning how to cope with both babies and jobs. . . . Either jobs were not interfering with having babies or having babies was less and less interfering with labor-force participation. Stewart Garfinkle had noted that 'the effect of the birth of a child on work life continuity is rapidly diminishing,' and the figures bore him out. In 1969 the fertility of women in the labor force was approaching more nearly the fertility of women not in the labor force than in 1960." [15] We know, further, from the frontispiece, that during the 1950s, women were increasing both their number in the labor force and the number of babies they bore.

As it turned out, political methods proved unnecessary. Women were, for reasons of their own, cutting down on the number of babies they bore. By the early 1970s the birth rate approached a non-replacement level. But the mother-worker role integration problem still remained, however attenuated the number of children per family involved.

## Modifying Motherwork

One of the suggestions made by Karl Marx had to do with industrializing housework. Today this is an accepted practice in public buildings. A firm specializing in cleaning, well-equipped with the most efficient appliances, staffed with trained employees, contracts to keep a building in good shape. The idea is now proposed that such services be extended to apartments and houses. This kind of service would alleviate at least the physical component of motherwork.

For the mother aspect, two suggestions have been made, one that turns it into a specialized profession and one that despecializes it. According to the first suggestion, a profession devoted to child-bearing and child rearing would be recognized; or a religious vocation devoted to mothering could be established. Or, conversely, according to the second suggestion, everyone would be called upon to share the obligations of mothering. Young people, instead of being drafted for military service, would be drafted for civilian work, including, for those so qualified, the care of children.[16]

Among the more familiar suggestions for alleviating motherwork are: better and more available services of all kinds—medical, educational, child-care, housekeeping; and more sharing on the part of fathers.

### Modifying Gainful Employment Patterns

Among the suggestions for making the worker role an easier option are: maternity leave with no loss of seniority,[17] part-time work with no loss of fringe benefits, provision of child care, and such less familiar proposals as flexible work schedules, not only for a day or week, but for a life-time, which "would make the child-bearing period a less complete break with other periods in the life cycle. Many specific things could be done to accomplish this goal, including (1) increasing availability of part-time work, (2) staggering working hours to make them more responsive to individual needs (a measure already being tried with apparent success by some European companies), and (3) permitting greater flexibility and variation, particularly concerning timing and age, in the requirements for obtaining educational degrees." [18]

The 1970 White House Conference on Children elaborated these suggestions and added other ways in which employers could help women in the mother role:

> *Flexible Work Schedules.* Business and industrial organizations and government agencies should establish flexible work schedules so that both male and female employees can be with children when they are most needed, as when children get home from school, or when they are sick (Recommendation #3 for Employer: Industry, Business, and Government).
>
> *Increasing Number & Status of Part-time Positions.* We recommend that business and industrial organizations and government agencies increase the number and status of part-time positions so that employees who wish to give a larger part of their time and energy to parenthood or other activities with children can do so without sacrificing their career opportunities and rate of income. Whenever possible, business and

industrial organizations are encouraged to be creative in developing home-based, part-time employment opportunities (Recommendation #7).

*Leave and Rest Privileges for Maternal and Child Care.* Business and industrial organizations share with other institutions in society responsibility for the birth of a healthy child. In view of the cost to society of welfare and institutionalization of children born with prenatal damage, these organizations have the obligation to develop policies of leave and rest for mothers during pregnancy and early months of infant care without jeopardy to their employment or income status (#8, *ibid.*)

*Day Care Facilities.* To increase opportunities for parents and other employees to spend time with their children, day care facilities should be established within or near the place of work, but with completely independent administrative arrangements which allow parents a determining voice in the planning and execution of the program. Parents and other employees should be encouraged to visit the day care facility during the lunch or coffee breaks-and to participate in activities with the children (#9 *ibid.*).

*Family-oriented Industrial Planning and Development.* To an ever increasing degree, business establishments determine not only where and how employees work, but also where and how their families live. Decisions on plant and office location have substantial influence upon the kind of housing, schools, and neighborhoods that become available to employees and their children. Indeed, more and more large organizations are becoming involved in planning and building housing projects and even the entire community in which their employees live. Such plans should give explicit consideration to factors which influence the course of family life, specifically those which provide or preclude opportunity for active participation of parents and other adults in the life of children and vice versa. This includes such issues as commuting, traffic safety, location of shops and businesses where children could have contact with adults at work, recreational and day care facilities readily accessible to parents as well as children, provision for a neighborhood family center, and other family-oriented facilities and services described in this report (#12).

Although these recommendations are primarily designed to benefit children and families, experienced managers and labor leaders will also recognize them as good business. For example, contrary to commonly held views, studies of part-time workers in several occupations and industries reveal a gain rather than a loss of quality and quantity of production. Similarly, implementation of these recommendations can be expected to counteract two of the most serious and growing problems in the nation's economy—high rates of turnover and absenteeism.[19]

This is quite a large list. All the items, if implemented, would make it easier for women to integrate their two roles. All are clearly part of the wave of the future, especially the suggestion of flexible work schedules to make it possible for "both male and female employees . . . [to] be with children when they are most needed. . . ." This is a system, for helping fathers to share motherwork.

### Role Sharing

Although the idea of role sharing in the family has only recently caught the popular imagination, it was already beginning to occur to students of the family almost half a century ago. In a study of the family published in 1930, for example, Albert C. Jacobs and Robert C. Angell found themselves having to deal with such problems as "the duty of family support . . . and sharing of household services," or asking "how gainful employment of the wife should affect the whole economic relationship between husband and wife" and should the rights and obligations of the two parties to the marriage be identical with regard to mutual support . . . ?"[20] They even noted that "there is some indication of a trend towards participation in household services by the husband. This may clear one obstacle from our path, if the practice should become the normal one. Joint service hand in hand with joint support, or support in proportion to respective incomes, may be the best solution."[21] But, like so many other feminist ideas, this one—then espoused by men—was eclipsed and has only recently re-appeared.

Fathers are increasingly being asked to share the "costs" of parenthood, up till now borne primarily by mothers, by sharing in the care itself.[22] The benefits for both father and child of extending fatherhood have been recognized by observers who had long deplored the isolation of men from their children. The precise form which such a contribution by fathers could take varies according to circumstances and the wishes of those involved.[23]

Sweden is farthest along in implementing this line of thought.

"It is nowadays most unusual for any Swede in a responsible position to defend [the radical distinction between the life roles of the sexes]." [24] Thus, at a conference in 1967, five highly influential executives agreed that "women must be regarded as every bit as valuable a part of the labor market as men, and that men must have the same practical and emotional responsibility [sic] for children as women . . . . They also thought it self-evident that a father of small children should be as [much] entitled to take a part-time job, or forego the advantages of overtime, as [was his] wife.[25] It is notable that responsibility, which is a great deal more than mere help, is also included. Policy with respect to men rests on the conviction that "the greatest disadvantage with the male sex role is that the man has too small a share in the upbringing of the children. The ability to show affection and to establish contact with children has not been encouraged in the man." [26]

Thought is being translated into action. In Sweden, both unions and management organizations are trying to implement the new ideas. "The big trade union organizations have prepared their own programs which will make it possible for men to share child care with women. The trade union organizations and the organization of the employers also have a joint collaboration body which works for equality between the sexes in accordance with this principle." [27] Responsibility for child rearing must be shared by both parents. And a Canadian sociologist, Leo Davids, goes so far as to advocate that "fathers might be prohibited from full-time employment outside the home as long as they have preschool children, in line with arguments that the young child needs close contact with both parents." [28] In our own society the nearest we have come to recognition of the father's time-and-service cost-sharing is in the concept of paternity leave.[29]

Part-time work plays a large role in plans for time flexibility. In 1972, at a Geneva Conference on New Patterns for Working Time, one of the ten reports noted that "the growth of the number of women who combine family responsibilities with gainful employment leads to a demand for intermittent or part-time work, variable hours, etc." [30] Flexibility refers to both short- and long-term intervals, from hours per day to years per life-time, from days per week, to months per year. Instead of the rigid eight-hour day, forty-hour week, fifty-week year, we ought to have "work a la carte," or "flexitime," and other "variable and unorthodox patterns for the allocation of working time over the day, the week and the year." [31]

If or when such sharing of the time-and-service costs of children does come about, it will call for rather fundamental re-organization of work scheduling by industry and this, in turn, will not come about because parents wish it to. It will happen because industry will find it to be "good business." Apparently it is. "There is now a growing body of experience which shows that permitting individuals to choose their daily hours of work can be of benefit to both employers and employes." [32] Already there is a wide-spread movement in the direction of such "flexible time schedules." [33]

More will be required, to be sure, than flexible time scheduling to make it feasible for fathers to share in child rearing. The pay for the work women do will have to be increased; otherwise the difference between the mother's earnings and the father's would be too great.[34]

### "For Greater Flexibility of Working Life"

On the surface, role sharing appears to be a relatively mild kind of change. It does not challenge the isolated household nor call for any tampering with conventional family relationships. All it does, seemingly, is call on the father to participate more extensively and intensively in a basic family function. Actually, of course, it would entail a revolution in the whole concept of work for both men and women.

In a report presented by the Director of Manpower and Social Affairs of the Organization for Economic Cooperation and Development at the Conference on New Patterns for Working Time, there was included the concept of extending "flexible time" to include flexibility not only in hours, days, weeks, or months of work but also a life time, a concept we've mentioned before. The individual's life time would be seen as a single entity, and his total work contribution could be viewed as flexible so far as its allocation over time is concerned. Some might wish to postpone their contribution to the labor force from one period in their life to another. Or receive income at one time rather than at another.

The plan proposed for implementing such an idea has to do with a set of "generalized drawing rights" based on a novel—time—insurance system:

> An integrated insurance system for transferring income between different periods of life (under appropriate risk-sharing) should be created in order to make the desired flexibility and freedom of choice a practical reality. The many separate

schemes for maintenance of income during periods of voluntary and involuntary non-work which already exist are becoming chaotic, bureaucratic, costly, inequitable, yet at the same time insufficient. Often they tend to reduce rather than increase the individual's freedom. . . . Freedom of choice and flexibility in shaping one's own life presupposes an increased degree of self-determination in the use of the income transfer and maintenance systems. This freedom should apply both to timing and to interchangeability—a right within limits to sacrifice benefits of one kind during one period in order to get more of another kind during another period.

This could best be achieved by combining into one single, unified system of individualized accounting all those fees, taxes, study loan payments and other compulsory savings [e.g., social security payments, unemployment insurance, worker's compensation payments, group health plans, etc.] which are already used to provide the individual with liquid income during periods of non-work. Part of those future increases of hourly earning which could be regarded as compensation for shortened working time (as is customary in connection with reductions in weekly hours) would also have to be directed into this unified system. Each person would be given a right to draw on his account for purposes of his own choosing in a way that would be similar in a technical sense to the right to borrow on that part of one's private life insurance which is not needed to cover the risk-sharing involved.[35]

Among the specified advantages of systems of "generalized drawing rights" were promotion of social equity by making it possible for more people to improve their education and making it possible for people to exchange expected old age pensions for earlier retirement.

The innovators dealing with ways to implement flexible time schedules are still thinking almost entirely in terms of the male work history and the relevance here is how these schedules make it possible for fathers to share in child care. But it does not involve a very large jump of the imagination to apply this scheduling to women as well. For example, the only change made in the following quotation is the substitution of female words for male:

Governments and industrial organizations should make it a *policy goal* to provide the individual with the greatest possible degree of freedom to determine the allocation of her own time among different uses. An endeavour should be made to

achieve this freedom through well planned and prepared policy programmes rather than by reluctantly and belatedly
yielding to the social pressures exerted in the direction of
greater flexibility.

The individual should be free to switch between periods of
income-earning work, education or training, [child care], and
leisure (including retirement) according to her own interests
and wishes. There should also be many different and variable
patterns of working time over the course of [a life-time], a
year, a week or a day so that the individual can always find
something that suits her preferences.

Of course this freedom cannot be unlimited; the task is
always to find the best compromise between individual
wishes and the technical, economic, and social exigencies
which have led to existing rules and regulations whose role in
promoting both economic efficiency and social protection
should not be overlooked. But the time has come to move the
point of compromise in the direction of freedom by offering
more flexibility whenever possible.

The reduction in total hours worked over the course of a
normal lifetime, which can be expected to continue, ought to
be designed in the light of a systematic and simultaneous consideration of all the options. Usually decisions concerning
[motherhood], retirement, vacations, weekly hours, years of
schooling and access to adult training and education are taken
piecemeal. Instead they should be seen as an inter-related set
of economic and social choices as to the utilisation of growing
resources, which should be taken into account in improving
the quality of life.[36]

The fact that men make a life-long commitment to labor-force
participation means that those who manage the economy can make
projections, assess costs, anticipate consequences. They know that
the "average man" will spend, say, fifty years in the labor force,
will be unemployed so many years, on vacation so many years, re-
tired so many years, and so on. Thus it becomes possible to devise
sound actuarial tables for the proposed "generalized drawing
rights."

As yet such expectability and hence predictability does not exist
in the case of women. But increasingly their total life-work patterns will approach a stability which will make the idea actuarially
feasible for women also. We do know already that even women
who do not enter the labor force until the age of thirty-five are

343

devoting about a quarter of a century to paid employment. In the meanwhile if the idea did no more than help women see their decisions "as an interrelated set of economic and social choices," to view themselves as not exclusively mothers throughout their life time, to get the perspective of themselves as workers with time off for motherhood at one stage of their lives, it might be worth while. But it could do more; if implemented, it could help correct a grave injustice in the present social security system which is, in effect, a specialized "drawing right" that sometimes proves no right at all.

Carolyn Bell Shaw has shown, for example, that a woman who contributes to the social security system for a whole working life may be no better off as a recipient in her own right than she is as recipient as her husband's survivor. [37] The "generalized drawing rights" plan could correct this injustice. The money paid in by working women but never received by them could go to a fund that would be available for income maintenance when women took time off for having babies. In the present social security system, those in their working years support those beyond. In a similar way, men and women in their working years would be contributing to those taking time out for the parental role, quite in line with the proposed generalized drawing rights plan.

In response, then, to the call for help from mothers overcome by a sense of insecurity, unhappiness, and uselessness, a variety of reforms are being proposed or actually tried. People, all the way from communards subsisting on AFDC checks in the backwoods of California to economists in international conferences, are tackling the problem. All the angles from child bearing to role integration are engaging the attention of thoughtful men and women throughout the industrial world. Since infants and small children cannot wait, however, for the answers that will finally emerge, mothers continue to gerrymander their own little self-help, stopgap, uncoordinateed programs to spell one another off from time to time. They devise a mosaic of arrangements to spare themselves from collapse, exchange baby-sitting services with one another, hire baby-sitters for occasional time off, set up their own co-operative child-care facilities . . . . Hardly an ideal way to deal with such an important function.

Their children, though, will be spared at least some of the trauma. Many different kinds of help are on the way. They will have options.

# PART EIGHT

## Motherhood and the Social Order

# Introduction

We began with the mother in the home. But an increasing number of women are now recognizing that modern motherhood involves more than in-house care of children. They are coming to realize that the welfare of their children demands that they participate in the wider political scene as well. There has therefore been accelerated participation by women in the political process and, socialized as they have been by their role as mothers, they have shown a generally humane concern for people. Their nurturance and idealism have been a counterpoise to the macho demanded of men in the harsh outside world.

The old Victorian conception of the proper balance of the sexes, a conception based on a strict specialization of each sex in a specific set of virtues—women in nurturance, men in power—has become obsolete. Erik Erikson, among others, calls for a new balance, one in which the virtues of both sexes coexist within each sex, a balance of nurturance and strength in both women and men. The Victorian balance may have fit the nineteenth century; but the world has changed. It no longer fits even the twentieth, and certainly not the twenty-first. Motherhood outside as well as inside the home calls for the contribution of both men and women.

# CHAPTER EIGHTEEN

## A New Balance

### Two Styles of Motherhood

Berthold Brecht made a distinction between motherly and non-motherly women, between mothers, that is, who defended their children and those who did not. He made a further distinction between those who protected their children passively and those who did so actively. The passive mother withdrew her children from harm, trying to protect them by avoiding trouble; she created a safe enclave in which the child could feel secure. It was a non-aggressive style, certainly non-political. But the modern style was different. It called for "confrontations with the unjust society by masses of people who think and organize in concert." [1] It was a defensively aggressive style.[2] It did not accept things as they were and adjust to them; it tried to change them. Not withdrawal but confrontation was called for. Participation in the political process, in this view, became an intrinsic part of motherhood, however much such participation conflicted with other aspects of the mother's role.

Since women are the primary caretakers in the family, they tend to be the representatives of children's interests in the larger society. But, for a number of reasons, such as maternal responsibility for the care of offspring, women seldom form efficient pressure groups in society. Children's interests thus tend to be unrepresented in industrialized, mobile societies, which are governed in part by pressure groups. Decisions of great importance to children are made without the direct involvement of those who have the closest contact with

children—the mothers. . . . Though extensive maternal responsibility and a low degree of social participation facilitate
socialization and insure adequate child-care, they also create
conditions that make children vulnerable to destructive pressures of non-familial organizations. . . .[3]

How to reconcile these incompatible functions is not a simple task.

Most mothers have shrunk from participation in the outside
world.[4] The snug, Victorian home and its contemporary heir may
have been appropriate for Brecht's first or withdrawing style of
mothering; it is not, in the minds of many mothers today, appropriate for the new style now called for. It denigrated the role of
mother, making her in effect a hand-maiden of the macho world,
bandaging the wounds it inflicted and thus making the situation
more tolerable. But it limited what she could do for her children.

Brécht himself felt that different historical situations called for
different styles; withdrawal may have been adequate at one time;
taking part in organized conflict was called for at another. Many
women feel that the present calls for a more aggressive style of
motherhood.

### An Aggressive Style of Motherhood

It had long been recognized that motherhood involved more
than in-house activities, that it extended beyond the home. Even
the Catholic Church had granted that it extended to the immediate neighborhood or parish. It might even include the local community, for protection of children required a mother to make sure
that their immediate environment was safe as well as salutary.
Protection of street crossings was thus, for example, a legitimate
concern.

But taking part in organized conflict was something else again.
In the 1960s mothers of many backgrounds, races, and religious
faiths were, in fact, confronting policy makers they saw responsible for threats to their children, including war, poverty, drugs. The
fact that war is not healthy for children was enough to justify their
participation in peace movements. The militancy of the National
Welfare Rights Organization was well within the script for the second type of motherhood Brecht delineated. The current scene was
definitely not one calling for, or even permitting, withdrawal.

Here is the impassioned cry of one woman who had tried withdrawal to a communal farm in Alabama. It was not enough!

More and more I yearn, I ache for the day when my family and I live in peace and freedom. No more nights hoping we won't be attacked by the KKK or other local racists. That will never happen unless we stand up and fight for our personhood, our humanbeingness, our survival. It's no matter of high-falutin theories or something I arrived at by reading or researching. I saw my black children (I am white) suffering from rickets, anemia, open sores, and malnutrition. My anger became deep-rooted and strong—not at myself but against a system of dog-eat-dog in which this suffering could take place—against racism and classism. I can fool myself by trying to find solutions to alienation and sexism and other evils. My husband can struggle against his chauvinism, I can try to insulate my children against racism and sex role conditioning; but we will end up only making minor adjustments. The basic, all-encompassing capitalist system remains. So our efforts at personal solutions are doomed to failure. But there is an out— and that out is struggle. Through struggle—hard, unrelenting, joyous struggle—we can change this country. It's a big job and we must be equal to the challenge.[5]

An increasing demand being made on the mother role was the ability to confront the enemies of children. Participation in the political process became a legitimate part of the mother's role. Mothers were coming to recognize that learning how to acquire and use power was one of their maternal responsibilities.

### The Power of Mothers

Samuel Johnson commented that it was just as well that the law gave women so little power because nature had given them so much. Among the oldest clichés about the relations between the sexes is one to the effect that women have tremendous power simply because of their influence over men, with an enormous cache of blue chips in the form of acceptance or rejection, approval or disapproval, sexual generosity or niggardliness; or that they had enormous power because of their influence as mothers on children.

Actually the hand that rocks the cradle has not ruled the world. In fact, rocking the cradle has been precisely what has prevented the hand from ruling the world. However much truth there might have been in the old saying, such private, fragmented, interpersonal power did not add up to genuine, public—political—power.[6]

True, women who achieved power may have had children— Eleanor of Aquitaine comes to mind—and everyone who has ever achieved power—including Macbeth's enemy, Malcolm—has had a mother, but almost by definition, the role of mother has been incompatible with the exercise of political power, although not incompatible with interpersonal domination and control. Catholic mothers, Jewish mothers, and all those other mothers from whom millions of men and women are at this very moment struggling for liberation; domineering mothers, sitting sternly in judgment on children years after they have left home; possessive mothers, self-martyred mothers, controlling by guilt if by nothing more; all exercised interpersonal domination and control. But the power of a million such mothers with great power at home does not amount to much if they are not organized. (Nor, as Lysistrata is meant to illustrate, even if they are.) Unorganized, they cannot sway policy. They cannot have an input in public decisions. They cannot exert pressure.[7] They cannot protect the outside environment of children. That calls for genuine political power, and the will to use it humanely.

### The "Redemptive" Function of Motherhood

A generation ago a sociologist, George Lundberg, answered the question, "can science save us?" with an assured, Yes, it can. To him recourse to science was, in fact, the only path to the salvation of society.[8] Science could not make us want to save society, but if we did want to, it could show us how.

Berthold Brecht had quite a different vision. He looked elsewhere, to mothers, in fact, for the transformation of the social order. "Wisdom does not spur a person to generous conduct. . . . Reason is *not* ultimately what makes men moral." [9] The qualities of motherliness, which had to do with "the person's energy and generosity of impulses" performed that function. For exploring the nature of moral situations, therefore, Brecht selected woman in her role as mother. The major criteria he set for defining what was moral—"do you work and plan to fulfill other humans' needs, desires, and potential wherever met?" [10]—coincided with his conception of the role of mothers. Mothers were expected to act in behalf of their children.[11] This was the moral imperative women were required to live up to as mothers.[12]

Early feminists had shared that vision. They had assumed a redemptive function. They had believed that increased participation by women in the political world would have precisely that effect on the social order. Rather than seeing female virtues sacrificed by participation in the political world, as some opponents did, they had argued that such virtues would have a leavening effect. They had "contended that the large affairs of government and business had been too long dominated by the crude, war-like, acquisitive, hardheaded, amoral qualities of men. Far from fearing that femininity would be endangered by contact with man's macho world, they argued that government and industry should no longer be deprived of the tempering influence of women's compassion, spirituality, and moral sensitivity. As Julia Ward Howe [had] declared, 'the very intensity of our feeling for home, husband, and children gives us a power of loving and working outside of our homes, to redeem the world as love and work only can.' Thus, the feminists did not always see themselves doing the same things in the same ways as men." [13] That conviction of their redemptive role had underlain the fight for the vote. Nor were they alone in this conviction. There were even men who agreed with this formulation: "the peril of present-day mankind springs in large part from the one-sidedly patriarchal development of the male intellectual consciousness, which is no longer kept in balance by the matriarchal world of the psyche. In this sense the exposition of the archetypical-psychical world of the Feminine . . . is . . . a contribution to a future therapy of culture." [14]

Modern feminists did not, however, accept the redemptive function. At least they did not claim moral superiority. They did not promise a transformation of the social order in return for their rights. Justice, not reform, was the basis of their claims. They did not seek power to create a better world or because they were morally superior to men. Women could be expected to act like others, supporting policies they felt were in their favor and fighting policies they felt were inimical to them. And anyway, it was the logic of the system that determined how anyone, male or female, operated in any position in the system. Indira Gandhi and Golda Meir behaved not as women but as the system demanded, according to the script for those in power. Women could be expected to be no better, or worse, than men. If women were better than men it was because their roles had made them so.

These new feminists are seriously concerned not only to redefine the feminine role selectively, but also to establish their position as quite different from that of their nineteenth-century predecessors. They reject the nineteenth-century notion that women's inherent nature befits them to improve the world; instead, they argue that confinement within the traditional role has given women a more objective view of society and of its failure to pursue humane objectives. [15]

Betty Friedan, at a meeting of the National Women's Political Caucus, illustrates the point:

I believe that women's voice in political decisions will help change our whole politics away from war and toward the critical human problems of our society—not because women are purer or better than men, but because our lives have not permitted us to evade the masculine mystique. Shana Alexander suggested that our slogan should be "Women's Participation—Human Liberation." [16]

And Gloria Steinem in 1971, under protest, summarized the kinds of changes she anticipated if women achieved more political power:

With women as half the country's elected representatives, and a woman President once in a while, the country's *machismo* problems would be greatly reduced. The old-fashioned idea that manhood depends on violence and victory is, after all, an important part of our troubles in the streets and in Viet Nam. I'm not saying that women leaders would eliminate violence. We are not more moral than men; we are only uncorrupted by power so far. When we do acquire power, we might turn out to have an equal impulse toward aggression. Even now, Margaret Mead believes that women fight less often but more fiercely than men, because women are not taught the rules of the war game and fight only when cornered. But for the next fifty years or so, women in politics will be very valuable by tempering the idea of manhood into something less aggressive and better suited to this crowded, post-atomic planet. Consumer protection and children's rights, for instance, might get more legislative attention.[17]

And one woman, a defector from the most radical branch of the New Left, was almost back to the redemptive ideal of the nineteenth century. "Women are beginning to rise in response to the

Mother's call to save her planet and create instead the next stage of evolution . . . . The uprising of women . . . must be an affirmation of the power of female consciousness of the Mother. The changes which it will embody can perhaps be better imagined as primarily spiritual and religious, rather than economic and social, though they will include and embody the latter." [18]

Actually, as it turned out, women were better. Despite their slow start [19] in political participation once the suffrage was won—quite understandable in view of their history—the voting record of women did show a "redemptive" bias. Analyses of voting behavior as of 1972 [20] showed that by and large women did tend to vote a more humanitarian line than men. They were more compassionate.[21] According to a Harris poll:

> Women are significantly more compassionate than men about social issues such as hunger, poverty, problems of the aged and racial discrimination. Women are standing squarely on their own feet. They are voting differently from men. They are motivated by different considerations. They are much more inclined now to vote and to become active not only for their own self-interest, but for the interest of society, the world, and most of all, out of compassion for humanity. And once you let a force like that loose, I would suggest that it can never be bottled up again.[22]

Specifically, as voters women showed deeper concern than men over drugs and war, they favored rehabilitative over punitive measures in dealing with drug abuse, and more than men they were for gun control. These findings were in line with earlier polls which showed that "in general women attach greater value to human life than do men."

When women legislators at a conference in 1972 described themselves as "more honest, less willing to compromise, more concerned with public interest, less interested in personal gain, more oriented to issues and less in fulfilling their egos than their counterparts" [23] there was, understandably, polite but cynical skepticism. Yet a study of women who were political activists does shore up this judgment. Women who participate actively in political life do show such an idealistic motivation and ideology. They are not in politics for self-enhancement nor for power or money to the same degree as men; they show the traditional female love-and/or-duty ethos. Their work is a labor of love, a way of helping others, a duty. It is not a step in a career, part of getting ahead. The female political activist is doing for the body politic what she does for her family at home.[24]

Gloria Steinem had hedged her predictions. Power corrupts. Women might be no better than men. Her predictions were based on the belief not that women were innately superior to men, only that they were—as yet—less corrupted. The woman the Harris poll was describing and the woman the researchers delineate for us are the kind of women we have so far been producing.

And as long as these women remained that way they would have little real political impact. One commentator, in fact, rather than gloating over the fact that no women were involved in the Watergate scandal of the Nixon administration, deplored the evidence it provided that women were absent from the seats of power. "I wouldn't have cared if there had been women involved in the planning of this terrible business. At least it would have shown they were in places that mattered politically." [25] The very idealism women in politics display may be what prevents their achievement of high office.[26]

There is a "balance" or "trade-off"—to use modern jargon— inherited from the past—between profoundly felt values, between the idealism possible for women sheltered in the home and open participation in the world outside the home.

### Women As the Product of a Role

Women have been able until now to be more idealistic than men because— in the Victorian model and its later heirs—they were protected; they did not have to fight on the front lines. "By partly excluding the caretakers of the children, the mothers, from occupational and political life, the social unit of mother and child is protected from the strains inherent in social participation." [27] In order adequately to perform their functions in the "domestic sphere" women had to be protected, sheltered. They were in no position to extend their mothering beyond the walls of their homes.

A perceptive literary critic shows us how Harriet Beecher Stowe had exposed the fragile ground on which the protected woman's idealism rested. In *Uncle Tom's Cabin*—"pointedly addressed to 'the mothers of America' "—Mr. Shelby must sell Uncle Tom to pay off some of the debts incurred in maintaining the amenities of his establishment, "amenities which include Mrs. Shelby's piety, her high moral code, her tender care of her slaves." [28] Mrs. Shelby is horrified to find how brutal the cash nexus world could be, how expendable were her own values in any confrontation with it. "How can I bear to have this open acknowledgement that we care for no tie, no duty, no relations, however sacred, compared with money?" [29] She had been able to indulge her moral principles only as long as her husband could pay for them. She could be noble because her husband could not be. Women practiced "vicarious virtue" as well as vicarious leisure for the rugged, macho individualists. They could be "the conscience of the nation" because they had no responsibility for running it.

Only such protected people as the Victorian mother could afford to be gentle, tender, nurturant. "As dutiful wife and mother, she created in the home a sanctuary for all the higher virtues." [30] The almost desperate need for the preservation of such motherliness shows up throughout the nineteenth century, even well into the twentieth. Secure, unthreatened, mother could be, like royalty, above the battle and hence available for the care and nurturance of those hurt and wounded outside its walls as well as those entrusted to her care within them. She could supply solace for the defeated. She could be altruistic because she was not in the fray. She could make the slings and arrows of outrageous fortune in the outside world tolerable. She could be tender and humane. Could she be if she were in the fray herself? If she were an active participant in that harsh competitive outside world? Clearly she could not.

Throughout the nineteenth century antifeminist writing was filled with the unnaturalness of women speaking in public, even attending public meetings. Anything that took women out of the shelter of the home was destructive to the social order. There was an almost passionate insistence that women remain out of the maelstrom that roiled the waters beyond the walls of the home. When, finally, the ruthless macho world of industrialism and urbanism and capitalism began inexorably to draw women outside of the protective walls, "the opposition . . . was concerned with far more than their place in the world of work. It was an integral part of a comprehensive effort to bring women back into the shelter of the home, to reemphasize their functions in the family, to reconstruct the supposedly tottering family around them, to reassert the authority of a strict moral code, and to restore a clear boundary between masculine and feminine character and behavior." [31] The fundamental issue was not so much the effect women's entrance into the outside world would have on the labor market as the effect of their departure on the old "balance of Male and Female, of Paternal and Maternal," a balance which called for nurturance in the home and macho in the outside world.

### Mothers As the Product of a Role

An old research tradition in sociology documents the imprint that our occupation has on our appearance, on our speech, on our thought patterns, on our personalities, on our characters. Sherlock Holmes has become the symbol of how deeply we can read a person's history from his or her carriage, dress, language. The occupation makes the man. Or woman. The "stigmata" of the school teacher, the librarian, the prostitute have become clichés. And so also does the role of mother shape the women who perform it. Women have had to be tender, compassionate, patient because the role of mother demanded those virtues.

A wide gamut of women enter the occupation of motherhood. The virtues prescribed for mothers are no more "natural" for them than for men. Some are not loving.[32] Some are. They retain many of their differences. But they tend also to converge in many ways. Relatively few achieve all the virtues prescribed for them as mothers but almost all believe they should. They work hard at it. They feel guilty if or when they fail. The effort shows in their characters. For even if they do not succeed in achieving all the role-prescribed virtues the actual process of bearing and rearing children tends to encourage them. Charged with the care and protection of infants and small children, most do show courage, patience, self-sacrifice. If all the people in the mother's world assume and act as if she were going to be self-sacrificing, as though she is going to behave in the interest of others, it becomes all but impossible to act any other way; there is no room for maneuver; the tether is short. Motherhood shapes women, however recalcitrant the material may sometimes be. Whatever materials women bring to motherhood, most do develop the cherishing qualities associated with the role. It is not so much biology as role that was the basis of a woman's virtues.

When we ask, then, what difference it would make if women had more political power, the question must always be phrased in terms of women who until now have been protected, reared in a cloistered way, socialized into a certain kind of role with humane attributes required for its performance.

### Case in Point: Female Macho

From history comes interesting insight into the role-shaped character of women. The medieval abbess and the women who surrounded her were released from family responsibilities by their vows; they were therefore free to participate in the characteristic activities of their age. And how did they behave? Did they present a shining example of what their female skills and talents could achieve? Yes, in fact, they did. But, as it turned out, their skills and talents were exercised very much like those of men. They could administer great institutions as well as men. And they could also brawl and fight as well as men. Here, for example, is Chrodield:

> Radegund entered the life at Poitiers that gave play to her great powers of organization, diplomacy, and leadership. Her nuns were her true spiritual children. After her death two rival claimants for the office of abbess contended even with violence. Leubover was the regularly appointed successor, but Chrodield, daughter and cousin of kings, heading a faction attacked and put to flight the clerics who excommunicated her party. Gregory of Tours tells how Chrodield, having collected about her a band of murderers and vagrants of all kinds, dwelt in open revolt and ordered her followers to break into the nunnery at night and forcibly to bear off the abbess. But the abbess, who was suffering from a gouty foot, on hearing the noise of their approach asked to be carried before the shrine of the Holy Ghost. The rebels rushed in with swords and lances, and, mistaking in the dark, the prioress for the abbess, carried her off, dishevelled and stripped of her cloak. The bishops were afraid to enter Poitiers and the nuns kept the district terrorised until the king sent troops to reduce them. Only after the soldiers had actually charged them, cutting them down with sword and spear, was the neighbourhood at peace. It was not with these ladies in mind that Wordsworth found the sunset-hour as "quiet as a nun." [33]

There were, to be sure, also the Poor Clares, who epitomize all the gentle virtues of mothering. Female biology lends itself to machismo as well as to nurturance.

As though to illustrate this point, in the first months of the feminist movement of the late 1960s, members of the avant garde used the tactic of parodying macho by surpassing men in the use of obscenities and, like the ferocious nuns, in violence and aggressiveness. They violated all the traditional norms for female behavior, especially the gentleness written into the role of mother. They expressed rather than repressed their anger; they were mirror-images of the Victorian mother. In effect, they were saying to men: this is what macho is really like; we can cultivate it as well as you; how do you like it?

The men did not like it at all. It was one of the most chilling experiences they had ever been subjected to. They were shaken. These women seemed archetypical proof of the nineteenth-century fear that participation in the outside world would un-sex women. If this was what political power was going to do to women, they wanted none of it. The confrontation had a profound and, in some cases, traumatic effect on men. It was, at least reportedly, a castrating experience; and again at least reportedly, increasing impotence came to the attention of therapists. If the alternative to the Victorian model was to be this hostile, angry, non-compassionate woman, the reaction was "for heaven's sake, No!" To the question, would political success spoil mothers? the answer was, Yes! if this is what it would do to them.

Little by little the caricature as a tactic was dropped by feminists. Having made their point—that macho was no more appealing in men than in women—the women did not have to come on so strong. As more conservative women picked up the trail, the tactics changed. Most women liked men and motherhood too much to pursue this radical course very long; [34] they wanted to work out a style that suited this day and age. And, relieved, so did the men. Success need not spoil mothers after all.

### Nurturance, Macho, and Sex

If women do not necessarily start out as intrinsically more talented than men in the skills of mothering, if they achieve them—when or if they do—in the practice of mothering, there is no reason to limit the humanizing process to women. There are no intrinsic reasons why men cannot become as nurturant as women. [35] Any more than there are intrinsic reasons why women cannot become macho.

To the extent that reproduction is an exclusively female function, it is, indeed, true that "biology is destiny" and no one can share it. Certainly not men. But motherhood, we remind ourselves again, is not the same as reproduction. And not intrinsically limited to the female sex. The mothering function can be—and, in fact, in some cultures, is—shared by men.[36] Still, at least in recent Western history, nurturance has been assigned to mothers and the nurturant qualities—love, tenderness, tender-mindedness, heart, compassion—have been written into their role.[37] And, in accordance with the functions assigned to men, a different set of qualities have been written into their role scripts.

In order to sidetrack a diversionary discussion of sex differences,[38] the point of departure here is simply the fact that there do exist two sets of values, ideals, principles, what-have-you variously labelled yin and yang, tender- and tough-mindedness, mercy and justice, nurturance and competence, expressiveness and instrumentality, intellect and emotion, mind and heart, and so on and on. The existence of such polarities may be accepted. There doubtless are such modalities.

But human thinking has not stopped at recognition of their existence. It has tended to locate them in the two sexes, assigning one set to males and the other to females. The assumption has been made that women qua women embodied the nurturance principle and men the aggressive or macho principle. And, more to the point, these differences have been assumed to be intrinsic [39] and, worse still, mutually exclusive. They represent an old balance inherited from the nineteenth century, one of rigid sex specialization, one which permitted only one set of virtues per sex.

### The Old Balance

Erik Erikson tells us that today "a new balance of Male and Female, of Paternal and Maternal is obviously presaged . . . in the wider awareness which spread wherever science, technology, and genuinely self-scrutiny advance," as they are now doing.[40] Unlike the old balance resting on sex specialization, the new balance is one which allows the strengths of both sexes to be cultivated in both men and women.

The old balance was not a contrived bit of irrelevance; it was an urgent necessity. And the traditional role of mother, apotheosized in the Victorian model, performed an essential set of functions, universally needed and eagerly sought, especially in the darkest days of early industrialization under the brutal dynamics of early capitalism.[41] There had to be anchors of security in human life. There had to be a source of reassurance. There had to be a principle above conflict and competition and survival of the fittest and deserving and exchanging and earning and winning and achieving. There had to be something above self-preservation.

There had to be somewhere, somehow, people who were uncontaminated by the dog-eat-dog practices of capitalism, by the rugged individualism that rewarded the most ruthless and punished the gentle. The conception of the role of mother embodied in the nineteenth-century model produced such healing people. It constituted a defense against the intolerable ambience that the new industrial-urban society was creating. Embodying this function in the role of mother was logical. It had a concrete and visible basis. A study of prehistoric as well as of historic remains shows how primordial this assignment of the nurturant and protective function to mothers has been. The Great Mother archetype represents not only fertility but also "the sheltering, protecting, and nourishing elementary character." [42]

The picture of the old balance that comes through is one in which the traits needed and cultivated in the outside world—aggressiveness, power, control, domination, competitiveness—were held in check by the traits cultivated in the home—nurturance, support, protective love—a picture in which motherhood was a counterpoise to macho. Motherliness balancing machismo. In this context, the exaggerations of the Prolegomena to Part I make sense.

But there has been a strange new twist to events in recent times. Along with the reconceptualization of motherhood now in process there is an ongoing reconceptualization of work also, not only of the work of women but also of the work of men. The outside world has changed. So has the home. The old balance is no longer appropriate.

### A New Twist

The outside world has become tempered. It is no longer the same world as that of early industrialism; the individualism is no longer permitted to be so rugged; dogs are not permitted to eat dogs, at least in such quantities; and, in general, the most brutalizing kinds of work have been gentled, if not wholly tamed or eliminated. George Cabot Lodge is quoted in an interview as saying that the complexities of modern business organization diminish the role of the rugged individualist. The "Horatio Alger" hero, he is quoted as saying, "was the loner, the self-reliant man fighting it out in the open market where only the fit survived. . . . But in today's world, few can live like [the characters in the works of] Horatio Alger." [43] For technology can be beneficent as well as brutalizing.

Among the more obvious changes that technology has produced have been those that have had to do with the relative decline in the male-dominated heavy industries and the relative—as well as absolute—rise in the light industries. Occupations which call for the qualities women have excelled in are the ones that are increasing. More and more of the world's work is done in two-sex rather than in sex-segregated situations. The overall effect has been to mollify the industrial world. All this, of course, not because of the entrance of women into the labor force but because of the direction in which technology has steered our society. It was not women but technology that had the gentling effect. To such an extent, in fact, that alienation, not violence, is the problem.

The outside world is now willing to undertake the salvaging effect once called for in the home. Working conditions have become a matter of legislative concern. Thus a bill was introduced into the 93rd Congress (S.736) to the effect that "it is in the national interest to encourage the humanization of working conditions and the work itself so as to increase worker job satisfaction, diminish the negative effects of job dissatisfaction, and to the extent possible, maximize potential for democracy, security, equity, and craftsmanship." [44] Not the harsh competitive struggle, not the hard-driving boss, not the diet of dogs, not the grim labor so much as boredom and frustration are allegedly the characteristics of the outside world. The Victorian mother had, in fact, been co-opted in the personnel office to hold the macho union at bay.

Relations with co-workers became as pleasant as those with family members or even more so. In fact, a study made in the 1950s found that men derived more satisfaction from contacts with their fellow workers than from those with their families. Not in marriage but in "friendships and in relationships with colleagues at work and with the larger social community" did the men find gratification of their social needs. "It is in day-to-day contact with the business world and the social world outside of the home that men seem to seek their broad interpersonal gratifications." [45] An evening with the office bowling club is more fun than a picnic with the family.

Home life and work life were tending to become homogenized:

> The salient feature of this scenario [of the future of work] is the gradual reunification of work and leisure into a holistic pattern as was characteristic of most preindustrial societies. Such a reunification may already be observed in the guise of coffee breaks, informal on-the-job socializing, and increasing concern for the amenities of the work setting. But these are only the surface manifestations of more profound changes. The proliferation of on-the-job training courses, for example, reflects an increasing concern with the need to elicit from workers a greater sense of commitment by increasing their opportunities for growth and fulfillment within the work setting. What is significant in these developments is not the claim or belief that such innovations are conducive to increased productivity, but rather the fact that they represent an attempt to humanize the work setting.[46]

When asked by pollsters, men reported, despite research documenting the existence of "blue-collar blues," [47] in overwhelming numbers that they were satisfied with their jobs or that they liked their work. The proportion happy in their work was not less than the proportion reported happy in marriage.[48]

Meanwhile, "back at the ranch" house, changes have also been going on. The home is still an escape from a complex and demanding outside world, but now an escape in which to express aggressive and hostile impulses in safety. Thus, Richard E. Farson, giving his view of the future, tells us:

> The family will, in a sense, become a rehabilitative agent, a buffer against a very complex and demanding world in which family members constitute our only advocates, the only people who are *for* us. So we shall depend upon them increasingly. Furthermore, in one sense, the family may be one of the few places in the world of the future—one of the last places—in which we can find privacy. As such, it will be a safe place for expressing our aggressive and hostile impulses. So family life will be highly emotional, intimate, infantile, aggressive, hostile, and irrational.[49]

363

A new balance was clearly in order. A balance that did not specialize one set of virtues in one sex, another set in the other. Both sets
were needed in both worlds.

## The New Balance

This book began with a brace of poetic accolades for mothers
that may well have elicited sardonic chortles in some, especially
younger, readers. They were intended to have precisely that effect
in that context. An opposite effect is aimed at now, a soberer critique of the traditional conceptualization of the role of mother. For
what, after all, is so bad about love, courage, concern for others,
patience, tenderness, cherishing, nurturance, compassion, fore-
bearance, and all the other virtues written into the traditional
script for the role of mother? Any diminution of them in a world
that generates too little love and tenderness would be a calamity.
They are, in fact, too important to be specialized only for mothers.

And what, while we are at it, is so bad about strength, aggressiveness, power except when exaggerated in the form of macho?
Too important to be denied to mothers, for they, too, need
strength. The new balance calls not for a diminution of the virtues
of either sex but for a sharing of both sets of virtues by both sexes.
A balance within each sex rather than a balance between them.
For just as the major defect in the Victorian model for the role of
mother was its exaggeration of the nurturant virtues at the almost
total expense of strength, so also the major defect of macho has
been its exaggeration of the power component at the almost total
expense of tenderness and gentleness.

Erikson's "new balance of Male and Female, of Paternal and
Maternal" does not mean unisex or monosex or androgyny. During
the 1972 Democratic Convention in Miami Beach, there was a
child-care center run by volunteers. One of the most dedicated of
these volunteers was a man in the Coast Guard who worked at his
job all day and at the child-care center a good part of the night.
Why? Simply because he loved children. Beethoven showed
great motherliness toward his nephew; Ernest Jones speaks of
Freud's motherliness; Carl Ringer's book on Thomas Jefferson
notes harmonious male-female trends in that great man's character.[50] Not one of these great men, in fact, is in the least impugned
or denigrated by the new balance. The compassionate man is still
different from the compassionate woman; the strong woman is still

different from the strong man. The father's mothering or nurturance is not identical with the mother's.

Nor does the new balance portend utopia. Or dystopia. It does not threaten us with matriarchy. The Great Mother is not going to take over. But the qualities she symbolizes will be shared by more and more men, as so many young people are trying to share them today. Both children and the social order will profit by opening up motherhood for men to share.

How one judges a future that has achieved the new balance depends on how one values the principles embodied and symbolized in the role of mother. If one prefers the hard-boiled, he-man, get-tough, win-at-any-cost machismo, the spread of the nurturant principle will be appalling. It will look like womanish weakness, like putting heroes into chains, turning us all into weaklings. We live in a harsh, competitive world, it will be argued, and we have to rear people tough enough to win in it. None of that soft stuff. The Hell's Angel symbolizes this view in pathological form; but so, in only a more tempered form, does the tough Marine Corps sergeant. The question is, can it survive indefinitely in our "wider awareness?"

The old balance was too restrictive for this day and age. It did not make room for the male strengths required of mothers and it did not extend the nurturant virtues to fathers who, at least in archetypal form, must also be protective. The trend of the times is in the direction of seeing the two ideals or principles in both sexes rather than as separately specialized in one or the other, of seeing the polarity in both men and women rather than in only one sex. There is a feeling that specializing each principle in one sex alone has a distorting effect, debilitating one and truncating the other.

"Western mankind," we are told—and the term should, of course be "Western humankind"—must arrive at a synthesis that includes the feminine world—which is . . . one-sided in its isolation. Only then will the individual human being be able to develop the psychic wholeness that is urgently needed if Western man [sic!] is to face the dangers that threaten his [sic!] existence from within and without." [51] We cannot, in brief, afford to deprive either sex of the strengths of the other. Motherhood, we repeat once more, is too important to leave to women. Inside or outside of the home.

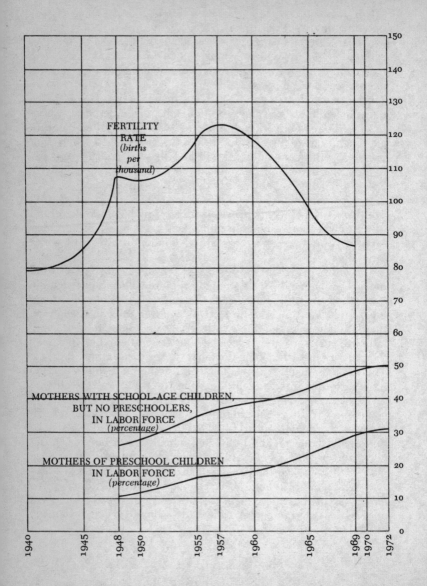

FERTILITY
RATE
*(births
per
thousand)*

MOTHERS WITH SCHOOL-AGE CHILDREN,
BUT NO PRESCHOOLERS,
IN LABOR FORCE
*(percentage)*

MOTHERS OF PRESCHOOL CHILDREN
IN LABOR FORCE
*(percentage)*

150
140
130
120
110
100
90
80
70
60
50
40
30
20
10
0

1940  1945  1948  1950  1955  1957  1960  1965  1969  1970  1972

# Notes

### Title Page Figure

The figure on the title page, representing "the three most important 'feminine curves' today," is a stylized version of data from the following sources. For labor-force participation of mothers with school-age, but not preschool, children (middle curve) and for mothers of preschool children (the bottom curve): the Manpower Report of the President, 1973, Table B-4, p. 168. For the top curve, fertility rate (births per 1,000 women 15 to 44 years of age): U.S. Public Health Service, Natality Statistics Analysis United States 1964 (U.S. Department of Health, Education, and

| YEAR | FERTILITY RATE | MOTHERS WITH SCHOOL-AGE CHILDREN, BUT NO PRESCHOOLERS, IN LABOR FORCE | MOTHERS OF PRE-SCHOOL CHILDREN IN LABOR FORCE |
|------|------|------|------|
| 1940 | 79.9 | — | — |
| 1945 | 85.9 | — | — |
| 1948 | 107.3 | 26.0 | 10.8 |
| 1950 | 106.2 | 28.3 | 11.9 |
| 1955 | 118.5 | 34.7 | 16.2 |
| 1957 | 122.9* | 36.6 | 17.0 |
| 1960 | 118.0 | 39.0 | 18.6 |
| 1965 | 96.7 | 43.7 | 23.3 |
| 1969 | 86.5 | 48.6 | 28.5 |
| 1970 | — | 49.2 | 29.6 |
| 1972 | — | 50.2* | 30.1* |

* High point in curve.

Welfare, Feb., 1967) and "Summary Report: Final Natality Statistics 1969," *Monthly Vital Statistics Report*, Vol. 22, No. 7, Supplement, Oct. 2, 1973.

### Foreword

1. But see Chapter 13 for possible impending changes.
2. By the early 1970s, about half of all women with school-age (but no pre-school) children were in the labor force; about a third of mothers with children 3 to 5; and about a fourth of those with children under 3. But see Chapter 8 for a discussion of possible future ceilings to these curves.
3. For further comments on the complexity of the concept of work as related to motherhood see Chapter 7 below.
4. In the United States almost 40 percent; Austria, 40 percent; Japan, 39 percent; Czechoslovakia, 44 percent; Rumania, 45.3 percent; in the USSR, 50 percent. The proportions are lower in other countries, as low as 27 percent in Luxembourg (Cynthia Epstein, *Woman's Place, Options and Limits in Professional Careers*, University of California Press, 1970, p. 45; Toni Blanken, Chapter 20 in Pamela Roby, ed., *Child Care—Who Cares?*, Basic Books, 1973).
5. See Chapter 8.
6. Valerie Kincade Oppenheimer, "Demographic Influence on Female Employment and the Status of Women," *American Journal of Sociology*, 78 (Jan., 1973), p. 958. See also Sidney Wolfbein, *Work in American Society* (Scott, Foresman, 1971), pp. 23 ff., p. 46, and the Economic Report of the President, 1973, Chapter 4.
7. Jeanne Binstock, "Motherhood: An Occupation Facing Decline," *The Futurist*, 6 (June, 1972), p. 99. The same idea was expressed in Jessie Bernard, *Women and the Public Interest, An Essay on Policy and Protest* (Aldine, 1971).
8. Jeanne Binstock, *loc. cit.*, p. 99.
9. Ruth Farwell, "Exiled from the Land," *The Washington Post*, Jan. 13, 1973. The quotation is from a review of Curtis K. Stadtfeld, *From the Land and Back* (Scribner's, 1972).
10. Louis Harris and others, The 1972 Virginia Slims American Women's Opinion Poll, p. 2.
11. *Ibid.*, p. 2.
12. Manpower Report of the President, 1973, pp. 225–226.
13. Erik Erikson, *Identity, Youth and Crisis* (Norton, 1968), p. 264.

### Prolegomena

1. Marc Antony de Wolfe Howe, "The Valiant."
2. Joaquin Miller, "The Bravest Battle," Stanza 1.
3. Elizabeth Akers Allen, "Rock Me to Sleep," Stanza 4, *Saturday Evening Post*, June 9, 1860.
4. Mary Riley (Mrs. Albert) Smith, Dedication in "Cradle and Arm Chair."
5. Sir Edwin Arnold, "Mothers," Stanza 6.
6. Arthur Wallace Peace, "The Reasons."
7. Alfred Lord Tennyson, "The Princess," Part VII, lines 301–312.
8. Thomas Dunn English, "Smiting the Rock."

9. Jean Richepin, translated from "Severed Heart" by J. Echegaray, a Spanish poet who won the Nobel prize for literature in 1904. The poem was also translated by Herbert Trench, Arthur Guiterman, and Arthur Stringer. The last line is variously translated as: "Are you hurt, my child, are you hurt at all?", "The Mother's heart: Oh, art thou hurt, my son?", "Son of mine, did I hurt you, dear?"

10. Victor Hugo, *Les Miserables*, Book 4, Chapter 1.

11. Walter E. Houghton, *The Victorian Frame of Mind 1830–1870* (Yale University Press, 1957), p. 355.

12. Edgar J. Schmiedeler, OSB, "Blessed Art Thou among Women," in Edgar J. Schmiedeler, OSB, ed., *The Mother the Heart of the Home* (St. Meinard, Ind.: A Grail Publication, 1955), p. 17.

13. *Ibid.*, pp. 17–31.

14. Junius Moreland Martin, *Mother: Heart Songs in Prose and Verse* (Published by the author, Salem, Iowa, 1932), p. 41.

15. *Ibid.*, pp. 20–21.

## Chapter One

1. Beatrice B. Whiting, ed., *Six Cultures, Studies of Child Rearing* (Wiley, 1963).

2. Robert A. LeVine and Barbara B. LeVine, "Nyansongo: A Gusii Community in Kenya," *Ibid.*, p. 139.

3. *Ibid.*, p. 161.

4. Leigh Minturn and John T. Hitchcock, "The Rajputs of Khalapur, India," *Ibid.*, p. 314.

5. Thomas W. Maretzki and Hatsumi Maretzki, "Taira: An Okinawan Village," *Ibid.*, p. 462.

6. Kimball Romney and Romaine Romney, "The Mixtecans of Juxtlahuaca, Mexico," *Ibid.*, p. 650.

7. William F. Mydegger and Corinne Mydegger, "Tarong: An Ilocos Barrio in the Philippines," *Ibid.*, p. 821.

8. *Ibid.*, p. 833.

9. *Ibid.*, p. 834.

10. Cora DuBois, *The People of Alors* (University of Minnesota Press, 1944), p. 36. "Lazy" women "use the care of the child as an excuse to slight their field work" (p. 34).

11. John L. Fischer and Ann Fischer, "The New Englanders of Orchard Town, U.S.A.," in Beatrice B. Whiting, ed., *op. cit.*, p. 946. Alorese mothers face the same problem of irresponsibility in older siblings as "baby sitters." It might be noted in passing that despite the much-publicized community child-care facilities in China today a newspaper report in 1972 pointed out that "an older child always seems to be taking care of a younger one" (Wes Gallagher, "Unexpected U.S. Visitors Stir a Tiny Chinese Hamlet," *The Washington Post*, August 17, 1972).

12. Leigh Minturn and William L. Lambert, *Mothers of Six Cultures: Antecedents of Child Rearing* (Wiley, 1964), p. 56.

13. *Ibid.*, p. 66.

14. *Ibid.*, pp. 282–283.

15. *Ibid.*, p. 283.

16. James W. Prescott and Cathy McKay, "Child Abuse and Child Care: Some Cross-Cultural and Anthropological Perspectives," Paper prepared for research workshop of the National Institute of Child Health and Human Development, June, 1973, Table 2.

17. Minturn and Lambert, *op. cit.*, p. 97.

18. Shirley Radl, *Mother's Day Is Over* (Charterhouse, 1973), *passim*.

19. Arthur W. Calhoun, *A Social History of the American Family:* Volume 1. *Colonial Period* (Cleveland: Arthur H. Clark, 1917), pp. 38–40.

20. Philippe Ariès, *Centuries of Childhood* (Knopf, 1962), pp. 398, 406–407.

21. Erich Neumann, *The Great Mother, An Analysis of the Archetype*, trans. Ralph Manheim (Princeton-Bollinger, 1963), p. 137.

22. Walter E. Houghton, *The Victorian Frame of Mind* (Yale University Press, 1957), p. 343.

23. *Ibid.*, p. 343.

24. John Ruskin, "Of Queens' Gardens," Section 68, in *Works*, Vol. 8, p. 122.

25. *Ibid.*, p. 122.

26. George Eliot, "Amos Barton," in *Scenes from Clerical Life*, Vol. 1, p. 85.

27. Alexander Mitscherleck, *Society Without Father, A Contribution to Social Psychology* (Harcourt Brace & World, 1968), p. 56.

28. The concept of altruistic surrender was originally developed by Anna Freud to refer to a form of identification with another person in which one all-but-gave up one's own identity. Arlie Hochschild has developed the concept as a component of the mother role among women sixty-five years of age and older as related to grown sons and daughters (*The Unexpected Community*, Prentice-Hall, 1973, pp. 100 ff.). It may be noted in passing that even Mary, who in the folk mind had been something of a roustabout, became, in effect, a Victorian mother in the nineteenth century, the very model of "the heart of the home." Although she had always been full of maternal warmth and kindness, though amoral, generous with mercy, assistance, and healing even for sinners, she had also been patroness of prostitutes and, in the Mexican folk mind, suspected of promiscuity. Folk tales had her giving milk from her own breast to horribly diseased patients, delivering the baby of a reverend abbess, substituting for a nun who went off to live it up as a prostitute (Wolfgang Lederer, *The Fear of Women*, Harcourt Brace Jovanovich, 1968, pp. 175–177). Not until the middle of the nineteenth century did she become completely domesticated.

29. As late as 1967, 34 percent of the respondents in a Gallup poll believed women's place was in the home. Even among college freshmen, usually an avant garde, 51.9 percent of the men queried in 1971 and 30.6 percent of the women, professed that belief. But see also Chapter 8 below for woman's place.

30. New Jersey NOW Task Force, *Dick and Jane As Victims* (1972). Published by authors.

31. See Chapter 18.

32. R. Heber Newton, *Womanhood* (Putnam's, 1881), p. 123.

33. *Ibid.*, p. 123.

34. *Ibid.*, p. 123.

35. Alexander Mitscherleck, *op. cit.*, p. 57.

36. Margaret Sanger, *Motherhood in Bondage* (Brentano's, 1928).

37. Shirley Radl, *op. cit.*, p. 10.

38. Simone de Beauvoir, *The Second Sex* (Bantam, 1952), pp. 484–485.

39. *Ibid.*, p. 485.

40. Philip Wylie, *A Generation of Vipers* (Farrar, 1942).

41. William Streckert, *Their Mothers' Sons* (Lippincott, 1956).

42. Philip Roth, *Portnoy's Complaint* (Random House, 1969).

43. Erich Neumann, *op. cit.*, pp. 148–149. The archetype of the Terrible Mother is the negative side of the Great Mother, witches, vampires, ghouls, specters.

44. Helen E. Peixotto, "Mothers Had Mothers Too," in Edgar J. Schmiedeler, ed., *The Mother the Heart of the Home* (St. Meinard, Ind.: Grail Publications, 1955), pp. 135–136.

## Introduction to Part Two

1. Corrado Gini, "Beauty, Marriage and Fertility," *Human Biology*, 10 (Dec., 1938), pp. 575–576.

2. Judith Blake, *Coercive Pronatalism and American Population Policy* (University of California, Berkeley: International Population and Urban Research, 1972).

## Chapter Two

1. See Chapters 4 and 8.

2. See Chapter 3.

3. This question, originally central in the fight for birth control half a century ago, seemed to have been answered when the Catholic Church accepted the principle of contraception by way of rhythm in the 1950s. It lay dormant for some time and has only recently been revived in reaction to current anti-natalism. This resuscitation of the issue is the only justification for the truncated discussion here. For a more detailed discussion see Betty Rollin, "Motherhood, Who Needs It?", *Look* Magazine, Sept. 22, 1970, pp. 15–17. See also Shirley Radl, *Mother's Day Is Over* (Charterhouse, 1973), Chapter 2.

4. E. E. Maccoby and C. N. Jacklin, *Sex Differences and Their Implications for Sex Role* (Unpublished manuscript, Stanford University, 1971). Present citation from Bernice E. Lott, "Who Wants the Children?", *American Psychologist* (July, 1973), pp. 573–582.

5. See, for example, the differences in reaction to newly born infants between Sunny Jim and Mgeni-mopaya described below.

6. It is easy enough to see why others might want women to want to have children. In the nineteenth century and early twentieth century there were several interested blocs that wanted high birth rates. The military could always use what disaffected women have called "cannon fodder" and industrial empire builders could always use an abundant and cheap labor supply. The use of a high birth rate to out-breed potential enemies is still going on. In Israel, fear is expressed that the Arab populations may outbreed the Israelis and in Russia, the fear is expressed that the Central Asian republics may out-breed European Russia (Murray Seeger, "Mother Russia Forsakes Hearth," *The Washington Post*, Aug. 17, 1972). See Jessie Bernard, *American Community Behavior* (Holt, Rinehart, and Winston, 1962, pp. 427–432) for further discussion of the birth rate as a political and economic weapon. At the personal level there is also an advantage in making women want babies. If they are getting what they want by having babies they have nothing to complain about if the cost is high; they are being rewarded enough by motherhood itself.

7. William Graham Sumner, *Folkways* (Ginn, 1906), Chapter 7.

8. *Ibid.*, p. 310.

9. *Ibid.*, p. 310. For comments on the relationship between sexuality and maternity see Chapter 4.

10. Judith Blake, "Are Babies Consumer Durables?", *Population Studies*, 22 (March, 1968), p. 24.

11. Unsigned, "All Dimples, My Lumpy-Dumpy Girlie," *Country Women* (n.d.), p. 4.

12. Judith Blake, "Coervice Pronatalism and American Population Policy," International Population and Urban Research, University of California, Berkeley (Dec., 1972), p. 4.

13. *Ibid.*, p. 6. The author specifies male homosexuality as a fourth example of labeling as pathological anything that threatens parenthood (pp. 22–24).

14. See Chapter 11.

15. Judith Blake, "Coercive Pronatalism," *loc. cit.*, p. 33.

16. New Jersey NOW Task Force, *Dick and Jane As Victims* (Princeton: published by the authors, 1972), p. 1.

17. *Ibid.*, p. 10.

18. Arthur A. Campbell, "The Role of Family Planning in the Reduction of Poverty," *Journal of Marriage and the Family*, 30 (May, 1968), p. 240. The concept of "sterility" is not clear-cut; increasingly demographers speak rather of "fecundity impairment," which is a matter of degree rather than of all-or-nothing. The estimate of 13 percent was low compared to earlier trends. Among women born 1880–1889, 23 percent (including single women) would bear no children; among women born 1900 to 1909, 26 percent would not. "Projections for the women now in the middle of their child bearing indicate that they may complete child-bearing with as few as 10 percent childless" (Paul C. Glick and Robert Parke, Jr., "New Approaches in Studying the Life Cycle of the Family," *Demography*, 2 (1965), p. 193. Reduction in the venereal diseases is credited with reducing involuntary childlessness.

19. Leta Hollingworth, "Social Devices for Impelling Women to Bear and Rear Children," *American Journal of Sociology*, 22 (July, 1916), pp. 19–29.

20. Ellen Peck, " 'I Have 7 Children,' She Said to Wild Applause," *New York Times* (Aug. 13, 1972).

21. *Ibid.*

22. *Ibid.*

23. Ellen Peck, "Television Commercials," paper prepared for Population Communication Center, National Academy of Television Arts & Sciences, New York Conference, March 15, 1972.

24. Lee Israel, "Lovelady Christabel Breaks Years of Anguished Silence to Tell: How Fan Magazines Can Make You A Real Woman," *Ms*, Sept., 1972, p. 38.

25. *Ibid.*, pp. 43, 102.

26. *Ibid.*, p. 103. Caught off-guard by the separation and announced divorce of Elizabeth Taylor and Richard Burton, the movie magazines were still grinding out the motherhood bit about Liz and Dick in August, 1973. "Elizabeth Taylor has said she would willingly give up her career and turn in all her fabulous jewels if she could have a baby with Richard," *Movie Mirror* was telling its readers authoritatively at the very moment she was reported to be cheerfully bounding about on the set of her new movie (Judith Martin, "Liz and Dick: Belated Idylls," *The Washington Post*, Aug. 3, 1973).

27. Ellen Peck, Nancy Cox, and Audrey Bertolet, "Pronatalism in Textbooks," unpublished paper.

28. Edward H. Pohlman, *Psychology of Birth Planning* (Schenkman, 1969), p. 53. Part I of this book (pp. 35–81) presents an excellent summary of reasons for wanting children.

29. Edward H. Pohlman, *Ibid.*, pp. 35–81.

30. Brenda Beust Smith, "NON Says Too Many Ob-Gyns Encourage Pregnancy," *Houston Chronicle*, April 13, 1973.

31. *The Washington Post*, Feb. 15, 1973.

32. Wolfgang Lederer, *The Fear of Women* (Harcourt Brace Jovanovich Harvest Book, 1968), p. 67. One study reported that the period parents found most satisfying was the pre-school age of the child; the least satisfying were the stages when the children were adolescent and adult (Joseph Veroff and Sheila Feld, *Marriage and Work in America*, Van Nostrand, 1970, p. 127). Sometimes, in fact, mothers get "stuck" at a certain stage of child-development and never move beyond it. Martha Wolfenstein, for example, contrasts two Jewish mothers, one with an immigrant and one with a native-American background. In the shtetl a woman had her son only during the first three years of his life; after that he was "snatched from the arms of his weeping mother and sent to school" ("Two Types of Jewish Mothers," in Margaret Mead and Martha Wolfenstein, eds., *Childhood in Contemporary Culture* (University of Chicago Press, 1955), p. 426. He remained thereafter in her mind "a baby incapable of taking care of himself, who would perish without her constant vigilance" (p. 438). The American mother, by way of contrast, tends to fixate at the level when children are acquiring skills; "a different aspect of the growing child is emphasized, that having to do with learning." Achievement by the son is her major preoccupation thereafter.

33. Letter to Ann Landers, *The Washington Post*, May 24, 1973.

34. Unsigned, "Baby Gorillas in New York and Washington," *Ibid.*, Sept. 9, 1972.

35. *Ibid.*

36. Jane Lawick-Goodall, *In the Shadow of Man* (Houghton-Mifflin, 1972). For a summary of some of the research on maternal rejection see Jessie Bernard, *American Family Behavior* (Harper, 1942; Russell & Russell, 1973), Chapter 10. For a more recent study of rejecting mothers see Marian Gennaria Morris, "Psychological Miscarriage, An End to Mother Love," in Helena Z. Lopata, ed., *Marriages and Families* (Van Nostrand, 1973), pp. 55–61.

37. "Woman Fights to Adopt Youth," *The Washington Post*, July 24, 1972.

38. Tobi Frankel, "Single but Not Alone, Adoption Brings Family Life to Unmarried," *New York Times*, March 28, 1973.

39. Helena Lopata found that even housewives tend to prefer motherhood to wifehood (*Occupation Housewife*, Oxford University Press, 1972), p. 217.

40. Tobi Frankel, "Single but Not Alone," *loc. cit.*

41. Including, it might be added, the burden of guilt written into practically all roles of women: "my conscience does bother me; I love her, but it is not the best decision," says one lawyer (*Ibid.*). It is doubtful if women who bear children for their own purposes would admit that having them was not necessarily in the best interests of the children. Even with respect to guilt, not all single adoptive parents are alike. Carole Klein found many single women performing the mother role in a manner quite different from the traditional. They did not experience guilt (Carole Klein, "Socialization of Child in Voluntary, Single-Parent Home," paper given at meeting of Society for Study of Social Problems,

Aug., 1973). These mothers perform differently in other respects also. They are not self-sacrificing to the same extent as traditional mothers; they are not possessive; they do not feel that the child owes them anything for their love; they inculcate androgynous, not sexist, values; humanistic, not achievement, goals are emphasized; independence for both self and child is important; they are flexible, non-authoritative, non-authoritarian, and not future-oriented. They view marriage as far more complex than motherhood. Certainly a new style of motherhood.

42. Robert T. Francoeur, *Utopian Motherhood* (Doubleday, 1970), p. 27.

43. Simone de Beauvoir, *The Second Sex*, trans. and ed. H. M. Parshley (Bantam, 1949), p. 466.

44. *Ibid.*, p. 466. Until recently the closest we have come to such one-parent situations has been in the case of black women. Because of the uncertainty of the ability of so many black men to support their families, some black women have preferred not to marry. So far as can be determined, these women perform the role of mother as adequately as anyone else similarly handicapped by poverty (Robert Bell, "The One-Parent Mother in the Negro Lower Class," unpublished paper). Presumably women in the future who choose to have children outside of marriage will be less handicapped by poverty. If they are employed, a major difficulty is providing day care (Carole Klein, *The Single Parent Experience*, Walker, 1972). In Southern California there is an organization called Momma, complete with Newsletter, organized to help single mothers deal with their problems. The older organization, Parents Without Partners, performs a similar function.

45. *The Washington Post*, Aug. 18, 1972.

46. *Ibid.*, May 25, 1973.

47. Jessie Bernard, *Academic Women* (The Pennsylvania State University Press, 1964), p. 225.

48. Niles Newton, *Maternal Emotions* (Hoeber, 1955), p. 70.

49. *Ibid.*, p. 68.

50. *Ibid.*, pp. 69–70.

51. See Chapter 4 for studies of differences between women with high and low fertility.

52. Women who liked caring for their babies were more apt to have positive feelings about menstruation and childbirth and other aspects of their biological role. They were also more likely to have copious menstrual flows, more children, and to present no obstetrical problems. Other physiological research also indicates that motherly behavior is related to menstrual flow, breast feeding, hormonal changes, and some other physical and social factors (*Ibid.*, pp. 70–71).

53. Helene Deutsch, *Neuroses and Character Types, Clinical Psychoanalytic Studies* (International Universities Press, 1965), pp. 197–198.

54. *Ibid.*, p. 198.

55. Colin Turnbull, *The Mountain People* (Simon & Schuster, 1972).

56. J. H. Plumb, "The Bad Old Days," *Book World*, March 4, 1973. The author is reviewing Jeffry Kaplow, *The Names of Kings* (Basic Books, 1973).

57. *Ibid.*

58. Leigh Minturn, William W. Lambert, and Associates, *Mothers of Six Cultures, Antecedents of Child Rearing* (Wiley, 1964), p. 56.

59. Harris poll, reported in *The Washington Post*, Nov., 1971. A far smaller propor-

tion—about 23 percent—reported major satisfaction from being wives and only 22 percent from housework.

60. Helena Lopata, *op. cit.*, p. 205. Only 9 percent of the comments referred to happy marriages and husbands. If comments dealing with children and with "relations" which included all kinds of relations, are combined with those specifically with children, the percent of comments dealing with satisfactions from motherhood is 59 percent.

61. Joseph Veroff and Sheila Feld, *op. cit.*, p. 150.

62. *Ibid.*, p. 195.

63. *Ibid.*, p. 199.

64. *Ibid.*, p. 201.

65. *Ibid.*, p. 203.

66. See Chapter 8.

67. John Money and Anke A. Ehrhardt, *Man and Woman, Boy and Girl* (Johns Hopkins University Press, 1972), Chapter 6. Follow-up studies of females who had inadvertently been subjected to male hormones *in utero* found that, as compared with a control group, they were more tomboyish and less maternal. "All control girls were sure that they wanted to have pregnancies and be the mothers of little babies when they grew up, whereas one third of the fetally androgenized girls with the adrenogenital syndrome said they would prefer not to have children. The remainder, as well as the ten girls with a history of fetal progestin, did not reject the idea of having children, but they were rather perfunctory and matter-of-fact in their anticipation of motherhood, and lacking the enthusiasm of the control girls" (101). Herbert Osofsky has raised questions about the control group, suggesting that they should have been girls reared in the same home, that is, siblings of the androgenized girls. Needless to say, Money and Ehrhardt do not even think in terms of "androgenizing" women.

## Chapter Three

1. Angus Campbell, Philip Converse, and Willard Rodgers, a study of changes over the life cycle, forthcoming. Present citation from a press release. The dysfunctional effects of children on marriage have been well documented. See Jessie Bernard, *The Future of Marriage* (World, 1972), Chapter 4, for an overview of the research.

2. The proportion of women involuntarily childless varies from time to time and from study to study. A 1939 study reported 3.4 percent among 4,500 married women; another study in the same year reported twice that many—7 percent— from a New York sample; in 1941, 9 percent was reported from a sample of married women patients; in 1950, a study of 1,080 Indianapolis couples reported 9.8 percent; a study in 1960 found 13 percent; and in 1972, Judith Blake Davis, reviewing the literature, concluded with an estimate of 26.7 percent ("Fallacy of the 5 Million Women," *Demography*, 9, Nov., 1972, p. 574). Over a lifetime, roughly a fifth of married women do not conceive at all (Paul H. Gebhard, Wardell B. Pomeroy, Clyde E. Martin, and Cornelia V. Christenson, *Pregnancy, Birth, and Abortion* Harper, 1958, p. 80). Before syphilis came under control, the sterility rate was much higher. For longtime trends in childlessness, see footnote 15, Chapter 2 above.

3. Leslie Aldrich Westoff and Charles Westoff, *From Now to Zero: Fertility, Contraception, and Abortion* (Little, Brown, 1971). Research on fertility is produc-

ing a variety of treatments which overcome "impaired fertility" and tend to increase multiple births.

4. J. E. Veevers, "Factors in the Incidence of Childlessness in Canada," *Social Biology*, 19, (Dec., 1972).

5. Robert C. Sorensen, *Adolescent Sexuality in Contemporary America* (World, 1973), p. 378.

6. Among the founders were a midwestern financial executive, a psychiatrist, a Princeton professor, a University of Kentucky professor, a University of the Pacific professor, two professional writers, and a former director of Zero Population Growth. Hugh Downs was also on the Honorary Board of Directors.

7. Judith Blake, "Coercive Pronatalism and American Population Policy," Preliminary Paper No. 2 on Results of Current Research in Demography (International Population and Urban Research, University of California, Berkeley, Dec., 1972), pp. 17–22.

8. Bureau of the Census, "Birth Expectations Data: June, 1971," Current Population Reports, Series P-20, No. 232, Feb., 1972). In studies of college students in 1965 and in 1970, the rise in the proportion wanting no children was from 0 to 6 percent in the College of the Pacific and from 10 to 18 in other colleges (Edward Pohlman, unpublished preliminary report of a study in the fall of 1972).

9. Unsigned, "All Dimples, My Lumpy-Dumpy Girlie," *Country Women* (no date), p. 4.

10. Martha Shuch Mednick and Sandra Schwartz Tangri, "New Social Psychological Perspectives on Women," *Journal of Social Issues*, 28 (1972), p. 12.

11. J. E. Veevers, "Voluntarily Childless Wives: An Exploratory Study," *Sociology and Social Research*, 57 (April, 1973), pp. 356–366.

12. Edward Pohlman, unpublished preliminary report. Comparison of students and parents showed interesting trends. Almost 10 percent of the students expected to have only one child whereas only 3.4 percent of the students themselves were only children; half expected to have 2 children, between a fourth and a fifth of their parents had had two. At the 3-child level, reverses as between the students and their parents turned up; 27.3 percent of the parents as compared to only 10 percent of the students themselves fell into the category of the 3-child family and the disparities between parents' families and children's expected families grew wider with each family size. Less than a fourth as many students as 4-child parents expected to have that many children; a tenth as many expected to have 5; fewer than a tenth as many expect to have 6. So few parents had 7 children and so few of the students expected to, that the ratio of 1 to 5, which seems like a reversal, may be disregarded.

13. In the Sorensen survey, the difference between young men and women was slightly less extreme; among the young men, 12 percent would probably not marry and have children, among the young women, 7 percent (*op. cit.*, p. 378).

14. Personal document.

15. Helene Deutsch, *Neuroses and Character Types, Clinical Psychoanalytic Studies* (International Universities Press, 1965), p. 199.

16. Quoted by Rita Kramer, "The No-Child Family," *New York Times* Magazine, Jan., 1973.

17. *Ibid.*

18. *Ibid.*

19. *Ibid.*
20. *Ibid.* It is interesting to note that a study made a generation ago of 862 childless professional couples—two-thirds of whom were voluntarily so—also attributed to them such motives as "self-centeredness" in 31 percent of the cases including social ambition, desire to travel, desire to make money, avoidance of work, protection of looks and figure. See Paul Popenoe, "Motivation of Childless Marriage," *Journal of Heredity*, 27 (1936), pp. 469–472.
21. Bernice E. Lott, "Who Wants the Children?", *The American Psychologist*, July, 1973, p. 579.
22. *Ibid.*, p. 580.
23. *Ibid.*, p. 580. Lott herself regrets the loss to motherhood of such able women. She wonders if they may not have been victimized by male chauvinist values to under-value the one function men cannot share with women. It may be relevant at this point to note that motherhood has recently been emerging as an issue in the feminist movement. An issue potentially as divisive as lesbianism was, but one which, there is reason to hope, will, like lesbianism, be successfully accommodated. One "straw in the wind" is the article by Lott which presents a critique of the earlier anti-motherhood position of the liberation movement. She fears that if the denigration of motherhood continues, "those who want to rear the children will be those who are fearful of autonomy and distrustful of their own capacities to function in the larger community"(582). If children can be seen as desirable rather than as necessary, not incompatible with other activities, then a more autonomous kind of woman will opt for motherhood, while "many will still decide . . . that parenthood is not for them"(582). A second "straw in the wind" is an article by Jane Alpert, a fugitive from the law living in the underground because of her association with the New Left bombing activities in the 1960s. She also, like Lott, presents a critique of the anti-motherhood stance of the feminist movement and sees motherhood as the optimum channel for the acquisition of power ("Mother Right: A New Feminist Theory," *Ms*, Aug., 1973, pp. 52 ff.). See Chapter 18 for further comment on this important paper.
24. Ellen Peck, *The Baby Trap* (Pinnacle Books, 1971), Chapter 12.
25. Jessie Bernard, *The Sex Game* (Atheneum, 1972), pp. 28, 329.
26. One team of theorists has, actually, proposed a system of parenthood licenses which could be exchanged. Every couple would be given coupons entitling them to, let us say, the authorized two children. If they did not want to use them they could transfer them to others who did and those who wanted more than two could acquire more than their allotment. The acceptance of voluntary nonmotherhood could achieve the same end without resorting to such structured systems. See Chapter 14 for comments on policies with respect to population control.
27. Jessie Bernard, *American Family Behavior* (Harper, 1942; Russell & Russell, 1973), Chapter 8.
28. See Chapters 7 and 8.
29. Paul C. Glick and Arthur J. Norton, "Perspectives on the Recent Upturn in Divorce and Remarriage," *Demography*, 10 (Aug., 1973), pp. 301, 303.
30. Eleanor D. Macklin, of Cornell University, has found enough research on cohabitation on campuses going on that she publishes a Research Newsletter on the subject.
31. Shirley Radl, *Mother's Day Is Over* (Charterhouse, 1973), pp. 231–232.

## Chapter Four

1. See Chapter 14 for discussion of "antinatalism."
2. Manpower Report of the President, 1973, p. 59.
3. Charles Vickery Drysdale, *Small Family System, Is It Injurious or Immoral?* (Viking, 1914).
4. Anne Firor Scott, *The Southern Lady, from Pedestal to Politics 1830–1930* (University of Chicago Press, 1970), p. 37.
5. *Ibid.*, p. 38.
6. *Ibid.*, p. 39.
7. Document supplied by Carol Smith-Rosenberg.
8. Margaret Sanger, *Motherhood in Bondage* (Brentano, 1928), pp. 40–41.
9. *Ibid.*, p. 43.
10. Although the concept of "ideal" number of children is not identical with "desired" number, the figures coincide in the case of 94 percent of the women queried in one study and may, therefore, be taken as referring to roughly the same attitudes (Ronald Freedman and others, *Family Planning, Sterility, and Population Growth*, McGraw-Hill, 1959, p. 218). For an excellent guide through the literature on family planning consult Edward H. Pohlman, *Psychology of Birth Planning* (Schenkman, 1969), Chapter 1.
11. C. F. Westoff, R. G. Potter, Jr., P. C. Sagi, and E. G. Mishler, *The Third Child* (Princeton University Press, 1963), p. 102.
12. The average number of children reported as wanted over time may be summarized as follows: 1930s, 2.79; 1950s, 2.78 among planners, 2.91 among nonplanners; 1954, 3.2 before marriage, 2.7 after marriage, 3.1 at time of interview (Westoff, Mishler, and Kelly, "Preferences in Size of Family and Eventual Fertility Twenty Years After," *American Journal of Sociology*, 62 (March, 1962), pp. 491–497; Freedman and others, *op. cit.*, p. 225).
13. *Life* Magazine, Jan. 8, 1971.
14. Judith Blake, "Ideal Family Size among White Americans: A Quarter of a Century's Evidence," *Demography*, 3, 1966, pp. 154–173. The modal number of children considered ideal during the era of the feminine mystique was 4, compared with 2.0 in 1941 and 3. 0 in 1945. The mean number was 3.4, 3.0, and 3.3 in these three years respectively. Non-Catholic men held the smallest ideal of family size and they remained relatively unchanged over time (Judith Blake, "The Americanization of Catholic Reproductive Ideals," *Population Studies*, 20, 1966, p. 43).
15. Ronald Freedman and others, *op. cit.*, p. 223.
16. Judith Blake, "Ideal Family Size among White Americans," *loc. cit.*, p. 169.
17. *Ibid.*
18. Ronald Freedman and others, *op. cit.*, p. 225.
19. G. Gurin, J. Veroff, and S. Feld, *Americans View Their Mental Health* (Joint Commission on Mental Illness and Health, Monograph series, No. 4, Basic Books, 1960), p. 137.
20. Bureau of the Census, Population Characteristics, "Birth Expectations and Fertility: June, 1972," Series P-20, No. 240, 1972, p. 1.
21. Manpower Report of the President, 1973, p. 62.
22. Westoff, Mishler, and Kelly, "Preferences in Size of Family," *loc. cit.*

23. Charles F. Westoff and Larry L. Bumpass, *The Later Years of Childbearing* (Princeton University Press, 1970), pp. 44–45. See also Chapter 3.

24. *Ibid.*, p. 45.

25. J. E. Vievers, "Voluntarily Childless Wives," *Sociology and Social Research*, 57 (April, 1973), pp. 356–366.

26. Judith Blake, "Reproductive Ideals and Educational Attainment among White Americans 1943–1960," *Population Studies*, 21 (Sept., 1967), pp. 159–174.

27. In one study, the average number of children women said they wanted was 2.8, the average number borne, 2.6 (Westoff, Mishler, and Kelly, "Preferences in Size of Family," *loc. cit.*). The discrepancy between wanted and actual number is greater among women who plan conception than among those who do not (Westoff and Bumpass, *op. cit.*, p. 44).

28. Westoff and Bumpass, *op. cit.*, p. 47. Jewish women were most successful in achieving the exact number of children wanted (55 percent); Catholic women, least (35 percent). In terms of averages, active Protestants and Jewish women had fewer children than they originally wanted; other Protestants had more; and Catholic women had about the desired average number. College women also had fewer children than originally wanted (p. 43).

29. Gary Becker, "An Economic Analysis of Fertility," *Demographic and Economic Change in Developed Countries* (Princeton: National Bureau of Economic Research, 1960), pp. 209–240.

30. Judith Blake, "Are Babies Consumer Durables?", *Population Studies*, 22 (March, 1968), p. 14.

31. *Ibid.*, p. 17.

32. The fact that religion has been found to be such an important factor in all studies of fertility justifies at least parenthetical comment here. Conservative religious denominations tend to support pronatalism, taking seriously the biblical injunction to replenish the earth. Although the Catholic Church, by permitting the rhythm method of birth control, has modified its former position (which implied almost compulsory procreation), it still teaches that motherhood is woman's true vocation (Pope Paul VI, Dec. 10, 1972). High fertility has not, however, always been a desideratum of the Church. There were, in fact, many centuries in which motherhood was denigrated. St. Paul spoke of the troubles and anxieties of family life, St. Jerome of crying infants and household chores. But it was the relationship of motherhood to concupiscence that stoked the downgrading of motherhood. St. Jerome referred to "the tumefaction of the uterus." The depravity associated even with procreative sexual relations (the only legitimate ones) contaminated motherhood itself. And marriage, which according to Paul was only better than burning because it provided some sort of regulation of sexuality, was to be tolerated only as an inferior status, a concession to human weakness. "Married people ought to blush at the state in which they are living." Both Tertullian and Ambrose believed that the end of the human species was not too great a cost for extirpating human sexuality. The Church struggled hard to dissociate motherhood from sexuality. It finally came to terms with the connection of sexuality with motherhood in 1563 at the Council of Trent when it made marriage a holy sacrament. Until then there was still argument about its sinfulness. The very term *matrimony* illustrates the relationship between marriage and motherhood. Of course sexual relations even within marriage were to be engaged in only for purposes of procreation. Motherhood was, in effect, the payment exacted for carnal indulgence. And even though the Council of Trent sanctified matrimony, it nevertheless anathematized the belief that virginity was not better (Wolfgang Lederer, *The Fear*

*of Women*, Harcourt Brace Jovanovich, 1968, pp. 163, 178ff). It was not until the First Vatican Council in 1854 proclaimed the immaculate conception as official doctrine that the Church succeeded finally in completely dissociating motherhood from sin. Mary herself was exonerated from the concupiscence which normally accompanies conception (Hilda Graef, *Mary: A History of Doctrine and Devotion*, Vol. 2. *From the Reformation to the Present Day*, Sheed & Ward, 1965, p. 82).

33. Westoff and Bumpass, *op. cit.*, p. 47.

34. Martha Schuch Mednick and Sandra Schwartz Tangri, "New Social Psychological Perspectives on Women," Journal of Social Issues, 28, 1972, p. 12.

35. P. K. Whelpton and C. V. Kiser, ed., *Social and Psychological Factors Affecting Fertility*, Vols. 1–5 (New York: Milbank Memorial Fund, 1946–1958).

36. Westoff, Potter, and Sagi, *op. cit.*, p. 290.

37. For a brief overview of the research on feelings of economic security as related to desire for children and family size see Edward Pohlman, *op. cit.*, pp. 166–167.

38. Westoff, Potter, and Sagi, *op. cit.*, Table 42.

39. There was no relationship at all among Catholics; five times as much among Jews as among Protestants (*Ibid.*, Table 29).

40. *Ibid.*

41. Westoff and Bumpus, *op. cit.*, pp. 267–268. We hasten to add that "unwanted" means unplanned pregnancies or Acts of God, not necessarily actively rejected children.

42. Throughout this book, as throughout all my writing, enormous emphasis has been placed on individual differences, on recognizing the uniqueness of all human beings. Lumping all women together and generalizing about them leads to stereotyping which impedes clear observation or accurate analyses. So how come the emphasis here is on similarities? After all the discussion of human differences does it finally end in a stereotype? The answer is no. It is not individual women who are all alike but sets of women. In the present context, for example, the whole spectrum of female differences is present among the women who have many as well as among the women who have few children. Among both a wide range of individual differences exist. What is true of women who want few is also true of women who want many in the sense that on the measured attitudes and qualities the whole gamut is present. And most, if not all, in both categories are moderate.

## Introduction to Part Three

1. Catherine E. Beecher, *Treatise on Domestic Economy*, rev. 3d ed. (Harper, 1947), p. 43. Present citation from Nancy F. Cott, ed., *Root of Bitterness, Documents of the Social History of American Women* (Dutton, 1972), p. 177.

## Chapter Five

1. *Le Grand Propriétaire de toutes choses*, quoted by Philippe Ariès, *Centuries of Childhood* (Knopf, 1962), p. 129.

2. Philippe Ariès, *op. cit.*, p. 38.

3. *Ibid.*, p. 39.

4. *Ibid.*, p. 39.

5. *Ibid.*, p. 39.

6. Laura L. Dittman, Introduction to Laura L. Dittman, ed. *Early Child Care, The New Perspectives* (Atherton, 1968), p. 5.

7. See Chapter 13.

8. Jeanne Binstock, "Motherhood: A Profession Facing Decline," *The Futurist*, 6 (June, 1972), p. 100. Ms. Binstock concluded that, with modern technologies at her disposal, a woman could tend to the care of an infant in three hours a day.

9. Ashley Montagu, "The Awesome Power of Human Love," *Reader's Digest*, July, 1971.

10. Anna Freud and Dorothy Burlingame, *Infants without Families* (International Universities Press, 1944).

11. John Bowlby, *Maternal Care and Mental Health* (Geneva: World Health Organization, 1951); Forward to *Determinants of Infant Behavior*, B. Foss, ed. (Methuen & Co., 1961).

12. H. F. Harlow and M. K. Harlow, "The Effect of Rearing Conditions on Behavior," *Bulletin of the Menninger Clinic* 26 (1962), pp. 213–224.

13. James W. Prescott, "Early Somatosensory Deprivation as an Ontogenetic Process in the Abnormal Development of the Brain and Behavior," Medical Primatology 1970 Proc. 2nd Conf. exp. Med. Surg. Primates, New York, 1969, pp. 356–375 (Basel: Karger, 1971); "Human Affection, Violence and Sexuality: A Developmental and Cross-Cultural Perspective" (with Cathy McKay), paper prepared for Society for Cross-Cultural Research, Feb., 1973; "Child Abuse and Child Care: Some Cross-Cultural and Anthropological Perspectives" (with Cathy McKay), paper prepared for National Conference on Child Abuse, June, 1973.

14. See Chapter 1.

15. See Chapter 2.

16. Leigh Minturn, William W. Lambert, and Associates, *Mothers of Six Cultures, Antecedents of Child Rearing* (Wiley, 1964), p. 291.

17. James W. Prescott, "Child Abuse and Child Care" (with Cathy McKay), *loc. cit.*

18. Alexander Mitscherleck, *Society without Father, A Contribution to Social Psychology* (Harcourt, Brace, & World, 1968), pp. 56–57.

19. See Chapter 1.

20. Alix Kates Shulman, quoted by Susan Jacoby in "That Was No Lady Writer, That (He Smiled) Was My Wife," in *The Washington Post*, June 11, 1972.

21. *Ibid.* It is not accurate to say that little was said about "dark underside of motherhood." There is a remarkably full research literature on it. (For an excellent résumé of it, see Edward Pohlman, *The Psychology of Birth Planning*, Schenkman, 1969, Chapters 5–8.) What is notable is not that the dark underside was not talked about but that, despite the adverse effects reported in the research literature, it was not really taken all that seriously. The romanticized media version, a bright, gay, fun-and-games version prevailed, helped in part by a special literary genre which made it all seem a happy romp and thus led each individual mother to feel that she alone did not find it as much fun as Mary Kerr, Phyllis McGinley, or Judith Martin. In the discussion here the personal documents of the women themselves have been selected rather than the tables and charts of the researchers; they communicate more. It is worth pondering the fact that women have been so reticent about their feelings; only in woman-to-woman discussions, if even then, did they dare to express their disillusionment with motherhood. The power of a myth to distort perception has rarely been better illustrated. Women have seen the idealized conception

of motherhood rather than the grim reality of their own experience propagated by the media.

22. Boston Women's Health Book Collective, *Our Bodies, Our Selves* (Simon & Schuster, 1973), p. 218.

23. As long ago as the seventeenth century, Montaigne was commenting—unfavorably—on the way adults used babies for their own amusement, like monkeys, and on their "frolickings, games, and infantile nonsense." Early in the seventeenth century a manual on etiquette expressed disapproval of the way people effused over their children and insisted on telling everyone about them. "My little son made me laugh so much! Just listen to this" (Philippe Ariès, *op. cit.*, pp. 130–131). (Haven't we all?) Ariès also refers to the "antipathy to children shown by solemn or peevish spirits (112)."

24. Their story becomes complicated only later when they must surrender close contacts with their children. If they invest themselves completely in their children the cost will be exacted when their children cease to need them.

25. This recognition of the joys of motherhood is inserted here to forestall the blizzard of protests always forthcoming from women who find motherhood completely fulfilling. I have already received hate mail from women when the material here presented was presented to live audiences.

26. Shirley Radl, in an admittedly non-random sample of about two hundred women interviewed, says she found only six who were "fulfilled by their roles and possessing a talent for nurturing and guiding their children in something approaching an inspired manner" (*Mother's Day Is Over*, Charterhouse, 1973, p. 230). Four of the six were nurses. Postpartum emotional disturbances do not appear in the reports of anthropologists. To the extent that they have intrinsic biological and physiological bases, they are, no doubt, present to some extent in all cultures, no matter how motherhood is structured. But, in addition to these causes there are, in our society, built-in stresses that exacerbate them. The Boston Women's Health Book Collective cites a British study of 137 women that found 64 percent displaying symptoms of anxiety, depression, mood swings, distractability, and shortened attention span (Kane, Harmon, et al., "Emotional and Cognitive Disturbance in Early Puerperium," pp. 99–102). In a study conducted in Detroit in the heyday of the era of the feminine mystique of the 1950s when having babies was a delightful, fulfilling experience almost by definition, two-thirds of 582 women replied that having babies had been very pleasant, 19 percent, mildly pleasant. Only 14 percent reported the experience as unpleasant. The authors found it a "striking possibility that more than one out of every ten mothers finds the arrival of a new baby more depriving than rewarding" (Miller and Swanson, *The Changing American Parent*, Wiley, 1958, p. 217). But in another Detroit study of 217 mothers, asked "how is a woman's life changed by having children?" most replied negatively. "Four times as many gave totally negative responses as gave totally positive. There was essentially no difference between working mothers and nonworking mothers in the number of positive or negative responses given" (Lois Hoffman in Hoffman and Nye, ed., *The Employed Mother in America*, Rand-McNally, 1963, p. 30). Among gifted women, on the other hand, Judith Birnbaum found that professional mothers expressed more positive aspects of motherhood than homemaking mothers (*Life Patterns, Personality Style and Self Esteem in Gifted Family Oriented and Career Committed Women*, Doctoral Dissertation, University of Michigan, 1971, p. 184). For dysfunctional aspects of motherhood see Edward Pohlman, *op. cit.*, Chapters 5–8; for research on negative impact of children on marriage, see Jessie Bernard, *The Future of Marriage* (World, 1972; Bantam, 1973), Chapter 4.

27. Boston Women's Health Book Collective, *op. cit.*, p. 207.
28. Lois Hoffman, *loc. cit.*, p. 28.
29. Judith Birnbaum, *op. cit.*, p. 48.
30. Niles Newton, *Maternal Emotions* (Hoeber, 1955), p. 100. The same point has been made by Elise Boudling in unpublished papers.
31. Boston Women's Health Book Collective, *op. cit.*, p. 10.
32. Alice Rossi, "Transition to Parenthood," *Journal of Marriage and the Family*, 30 (Feb., 1968), p. 35. The author also comments on the abruptness with which motherhood takes place as compared with the relatively longer learning process involved in most roles.
33. John L. Fischer and Ann Fischer, "The New Englanders of Orchard Town U.S.A.," in Beatrice Whiting, ed., *Six Cultures* (Wiley, 1963), p. 970. Among mothers with only grade-school education, guilt is less pervasive. Because their standards are different they feel less inadequate. Difficulties can more reasonably be attributed to such outside factors as housing, in-law problems, poor schools, or financial insecurities (Joseph Veroff and Sheila Feld, *Marriage and Work in America*, Van Nostrand, 1970, p. 151). For college women, the guilt load is especially heavy. They had wanted their children. They must therefore pay the price. Women who have had their children as the will of God are penalized in other ways, but their load of guilt is less. They did not ask for all those children. The children were thrust upon them.
34. Boston Women's Health Book Collective, *op. cit.*, p. 207.
35. Fischer and Fischer, *loc. cit.*, p. 971.
36. *Ibid.*, p. 943. In 1972 a case brought by the Federal Trade Commission alleged that the advertisement of a certain product pandered to the "guilty mother." The Commission charged that the advertisements "tend to exploit the emotional concern of such parents for the healthy physical and mental growth and development of their children by falsely portraying, directly and by implication . . . [its product] as a necessary food for their children to grow and develop to the fullest extent during the preadolescent years" (Nancy L. Ross, "Ads: Pandering to the 'Guilty Mother'?", *The Washington Post*, June 13, 1972). Such pandering is an old story. It has been used to sell books, encyclopedias, toys, what-have-you. A near-scandal was precipitated a generation ago when the name of Eleanor Roosevelt was invoked to show that homes with television sets gave children an added advantage in school achievement, implying that parents who did not supply their children with television were guilty of neglect.
37. Fischer and Fischer, *loc. cit.*, p. 943.
38. Jacob L. Gewirtz, "On Designing the Functional Environment of the Child to Facilitate Behavioral Development," in Laura L. Dittman, ed., *op. cit.*, pp. 197–198. The author is too discreet to speak of a power struggle. He speaks, rather, of "control of the environment by the infant."
39. *Ibid.*, p. 198.
40. *Ibid.*, p. 202.
41. *Ibid.*, p. 202.
42. See Chapter 1, also Chapter 7.
43. John C. Koss, president of a stereo head-phone company, reports on "The Auditory Environment in the Home." Among the noise hazards, in addition to appliances and power tools, he specifies the activities of normal healthy children. He therefore recommends that "because healthy children are normally active while adults need more quiet, set aside a retreat for yourself within the home"

("Increasing Home Noise Cause for Concern," *The Washington Post*, Aug. 19, 1972). Architects once did incorporate this idea in the concept of playrooms for children. Did the children stay in the playroom? Ask any mother. They always ended up, naturally, in the kitchen with their mothers. The longing of women for a "room of their own" had been a desideratum long before Virginia Woolf articulated it so eloquently, and not only among creative women but also among "only housewives."

44. Francis I. Nolly, "Plucky in Love," in Edgar Schmieder, ed., *The Mother the Heart of the Home* (St. Meinard, Ind.: Grail Publication, 1955), p. 143.

45. David G. Gil, *Violence against Children, Physical Child Abuse in the United States* (Harvard University Press, 1972), p. 118.

46. Mary Haworth in *The Washington Post*, July 2, 1972.

47. Boston Women's Health Book Collective, *op. cit.*, p. 207.

48. *Ibid.*, p. 217.

49. Francis Nolly, "Plucky in Love," *loc. cit.*, p. 148.

50. *Ibid.*, pp. 151–152.

51. *Washington Star and News*, Feb. 9, 1972.

52. Margaret Mead, *Blackberry Winter, My Earlier Years* (Morrow, 1972), pp. 262–263.

53. Graham B. Blaine, *Are Parents Bad for Children?* (Coward, McCann & Geoghegan, 1973), p. 95.

54. *Ibid.*, p. 95.

55. Alexander Mitscherleck, *op. cit.*, p. 56.

56. *Ibid.*, p. 56.

57. Niles Newton, *op. cit.*, p. 70.

58. Personal document from member of Mothers Anonymous. Another group is called Recovery. Another, Momma, serves a special single-parent population.

59. Letter to Ann Landers, *The Washington Post*, May 16, 1973.

60. See Chapter 1.

61. David G. Gil, *op. cit.*, p. 23.

62. *Ibid.*, p. 31.

63. *Ibid.*, p. 31.

64. *Ibid.*, p. 32.

65. *Ibid.*, p. 33.

66. Only 5,993 were reported in 1967 and 6,617 in 1968 (*Ibid.*, p. 135). Only an unknown proportion of all cases are reported.

67. *Ibid.*, pp. 146–147. Emphasis added.

68. James Prescott, "Human Affection, Violence and Sexuality" (with Cathy McCay), *loc. cit.*

## Chapter Six

1. Bruno Bettelheim, "A Look into Your Future: Child Rearing," *Today's Health*, Feb., 1973, p. 56.

2. G. Stanley Hall, *Adolescence: Its Psychology and Its Relations to Physiology, Anthropology, Sociology, Sex, Crime, Religion and Education*, 2 vols. (Appleton, 1904).

3. Kenneth Keniston, *The Uncommitted, Alienated Youth in American Society* (Delta, 1960).

4. Philippe Ariès, *Centuries of Childhood* (Knopf, 1963), p. 128.

5. *Ibid.*, p. 129.

6. J. B. de La Salle, *Conduite des écoles chrétiennes*, quoted *Ibid.*, p. 131.

7. d'Argonne, *L'Education de Monsieur de Moncade*, 1690, quoted *Ibid.*, p. 131.

8. *Ibid.*, p. 132.

9. Abbé Goussalt, *Le Portrait d'une honnête femme* (1693), quoted *Ibid.*, 132.

10. Robert Sunley, "Early Nineteenth-Century American Literature on Child Rearing," in Margaret Mead and Martha Wolfenstein, eds., *Childhood in Contemporary Cultures* (University of Chicago Press, 1955), p. 169.

11. Martha Wolfenstein, "Fun Morality: An Analysis of Recent American Child-training Literature," *Journal Social Issues*, 7 (1951), pp. 15–25.

12. Benjamin Spock, "Letter to the Reader," *Baby and Child Care* (Hawthorne, 1957).

13. Ruth Sidel, *Women and Child Care in China, A Firsthand Report* (New York: Hill & Wang, 1972), p. 188.

14. *Ibid.*, p. 188.

15. Clark Vincent, "An Open Letter to the 'Caught Generation,'" *The Family Coordinator*, 21 (April, 1972), p. 148.

16. *Ibid.*, pp. 147–150.

17. Alexander Mitscherleck, *Society Without Father* (Harcourt Brace & World, 1968), p. 57.

18. See Chapter 5, for example, on child abuse.

19. See Chapter 11 for possible changes in the future under the Equal Rights Amendment.

20. Robert S. Lynd, *Knowledge for What?* (Princeton, 1939).

21. Robert Sunley, *loc. cit.*, p. 151.

22. Included in this literature are the works of Margaret Mead, Ruth Benedict, Urie Bronfenbrenner, and the long series on "national character." In addition there are numerous studies showing how ethnic groups and socioeconomic classes differ from one another in child-rearing practices.

23. David Riesman, Nathan Glazer, and Reuel Denney, *The Lonely Crowd* (Doubleday Anchor, 1950).

24. Daniel R. Miller and Guy E. Swanson, *The Changing American Parent* (Wiley, 1958).

25. See, for example, "Work in America," report of a subcommittee on Employment, Manpower, and Poverty, Feb., 1973, 93rd Congress, 1st Session; also "Worker Alienation," 1972, Hearings on S.3916, July 25–26, 1972, 92nd Congress, 2nd Session.

26. Laura L. Dittman, Introduction to Laura L. Dittman, ed., *Early Child Care, The New Perspectives* (Atherton, 1968), pp. 5–6.

27. *Ibid.*, pp. 9, 10, 25, 33, 43, 278.

28. Marian Radke-Yarrow and Leon J. Yarrow, "Child Psychology," *Annual Review of Psychology*, 6 (1955), p. 11.

29. Robert F. Winch, "Marriage and the Family," in Joseph B. Gittler, ed., *Review of Sociology: Analysis of a Decade* (Wiley, 1957), p. 363.

Notes

30. Sally Provence, "The First Year of Life: The Infant," in Laura L. Dittman, ed., *op. cit.*, pp. 31–34.
31. Eleanor Pavenstedt, "Development During the Second Year: The One-Year-Old," in Dittman, pp. 41, 44, 45, 47, 48, 49, 51, 52.
32. Peter B. Neubauer, "The Third Year of Life: The Two-Year-Old," in Dittman, pp. 61, 74, 75.
33. Clara C. Park, "Through a Glass Darkly," *Book World*, April 29, 1973, p. 4. The article is a review of Sally Carrighar's *Home to the Wilderness*.

## Introduction to Part Four

1. Jessie Bernard, "Changing Family Lifestyles: One Role, Two Roles, Shared Roles," *Issues in Industrial Society*, 2 (Jan., 1971), pp. 21–28.
2. Alva Myrdal and Viola Klein, *Women's Two Roles* (Routledge and Kegan Paul, 1956), *passim*.
3. "It has been estimated that working women . . . end up doing a much higher proportion of society's total work (paid and unpaid) during a given year than men" (Special Task Force Report to the Secretary of Health, Education, and Welfare, "Work in America," U. S. Govt. Printing Office, 1973, p. 52).

## Chapter Seven

1. It was not only that work done in the home was not paid for that distinguished it from work done outside the home but also that it separated the work of women from the work of men. They left her to go off to work. The two kinds of work were not synchronized. See Jessie Bernard, *American Family Behavior* (Harper, 1942; Russell & Russell, 1973), pp. 535–536 for comments on the effects of such non-synchronizations of work.
2. Samuel H. Preston, "Female Employment Policy and Fertility," Report to the President's Commission on Population Growth and the American Future (reproduced, n.d.). See also Chapter 8.
3. See Chapter 11.
4. Among the most outstanding have been Thorstein Veblen, Sigmund Freud, Max Weber, Henry Marcuse.
5. Lionel S. Lewis and Dennis Brissett, "Sex as Work: A Study of Avocational Counseling," *Social Problems*, 15 (Summer, 1967), pp. 8–18.
6. Martha Wolfenstein, "Fun Morality: An Analysis of Recent American Child-training Literature," *Journal of Social Issues*, 7 (1951), pp.15–25. The literary genre which plays up the fun-and-games aspect of motherhood in the popular women's magazines illustrates the same approach.
7. The relative amount of motherwork devoted to child care varies also by class and rural-urban background. A study of Wisconsin farm housewives published in 1956 found that 14 percent of the fifty-three weekly hours of homemaking was devoted to care of the family (May L. Cowles and Ruth P. Dietz, "Time Spent in Homemaking Activities by a Selected Group of Wisconsin Farm Homemakers," *Journal of Home Economics*, 48, 1956, 29–35). Another study two years later divided farm work into outside and inside work. Of the work inside the home, about 8 percent of the roughly seven hours a day was devoted to child care (John E. Ross and Lloyd R. Bostian, "Time Use Patterns and Communications Activities of Wisconsin Farm Families in Winter," *Agricultural Journalism Bulletin*, 28, pp. 110). Since inside work constituted about

386

two-thirds of the entire work load, child care constituted even less than 8 percent of the entire work load. This study found no difference among families according to degree of urbanization but studies of urban families report considerably larger proportions of time devoted to child care. A Michigan study of 1954 found, for example, that upper-middle-class mothers were spending 37 percent of their housekeeping time in the mother role and lower-middle-class women, 46 percent (Dorothy G. Van Bortel and Irma H. Gross, "A Comparison of Home Management in Two Socio-Economic Groups," *Mich. Agr. Expt. Sta. Tech. Bul.* 240, 50 pp.). In Vermont farm homes, about 23 percent of homemaking activities went into family care (Marianne Muse, "Time Expenditures on Homemaking Activities in 183 Vermont Farm Homes," *Vt. Agr. Expt. Sta. Bul.* 530, 72 pp.). A range of 5 to 46 percent in proportion of time devoted to a variable defined in one study as care of family and in another as child care is difficult to interpret. Another difficulty results from the fact that in computing hours of work, care of children to some extent counts twice since it is usually performed along with other work around the house. Thus in the studies here cited care of children may be allotted relatively less amounts of time than were actually devoted to it.

8. See Chapters 8 and 10.

9. One New York case, cited by Ira Glasser (in a paper presented at the meetings of the Eastern Sociological Society, April, 1973), had to do with eight children whose institutional care by the city cost $80,000 annually. Given to women (if they could be found) who would care for them in their homes, the cost per child would have been far less and far superior in quality. The principle is an old one, embodied in the practice of foster-care, except that in the past the theory prevailed that no family should be paid for the care of foster children. Reimbursed for direct costs, to be sure, but not for the love and affection that were the raison d'être for foster care in the first place. The idea was that if women did not supply the care because they loved the child it could only be mercenary and hence inadequate. It was the willingness to supply the care out of love that counted as much as the care itself.

10. Unpublished study.

11. *Ibid.*

12. Philip Slater, *The Pursuit of Loneliness* (Beacon Press, 1970), p. 62.

13. While we are on the subject, the value placed on lactation in developing countries is relevant. Here the value of the milk mothers supply infants is put in the billions of dollars. "If 20 percent of the estimated 27 million mothers in urban areas of developing countries do not breast-feed, the loss in breast milk is $365 million. If half of the other 80 percent do not continue to breast-feed after the first six months, the total loss reaches $780 million. These estimates . . . clearly understate the situation; losses to developing countries more likely are in the billions" (Alan Berg, "Nutrition, Development, and Population Growth," *Population Bulletin*, 29 (1973), p. 22. For further discussion of related points, see Chapter 15.

14. Jessie Bernard, *Women and the Public Interest, An Essay on Policy and Protest* (Aldine, 1971), Chapter 5.

15. Alva Myrdal and Viola Klein, *Women's Two Roles* (Routledge and Kegan Paul, 1956), p. 35.

16. Samuel H. Preston, "Female Employment," *loc. cit.*

17. Edward Pohlman, *Psychology of Birth Planning* (Schenkman, 1969), p. 110. Pohlman is reporting a study by Robert Blood (1962) based on earlier work in 1929 and 1954.

18. James N. Morgan, Martin H. David, Wilbur J. Cohen, and Harvey E. Brazer, *Income and Welfare in the United States* (McGraw-Hill, 1962), p. 342.

19. Jessie Bernard, *Academic Women* (The Pennsylvania State University Press, 1964, Meridian Press, 1973), pp. 96–97. For a discussion of nineteenth-century efforts to professionalize domestic work, see Kathryn Kish Sklar, *Catharine Beechers, A Study in American Domesticity* (Yale University Press, 1973), Chapter 11.

20. Unpublished study.

21. Juanita Kreps, *Sex in the Marketplace: American Women at Work* (Johns Hopkins University Press, 1971), p. 74.

22. There is a fallacy involved here since the unmarried worker must also pay for the services which wives supply to married men. Being cared for costs, whether the care comes from a wife or from a hired servant. But let that pass.

23. Gardner Ackley, *Macroeconomic Theory* (Macmillan, 1961), p. 55. An in-depth examination of the economics of unpaid household labor would be too diversionary but as a backdrop for the thinking increasingly devoted to ways to pay women for work in the home it is entitled to at least parenthetical comments. In the original thinking about how to conceptualize the gross national product, it was decided not to include services contributed to the family by its own members. Certain concessions were made in the case of agricultural products consumed in the home and rent in the form of home ownership. And, more recently, in the case of transportation provided by an automobile. But inclusion of the services of housewives has never been accepted, despite the frequently cited absurdities such as that of the bachelors who married their housekeepers, thus reducing the gross national product; or that of the maid who entered the munitions factory during the war and afterwards married and became a homemaker. Now both she and her former mistress are excluded from the gross national product, reducing it rather than increasing it. Excluding the non-market work of women also renders international comparisons of gross national product infeasible. See Sylvia M. Gelber, "The Labour Force; the G.N.P.; and Unpaid Housekeeping Services," Women's Bureau, 1970, pp. 20–26. This is a paper given at the North American Conference on Labor Statistics, Houston, Texas in 1970. It is available also in a Bureau of Labor Statistics publication, *Labor Developments Abroad*, Aug., 1970, Vol. 15, No. 8. See also Juanita Kreps, *op. cit.*, pp. 66–69.

24. Ismali Abdel-Hamid Sirageldin, *Non-Market Components of National Income* (Institute for Social Research, University of Michigan, 1969), p. 72.

25. John Leonard, "More on Lessing," *New York Times Book Review*, May 13, 1973. The book under review is Doris Lessing's *The Summer before the Dark*.

26. Sirageldin, *op. cit.*, p. 54.

27. *Ibid.*, p. 64.

28. *Ibid.*, p. 64.

29. *Ibid.*, p. 67.

30. Chong Soo, "The Monetary Value of a Housewife," *American Journal of Economics and Sociology*, 28 (July, 1969), pp. 271–284.

31. The five studies: National Bureau of Economic Research, *Income in the United States, Its Amount and Description, 1909–1919* (1921): 25.1 percent of gross national product; Simon Kuznets, 1929, one-fourth of net product of social system; Ahmad Hussein Shamseddine, about 24 percent as of 1964 (*The Economic and Business Bulletin*, Temple University, Summer, 1968); Juanita Kreps, over a sixth as of 1960 (*op. cit.*, pp. 71–73); Morgan, Sirageldin, and

Baerwaldt, *Productive Americans* (Institute for Social Research, University of Michigan, 1966), 38 percent. See Sylvia M. Gelber, *loc. cit.*, for details.

32. See Chapters 8 and 18 for trends in the several kinds of occupations.

33. Sylvia M. Gelber, *loc. cit.*, p. 21.

34. Lorna R. Marsden, "Damned If They Do, Damned If They Don't; Women and Careers in Contemporary Canada," unpublished manuscript.

35. *Ibid.*

36. In France legislation was being drafted in 1973 to expand its social security system to include mothers. Earlier women whose current earnings were too low had been brought into the system by government contributions; the new legislation was intended for mothers who had never worked and plans were being considered for ultimately including women who had never worked (William Steif, "French Motherhood Pension Gains," *Washington Star Times,* Aug. 1, 1973).

37. Elizabeth Koontz, former head of the Women's Bureau, has suggested that "there should be Social Security accounts set up for housewives into which husbands could pay. That way, not only is the wife protected but, should she die, a man could hire a housekeeper to help care for the children instead of remarrying quickly for mere convenience rather than for love" (*Parade*, June 25, 1972). Senator Russell Long was making the same suggestion in 1971.

38. Erma Bombeck, *Washington Evening Star*, Feb. 19, 1973.

39. J. K. Galbraith, "The Economics of the American Housewife," *Atlantic Monthly* (Aug., 1973), pp. 78–83.

40. Jessie Bernard, *American Family Behavior*, p. 518.

41. T. B. Veblen, *Theory of the Leisure Class* (Macmillan, 1898).

42. Colin Clark, "The Economics of Housework," *Bulletin of the Oxford Institute of Statistics*, 20 (May, 1958). See also Chapter 8.

43. Ruth S. Cowan, "Domestic Technology and Social Change: The Washing Machine and the Working Wife," paper presented at The Berkshire Conference of Women Historians (Douglass College, March 3, 1973).

44. Joseph K. Folsom, *The Family and Democratic Society* (Wiley, 1934), p. 580.

45. Lucy Maynard Salmon, *Domestic Service* (Macmillan, 1897), p. 4.

46. T. B. Veblen, *op. cit.* A distinction should be made between the women who merely perform conspicuous consumption and those whose services are part of their husband's profession. W. Lloyd Warner, William Whyte, Jr., and C. Wright Mills all pointed out the importance of "social life" for a number of male careers, and Hanna Papanek has made a detailed analysis of the two-person career ("The Two-Person Career," *American Journal of Sociology*, Jan., 1973, pp. 852–872). In the spring of 1973 there was a great brouhaha when it was reported that military personnel were being assigned to serve as servants in the homes of the Big Brass. The military justified the practice on the grounds that senior officers had "to host a number of social functions at their homes" (*Washington Post*, May 24, 1973) and that "their wives . . . take on considerable social obligations" (*Ibid.*, May 18, 1973). The women in these two-person careers may or may not be mothers. Their part of the two-person career is not motherwork.

47. Myrdal and Klein, *op. cit.*, pp. 5–6.

48. Charlotte Perkins Gilman, "Economic Basis of the Woman Question," *Woman's Journal*, Oct. 1, 1898.

49. Jeannette Mirsky, in Introduction to Emily James Putnam, *The Lady, Studies*

*of Certain Significant Phases of Her History* (Sturges & Walton, 1910, University of Chicago Press, 1970), pp. xxxi–xxxiii. Actually, this description does not fit all women who have been labeled "ladies." Even the book that includes the above description has a chapter on "The Greek Lady" which quotes Ischomachos on the way he trained his young wife to operate his household. Her job included the organization of the slaves, selecting some for outdoor work, some for the household; she was to receive and store supplies as they came from the farm; she was to supervise every step from receiving the wool to the finished garment, and she was to take care of the sick in the household. "I told my wife that good laws will not keep a state in order unless they are enforced, and that she as the chief executive officer under our constitution must contrive by rewards and punishments that law should prevail in our house. By way of apology for laying upon her so many troublesome duties, I bade her observe that we cannot reasonably expect servants spontaneously to be careful of the master's goods, since they have no interest in being so; the owner is the one who must take trouble to preserve his property" (8–9). And in a later chapter on the ante-bellum Southern Lady, we learn that she worked at very much the same kind of jobs as Ischomachos' wife, and that, like her, she was seriously overworked. See also Anne Firos Scott, *The Southern Lady* (University of Chicago Press, 1970). These hard-working women were more like the chatelaines of the medieval castle who ran the business while the lords went about fighting one another. The new "ladies" were of a different ilk.

50. T. B. Veblen, *op. cit.*

51. Myrdal and Klein, *op. cit.*, pp. 5–6.

52. See Chapter 11.

53. Robert Smuts, *Women and Work in America* (Columbia University Press, 1959), pp. 14–15, 16, 25, 47.

## Chapter Eight

1. Karl Marx, *Capital*, Frederick Engels, ed. (Modern Library, 1906), p. 431.

2. Jergen Kuczynski, *The Rise of the Working Class*, trans. from the German by C. T. A. Ray (McGraw-Hill, 1967), pp. 62–63.

3. In 1929, for example, a study was reported which showed that 60 percent of the daughters who were gainfully employed contributed all their earnings to the family; only a quarter of them contributed less than half. Far fewer sons contributed. About a third of them contributed all their earnings; almost two-fifths contributed less than half (Agnes L. Peterson, "What the Wage-Earning Woman Contributes to Family Support," *Women's Bureau Bulletin*, No. 75, p. 11).

4. Karl Marx, *op. cit.*, p. 416.

5. Alexander Hamilton, *Report on the Subject of Manufactures*, Vol. I, 1791 (New York: Williams & Whiting, 1810), pp. 210–211. Present citation from Elizabeth Faulkner Baker, *Technology and Woman's Work* (Columbia University Press, 1964), p. 4.

6. Hamilton, *op. cit.*, p. 175. Present citation, E. F. Baker, *op. cit.*, p. 6. Recognition of the fact that the worker role of women was, at least in the case of some women, more valuable than the maternal role has a long history. In Argentina a learned man once expressed surprise that any society could operate without the services supplied by nuns. The institutionalization of a special service or worker role for women is an example of accepting the priority of the worker over the mother role.

7. E. F. Baker, *op. cit.*, p. 6.

8. *Ibid.*, p. 6.

9. Jergen Kuczynski, *op. cit.*, p. 62.

10. *Ibid.*, p. 62.

11. Report by Committee on Education relative to the education of children employed in manufacturing establishments, House of Representatives, Commonwealth of Massachusetts, March 17, 1936. Present citation, Jergen Kuczynski, *op. cit.*, p. 60.

12. Albert Gallatin, *Memorial for the Free-Trade Convention*, 1831. Present citation, E. F. Baker, *op. cit.*, p. 9.

13. *Ibid.*, p. 9.

14. E. F. Baker, *op. cit.*, p. 7. Sometimes that "place" was rather sinister. In eighteenth-century Paris, for example, we are told that "survival would have been scarcely possible, especially in times of dearth, but for the labor of . . . wives and children, even if this was confined to begging, prostitution or petty theft" (J. H. Plumb, "The Bad Old Days," *Book World*, March 4, 1973). The author is reviewing Jeffry Kaplow, *The Names of Kings* (Basic Books, 1973).

15. Fourteenth Annual Report, Bureau of Statistics of Labor, Boston, Massachusetts, 1883, p. 380.

16. Lucy Larcom, *A New England Girlhood* (Houghton Mifflin, 1889). Present citation from Nancy F. Cott, ed., *Root of Bitterness* (Dutton, 1972), pp. 126–129.

17. John R. Commons, ed., *A Documentary History of American Industrial Society*. Vol. 1 (Cleveland, 1919), p. 429.

18. Even in the cotton mills, immigrant women and girls began to take over the jobs formerly held by the native girls and women who then turned to more genteel occupations like school teaching. Thus, in the female, as in the male labor force, "working women" and "middle-class women" began to be distinguished. There began to be among women blue-collar and white-collar workers, with differences as marked as those between the classes among housewives. White-collar workers were "ladies"; blue-collar workers were "working women."

19. Elizabeth Janeway, *Man's World, Woman's Place, A Study in Social Mythology* (Delta, 1971).

20. Quoted by Baker, *op. cit.*, p. 84. Our thinking about sex roles is so stereotyped that we can think of no other kind of change than one that involves reversal of roles. Nor is it at all amusing to note that then, as now, the plea was being made to women to help preserve male sexuality. The entrance of women into the labor force was once seen as unsexing them; it is now being seen by some men as unsexing men (George Gilder, "The Suicide of the Sexes," *Harper's*, July, 1973, pp. 42–45).

21. E. F. Baker, *op. cit.*, p. 84.

22. *Ibid.*, p. 84.

23. *Ibid.*, p. 84.

24. *Ibid.*, p. 85.

25. It should be noted, however, that even women who are not mothers, must still integrate a domestic with a worker role, even if the domestic role refers to only their individual households. Working wives almost invariably retain responsibility for the household.

26. Leonard D. Cain, Jr., "Life Course and Social Structure," in Robert E. L. Faris, ed., *Handbook of Modern Sociology* (Rand-McNally, 1964), pp. 272–309.

27. The Latin language, for example, reflecting a fairly sophisticated society, had been able to distinguish seven stages, the French language as late as the middle of the sixteenth, only three (Philippe Ariès, *Centuries of Childhood*, Knopf, 1962, p. 25). We are all familiar with Shakespeare's seven stages. Other schemes differentiated the age of toys, of school, of love and sports, of war, of law, science, and learning (*Ibid.*, pp. 24–25). And we know that as our own society becomes increasingly complex we have had to add new stages such as adolescence and youth (Chapter 6).

28. In the past, and even today in some cultures, only one other criterion has approached child-bearing as a basis for classifying the critical points in the lives of women: a woman was a maiden, that is, a virgin, or she was not, for sociologically if not biologically the sexual initiation of a woman marked one of the most significant transitions of all for her. And even this criterion for demarcating stages was related to child-bearing.

29. Parenthetically, one might note that there has been a substratum of disparagement for each of the succeeding stages. With the menarche, a woman became unclean; with sexual initiation she lost her chief asset, her virginity. With childbearing she lost her sex appeal. With menopause she lost her reason for being. Every stage was a downward step.

30. National Manpower Council, *Womanpower* (Columbia University Press, 1957), p. 10.

31. Stewart Garfinkle, "Work in the Lives of Women," paper prepared for International Union for the Scientific Study of Population, 1969.

32. Jessie Bernard, *Women and the Public Interest, An Essay on Policy and Protest* (Aldine, 1971), Chapter 4.

33. Louis Harris and others, The 1972 Virginia Slims American Women's Opinion Poll, p. 8.

34. Helena Z. Lopata, *Occupation Housewife* (Oxford, 1971), pp. 51–53.

35. R. S. Weiss and N. M. Samuelson, "Social Roles of American Women: Their Contribution to a Sense of Usefulness and Importance," *Marriage and Family Living*, 20 (1958), pp. 358–366.

36. See Chapter 2.

37. Judith Blake Davis, "Are Babies Consumer Durables?", *Population Studies*, 22 (March, 1968), p. 24.

38. New Jersey NOW Task Force, *Dick and Jane As Victims* (published by authors, Princeton, 1973), pp. 25–26.

39. T. B. Veblen, *The Instinct of Workmanship*. "Idle curiosity" was a third "instinct."

40. Samuel H. Preston, "Female Employment Policy and Fertility," Report to the President's Commission on Population Growth and the American Future (reproduced, n.d.). For a summary of studies on financial reasons for employment of mothers, see Edward Pohlman, *op. cit.*, pp. 128–130.

41. Sidney Cornelia Callahan, *The Working Mother* (Warner Paperback Library, 1972), p. 16.

42. Jessie Bernard, *The Future of Marriage* (World, 1972), pp. 47–48. See also Chapter 11.

43. Sidney Cornelia Callahan, *op. cit.*, p. 24.

44. Joseph C. Rheingold, *The Fear of Being a Woman* (Grune & Stratton, 1967), p. 144.

45. Seymour Wolfbein, *Work in American Society* (Scott, Foresman, 1971), p. 24.

46. *Ibid.*, p. 25.

47. *Ibid.*, p. 23.

48. The occupations which are projected to increase most in the 1970–1980 decade are as follows: technical and professional, 3.4 percent; clerical, 2.4 percent; service, except household service, 3.0 percent; but operatives, a relatively low-level occupation, will increase by only 1.0 percent (Manpower Report of the President, 1972, p. 259).

49. Whether or not the women, who will be more educated, will accept the clerical jobs is moot. See Valerie Kinkade Oppenheimer, "Rising Educational Attainment, Declining Fertility, and the Inadequacies of the Female Labor Market," submitted to the Commission on Population Growth, Jan., 1972.

50. Seymour Wolfbein, *op. cit.*, p. 46.

51. *Ibid.*, p. 141.

52. Among the industries (as distinguished from the occupations) sex-typed for women are: textiles, apparel, and tobacco; those sex-typed for men are: iron, steel, automobile manufacture (*Ibid.*, 139).

53. Samuel H. Preston, "Female Employment," *loc. cit.*

54. Except in cases where wives and children were contracted out by husbands and fathers, as they were, indeed, in some cases. "Workers with many children were given preference in the matter of employment. A frequent advertisement, as in the Rhode Island Manufacturers' and Farmers' Record of May 4, 1820, went as follows: 'Wanted, family from five to eight children capable of working in a cotton mill' " (Jergen Kuczynski, *op. cit.*, p. 63).

55. Manpower Report of the President, 1973, p. 65.

56. Samuel H. Preston, "Female Employment," *loc. cit.*

57. Charles F. Westoff and Larry L. Bumpass, *The Later Years of Childbearing* (Princeton, 1970), p. 96. A belief in the fertility-inhibiting effect of labor-force participation underlies a good deal of the policy recommendations of anti-natalists.

58. The fertility of women in the Soviet Union does not seem to show the same inverse relationship. Peter Mazur reports that fertility is not related to labor-force participation one way or another ("Fertility and Economic Dependency of Soviet Women," *Demography*, 10, Feb., 1973, pp. 37–51).

59. Jessie Bernard, "One Role, Two Roles, Shared Roles," *Issues in Industrial Society*, Jan., 1972, pp. 21–28.

60. Stewart Garfinkle, "Work in the Lives of Women," *loc. cit.*

61. *Ibid.*

62. Manpower Report of the President, 1973, pp. 64, 66.

63. Fertility in the hundred largest metropolitan areas in the United States also related to median earnings, the ratio of female to male earnings, the "female-ness" of the industrial structure, and to the unemployment level (Samuel H. Preston, "Female Employment," *loc. cit.*).

64. Paul C. Glick and Arthur J. Norton, "Perspectives on the Recent Upturn in Divorce and Remarriage," paper presented at the April, 1972, meetings of the Population Association of America, Toronto, Canada.

65. Samuel H. Preston, "Female Employment," *loc. cit.*

66. Ravenna Helsen, "The Changing Image of the Career Woman," *Journal of Social Issues*, 28 (1972), p. 37.

67. The term career implies a course of development, commitment, and a heavy

investment over time. A job may be a sometime thing, agreeable enough while it lasts but replaceable by another.

68. The comments here are based on the following studies: Mervin Freedman, *The College Experience* (Jossey-Bass, 1967), Chapter 10; Rose K. Goldsen and others, *What College Students Think* (Van Nostrand, 1960), Chapter 4; James A. Davis, *Stipends and Spouses* (University of Chicago, 1962); Edna Rostow, "Conflict and Accommodation," in Robert Lifton, ed., *The Woman in America* (Houghton Mifflin, 1965); Shirley S. Angrist, "Variations in Women's Adult Aspirations during College," *Journal of Marriage and the Family* (Aug., 1972), pp. 465–468; Institute of Life Insurance, *Finance-Related Attitudes of Youth*, 1970, p. 14; Gilda F. Epstein and Arline L. Bronzaft, "Female Freshmen View Their Roles as Women," *Jour. Mar. & Fam.*, 34 (Nov., 1972), pp. 671–672; Lorraine M. Rand and Anna Louise Miller, "A Developmental Cross-Section of Women's Career and Marriage Attitudes and Life Plans," *Journal of Vocational Behavior*, 2 (1972), pp. 317–331; Doris B. Entwhistle and Ellen Gruenberger, "Adolescent's View of Women's Work Role," *American Journal of Orthopsychiatry*, 42 (1972), pp. 648–656; Z. Luria, "Women College Graduates: A Study of Rising Expectations," presidential address, New England Psych. Assn., Nov., 1972; Ravenna Helsen, "The Changing Image of the Career Woman," *Jour. Soc. Issues*, 28 (1972), pp. 33–46; Shirley Angrist and Elizabeth Almquist, *Careers and Contingencies: A Longitudinal Study of Women in College* (in process).

69. Rose K. Goldsen and others, *op. cit.*, p. 48.

70. Mervin Freedman, *op. cit.*, p. 139.

71. Z. Lurie, "Women College Graduates," *loc. cit.*; D. J. Watley, *Career or Marriage? A Longitudinal Study of Able Young Women* (National Merit Scholarship Corporation Research Reports, 1969, 5, pp. 1–16). Half of these merit-scholarship winners, 1956–1960, retested in 1965, had begun or planned to begin careers immediately after completing their education and 86 percent expected to have careers as soon as their children were old enough.

72. Z. Lurie, "Women College Graduates," *loc. cit.*

73. Referred to by Shirley Angrist and Elizabeth Almquist, *op. cit.*, Chapter 9.

74. *Ibid.*

75. Ravenna Helsen, "The Changing Image of the Career Woman," *loc. cit.*, p. 37.

76. Carolyn F. Etheridge, "Divide and Conquer: The Oppression of Working-Class Women," paper presented at Aug., 1972, meetings of Sociologists for Women in Society, New Orleans.

77. See Chapter 7.

78. Arthur B. Shostak, "Ethnic Revivalism, Blue-Collarites, and Bunker's Last Stand," *Sounding*, Spring, 1973, pp. 73–74. It is a matter of at least peripheral interest to note parenthetically that in this popular show a neighboring couple was introduced in 1973 in which stereotyped sex roles were also reversed. The husband cooked and the wife repaired appliances. In and of itself such sex role reversals for humorous effect is not new. The ploy of posing the brassy termagant opposite the henpecked husband is as old as the Maggie-Jiggs cartoon. Not so in the case of the Bunker neighbors; the butt of the joke is not on them but on Archie himself; we laugh at him, not at them.

79. *Ibid.*, p. 75.

80. See Chapter 14.

81. Manpower Report of the President, 1973, p. 220.

82. Manpower Report of the President, 1972, p. 44. Juanita Kreps, comparing the

1970 and 1960 data on labor-force participation by women, notes that "the pool of nonworking women with small children is diminishing" (*Sex in the Marketplace: American Women at Work*, Johns Hopkins University Press, 1971, p. 82).

83. See Chapter 11.

84. Manpower Report of the President, 1972, p. 44.

## Chapter Nine

1. Talcott Parsons, "The Social Structure of the Family," in Ruth Nanda Anshen, ed., *The Family: Its Function and Destiny* (Harper, 1959), pp. 262–263.

2. Judith Lynn Abelew Birnbaum, *Life Patterns, Personality Style and Self Esteem in Gifted Family-Oriented and Career-Committed Women* (Doctoral Dissertation, University of Michigan, 1971), p. 35.

3. *Ibid.*, p. 141.

4. Jessie Bernard, *Women and the Public Interest, An Essay on Policy and Protest* (Aldine, 1971), Chapter 5.

5. It seems helpful to distinguish between the offensive types of aggression which seem to characterize more men than women and the defensive types which seem to characterize more women, especially mothers, than men. The aggression which some animals, especially the great cats like the lioness, display in protecting their young is legendary.

6. *Time* Magazine, Nov. 10, 1952, p. 109. The author of the study was Stanley Talbot.

7. Christiane Collange, *The Well Organized Woman*, trans. Ghislaine Boulanger (Avon Publishers, 1971), pp. 250–251.

8. On one military base, mothers were told to take their family problems to the chaplain, not to call their husbands.

9. Margaret M. Poloma and T. Neal Garland, "Role Conflict and the Married Professional Woman," paper presented at Ohio Valley Sociological Society, 1970.

10. *Ibid.* If they did bring home their professional aggressiveness, they learned to temper it and "defuse" overly strong emotional responses by humor and intellectualization (Judith Birnbaum, *op. cit.*, p. 249).

11. Margaret M. Poloma and T. Neal Garland, *op. cit.*

12. Judith Birnbaum, *op. cit.*, p. 164. The Birnbaum findings are based on a study of 25 gifted professional women who had one or two children, a third of whom were under five and half of school age.

13. Lynda Lytle Holmstrom, *The Two-Career Family* (Schenkman, 1972), p. 137.

14. Eli Ginzberg and others, *Life Styles of Educated Women* (Columbia University Press, 1966), p. 118.

15. Judith Birnbaum, *op. cit.*, p. 166.

16. *Ibid.*, p. 166.

17. Z. Lurie, "Women College Graduates," presidential address, New England Psychological Society, Nov., 1972.

18. Eli Ginzberg and others, *op. cit.*, p. 119.

19. *Ibid.*, p. 120.

20. Talcott Parsons, "The Social Structure of the Family," *loc. cit.*, p. 271.

21. George Gilder, "The Suicide of the Sexes," *Harper's*, July, 1973, p. 43, 44.

22. Judith Birnbaum, *op. cit.*, p. 250.

23. *Ibid.*, p. 173.

24. Lynda Lytle Holmstrom, *op. cit.*, pp. 113–114.

25. Eli Ginzberg and others, *op. cit.*, p. 120.

26. Lynda Lytle Holmstrom, *op. cit.*, pp. 113–114.

27. *Ibid.*, p. 112.

28. *Ibid.*, p. 115.

29. Talcott Parsons notes that keeping the wife out of the labor force is functionally necessary to shield spouses from competition in the work world which constitutes the single focus of feelings of self-respect among American men (*op. cit.*, p. 265).

30. Margaret M. Poloma and T. Neal Garland, "The Myth of the Egalitarian Family: Familiar Roles and the Professionally Employed Wife," in Athena Theodore, ed., *The Professional Woman* (Schenkman, 1971), p. 755.

31. Margaret M. Poloma and T. Neal Garland, "Role Conflict and the Married Professional Woman," *loc. cit.*

32. *Ibid.*

33. *Ibid.*

34. *Ibid.*

35. *Ibid.*

36. Judith Birnbaum, *op. cit.*, p. 21.

37. Margaret M. Poloma and T. Neal Garland, "Role Conflict and the Married Professional Woman," *loc. cit.*

38. Helene Deutsch, *Neuroses and Character Types, Clinical Psychoanalytic Studies* (International Universities Press, 1965), p. 348.

39. Judith Birnbaum, *op. cit.*, p. 192.

40. See Chapter 10.

41. Faye Higier von Mering, "Professional and Non-professional Women as Mothers," *Journal of Social Psychology*, 42 (1955), p. 32.

42. Judith Birnbaum, *op. cit.*, p. 208.

43. *Ibid.*, p. 249.

44. *Ibid.*, p. 184. The non-employed mothers in this study did speak of self-sacrifice. See Chapter 11.

45. *Ibid.*, p. 249.

46. Lynda Lytle Holmstrom, *op. cit.*, p. 90.

47. Margaret M. Poloma and T. Neal Garland, "Role Conflict and the Married Professional Woman," *loc. cit.*

48. *Ibid.*

49. See Chapter 11.

50. Margaret M. Poloma and T. Neal Garland, "Role Conflict and the Married Professional Woman," *loc. cit.*

51. Judith Birnbaum, *op. cit.*, p. 249.

52. See Chapter 11.

53. Ann Harris, quoted from her statement at the Hearings called by Congresswoman Edith Green, in Judith Hole and Ellen Levine, *Rebirth of Feminism* (Quadrangle, 1971), p. 207.

54. Z. Lurie found that her "sample of college women graduating between 1967

and 1970 leads us to conclude that the brighter the woman . . . the greater her desire to work while raising young children" (Presidential address New England Psychological Society, Nov., 1972). Joseph Rheingold believes the active, vigorous women excel in both family and work roles.

55. Judith Birnbaum, *op. cit.*, pp. 231–232.

56. Margaret M. Poloma and T. Neal Garland, "Role Conflict and the Married Professional Woman," *loc. cit.*

57. Jessie Bernard, "Changing Family Lifestyles, One Role, Two Roles, Shared Roles," *Issues in Industrial Society*, 2 (1971), pp. 21–28.

58. Judith Hole and Ellen Levine, *op. cit.*, p. 24.

59. Colman McCarthy, "The State of Fatherland and the Comfort of Continuity," *The Washington Post*, June 17, 1973.

60. *Ibid.*

61. E. Page Doss, personal advertisement soliciting subscriptions for *Personal Report*.

62. Fathers are the major child caretakers in about 15 percent of the families of women in the labor force (Women's Bureau, 1969 *Handbook on Women Workers*, U. S. Govt. Printing Office, 1969, p. 49). Whether this situation represents a temporary stop-gap while the father happens to be unemployed, a permanent situation due to some disability rendering him unemployable, or a preferred division of labor between the parents is not clear from the data. In the research literature on working mothers, such role reversal is not even suggested as an ideal way to integrate the roles of mother and worker. It is included as a rational option in some cases, but not necessarily as ideal.

63. See Chapter 17 for further discussion of role sharing from a structural point of view.

64. Marriage contracts dealing with property still remain in common practice. They may specify anything that does not controvert morality or other laws.

65. Susan Edmiston, "How to Write Your Own Marriage Contract," *Ms* (Spring, 1972), pp. 66–72. The author summarizes the contracts made by William Godwin and Mary Wollstonecraft, by Margaret Sanger and J. Noah H. Slee, by Lucy Stone and Henry Blackwell. In the first two, separate households were specified. The Onassis contract is also noted.

66. Alix Kates Shulman, *Redbook*, April, 1971.

67. Advertisement in *Potomac* Magazine, March 11, 1973.

68. See Chapter 17.

69. Sidney Cornelia Callahan, *The Working Mother* (Warner Paperback, 1972), p. 46.

70. Leon Friedman, *New York Times*, Jan. 28, 1973.

71. *Ibid.*

72. Bruno Bettelheim, "Child Raising," *Today's Health*, April, 1973, p. 61.

73. William A. Westley and Nathan B. Epstein, *The Silent Majority* (Jossey-Bass, 1969), pp. 123–125.

74. Inge Broverman and others, "Sex Role Stereotypes and Clinical Judgments of Mental Health," *Journal of Consulting and Clinical Psychology*, 34 (1970), pp. 1–7.

75. Westley and Epstein, *op. cit.*, p. 51.

76. Alice Rossi, "Equality between the Sexes: An Immodest Proposal," *Daedalus*, 93 (Spring, 1964), p. 608.

77. Laura A. Kiernan, "Virginia Parents Give Up Child So It Can Live," *The Washington Post*, Sept. 21, 1973.

78. Leon Friedman, *loc. cit.*

79. William A. Simon and John Y. Gagnon, "A Look into Your Future Sex," *Today's Health*, April, 1973, p. 64.

## Chapter Ten

1. In 1972, 21.0 percent of all employed married women, husband present and, presumably, also children, were in professional, technical, managerial, or administrative occupations (Manpower Report of the President, 1973, p. 169).

2. In 1967, about 17 percent of mothers with children under eighteen who were in the labor force were widowed, divorced, or separated and hence, very likely, heads of households (Women's Bureau *1969 Handbook of Women Workers*, Table 16, p. 39).

3. See Chapter 14.

4. Almost twice as many employed married women living with their husbands were in clerical and sales occupations as in career-type occupations, 40.9 as compared with 21.0 percent (Manpower Report of the President, 1973, p. 169). About a fifth (19.7 percent) were in service occupations. In a study of fifty-eight blue-collar marriages, among the 17 percent of the mothers who were employed, the occupations were: part-time work in restaurants, cafeterias, department stores, factories, baby-sitting, office cleaning, typing, and piece-work at home (Mirra Komarovsky, *Blue-Collar Marriage*, Random House, 1962, p. 64). These occupations were lower than the national figures suggest. "Operatives" or unskilled blue-collar workers constitute only 14.4 percent of the working wives living with husbands and service workers only 19.7. Among women workers sixteen to thirty-four, two-thirds are in white-collar occupations (professional, technical, clerical, and sales); among those thirty-five and over, 60 percent are (Elizabeth Waldman, "Women at Work: Changes in the Labor Force Activity of Women," *Monthly Labor Review*, 93, June, 1970, pp. 10–18).

5. Mirra Komarovsky, *op. cit.*, p. 328.

6. Erik H. Erikson, *Identity, Youth and Crisis* (Norton, 1968), p. 265.

7. *Ibid.*, p. 265.

8. *Ibid.*, p. 266. The term Erikson uses is "female fidelity" but the context makes it probable that he is referring to female identity.

9. Anonymous, "When You Think You're God, You Can Go to the Devil in Style, A True Love Mini Story," *True Love*, Oct., 1972. In connection with the sentence in this quotation that "she's reacting the way anyone does when he realizes how much *he's* let *himself* be had," it is amusing to note in the August, 1973, issue of *The Atlantic Monthly* an article by John Kenneth Galbraith on the economics of the American housewife which is featured on the cover as showing "how the housewife is had." Academia is catching up with the women.

10. Mirra Komarovsky, *op. cit.*, p. 61.

11. *Ibid.*, p. 64.

12. See Chapter 14.

13. In 1970 "more than half of all husband-wife families today are multi-earner families in an average month . . . because wives . . . are out working" (Elizabeth Waldman, "Women at Work," *loc. cit.*, p. 15). As of 1968, among mothers who worked one week or more, 41.9 percent had some children under three;

almost half (46.5 percent) had children three to six; and 58.2 percent had children six to seventeen (14).

14. Alva Myrdal and Viola Klein, *Women's Two Roles* (Routledge & Kegan Paul, 1962), p. xi.

15. Mirra Komarovsky, *op. cit.*, p. 70.

16. Edmund Dahlström, *Changing Roles of Men and Women* (Beacon, 1967), p. 202.

17. Ruth Hartley found that working women did, indeed, see their labor force participation as part of their nurturant function ("Some Implications of Current Changes in Sex Role Patterns," *Merrill-Palmer Quarterly*, 1960, pp. 153–164.

18. Elizabeth Waldman, "Women at Work," *loc. cit.*, p. 10.

19. If she feels guilty it is about detesting housework, not about wanting a job (Mirra Komarovsky, *op. cit.*, p. 62).

20. Jessie Bernard, *The Future of Marriage* (World, 1972), Chapter 3; Walter Gove, "The Relationship between Sex Roles, Marital Status, and Mental Illness," *Social Forces*, 51 (Sept. 1972), pp. 34–44.

21. Loïs Hoffman, "Why They Work," in Lois Hoffman and Ivan Nye, ed., *The Employed Mother in America* (Rand-McNally, 1963), p. 29.

22. Louis Harris and others, The 1972 Virginia Slims American Women's Opinion Poll, Table 2. By 1972, however, the married women exceeded the married men in proportion, favoring the women's movement.

23. Carolyn Shaw Bell, "Age, Sex, Marriage, and Jobs," *The Public Interest*, 30 (Winter, 1973), p. 83.

24. *Ibid.*, p. 85.

25. M. G., "Should a Woman Work Part-Time?", Anne's Reader Exchange, *The Washington Post*, Oct. 8, 1972. This advice reflects a nugget of ancient wisdom. Some years ago a moving picture based on the Bluebeard theme introduced a novel twist to this idea. The wealthy man, instead of destroying his last wife, endowed her with a fortune of her own, thus freeing her from dependence on him. Thereafter she became a much more interesting and attractive companion to him. She did not lose her appeal, as the earlier wives had, and became a pleasure rather than an incubus. The moral was unequivocal.

26. Joyce Brothers, "When Your Husband's Affection Cools," *Reader's Digest*, Oct., 1972, p. 152.

27. Economic Report of the President, in 1972, p. 105.

28. George Gilder, "The Suicide of the Sexes," *Harper's*, July, 1973, pp. 48–49.

29. Since the concern here is with mothers rather than with children, there is little need to review the very considerable corpus of research dealing with the effect of maternal employment on children. Actually, the research evidence on the effect of maternal development is reassuring. For a resumé of the major studies see Lois Hoffman and F. Ivan Nye, eds., *op. cit.*, Chapters 4–14. Another review of the literature concluded that "a mother's sense of guilt is likely to be worse for the child than her working or not working" (Elizabeth Herzog and Cecelia E. Sudia, "Fatherless Homes: A Review of the Literature," *Children*, Sept.–Oct., 1968, p. 163. See also Abbott Ferriss, *Indicators of Trends in the Status of American Women*, Russell Sage Foundation, 1971, pp. 106–107). The age, sex, and special needs of children are important factors. So, obviously, are the arrangements the mother can make for the care of the child. Our knowledge of the child-care arrangements of mothers in the labor force is defective. The few studies available show that "for preschool-age children . . . care in their own homes ranks first, with care in someone else's home a close second.

A weak third place goes to group care in day care centers, nursery schools, and the like. Adequate state and local data on child care arrangements are almost totally nonexistent. . . . Annual Bureau of Labor Statistics studies have shown that the labor force participation rates of married women are usually higher if female relatives at least eighteen years old are in the family. Over the past decade, the proportion of working wives with such relatives was . . . about 1 out of 8 with children under eighteen; about 1 out of 20 with children under six. . . . Labor force participation rate of the mothers with preschool-age children was 38 percent when female relatives were present, compared to 30 percent without them" (Elizabeth Waldman and Kathryn R. Gover, "Children of Women in the Labor Force," reprint with Supplementary tables No. 2747 from *Monthly Labor Review*, July, 1971, p. 24). Some of the children of working mothers were probably "cared for by older sisters or brothers or other relatives. . . . In other cases, young children may have been cared for by their fathers who worked different shifts from the mother" (p. 25). One study of young mothers in a suburban community found that willingness of husbands to share in the care of children was a major factor in either actual or planned labor force participation (Mildred W. Weil, "An Analysis of the Factors Influencing Married Women's Actual or Planned Work Participation," *American Sociology Review*, 26, 1961, pp. 91–96). In 1965, 14.4 percent of the children under six were being taken care of by fathers in their own homes (Women's Bureau, *1969 Handbook on Women Workers*, Bul. 294, p. 49). Even grandfathers were reported as caretakers.

30. M. G., "Should a Woman Work Part-Time?", *loc. cit.*

31. *Ibid.*

32. Lois Hoffman, "Effects on Children: Summary and Discussion," in Hoffman and Nye, eds., *op. cit.*, p. 198.

33. Joseph Veroff and Sheila Feld, *Marriage and Work in America* (Van Nostrand, 1970), p. 202.

34. *Ibid.*, p. 199.

35. *Ibid.*, p. 173.

36. F. Ivan Nye and James F. Short, Jr., "Scaling Delinquent Behavior," *Amer. Sociol. Rev.*, 22 (June, 1957), p. 327.

37. Alice Marcella Propper, "The Relationship of Maternal Employment to Adolescent Roles, Activities, and Parental Relationships," *Journal of Marriage and the Family*, 34 (Aug., 1972), p. 419.

38. Helena Z. Lopata, *Occupation Housewife* (Oxford, 1971), p. 178.

39. Mirra Komarovsky, *op. cit.*, pp. 68–69.

40. Judith Tolmack, "Crumbling Families and the Generation Factor," *Potomac* Magazine, June 25, 1972, p. 8.

41. National Center for Health Statistics, *Selected Symptoms of Psychological Distress* (U. S. Department of Health, Education, and Welfare, 1970), Table 17, pp. 30–31.

42. Mirra Komarovsky, *op. cit.*, p. 70.

43. Manpower Report of the President, 1973, p. 220.

44. *Ibid.*, p. 220.

45. See Chapter 13.

46. Joseph Veroff and Sheila Feld, *op. cit.*, p. 174.

## Chapter Eleven

1. Manpower Report of the President, 1973, p. 220.
2. Wolfgang Lederer, *The Fear of Women* (Harcourt Brace Jovanovich, 1968), p. 69.
3. *Ibid.*, p. 70.
4. Audrey C. Cohen, Alida Mesrop, Carol Stoel, Newman II Committee—Task Force on Higher Education, *Women and Higher Education, Creating the Solutions*, reproduced, March, 1973, 28–29.
5. Frances Kaufman, "When Smugness Collapses," *New York Times*, Feb. 7, 1972.
6. See Dana Densmore quotation below.
7. The consciousness of a man with respect to the position of women is sometimes raised by the experience of his daughter rather than in response to his wife's. When he finds that this talented, brilliant young woman in whose education he has invested so much now has to walk three paces behind a young man, certainly not her superior and even, perhaps, not her equal, his mind clicks and he begins to understand what all the shouting is about.
8. Judith Lynn Abelew Birnbaum, *Life Patterns, Personality Style and Self Esteem in Gifted Family-Oriented and Career-Committed Women* (Doctoral Dissertation, University of Michigan, 1971), p. 184.
9. *Ibid.*, pp. 186, 244.
10. *Ibid.*, p. 208.
11. *Ibid.*, p. 164.
12. *Ibid.*, pp. 242–243.
13. *Ibid.*, pp. 244–245.
14. Personal document.
15. Birnbaum, *op. cit.*, p. 246.
16. Cited by Birnbaum, *op. cit.*, p. 38.
17. Anne's Reader Exchange, *The Washington Post*, Oct. 1, 1973.
18. W. C. Fields is quoted as once saying that if he were hard up and had to ask someone for a handout, he would not ask those in the audience howling with laughter at his performance but the little old lady in the back row who didn't understand one cynical word he said.
19. Abbott L. Ferriss, *Indicators of Trends in the Status of American Women* (Russell Sage, 1971), p. 173. Women who participate in groups differ rather markedly from women who do not. *Psychology Today* found that women who participated in groups were less likely than those who did not to believe that the children of working mothers were less well-adjusted than children of nonworking mothers, or that raising a child is a full-time job. Group experienced women seemed, thus, to resemble working women in their attitudes more than nonworking women.
20. Alva Myrdal and Viola Klein, *Women's Two Roles* (Routledge & Kegan Paul, 1962), pp. 26–27.
21. Valerie Kinkade Oppenheimer, "Rising Educational Attainment, Declining Fertility and the Inadequacies of the Female Labor Market," paper prepared for the Commission on Population Growth and the American Future, Jan., 1972.
22. François D. Lacasse, *Women at Home: The Cost to the Canadian Economy of the Withdrawal from the Labour Force of a Major Proportion of the Female*

*Population* (Royal Commission on the Status of Women in Canada, 1971), p. 12.

23. Judith Martin, "Rich Wildlife," *The Washington Post,* Feb. 4, 1973.

24. Samuel H. Preston, "Female Employment Policy and Fertility," Report to the President's Commission on Population Growth and the American Future (reproduced, n.d.).

25. Helena Z. Lopata, *Occupation Housewife* (Oxford, 1971), pp. 50–52.

26. Ravenna Helsen, "The Changing Image of the Career Woman," *Journal of Social Issues,* 28, 1972, p. 39.

27. *Ibid.,* p. 36. A later reinterpretation of the earlier research showed that so far from being the forlorn characters there represented, the career-oriented "freshmen . . . were serious, idealistic, ambitious, anxious to make a good impression, and . . . 'late developers'" (p. 39).

28. *Ibid.,* p. 39.

29. L. Stoltz, "Effects of Maternal Employment on Children: Evidence from Research," *Child Development,* 31 (1960), pp. 749–782.

30. Z. Lurie, "Women College Graduates," presidential address, New England Psychological Society, 1972.

31. Shirley Angrist and Elizabeth Almquist, *Careers and Contingencies: A Longitudinal Study of Women in College* (forthcoming), Chapter 9.

32. See Chapter 9.

33. Birnbaum, *op. cit.,* p. 256.

34. Elsieliese Thrope, "The Favored Sex," *Reader's Digest,* May, 1972, p. 84; "Postscripts from the 'Favored Sex,'" a symposium, *Ibid.,* Oct., 1972, p. 106. It is only fair to note that not all opponents of the women's liberation movement as symbolized in the Equal Rights Amendment base their position on sex grounds. Many favor equal rights but object to the amendment route. Some believe the Fourteenth Amendment already guarantees equal rights; others that the 1964 Civil Rights Act does, obviating the need for an amendment.

35. Lillian Hellman and others, "Women on Women," An American Scholar Forum, *American Scholar,* Autumn, 1972, p. 603.

36. Carolyn Heilbrun, *Ibid.,* p. 607.

37. Unsigned letter in *The Vocal Majority,* organ of the NOW National Capital Area Chapter, 4 (May, 1973), p. 16.

38. Dana Densmore, "The Slave's Stake in the Home," *Journal of Female Liberation,* No. 2 (Feb., 1969), pp. 15, 16, 19.

39. Edmund Dahlström, *The Changing Roles of Men and Women* (Beacon, 1967), p. 172.

40. Louis Harris and others, The 1972 Virginia Slims American Women's Opinion Poll, 1972.

41. Some opponents of the amendment objected to the inclusion of "by any state" on the grounds that this was a violation of state's rights.

42. See Chapter 15.

## Chapter Twelve

1. Philippe Ariès, *Centuries of Childhood* (Knopf, 1963), p. 392.

2. *Ibid.,* p. 392.

3. Arthur W. Calhoun, *A Social History of the American Family,* Vol. 1. *Colonial Period* (Cleveland: Arthur H. Clark, 1917), p. 38.

4. Philippe Ariès, *op. cit.*, p. 393.

5. Ruth Schwartz Cowan, "A Case Study of Technology and Social Change," paper prepared for the Berkshire Conference of Women Historians, March, 1973. Actually, of course, no amount of "hardware" takes the place of efficient servants. Servants were never so plentiful or so institutionally established in the United States as in Europe, but there was a time when a mother could hire "help." Today women feel lucky if they can count on a cleaning woman regularly. Babysitting is a permanent emergency for many mothers.

6. James L. Halliday, *Psychosocial Medicine* (Norton, 1948), pp. 112–121.

7. Jessie Bernard, *Social Problems at Midcentury* (Dryden Press, 1957), p. 376.

8. Efrem Sigel, "General Learning," *Saturday Review of Education*, May, 1973, p. 47; Mary Jo Bane, "Child Care Co-ops," *Idem.*, p. 71.

9. See Chapter 8.

10. Jeanne Binstock, "Motherhood: An Occupation Facing Decline," *The Futurist*, 6 (June, 1972).

11. Quoted by Wolf von Eckhardt, "High Rise Vanity and Power," *The Washington Post*, Jan. 30, 1973.

12. Wolf von Eckhardt, "Toward New Horizons, Challenging the High Rise," *Ibid.*, June 23, 1973.

13. Irving Tallman, "Working-Class Wives in Suburbia: Fulfillment or Crisis?", *Journal of Marriage and the Family*, 31 (Feb., 1960), p. 67.

14. David R. Boldt, "The Architect of Suburbia, He Is Not Proud," *The Washington Post*, Dec. 11, 1972.

15. In the United States, of households headed by persons 45 to 54 years of age, almost half had two or more cars, 14 percent had three or more (Bureau of the Census, "Household Ownership of Cars and Light Trucks: July 1972," Series P-65, Feb., 1973, p. 1).

16. Arthur Shostak, Preface to *America's New Towns: Green-Belt Cities and the Greening of America*, a report prepared for Decision Sciences Corporation, 1971.

17. Barbara Hollins, *Family Structure, Child Care, and New Communities*, Master's Thesis, Columbia University Graduate School of Architecture, June, 1971, quoted *Ibid.*, Chapter 9, p. 3.

18. Arthur Shostak, *op. cit.*, Chapter 8, p. 2.

19. *Ibid.*, p. 3.

20. There remains the original step of finding the three congenial families. The experience of communes illustrates how difficult that may be. An analogous problem arose in connection with charter airplane flights. If aggressive people could assemble congenial individuals to share a flight, the rates could be reduced. The organizer did the selling, so the airline company could reduce the rates. All too soon the organizing of groups was taken over by travel agents or reverted to the companies.

21. National Broadcasting Company program, June 19, 1973.

22. Daniel R. Miller and Guy E. Swanson, *The Changing American Parent* (Wiley, 1958), pp. 57, 58, 92.

23. Senate Bill S. 3916, 92nd Congress, 2nd Session, introduced August 14, 1972, Section 3 (2). This bill was "to provide for research for solutions to the problem of alienation among American workers. . . ."

24. Jeanne Binstock, "Motherhood: An Occupation Facing Decline," *loc. cit.*, p. 99.

25. *Ibid.*, pp. 101–102.

26. *Ibid.*, p. 100.

27. David B. Lynn, "Determinants of Intellectual Growth in Women," *School Review*, 80 (Feb., 1972), p. 245.

## Chapter Thirteen

1. Although there had been by 1973 a significant decline in the rate of unwanted births from about one in three in 1965–1970 to about 10 to 15 percent, according to Charles Westoff in a newspaper interview (Victor Cohn, "Studies of Unwanted Pregnancy," *The Washington Post*, September 27, 1973), still Frederick S. Jaffe, vice-president of Planned Parenthood, spoke of unwanted pregnancies as of "epidemic proportion . . . in terms of ordinary public health criteria" (*Ibid.*).

2. Abortions and vasectomies have contributed to the decline in unwanted pregnancies. The peak in vasectomies occurred in 1971 when there were 850,000 reported. Since then there has been a decline in the rate. By 1973, more than 3 million Americans had been sterilized, increasing by about a million annually. Until 1965, over half—about 60 percent—were women; by 1971, 80 percent were men. A year later, only 68 percent were men (Brian Sullivan, "Gaining Control: Modernized Contraception," *The Washington Post*, Aug. 3, 1972). The increasing use of labaroscopy or "bellybutton" sterilization for women was cutting down on resort to vasectomy (Nancy L. Ross, "Decline of Vasectomy," *Ibid.*, July 5, 1973). Overall throughout the world, the condom was still the most widely used contraceptive and in the United States, the second most widely used (Philip D. Harvey, "Condoms—A New Look," *Medical Aspects of Human Sexuality*, 7, July, 1973, p. 70).

3. Jessie Bernard, *The Sex Game, Communication between the Sexes* (Atheneum, 1972), pp. 25–26.

4. Robert T. Francoeur, *Utopian Motherhood* (Doubleday, 1970), p. viii.

5. Joanne Nadol, "Who Shall Live? Who Shall Be Aborted? Who Shall Reproduce? Who Shall Decide?", *Johns Hopkins University Magazine*, May, 1973, p. 14.

6. *Ibid.*, p. 14.

7. *Ibid.*, p. 14.

8. *Ibid.*, p. 13.

9. *Ibid.*, p. 16.

10. James R. Sorenson, *Social Science Frontiers, Social Aspects of Applied Human Genetics* (Russell Sage Foundation, 1971), p. 10.

11. *Ibid.*, p. 10.

12. *Ibid.*, p. 10.

13. Edward Grossman, "The Obsolescent Mother, A Scenario," *Atlantic Monthly*, June, 1971, p. 46. A sperm bank was opened in France in 1973, despite Church opposition. It is reported that 1,000 babies resulted from artificial insemination last year (Paul Majendie, "An 'Adulterous Bank,'" *The Washington Post*, June 10, 1973). Donors must be under forty, receive no pay, have at least one child, and receive wife's consent. The donated semen is mainly for infertile couples and for cases in which, for one reason or another, a man is expected to lose his ability to reproduce. Frozen semen is reported to remain viable and effective for at least ten years. In this country, 520 births from frozen semen are known

to have taken place (Jerome K. Sherman, "Reliability of Frozen Sperm," *Medical Aspects of Human Sexuality*, 7, July, 1973, pp. 111–112).

14. Edward Grossman, "The Obsolescent Mother, A Scenario," *loc. cit.*, p. 44.

15. Bernard D. Davis, "Threat and Promise in Genetic Engineering," in Preston Williams, ed., *Ethical Issues in Biology and Medicine* (Schenkman, 1973), pp. 17–31.

16. Strange deviations from this overall sex ratio occur from time to time. In the spring of 1973 when psychologists were testing children for fall admission to the school system's kindergarten in one affluent county, there were almost twice as many boys as girls.

17. Robert G. Martin, a biochemist, quoted in *The Washington Post*, Jan. 2, 1973.

18. Marc Lappe, "How Much Do We Want to Know about the Unborn?", *The Hastings Center Report*, 3 (Feb., 1973), p. 8.

19. Robert Theobold and others, *Dialogue on Women* (Bobbs-Merrill, 1967), p. 12.

20. Robert Francoeur, *op. cit.*, p. 21. An earlier statement is even more extravagant: "The possibility of human genetic modification . . . is potentially one of the most important concepts to arise in the history of mankind. I can think of none with greater long-range implications for the future of our species. Indeed, this concept marks a turning point in the whole evolution of life. For the first time in all time a living creature understands its origin and can undertake to design its future" (Robert L. Sinsheimer, "The Prospect for Designed Genetic Change," *American Scientist*, 57, Spring, 1969, p. 134).

21. Robert Francoeur, *op. cit.*, p. 102.

22. *Ibid.*, p. 100.

23. *Ibid.*, p. 100.

24. *Ibid.*, p. 106.

25. *Ibid.*, p. 106.

26. Nadol, *loc. cit.*, p. 15.

27. *Ibid.*, p. 16.

28. *Ibid.*, p. 16.

29. *Ibid.*, p. 17.

30. *Ibid.*, p. 17.

31. *Ibid.*, p. 17.

32. James R. Sorenson, *op. cit.*, p. 11.

33. *Ibid.*, p. 12.

34. *Ibid.*, p. 12.

35. *Ibid.*, p. 23.

36. *Ibid.*, p. 22.

37. Only 3 percent of respondents in a Harris poll in 1969 knew about artificial insemination from a donor's semen.

38. Robert Francoeur, *op. cit.*, p. 116.

39. *Ibid.*, pp. 118–119.

40. *Ibid.*, p. 114.

41. Sorenson, *op. cit.*, p. 24. In the Harris poll, 70 percent of the women approved of hormone treatments to improve fertility; 62 percent approved of insemination with husband's sperm; 28 percent approved of insemination with anonymous donor sperm; 39 percent approved of egg implantation, 25 percent, in

vitro babies; 37 percent, 43 percent, and 35 percent respectively felt the three preceding procedures were justified in case of infertility or danger to the mother; 39 percent opposed all three new methods; 40 percent considered them morally wrong. Over half of the women would feel love toward an in vitro baby with her own egg and own husband's sperm; about half would love an egg-implant child of her own; 38 percent would love an in vitro baby not of her own egg and husband's sperm. About two-fifths felt the child would love its parents in any event (Robert Francoeur, *op. cit.*, p. 116).

42. Edith Hamilton, *Mythology, Timeless Tales of Gods and Heroes* (Mentor, 1969), pp. 65–66.

43. Nadol, *loc. cit.*, p. 14.

44. Czeslaw Milosz, *The Captive Mind* (Vintage, 1953), pp. 4–5. This part of the book appeared originally in *The Partisan Review*, Sept.–Oct., 1951.

45. Jeanne Binstock, "Motherhood: An Occupation in Decline," *The Futurist*, 7 (June, 1972), p. 100.

46. Anke A. Ehrhardt, R. Epstein, and John Money, "Fetal Androgens and Female Gender Identity in the Early-Treated Androgenital Syndrome," *Johns Hopkins Medical Journal*, 122 (1968), pp. 160–167; Anke A. Ehrhardt, K. Evers, and John Money, "Influence of Androgen and Some Aspects of Sexually Dimorphic Behavior in Women with the Late-Treated Androgenital Syndrome," *Ibid.*, 123 (1968), pp. 115–122; John Money and Anke A. Ehrhardt, *Man and Woman, Boy and Girl* (Johns Hopkins University Press, 1972), Chapter 6. Dr. Harold Osofsky, of Temple University, has raised questions about the controls used in this important work, suggesting that they should have been sisters of the subjects.

47. Alice S. Rossi, "Maternalism, Sexuality, and the New Feminism," in Joseph Zubin and John Money, *Contemporary Sexual Behavior: Critical Issues in the 1970s* (Johns Hopkins University Press, 1973), pp. 154–155.

48. In Washington, there were in 1973 about a hundred "behavior modifiers." The Department of Health, Education, and Welfare was investing $3,000,000 in behavior modification; every school district in the city was using it. More than 400 teachers and parents were being trained in it (Philip J. Hilts, "The Controllers," *Potomac* Magazine, April 29, 1973, p. 18).

49. *Ibid.*, p. 44.

50. Constance Stapleton, "A New Game Plan for Parents and Children, What Makes a Good Parent?", *Ibid.*, p. 42.

51. Leaflet describing the work of the Individual Psychology Association of Greater Washington, Inc.

52. Newspaper report in *The Washington Post*, April 23, 1973, of a paper given by Georges Ungar and S. R. Burzynasky at the fifty-seventh annual meeting of the Federation of American Societies for Experimental Biology.

53. At least a passing nod should be directed toward another technology, brain surgery. Lobotomies—which leave patients in a quasi-vegetative condition—were once more popular than they now are. Housewives constituted a relatively disproportionate percentage of the population selected for this treatment since their lives did not demand much more than the limited mentality left after the operation. The implications were not lost on feminists.

54. Robert Francoeur, *op. cit.*, p. ix.

55. Daniel Bell, "Living with Technology," in the Frank Nelson Doubleday lecture at the Smithsonian Institution, reported in *The Washington Post*, Dec. 17, 1972.

## Chapter Fourteen

1. In the United States contraception is still controlled largely by women in marriages in which control is practiced at all. Feminists protest the unequal burden implied and increasingly the sharing of contraception is being urged on men. In marriages in which the wife is over thirty, men and women tend to assume equal responsibility.

2. See Chapters 2–5.

3. The same thing happened in Rumania in the sixties. Legitimizing abortion in 1956 had cut down the birth rate drastically; limiting abortion in 1966 restored it (*Population Bulletin*, 28 Aug., 1972, p. 9).

4. Maurice Hexter, *Social Consequences of Business Cycles* (Houghton Mifflin, 1921).

5. The Economic Opportunity Act, for example, the Manpower Development and Training Act, and the Elementary Education Act.

6. Rufus E. Miles, Jr., "Whose Baby Is the Population Problem?", *Population Bulletin*, 16 (Feb., 1970), p. 26.

7. Two single-spaced pages of typescript are required to list all the programs for services provided for in the seven administrative units of the Federal government that provide services or funds for child care, namely: Agriculture, HEW, HUD, Labor, Office of Economic Opportunity, Small Business Administration, and the Appalachian Regional Commission (Women's Bureau, *Federal Funds for Day Care Projects*, Pamphlet 14, revised, 1972).

8. Women's Bureau, *Day Care Facts*, Pamphlet 16, revised, 1973, p. v.

9. Judith Blake, "Population Policy for Americans: Is the Government Being Misled?" *Science*, 164 (May 2, 1969), p. 529.

10. *The Washington Post*, July 25, 1973.

11. *Ibid.*, Sept. 21, 1973.

12. James R. Sorenson, *Social Aspects of Applied Human Genetics* (Russell Sage Foundation, 1971), p. 30.

13. Joanne Nadol, "Who Shall Live? Who Shall Be Aborted? Who Shall Reproduce? Who Shall Decide?", *Johns Hopkins University Magazine*, 24 (May, 1973), p. 15.

14. In July, 1973, an amendment to the Social Security Act went into effect which places most of the costs of renal dialysis—which may range from $6,000 to $30,000 a year—under Medicare; kidney transplants also come under Medicare. The costs were estimated to rise to a billion in 1978 (*Newsweek*, July 16, 1973).

15. Dr. Y. Edward Hsia, quoted by Victor Cohn, "New Devices to Show Pre-Birth Defects," in *The Washington Post*, Dec. 30, 1972.

16. Public opinion polls were reporting quite inconsistent results in the summer of 1972. A Gallup poll conducted in June, 1972, asked: ". . . do you agree or disagree with the following statement regarding abortion: 'The decision to have an abortion should be made solely by a woman and her physician?' " Among the women respondents, 66 percent replied affirmatively; among the men, 63 percent (*The Washington Post*, Aug. 25, 1972). But a Harris poll, reported August 11, 1972, found only 45 percent of the women and 51 percent of the men favoring legalized abortion in reply to the question: "Do you favor or oppose allowing legalized abortions to take place up to four months of pregnancy?" It is hard to assess the significance of the enormous discrepancy between the two polls. The Gallup question had been introduced with the

statement "As you may have heard, in the last few years a number of states have liberalized their abortion laws." It may be, therefore, that respondents were assuming legalized abortion and were responding only to the criteria to be allowed in permitting it. The Harris poll was addressing another question, namely whether there should be legalized abortion at all, whatever the criteria. This resolution of the inconsistency is supported by the fact that a Gallup poll in 1969 which asked a question more comparable with the 1972 Harris poll— whether the respondent favored "a law which would permit a woman to go to a doctor to end a pregnancy at any time during the first three months"—and found 40 percent accepting legalized abortion. A University of Michigan poll dated in the fall of 1972 agreed with the Harris poll. As in the Harris poll, more men than women agreed that abortion should never be forbidden or that it should be permitted if the women would have difficulty having the child. As in all such polls, the young were far more liberal than the old and hence more in-dicative of the future (John Lear, "Women Lead Opposition to Abortion," *The Washington Evening Star and Daily News*, April 17, 1973).

17. Infanticide has been a fairly widespread practice. There is evidence, according to some students, in the Old Testament account of the willingness of Abraham to sacrifice Isaac, in the prohibition against giving one's seed to Moloch, and in the abandonment of Ishmael, Hagar's son (Charlotte Haldane, *Motherhood and Its Enemies*, Doubleday, 1928, p. 20). Less speculative is the research on in-fanticide presented by Otto Pollak. He notes that although it is declining in in-cidence as contraception practices improve, still it does survive. He notes also how unchanging it remains, almost the same today as in the past. Suffocation, strangulation, and the inflicting of wounds appear with monotonous regularity over the decades (*The Criminality of Women*, University of Pennsylvania Press, 1950, pp. 20–23). Reports of abandonment of infants in trash cans and bus depots, even airplanes, appear in the news at not infrequent intervals.

18. W. G. Sumner, *Folkways* (Ginn, 1906), pp. 309–312.

19. Similar perplexities have shown themselves in other countries, including Communist East Europe and non-Communist Japan. The politics of mother-hood is very much the same everywhere.

20. Surprisingly, in the Gallup poll referred to above, more Republicans (67 per-cent) than Democrats (56 percent) agreed with the statement that the decision to have an abortion should be made solely by a woman and her physician. The larger Catholic constituency in the Democratic Party might account for this unexpected difference.

21. Wolfgang Lederer, *op. cit.*

22. Philippe Ariès, *Centuries of Childhood* (Knopf, 1963), p. 114.

23. Jessie Bernard, *American Community Behavior* (Dryden Press, 1949), pp. 637–643.

24. Even in non-totalitarian societies child care has profound political implications as illustrated, for example, in Israel. See Rivka W. Bar-Yosef, "Pre-School Child Care in Israel," Chapter 16 in Pamela Roby, ed., *Child Care—Who Cares?* (Basic Books, 1973).

25. H. Kent Geiger, *The Family in Soviet Russia* (Harvard University Press, 1968), p. 72.

26. *Ibid.*, p. 72.

27. Samuel Saloman, *The Red War on the Family* (New York: Little & Ives, 1922), p. 97.

28. Geiger, *op. cit.*, pp. 72–73.

29. Urie Bronfenbrenner, *Two Worlds of Childhood*, U. S. and USSR (Russell Sage, 1970), p. 151.

30. "Kindergartens in the neighborhoods are run by revolutionary committees . . . since the Cultural Revolution. . . . This structure gives an idea of the importance of the Communist Party in basic decision making and in insuring that the decisions are carried out. . . . This cohesiveness makes it possible for child-care institutions as with one voice to teach young children in a unified value system that seemingly is accepted by all" (Ruth Sidel, *Women and Child Care in China*, New York: Hill & Wang, 1972, pp. 86–87).

31. *Ibid.*, p. 82.

32. *Ibid.*, p. 71.

33. James A. Harrell, letter to the editor of *The Washington Post*, September 11, 1972.

34. See Chapter 15.

35. Irja Echola, "Children's Day Care in Finland" in Pamela Roby, ed., *Child Care—Who Cares?* (Basic Books, 1973), Chapter 20.

36. Economic Report of the President, 1973, pp. 109–111.

37. Richard M. Nixon, President's Message Establishing the Office of Child Development, January, 1969.

38. Richard M. Nixon, Presidential Veto Message on the Comprehensive Child Development Bill, Dec., 1971.

39. Title V of the 1935 Social Security Act was only a minor component, thrown in almost incidentally. The real involvement was with Unemployment Insurance. Of several thousand pages of hearings on the Act, only two or three paragraphs were devoted to the aid to dependent children provision. It was not controversial; it was not new; it was consensually accepted. The "widow-and-orphan" had been a charge on communities for centuries. The mental image was of a white working-man's wife left widowed, with several children to take care of (Patricia Tanabe, "Views of Women's Work in Public Policy in the United States: Social Security and Equal Pay Legislation 1935–1967," paper presented at The Berkshire Conference of Women Historians, March, 1973).

40. Erika Streuer, "Current Legislative Proposals and Public Policy Questions for Child Care," in Pamela Roby, ed., *op. cit.*, Chapter 5.

41. Stephen Hess, National Chairman, Report of the White House Conference on Youth, April 18–22, 1971, Estes Park, Colorado (U. S. Gov. Printing Office, 1972), p. 241. A Minority Resolution stated that "the purpose of marriage should be to bear and be responsible for children."

## Chapter Fifteen

1. Rufus E. Miles, Jr., "Whose Baby Is the Population Problem?", *Population Bulletin*, 16 (Feb., 1970), p. 21. See Chapter 4 above.

2. See Chapter 3.

3. The purchase of babies on the black market and extortion in kidnapping are criminal exceptions to the no-exchange mores.

4. Edward H. Pohlman classifies the costs as: costs to husband-wife relations; psychological costs such as anxiety, conflict, separation, and grief, mess, noise, confusion, congestion; time, confinement, and hard work; health and appearance; out-of-home roles; parental role; role conflict; costs to father's role; and financial costs (*Psychology of Birth Planning*, Schenkman, 1969, Chapters 5–8). See Chapter 5 also.

5. Among those who have paid attention to this problem are: Ernst Engel, Louis L. Dublin, Alfred J. Lotka, Erven J. Long, Peter Dorner, Alfred Sauvy, W. F. Ogburn, George Malignas, Jean L. Permock, Sara A. Sohn, J. L. Nicholson, and A. M. Henderson. See a resume of this literature by Thomas J. Espenshade, "The Price of Children and Socio-economic Theories of Fertility," *Population Studies,* 26 (July, 1972), pp. 207–221.

6. Ritchie H. Reed and Susan McIntosh, *Costs of Children,* prepared for the Commission on Population and the American Future, 1972.

7. Garrett Hardin, *Birth Control* (Pegasus, 1970), p. 26.

8. *Ibid.,* p. 27.

9. If there are special health problems, the costs may be astronomical. See Chapter 14.

10. Bureau of the Census, "Household Ownership of Cars and Light Trucks: July 1972," Series P-65, Feb., 1973, p. 1.

11. Samuel H. Preston, "Female Employment Policy and Fertility," Report of the President's Commission on Population Growth and the American Future (reproduced, n.d.).

12. It was once said that Alma Glueck had sung hundreds of thousands of dollars worth of lullabies to her children. The children of women who command less for their talents in the market "cost" less. The typist's child, for example, has an "opportunity cost" of only about $7,500 a year. The Economic Report of the President, 1973, recognized these differences: "One study has found that women college graduates tend to reduce their outside work when their children are small more than less educated women and that they also devote more time to the training of their children. . . . This pattern . . . results in a considerable sacrifice of earnings and one may infer that these women have therefore placed a very high value on the personal attention they can give their children" (p. 107).

13. Carolyn Shaw Bell, "Employment Policy for a Public Service Economy: Implications for Women," *Social Policy* Sept.–Oct., 1972. See Chapter 10 for evidence.

14. A movement to "re-tool," that is, help women overcome these handicaps, has been a major trend in higher education since the 1960s. There is also a considerable amount of thought invested in preventing the loss of skills and knowledge during the drop-out years by provision of part-time jobs or professional practice during this period.

15. Economic Report of the President, 1973, p. 104.

16. Thought is being given to the idea that the experience women accumulate in child care is also "human capital" and might well be viewed in that light.

17. See Chapter 4.

18. Pauline Bart, "Mother Portnoy's Complaint," *Transaction,* 8 (Nov.–Dec., 1970), pp. 69–74.

19. Audry Siess Wells, quoted by Myra MacPherson, "Women Panelists Report on Bias," *The Washington Post,* Sept. 10, 1972.

20. Stewart Garfinkle, "Work in the Lives of Women," paper prepared for International Union for the Scientific Study of Population, London, 1969.

21. Eli Ginzberg and Associates, *Life Styles of Educated Women* (Columbia University Press, 1966), p. 102.

22. Meryle Secrest, "Pondering a Future with Too Many People," *The Washington Post,* July 23, 1972.

23. Marianne Käne and others, "Social Rights in Sweden before School Starts," in Pamela Roby, ed., *Child Care—Who Cares?* (Basic Books, 1973).

24. Carolyn Shaw Bell, *loc. cit.* The impact of this insight becomes greater when we remember that in the Soviet Union Jews who wished to emigrate to Israel were being charged for exit visas an amount equal to the costs incurred by the government in training them. If such an investment in their training was a cost to the government, so, similarly, is such an investment in the training of their own sons and daughters by mothers a monetary cost to them—as well as a contribution to the economy which gains by the improved productivity of the offspring.

25. See Chapter 1.

26. See Chapters 7 and 8.

27. Abt Associates, cited by Mary P. Howe and Ralph D. Husby, "Economics of Child Care: Costs, Needs and Issues," in Pamela Roby, ed., *op. cit.*, Chapter 8.

28. *Ibid.*

29. *Ibid.*

30. Dale R. Meers and Allen E. Marans, "Group Care of Infants in Other Countries," in Laura L. Dittmann, ed., *Early Child Care, The New Perspectives* (Atherton, 1968), p. 278. See also Chapter 7.

31. Rowe and Husby, *loc. cit.*, pp. 99–100.

32. *Ibid.*, Table 2.

33. Frederick C. Green, "A National Overview," *Sharing*, March, 1972, p. 13. Among the very wealthy, of course, the price of child-care services may be stratospheric even at home. Private apartments, even private cars, are among the inducements advertised to attract qualified women in the more affluent families.

34. About 5 percent at least can be counted on in the form of voluntary contributions, either in kind or in services. The question is sometimes raised—as a putdown of women who want relief from the 24-hour day of the mother role—isn't it ridiculous to exchange the care of one's own children for the care of other children in, let us say, a nursery school or kindergarten? The answer is no, it is not ridiculous. The care of other children in a limited time interval in the company of other adults is different from the care of one's own child in an interminable time interval all alone, and bound by different ties.

35. In 1973, federal standards on the maximum number of children to be cared for by each adult were doubled leading day care groups to charge that such standards would lead to "warehousing" rather than child care (Austin Scott, "HEW Defends New Cutback Rules," *The Washington Post*, Feb. 16, 1973).

36. Almost all—94 percent—of the teachers received less than $7,200; 65 percent, less than $4,800. That is how much the people who supply the tender-loving-care are worth.

37. Gwen Morgan, "Private Approaches to Environmental Solutions: Some Sensible and Outrageous Ideas," paper prepared for conference by Educational Facilities Laboratories, Ann Arbor, Michigan, Nov., 1970.

38. Gwen Morgan rejects subsidized programs with income eligibility limits. They constitute subsidies "for the exploitation of women, since the only employment which a mother can accept while her child is in such a program must not raise her income above a certain level. She must be poor and stay poor to receive public help with her children. Such a policy can only perpetuate poverty" (*Ibid.*)1 She finds this outrageous.

39. Rowe and Husby, *loc. cit.* Plans and curricula for using high school students are already available from, for example, the Educational Development Center of Newton, Mass.

40. See Chapter 12.

41. Florence A. Ruderman, *Child Care and Working Mothers* (Child Welfare League of America, 1968), p. 212. Although this study is no longer current, it was still being cited by the Women's Bureau Pamphlet, 16, in 1973.

42. The number of baby-sitters quintupled between 1950 and 1960 (Elizabeth Faulkner Baker, *Technology and Women's Work*, Columbia University Press, 1964, p. 110) and has no doubt vastly increased since that time.

43. Florence A. Ruderman, *op. cit.*, p. 212.

44. See Chapter 16.

45. George Canby Robinson, at a conference on national defense problems sponsored by the Milbank Foundation, reported in *Time* Magazine, May 12, 1941, p. 43.

46. See Chapter 2.

47. Stuart Hampshire, "A New Philosophy of the Just Society," *The New York Review of Books*, Feb. 24, 1972, pp. 37–38. This is an article reviewing John Rawls, *A Theory of Justice* (Harvard, 1971).

## Introduction to Part Seven

1. Graham B. Blaine, Jr., *Are Parents Bad for Children? Why the Modern American Family Is in Danger* (Coward, McCann & Geoghegan, 1973), pp. 14–15.

2. *Ibid.*, pp. 15–16. See pages below for Dr. Blaine's suggested alternative.

3. Martha Shuch Mednick and Sandra Schwartz Tangri, "New Social Psychological Perspectives on Women," *Journal of Social Issues*, 28 (1972), p. 12.

## Chapter Sixteen

1. Herbert A. Otto, "Communal Alternative," *The Modern Utopian*, 1972, pp. 9–13. Reprinted from the *Saturday Review*, April, 1971.

2. Except at Twin Oaks, founded on the principles expounded in B. F. Skinner's *Walden Two*. Here the socialization of children by means of the principles of conditioning is a primary concern.

3. Sandy Eccli, "Familia," *Communitas*, 2, Sept., 1972, p. 39.

4. Kat Grieve, "Selecting Members for Your Commune," *Communities*, 1, Dec., 1972, p. 13.

5. Unsigned, "Virginia, The New Dominion of Community," *Ibid.*, p. 6.

6. Bennett M. Berger, Bruce M. Hackett, and R. Mervin Millar, "Child Rearing in Communes," in Louise Kapp Howe, ed., *The Future of the Family* (Simon & Schuster, 1972), p. 168.

7. Kate Mewhinney, "Women and Communal Societies," *Communities*, 1 (Dec., 1972), p. 38.

8. Unsigned, "Religious Society of Families," *Communities*, 1 (Dec., 1972), p. 49. Death is to be by suicide; there is a moral obligation to self-destruct at age 72. All power is solar power, wind power, water power. Horses and bicycles furnish transportation.

9. Joseph Marshall, "The Bruderhof: Society of Brothers," *Communitarian*, 1 (March–April, 1972), pp. 19–22. See also Robert Friedmann, "Society of Broth-

ers," in Richard Fairfield, ed., *Utopia U.S.A.* (San Francisco Alternatives Foundation, 1972), pp. 33–35.

10. Graham B. Blaine, Jr., *Are Parents Bad for Children?* (Coward, McCann & Geoghegan, 1973, p. 130). See also Marcy Feuer, "Up in the Vermont Woods," in Fairfield, *op. cit.*, pp. 84–86, and Terry Mollner, "In Warwick," *Ibid.*, pp. 86–88.

11. Irving Herman, "Omega House," *Ibid.*, 1972, p. 208.

12. Peter Finkle, "Communes on Walden Two," *Ibid.*, 1972, p. 210.

13. Matthew Israel, "Walden Two: Behavioral Community," *Ibid.*, p. 214.

14. Stephen M. Pittell, quoted by Michael Kernan and Leroy Aarons, "The Village: A Rural Alternative," *The Washington Post*, Sept. 13, 1972.

15. Michael Kernan and Leroy Aarons, *Ibid.*

16. See Chapter 6.

17. Bennett Berger, Bruce M. Hackett, and R. Mervin Millar, *loc. cit.*, p. 161.

18. Bennett Berger, "The Decline of Age Grading in Rural Anarchist Communes," paper presented at American Sociological Association, New Orleans, Aug., 1972.

19. *Ibid.*

20. Berger, Hackett, and Millar, *loc. cit.*, p. 162.

21. *Ibid.*, p. 162.

22. *Ibid.*, p. 163.

23. Bennett Berger, *op. cit.* A report on nine rural communes in California and Oregon found the same situation. There were relatively few children; women still performed traditional women's roles; none were self-supporting, public and private welfare being the major source of income in all but one. Supportive relatives, unemployment compensation, welfare, and gifts were the forms such income took ("Commune Tripping," *The Communitarian*, 1, March-April, 1972, pp. 23–30). Food stamps constitute another form of subsidy.

24. Berger, Hackett, and Millar, *loc. cit.*, p. 170.

25. Bennett Berger, *op. cit.*

26. Berger, Hackett, and Millar, *loc. cit.*, p. 169.

27. Unsigned, "Youth Liberation Front," *The Modern Utopian*, 1972, p. 203. Other items in this manifesto call for full civil rights, repeal of laws prohibiting marijuana and other consciousness expanding drugs, sexual self-determination, anti-colonialism, resistance to militarism, reform of the penal system, abrogation of child-labor laws which "force youth into the status of a dependent colony," environmental and ecological programs, anti-technology, socialism, revolutionary solidarity. The document ends: "Youth will make the revolution—youth will keep it young."

28. Unsigned, "Kids in Communes," *Ibid.*, pp. 200, 202.

29. Jud Jerome, in "Conversation with Jud Jerome," *Communitas*, 1 (July, 1972), p. 28.

30. Michael Kernan, "Like a Tiny Adult Already Pursuing Its Karma," *The Washington Post*, Sept. 10, 1972.

31. Kernan and Aarons, *loc. cit.*

32. Ross V. Speck and others, *The New Families, Youth Communes, and the Politics of Drugs* (Basic Books, 1972), p. 89. Rosabeth Kanter, who has done a considerable amount of research on urban communes, writes in a personal letter that the references to Speck's book are misleading because the research for it

was done several years ago. "Communes in cities have little or no resemblance to hippy crash pads of the drug culture era."

33. *Ibid.*, p. 90.

34. *Ibid.*, p. 90.

35. *Ibid.*, p. 106.

36. *Ibid.*, p. 105.

37. *Ibid.*, p. 102.

38. *Ibid.*, p. 101.

39. *Ibid.*, p. 110.

40. *Ibid.*, pp. 110–111.

41. *Ibid.*, p. 111.

42. Berger, Hackett, and Millar, *loc. cit.*, p. 168.

43. *Ibid.*, p. 160.

44. *Ibid.*, p. 163.

45. *Ibid.*, p. 165.

46. Margarita Donnelly, "Alternate-Culture Mirrors America," in Louise Kapp Howe, ed., *op. cit.*, pp. 67–68. The references to fleeing fathers in this moving document wring grudging assent to a statement by George Gilder: "The idea that the father . . . will necessarily be inclined to remain with it [the family], is nonsense. The man must be made equal by the culture; he must be given a way to make himself equal" ("The Suicide of the Sexes, Are Feminism, Gay Liberation, and the Playboy Philosophy Really All the Same?", *Harper's*, July, 1973, p. 43).

47. Lois Haas, "Familia," *Communitas*, 2 (Sept., 1972), p. 39.

48. Sandy Eccli, "Familia," *Ibid.*, p. 39.

49. Lois Haas, "Familia," *loc. cit.*

50. Unsigned, "Kids in Communes," *loc. cit.*, p. 202.

51. *Ibid.*

52. Personal letter.

53. Rosabeth Moss Kanter, "Structure, Functions, and Impact of Urban Communes," Progress Report to National Institutes of Mental Health, on study of Historical Context and Social Role: Boston Urban Communes, 1973, The Domestication of the Counterculture; Rosabeth Moss Kanter and Karilyn Halter, "The De-Housewifing of Women: Equality between the Sexes in Urban Communes," paper presented at 1973 meetings of the American Psychological Association; Marilyn B. Halter, "The Swan Family," Preliminary Case Report I for Rosabeth Moss Kanter's project on Structure, Functions, and Impact of Urban Communes.

54. Kathleen Kinkade, *A Walden Two Experiment* (Morrow, 1973), pp. 130 ff.

55. *Ibid.*, p. 146.

56. Unsigned, "Child Meetings in Earnest," *Communites*, 3, 1973, pp. 47–48.

57. Sara, "Metas and Maya," *Leaves of Twin Oaks*, Vol. 2 (June–July, 1973), p. 11.

58. B. F. Skinner, Foreword to Kathleen Kinkade, *op. cit.*, p. x.

59. Consider the obstacles Jacqueline Onassis has had to overcome to assure privacy for her children. Twin Oaks may have to overcome the same kind, even though to a lesser extent. A professor of child development at one university once remarked, when it was called to his attention that his children at a faculty picnic behaved no better than the children of graduate students, that they

hadn't read the books yet. More is expected of the children of achieving parents.

60. Herbert Otto, "Communal Alternatives," *loc. cit.*, p. 13.

## Chapter Seventeen

1. It was, however, repudiated by the President primarily because it favored legalized abortion on demand.

2. See Chapter 4.

3. Dwight J. Ingle, *Who Should Have Children?* (Bobbs-Merrill, 1973), pp. 101–102.

4. *Ibid.*, pp. 97–98.

5. *Ibid.*, p. 104. See Chapter 3 for the activities of the National Organization for Nonparents in this direction.

6. Harriet F. Pilpel, "Limiting Population: The Voluntary Approach," *Civil Liberties*, Nov., 1971, reproduced in *Population Profile* by the Population Reference Bureau, Nov., 1971, pp. 4–5.

7. Michael F. Brewer, "Voluntarism and Coercion: The Ground Between," Population Reference Bureau, p. 7.

8. *Ibid.*

9. Rufus E. Miles, Jr., "Whose Baby Is the Population Problem?", *Population Bulletin*, 16 (Feb., 1970), p. 21.

10. *Ibid.*, p. 26.

11. *Ibid.*, p. 26.

12. See Chapter 8.

13. Rufus E. Miles, Jr., "Whose Baby Is the Population Problem?", *loc. cit.*, p. 26.

14. See Chapter 8.

15. Jessie Bernard, "One Role, Two Roles, Shared Roles," *Issues in Industrial Society*, Jan., 1971, pp. 26–27.

16. Judith Lorber, paper presented at meetings of Sociologists for Women in Society, Aug., 1973. See also Chapter 15.

17. Few are outraged that men who have taken two years out to discharge military obligations are given preferential treatment on Civil Service rosters or allowed to return to industrial jobs without loss of seniority. No more will it eventually outrage us that women who have taken time out to bear children should be given, not preferential treatment, but simply help in keeping up with their professions during their time out.

18. Lincoln H. Day, "The Social Consequences of a Zero Population Growth Rate in the United States," in Charles F. Westoff and Robert Parke, Jr., eds., *Commission on Population Growth and the American Future, Research Reports*, Vol. 1. *Demographic and Social Aspects of Population Growth*, p. 672.

19. Working Copy of "Report of Forum 15," 1970 White House Conference on Children: Children and Parents: Together in the World (n.d.).

20. Albert C. Jacobs and Robert C. Angell, *A Research in Family Law* (no publisher given), 1930, p. 646.

21. *Ibid.*, p. 646.

22. In 1965, fathers in the families of about 15 percent of working mothers were taking care of preschool children in the home. In such cases the mother was

probably the major if not the sole earner. Role sharing is not, however, the same as such role reversal.

23. If both partners have a clear-cut preference for one role or the other, a solution is logically if not practically simple. If the preferences go counter to convention there will be some flak from *hoi polloi* but it would be bearable. The hard solution is one required when both partners prefer the same role, whichever one it is. Then the logic calls for equal sacrifice by mutual sharing of both the preferred and the non-preferred roles, either simultaneously or alternately.

24. Marianne Käne and others, "Social Rights in Sweden before School Starts," Chapter 14 in *Child Care—Who Cares?*, Pamela Roby, ed. (Basic Books, 1973). The policy planners hoped that women would not continue long to accept a dual role and "rest content with a martyr's halo."

25. *Ibid.*

26. *Ibid.*

27. *Ibid.*

28. Quoted by Meryle Secrest, "Pondering a Future with Too Many People," *The Washington Post*, July 23, 1972. See also Leo Davids, "New Family Norms," *Trial* Magazine, Sept.–Oct., 1972, pp. 14–18.

29. In 1968, forty-eight out of seventy-five companies in England and Wales had paternity leave.

30. Gösta Rehn, "For Greater Flexibility of Working Life," *OECD Observer*, Feb., 1973, p. 3. *OECD* stands for Organization for Economic Cooperation and Development.

31. *Ibid.*, p. 7.

32. *Ibid.*, p. 3. Among the benefits specified were included: making service available to consumers more hours during the day; avoidance of traffic jams and overcrowding in tourist resorts; better use of expensive equipment; reduction of absenteeism and high labor turnover; better matching of supply and demand in the labor market.

33. A press release in the German American Trade News, No. 11, Nov., 1972, reports on "Germany's Office Hour Liberation Movement," a movement toward flexible working hours. "A new flexible system of determining the office hours of individual employees has freed some half million West German workers from the tyranny of the clock. These lucky workers now go to work when they are good and ready. . . . The widespread adoption of flexible time scheduling will primarily depend on whether it helps business· get its job done. Four years' experience in Germany argues that it works, and we may soon be wondering why it wasn't introduced years ago." In the United States, the UAW bargaining with General Motors in July, 1973, found voluntary as opposed to required overtime a bigger issue than wages. One young man in a television interview expressed desire to be with his family more. The Social Security Administration in its Baltimore office, a round-the-clock operation, was introducing "flexitime" in 1974.

34. The earnings of women at best are only four-fifths as high as those of men (Economic Report of the President, 1973, pp. 104, 106).

35. Gösta Rehn, "For Greater Flexibility of Working Life," *loc. cit.*, p. 4.

36. *Ibid.*, p. 4.

37. Carolyn Shaw Bell, "Social Security: Society's Last Discrimination," *Business and Society Review*, Sept., 1973.

### Chapter Eighteen

1. Lee Boxandall, Introduction to Berthold Brecht, *The Mother* (Grove, 1965), p. 17.

2. In studies of aggressiveness, more boys than girls beyond the age of eight show offensive aggressiveness, but girls show more defensive than offensive aggressiveness. The defense of offspring is one of the most characterizing traits of females of many species. In the study of sex relations in certain communes, the researcher commented on the almost pathological degree of dependency the women displayed. Only in defense of their children did they show any aggressiveness vis-à-vis the fathers. See Chapter 16.

3. Harriet Holter, *Sex Roles and Social Structure* (Oslo: Universitetsforlaget, 1970), pp. 231–232.

4. Withdrawal may be simply passive or it may involve a process of "hardening." Aristotle recommended that the infant be "hardened" to withstand changes in temperature. Analogously, children may be "hardened" to withstand the blows and buffets of outrageous fortune rather than actively to fight outrageous fortune. Or, as with the anti-prohibitionists a generation ago, to withstand rather than eliminate temptation. In any case the environment is left untouched and the onus of adjustment is placed on the individual.

5. Cheryl Buswell-Robinson, "People's Farm," *Communitas*, 1 (Dec., 1972), p. 48. People's Farm consisted originally of twenty-two persons—"poor white from Chicago; young, hustling black dudes from Northern ghettoes; farmer's daughter; ex-Democratic committee-woman from Virginia; college student; civil rights worker; and certified public accountant. We had just come from the Poor Peoples' Campaign (Resurrection City) and were determined to carry on the spirit of that city where all poor people, students, and other middle-class people came together to make demands on the government."

6. Some women were beginning to think of motherhood as, in effect, a tactic for the overthrow of patriarchy and institutionalizing, or re-institutionalizing, matriarchy. ". . . the point of Mother Right is to reshape the family according to the perceptions of women, and to reshape society in the image of this new matriarchal family. Because motherhood cuts across economic class, race, and sexual preference, a society in which women were powerful by virtue of being mothers would not be divided along any of these lines. Nor would any new division between women such as between mothers and childless women, arise. . . ." (Jane Alpert, "Mother Right: A New Feminist Theory," *Ms* (Aug., 1973), p. 93. Surely not at all what Samuel Johnson had in mind.

7. When women exert power it is as consumers, as housewives in the supermarket, as household procurement officers.

8. George Lundberg, *Can Science Save Us?* (Harper, 1947). Science and technology have been the great male achievements of the last two or three centuries. The absence of the names of women on the roster of great scientists is frequently referred to as evidence of their intellectual inferiority. Still today the feeling is expressed that science as embodied in technology is undermining rather than promoting our salvation. An uncomfortable sense of malaise with the course technology, if not science itself, is taking pervades the current scene, a feeling that, great as the achievements of technology are, it is getting out of hand, that there must be some bridling of it. At least some redirection. As expressed in polls, for example, the priority of women lies in the direction of human-welfare programs rather than in the direction of such alternatives as space programs.

9. Lee Boxandall, *loc. cit.*, p. 16.

10. *Ibid.*, p. 16.

11. It has, indeed, been in child-related issues such as school busing and drug control that mothers have participated most passionately. No significant difference between men and women was found in election to local offices in California (Edmond Costantini and Kenneth Craik, "Women as Politicians: The Social Background, Personality, and Political Careers of Female Party Leaders," *Journal of Social Issues*, 28, 2, 1972, p. 230.

12. Thus, for example, in Brecht's *The Caucasian Chalk Circle*, Grusha takes an abandoned child "without thinking of the burden it will prove to be. The *motherly* person for Brecht generally displays such an impulsiveness, openness to experience, unusual energy, and disregard for the costs of responsibility" (Lee Boxandall, *loc. cit.*, p. 15). The idea was not that all women had this moral character, only women who were motherly. Some women were barbarous or immoral; they did not take measures for the defense of their children (p. 17).

13. Robert Smuts, *Women and Work in America* (Columbia University Press, 1959), pp. 129–130.

14. Erich Neumann, *The Great Mother, An Analysis of the Archetype* (trans. from the German by Ralph Manheim, Princeton University Press, 1963), p. xiii.

15. Maren Lockwood Carden, *The New Feminist Movement* (Russell Sage Foundation, 1974), p. 169.

16. *Ibid.*, p. 169.

17. Gloria Steinem, "What It Would Be Like If Women Win, 1970," *Time* Magazine, Aug. 31, 1970, p. 22.

18. Jane Alpert, "Mother Right: A New Feminist Theory," *loc. cit.*, p. 94.

19. Once given the vote, the effect had not been immediately all that dramatic. Politics was cleaned up a little—there were fewer cases of violence at the polls—but there might have been fewer anyway as times changed. Violence was just taking different forms. In any event, there were so few changes that the female vote became a matter of cynical humor. Why, the weathered boss even wondered, had he worried about the "women's vote" at all? It didn't matter. But *"finis"* has not yet been written to that story. See below for the way women vote. Most of the research on women in political life has been done by men and the results, judged wholly on the basis of male values, are not worthy of male concern. One team of researchers, summarizing the research, note that "stripped of its male chauvinism," the conclusion of Maurice Duverger, which follows "highlights what has become a virtual truism regarding women and politics." "Women . . . have the mentality of minors in many fields, and, particularly in politics, they will accept paternalism on the part of men. The man—husband, fiancé, lover, or myth—is the mediator between them and the political world" (Edmond Costantini and Kenneth Craik, *loc. cit.*, p. 218).

20. The day after Vice-President Agnew resigned, *The Washington Post* sampled person-on-the-street reactions. Of the thirteen men queried, nine gave hostile and unsympathetic replies and the other four, equivocal replies. Of the seven women, only one gave a hostile or unsympathetic response; two were uncertain or equivocal; the remaining four expressed compassion (*The Washington Post*, Oct. 11, 1973).

21. Unsigned, "Womanpower," *Parade*, June 18, 1972. See also Carolyn Setlow and Gloria Steinem, "Why Women Voted for Richard Nixon," *Ms*, March, 1973, pp. 66 ff.

22. Louis Harris and others, *The 1972 Virginia Slims American Women's Opinion Poll*, p. 75.

418

23. Geri Joseph, "Women: Still on the Sidelines of Politics," *The Washington Post*, Aug. 5, 1973.

24. Edmond Costantini and Kenneth Craik, "Women as Politicians," *loc. cit.*, pp. 227–235.

25. Geri Joseph, "Women: Still on the Sidelines of Politics," *loc. cit.*

26. The woman created by this role approaches conflict and competition in a different way from the way the kind of men we have been producing does. She tends to be more communal in a competitive situation and more conciliatory in a conflict situation. These differences might reflect only the optimum strategy of a smaller animal vis-à-vis a larger one. But they may also reflect a character socialized into greater concern for others by a role that forces a protective stance on its performers. As long as women retain the nurturant character which socialization by motherhood emphasizes, it is likely that women would be more humane in their use of power.

27. Harriet Holter, *op. cit.*, p. 231.

28. Ellen Moers, "Money, the Job, and Little Women," *Commentary*, Jan., 1973, p. 59.

29. *Ibid.*, p. 59.

30. Robert Smuts, *op. cit.*, p. 124. The gain in character may be at the expense of more intellectual and prestigious qualities. See Alice Rossi, "Transition to Parenthood," *Journal of Marriage and the Family*, 30 (Feb., 1968), pp. 29, 34.

31. Robert Smuts, *op. cit.*, pp. 133–134.

32. Strangely enough, a woman once active in the radical New Left and now, as a result, a fugitive from justice, living an undercover life, was returning to a biological interpretation of motherhood. "Motherhood must be understood here as a potential which is imprinted in the genes of every woman; as such it makes no difference to this analysis of femaleness whether a woman ever has borne, or ever will bear, a child." She finds "more women within the Movement are beginning to experience their feelings as mothers as feelings which are integral to their identities as women" (Jane Alpert "Mother Right," *loc. cit.*, pp. 92, 94). But her interpretation of this biological emphasis is diametrically opposed to that of the traditional one. In the traditional view, the exigencies of the maternal role were seen as enough to justify keeping women in the home; in Ms. Alpert's view, they are seen as demanding participation in the political world. Another demonstration of the truism that it is not facts in and of themselves but the interpretation placed upon them that is crucial.

33. Emily James Putnam, *The Lady, Studies of Certain Significant Phases of Her History* (Putnam's, 1910; University of Chicago Press, 1970), pp. 78–79.

34. Betty Friedan, *McCall's*, Jan., 1973.

35. A most perceptive statement of the nature of machismo and the ways in which it is socialized into men—to their serious detriment—is presented by Warren Farrell in *Beyond Masculinity* (Random House, 1974). He also shows how male chauvinism can be attenuated and men, as well as women, liberated from its destructive effects.

36. See Chapter 1.

37. At Twin Oaks the term "mother" is used to refer to anyone, regardless of sex, who is nurturant. There is, thus, a strawberry mother, a cow mother, a chicken mother, an orchard mother; these are people who love and cherish strawberries, cows, chickens, orchards. Even mothers or cherishers and protectors of machinery and tools. It is the function, not the sex, of the caretaker that constitutes motherhood so conceived.

38. See Jessie Bernard, "Sex Differences: An Overview," Warner Modular Publications, 1974.

39. There was an apparently overlooked inconsistency in the insistence that female traits were intrinsic and insistence that they had to be protected in the home in order to preserve them. One could not, apparently, trust Nature to do so.

40. Erik Erikson, *Identity, Youth and Crisis* (Norton, 1968), p. 264.

41. Later descendants of the nineteenth-century "mother" viewed this function as a serious defect in the script. Performing the healing function of the Victorian model in effect served as a prop for the macho world by supplying shock absorbers in the home. As long as there was a retreat, the macho world was tolerable.

42. Erich Neumann, *op. cit.*, p. 96.

43. Robert J. Donovan, "George Cabot Lodge's Shockwaves from Harvard," *The Washington Post*, Dec. 17, 1972.

44. This same bill makes provision for a land-mark project: "Research on methods now being used in the United States and abroad to meet the problems of work alienation, including more flexible hours of work. . . ." (Section·3 (a) A2.) See discussion of flexible work time in Chapter 17.

45. Joseph Veroff and Sheila Feld, *Marriage and Work in America* (Van Nostrand, 1970), p. 339.

46. Denis F. Johnston, "The Future of Work: Three Possible Alternatives," *Monthly Labor Review*, May, 1972, p. 6. Reprint 2806.

47. "Work in America," Report of a Special Task Force to the Secretary of HEW, 93d Congress, 1st Session, (U. S. Govt. Printing Office, 1973), *passim.*; Worker Alienation, Hearings before Subcommittee on Employment, Manpower, and Poverty, July 25–26, 1972.

48. One poll found that 91 percent of their sample liked their jobs (Thomas C. Sorensen, "Do Americans Like Their Jobs?", *Parade*, June 3, 1973, p. 17). A Gallup poll reported 80 to 90 percent with a positive attitude toward their work. Studies of marital happiness report, according to the way the questions are stated, anywhere from 27 to 91 percent as above average in happiness. See also Harold Wool, "What's Wrong with Work in America? A Review Essay," *Monthly Labor Review*, March, 1973, pp. 38–44.

49. Richard E. Farson, "Behavioral Science Predicts and Projects," in W. Keith Daugherty, ed., *The Future of the Family* (Family Service Association of America, 1969), p. 59.

50. *Psychology Today*, June, 1972, p. 12.

51. Erich Neumann, *op. cit.*, p. xiii.

# Index

Abortion, 23, 26, 248, 258, 265, 267, 272, 273–275
Abt Associates, 298
Achievement, need for, 38–39
Adler, Alfred, 262, 263
Adolescence, 91–92
Adoption, 32–33, 49
Adult retraining programs, 121
Aid to Dependent Children, 282
Alexander, Shana, 353
Alienation, 241
Alimony, 218
Alors (tribe), 8
*American Scholar, The,* 213
American Society of Adlerian Psychology, 262
Androgen, 39, 259–260
Androgyny, 177–180
Angell, Robert C., 339
Anthropology, 101
Antinatalism, 16, 42, 53, 186–187, 266, 268–269
Anxiety, 77–79
Appliances, household, 229
Arendt, Hannah, 277
Ariès, Philippe, 70, 92, 227
Aristotle, 69–70
Arnold, Eberhard, 311
Artificial insemination, 249, 251, 256
Astor, Mrs. Vincent, 209
Automobile, 234, 237

Beauvoir, Simone de, 33–34
Beethoven, Ludwig van, 364
Behavior modification, 39, 261–262
Bell, Carolyn Shaw, 120, 289–290, 293, 344
Berger, Bennett, 316–317
Bergman, Ingrid, 33
Bettelheim, Bruno, 177–178, 180
Binstock, Jeanne, 259
Birth rate, 42, 51, 145, 333, 335, 336
Blake, Judith, 20, 25, 40, 64, 139, 269
Boëthius, Monica, 123, 215
Boulding, Kenneth, 225, 290
Bowlby, John, 72
Brecht, Berthold, 348, 349, 351
British Royal Commission Report on Population, 110
Brotherhood of the Spirit, 313–314
Bruderhof, Society of Brothers, 311, 312–313

Calvin, John, 68, 95–98
Career mothers. *See* Professional mothers
Carlyle, Thomas, 109
Carrighar, Sally, 104–105
Chapin, Henry, 71
Child abuse, 85–89
Child Care Resource Center, 298
Child support, 218, 220

Child-free marriage. *See* Nonmotherhood

Childhood, emergence of, 92–94

Children: of professional mothers, 165–170; of working mothers, 190–192

Chilman, Catherine, 239

Civil Rights Act of 1964, 217, 332

Clark, Colin, 125

Coalition for a National Population Policy, 42

"Coercive" motherhood, 24–26

Cohabitation, 51

Cohen, Jack, 233

College women, 145–147, 211–212

Commission on Population Growth and the American Future, 25, 288, 333

Commission on the Status of Women, 110, 136, 173

Communes, 309–331, 332

Communication technologies, 238–240

Comprehensive Child Development Bill, 281

Contraception, 24, 26, 42, 59, 62, 244, 270, 275

Cornell University, 146

Costs of motherhood: to economy, 292–293; monetary, 288–290; non-monetary, 290–292; quasi-monetary, 292

Cottage system, 131–132

Cyrus, Virginia J., 219

Dahlström, Edmund, 215

Davids, Leo, 340

Day care, 279–284, 297

Day Care and Child Development Council of America, Inc., 279

De Tocqueville, Alexis, 205

Delinquency, 191

Deutsch, Helene, 36, 45, 166

Devlin, Bernadette, 33

Diabetes, 253–254

Discipline, 90, 93–100, 104

Divorce rates, 50, 145

DNA, 254

*Doll's House, The* (Ibsen), 13

Domestic help, 125, 127

Down's syndrome, 248, 253, 257

Doxiadis, Constantinos A., 232

Dreikurs, Rudolph, 262, 263

Duke, Patty, 33

Education, 25, 149, 198

Edwards, Robert G., 249

Eliot, George, 12

Empty-nest syndrome, 291–292

Environment movement, 16, 20, 53

Equal Rights Amendment, 216–221

Erikson, Erik, 140, 183, 347, 360, 364

Eugenics, 243, 246, 270, 271

Euripides, 41

Ewbank, Weeb, 174

Factory work, 131–136

Family law, 98–99

Family size, 53–64, 333–335

Family wage system, 118

Fan magazines, 28

Farrow, Mia, 33

Farson, Richard E., 363

Fatherhood, 173–180, 339–341

Fatigue, 82–83, 291

Fertility, 144

Fields, W. C., 30

Folsom, Joseph K., 125, 126

Foster-care, 32, 49

Freud, Anna, 72

Freud, Sigmund, 364

Friedan, Betty, 353

Friedenberg, Edgar, 192

Fuller, Buckminster, 235, 305

Galbraith, John Kenneth, 123

Gallatin, Albert, 133, 136, 140, 207, 210, 294

Gandhi, Indira, 352

Garagiola, Joe, 174

Garfinkle, Stewart, 292, 336

General Learning Corporation, 230, 298

Generalized drawing rights plan, 341–344

Genethics, 253, 272

Genetic counseling, 254–255, 265, 272

Genetic defects, 246–249, 253–254, 257–258, 271–272

Genetic engineering, 250–251, 256, 265, 272

Geneva Conference on New Patterns for Working Time (1972), 340
Gesell, Arnold, 101
Gilder, George, 163
Gilman, Charlotte Perkins, 126–127, 213
Girls, socializing process and, 25–30, 77, 78
Glick, Paul C., 50, 136, 145
Gordon, Thomas, 262
Grandmothers, 9, 245
Great Depression, 267
Gross national product, 118, 120
Guilt, 79–82, 165–166, 169, 186, 291
Gynecologists, 29

Haas, Lois, 323–324
Hamilton, Alexander, 132, 135, 136, 140, 207, 210, 294
Harlow, H. F., 72, 96
Harlow, M. K., 72, 96
Hartman, Heinz, 140
Health, 23–24, 101, 244
Health, Education, and Welfare, Department of, 271
Heide, Wilma Scott, 113–115, 116
Heilbrun, Carolyn, 213
Hellman, Lillian, 213
Hemophilia, 249, 253
Heredity. *See* Genetic defects
Hexter, Maurice, 267
Hitler, Adolf, 267, 270
Hollingsworth, Leta, 26
Holmberg, Per, 293
Holt, John, 96
Holtzman, Neil A., 253
Home, 10–13, 16, 129, 227–228, 234–235
Household appliances, 229
Housework, 112–113, 124–126, 336
Howe, Julia Ward, 352
Husbands: professional mothers and, 162–165; working mothers and, 187–189. *See also* Fatherhood
Hutterites, 315
Huxley, Julian, 260
Hysterectomy, 28

Ibsen, Henrik, 13
Identity crisis, 183–186
Income, 59, 60

Individual Psychology Associations, 262, 263
Industrialization, 16, 50, 111, 231
Infancy, prolongation of, 91–92
Infant care, 69–72, 79–80, 101–104
Infant mortality rate, 70–71
Infanticide, 23, 26, 273, 274
Infertility, 27, 30, 256
Inovulation, 249, 251, 252, 256
Institute of Life Insurance, 288
Institutional pressures, 19, 22, 24

Jacobs, Albert C., 339
Jefferson, Thomas, 364
Johnson, Samuel, 350
Jones, Ernest, 364
Justice, quality of, 300–301

Kaiser Industries, 297
Kanter, Rosabeth Moss, 325
Keniston, Kenneth, 92
Kennedy, John F., 110, 136, 151, 155, 156, 173
Key, Ellen, 95
Kibbutz, 315
King, Alan, 174
Klein, Viola, 110, 214
Koestler, Arthur, 260
Kreps, Juanita, 117

Labor-force participation, 25, 39, 112, 125, 129–130, 136–152; college women, 145–147; fertility and, 144; supply and demand, 140–144; working-class women, 147–149
Landers, Ann, 29, 34
Larcom, Lucy, 134
Law, 25, 98–99
Lawrence, D. H., 34
Learning, 263–264
Leisure, 126–129, 207–210
Lesbianism, 34
Literature, 26
Lodge, George Cabot, 361–362
Longevity, 23–24, 244
Lott, Bernice E., 47–48
Lowell, Massachusetts, 133–134
Lundberg, George, 351
Lynn, David B., 242

Machismo, 158, 163, 353, 358–361
McKay, Cathy, 89
Marasmus, 71–72
Marriage, 50–51, 145
Marx, Karl, 109, 131, 213, 336
Maternal instability, 9, 37
Maternal instinct, 19–20, 22–24, 140
Maternal warmth, 9–10, 31–37
Mead, Margaret, 84–85, 353
Medical technologies, 244–258
Meir, Golda, 352
Menopause, 245
Military deferment, 221
Miller, Daniel R., 100
Mixtecans (tribe), 8
Monetization of motherwork, 118–123
More, Thomas, 93
Morgan, Gwen, 297
Motherliness. *See* Maternal warmth
Mothers Anonymous, 86
Mother's Pension movement, 118, 282
Moynihan, Patrick Daniel, 284
Myrdal, Alva, 110, 214

National Institute of Health, 192
National Manpower Council, 137
National Organization for Non-Parents (NON), 42–43
National Organization for Women, 206
National Trades' Union, 135
National Welfare Rights Organization, 349
Natural mothers, 32–35
Nestlings, 49
New Franconia, Virginia, 237
New Towns, 235–237
Newton, Niles, 77
Nixon, Richard M., 281, 333
Noise, 82
Nonmotherhood, 20, 40–52, 242
Non-working mothers, 126–129, 196–221
Norton, Arthur, 50, 145
Nyansongo (tribe), 7

Obstetricians, 29, 76
Office of Child Development, 281
Office of Economic Opportunity, 271
Omega House, 315
Oppenheimer, Valerie, 143

Orwell, George, 260
Oughton, Diane, 105
Out-of-wedlock pregnancies, 28–29, 266–267

Parent Effectiveness Training, 262
Parsons, Talcott, 157, 158
Pediatricians, 76
People's Republic of China, 278, 297
Permissiveness, 90, 93–100, 104, 240–241, 315
*Personal Report*, 174
Pharmacological technologies, 258–260
Phenylketonuria (PKU), 247, 253, 271
Physical contact, infants and, 70–72, 89, 96
Physical technologies, 227–238
Physiology, 35, 36
Piaget, Jean, 101
Planned Parenthood, 42
Plato, 84
Polaroid Corporation, 297
Political process, participation in, 347–357
*Politics* (Aristotle), 69–70
Politics of motherhood: abortion, 273–275; day care, 279–284; population policy, 265–275; sex, politicizing of, 275–276; socialization, control of, 277–279
Polygyny, 9
Population policy, 265–275
Poverty, 74
Power motivation, 38, 39
Pregnancy, 24
Prescott, James W., 72, 89
President's Task Force on the Mentally Handicapped, 270
Professional mothers, 157–161, 204–205, 210–212; children of, 165–170; discrepant role demands, 160–162; husbands of, 162–165; momism in reverse, 170–171; rewards and challenges, 171–173
Pronatalism, 266, 268–269
Prostitution, 276
Psychoanalysis, 25
Psychological technologies, 260–264

Psychology, 35, 101
Psychosomatics, 35

Rajputs, 7–8, 227
Rape, 275–276
Recovery, Inc., 86–87
Redgrave, Vanessa, 33
Religion, 44, 59, 60
Religious Society of Families, 311–312
Remarriage rates, 50, 145
Reproduction, 246–258
*Republic* (Plato), 84
Research Institute of America, Inc., 174
Responsibility, 73–74, 77–78
Retirement, 196
Riesman, David, 100
Ringer, Carl, 364
Role attrition, 196–197
Role sharing, 175–178, 339–341
Rossi, Alice, 260
Rousseau, Jean Jacques, 68, 95–98
Royal Commission on Population in Great Britain, 136, 151, 155
Ruskin, John, 11–12
Russell, Bertrand, 260

Sanger, Margaret, 54–55
Scott, Anne Firor, 54
Self-fulfillment, 37–39, 192–193, 291, 300
Self-selection for motherhood, 61–64
Sex, politicizing of, 275–276
Sex roles, 25, 179–180, 212
Sexuality, 23, 163, 245
Sickle-cell anemia, 249
Single mothers, 33
Skinner, B. F., 97, 325, 329
"Smother-love," 15
Soap operas, 27
Social Darwinism, 300, 301
Social Security Act, 268, 269, 282
Social technologies, 240–242
Socialization, 25–30, 77, 78, 94, 277–279
Sociology, 25, 35
*Sons and Lovers* (Lawrence), 34
*Sounder* (movie), 180
Spitz, René, 71
Spock, Benjamin, 96, 97
Springtree, 310

Stanford University, 146
Steinem, Gloria, 353, 355
Steptoe, Patrick C., 249
Sterilization, 244, 270–271, 332, 333
Stowe, Harriet Beecher, 355
Straus, Ellen, 206
Stress, 82–84, 291
Suburbanization, 231–237
Suicide rate, 203
Sumner, William Graham, 23, 273
Sunley, Robert, 95, 100
Surrogate wombs, 252
Swanson, Guy E., 100
Sweden, 339–340

Taira, Okinawa, 8
Tarong, Philippines, 8
Taylor, Elizabeth, 28
Tay-Sachs syndrome, 248, 253
Technology, 16, 124–126, 225–226, 362; communication, 238–240; medical, 244–258; pharmacological, 258–260; physical, 227–238; psychological, 260–264; social, 240–242
Telecommunication, 238–239
Telephone, 238, 239
Television, 26, 27, 238
Tender-loving care, 71, 74, 88
Textbooks, 29
Theology, 25
Trade unions, 134–135
Tranquilizers, 259
Twin Oaks, 310, 325–330

*Uncle Tom's Cabin* (Stowe), 355–356
Union of Soviet Socialist Republics, 278, 297
United States Supreme Court, 275, 332
Urbanization, 16, 50, 111, 231–232

Vassar College, 146
Veblen, Thorstein, 124, 127, 128, 139
Victorian motherhood, 3–6, 11–13, 15–16, 32, 356, 360–361
Vincent, Clark, 97–98, 315
Voluntarism, 205–207
Voting behavior, 354

*Walden Two* (Skinner), 325
Ward, Lester Frank, 300

Watergate scandal, 355
Watson, John, 101, 261
Weber, Max, 128
Webster, Noah, 132
Welfare, 149, 280, 282–284
White, R. W., 140
White House Conference on Children (1970), 337
White House Conference on Youth (1971), 284
Women's Bureau, 296, 298
Women's Centers for Change, 198
Women's liberation movement, 43, 47, 172–173, 200, 213–215, 242, 323
Woodcrest Community, 312–313
Work, 109–130, 336–339, 362–363. *See also* Factory work; Labor-force par-
ticipation; Professional mothers; Working mothers
Work ethic, 112
Work schedules, flexibility of, 337, 339–344
Working mothers, 15, 182–195; children of, 190–192; husbands of, 187–189; identity crisis, 183–186; mature women, 193–194; money, 187, 188–190; self-fulfillment, 192–193
Working-class women, 147–149
Wright, Carroll D., 135, 140

*Yale Law Review,* 219

Zero Population Growth, 42

Some other books published by Penguin
are described on the following pages.

# WOMEN AND CHILD CARE IN CHINA
## A Firsthand Report

*Ruth Sidel*

The changing status of women and children in today's China has important implications for our own society. The emphasis in this book is on the amazingly rapid liberation of Chinese women from their "bitter past." Now, Ruth Sidel reports, the Chinese woman takes an active part in the life of the nation, and vast programs provide birth-control information, prenatal assistance, maternity leaves, and child-care facilities. Most especially, *Women and Child Care in China* looks at nurseries, nursery schools, and kindergartens and at the revolutionary methods they employ. Mrs. Sidel also comments on the aspects of the Chinese experience that might be of value in the United States. Ruth Sidel and her husband, Victor W. Sidel, who took the many photographs in the book, visited the People's Republic of China as guests of the Chinese Medical Association.

**THE SUBORDINATE SEX**
A History of Attitudes toward Women

*Vern L. Bullough,*
*with a final chapter by Bonnie Bullough*

Ancient Egypt and ancient Greece, early Judaism and early Christianity, the Middle Ages and the Victorian era, the concept of romantic love, the teachings of the prophet Muhammad, and the Hindu theory of female eroticism are all considered in this cross-cultural study of attitudes toward women, from the most remote periods to the present day. The authors' many sources range from ancient law codes to a modern study of ideas about women in Soviet fiction. *Publishers Weekly* says: "Taken all together, the evidence overwhelmingly supports Bonnie Bullough's contention that the 'historical barriers' to women's equality will be harder to overcome than any biological, political, or economic impediments. Fascinating and an excellent source book." Vern L. Bullough is Professor of History at California State University, Northridge.

## PSYCHOANALYSIS AND WOMEN

*Edited by Jean Baker Miller, M.D.*

The articles in this volume revise the traditional
psychoanalytical approach to women. Feeling that
women have been too long "kept in their place"
by Freudian myths about penis envy, biological
determinism, dependency, and masochism, the
editor aims for a more realistic view. Included are
articles by such eminent figures as Karen Horney,
Alfred Adler, Clara Thompson, Gregory Zilboorg,
Mary Jane Sherfey, Frieda Fromm-Reichmann,
and Robert Seidenberg. Together, these writings
dispel the old stereotypical attitudes with their
phallocentric bias and show that psychoanalysis
can have a new relevance for women today. Jean
Baker Miller is a practicing psychoanalyst.

## SEX AND MARRIAGE IN
## UTOPIAN COMMUNITIES
### Nineteenth-Century America

*Raymond Lee Muncy*

Of the many utopian communities in nineteenth-century America, this book considers only those whose approach to sex and marriage was original or unique. Among the groups that Raymond Lee Muncy investigates are the Shakers, Rappites, Zoarites, and Jansonists, all of whom practiced continence; the Mormons, who adopted polygyny and propounded the doctrine of "celestial marriage" to support it; and the Perfectionists at Oneida, each of whom was married to all the others of the opposite sex. Some communities engaged in free love; others made sexual orgies occasions of divine worship. In general, Muncy finds that communities were forced to modify or abandon the monogamous family in order to survive. Raymond Lee Muncy is Chairman of the Department of History at Harding College, Searcy, Arkansas.

**BY A WOMAN WRITT**
Literature from Six Centuries
by and about Women

*Edited by Joan Goulianos*

This unique collection of literature reveals the
range and complexity of female experiences. The
twenty contributors include Margery Kempe, a
fourteenth-century wife and mother who described her struggles as a religious mystic; Aphra
Behn, a seventeenth-century author and spy who
wrote about passion; Mary Shelley, who evoked
the loneliness of widowhood in the nineteenth
century; and Anaïs Nin, who analyzed the con-
fusions and pleasures of the modern woman. Fiction, poetry, autobiography, diaries, and letters
are drawn upon. This is the first collection to
bring together the works of women writers from
so many different eras and in so many different
forms.

## FROM REVERENCE TO RAPE
### The Treatment of Women in the Movies

*Molly Haskell*

Seeing the movie industry as dedicated to reinforcing the idea of women's inferiority, Molly
Haskell examines each decade of cinematic history
in this surprising look at how the movies have
portrayed—and betrayed—women. She shows
that from the virgins and flappers of the twenties
to the raped and brutalized sex objects of the sixties and seventies, women on film have followed
a downhill path. Where once movies highlighted
the strength and independence of stars like Kath-
arine Hepburn, Joan Crawford, and Barbara Stan-
wyck, today we are given little but sexist images
of demeaned and dehumanized females. *From
Reverence to Rape* chronicles these changes with
wit and intelligence as it tells us how films have
distorted truth and reflected delusions. Illustrated with photographs.

*Sidney Cornelia Callahan*

Here is a new approach to parenthood. Herself
the mother of six, Sidney Callahan draws on her
own experience as well as on the theories and observations of experts like R. D. Laing, Erik Erikson, Jean Piaget, and Haim Ginott. Are American
parents unique, or do they share problems with
parents in other cultures? What do good parents
do? What are the rights and responsibilities of
parents and children in regard to their communities? What is the future of parenthood? Such are
the questions Mrs. Callahan confronts in this opti-
mistic book that proposes specific objectives—
from parental education and consciousness-raising
to day-care programs, substitute foster parenting,
and new "extended family" forms.